Facing Total War
German Society 1914–1918

je

Jürgen Kocka

Facing Total War
German Society
1914–1918

Translated from the German by
Barbara Weinberger

Harvard University Press
Cambridge, Massachusetts
1984

Translated from the German edition by permission of
Vandenhoeck & Ruprecht, Göttingen
Originally published as *Klassengesellschaft im Krieg. Deutsche
Sozialgeschichte, 1914-1918*; copyright © 1973 Vandenhoeck &
Ruprecht, Göttingen

Library of Congress Cataloging in Publication Data

Kocka, Jürgen.
Facing total war.

Translation of: Klassengesellschaft im Krieg.
Bibliography: pp.
Includes index.
1. Social classes—Germany. 2. World War, 1914–
1918—Economic aspects—Germany. I. Title.
HN460.S6K613   1985   306′.0943   84–19269
ISBN 0–674–29031–3

For **Hans Rosenberg**
on his eightieth birthday
26 February 1984

Translator's Note

I would like to thank Professor V. Berghahn for making his expertise so freely available to me during the time that I was working on this translation.

B.W.

Contents

Preface to the English Edition

This book deals with a society at war. What did the First World War do to German society? How did social structures and changes influence the country's military performance? What are the social resources of military strength? Did the War halt, re-direct or speed up long-term trends? An analysis of the extraordinary pressure which the nearly total War of 1914–18 exerted on the fabric of German society is the subject of this book; wartime changes are related to the basic structures and tensions of pre-1914 German society and to the Revolution of 1918/19 which resulted from the War and from the internal changes it promoted.

This is thus a comprehensive overview of a whole society confronted with a basic challenge. It surveys and summarises the research literature on the economic, cultural, social and political developments in Germany during the First World War. It is based partly on unpublished sources that have been rarely used hitherto for the writing of German history 1914–1918: on the – then secret – reports by the home-based regional military commands on the mood of the population and on the problems faced by different social groups.

Writing a synthesis like this one needs theory. A Marxist scheme of class analysis structures the argument of the book, although the Marxian concepts are used in a Weberian way and in accordance with the idealtypical method. A particular type of theory-orientated, analytical history is attempted in this book. In the beginning and at the end there are some reflections on the opportunities and limits of such an approach.

This is not 'social-scientific history' which applies general social science rules to historical data, formulating and testing hypotheses. The book has some tables and quantitative evidence is used wherever possible and where useful for clarification; but it is not an exercise in quantitative history. Neither, however, is it narrative history.

Certainly it talks in categories of before and after and like all history it is interested in change over time. Its main concern, however, is with economic, social, political and cultural structures and processes (including, of course, collective experiences and attitudes); not with individual actors or single occurrences or events. It works with explicit concepts. It does not avoid sharp definitions and theoretical reflections for the sake of narrative elegance. It has the form of a discourse, not a narrative.

The book was conceptualised in the late 1960s and its first German edition was published in 1973. Since then the mood has changed. Marxist ideas are less influential among both intellectuals and the public at large than they were. A revival of narrative is frequently observed and supported by historians who, some years ago, were more sympathetic to theory-orientated history. This may be, therefore, a good moment for publishing the English version of a book which tries to demonstrate both the usefulness of Marxist concepts (if used cautiously) and the superiority of theory-orientated history over plain narrative.

I am grateful to Marion and Volker Berghahn, who proposed the publication of this English edition, and to the translator, Barbara Weinberger; it must have been a most difficult task to translate this book, which seems to be rather German in style and structure. I would also like to thank Juliet Standing, editor at Berg Publishers, for her diligent care. I have taken the opportunity to bring this new edition up to date. The new literature has been incorporated; I am grateful to Ute Daniel (Bielefeld) for helping me with this. A few references to debates which were active in the early 1970s but have now moved to the background have been cut out, some newer arguments added. But by and large the text has remained unchanged.

I would like to dedicate this English edition to Hans Rosenberg, who celebrates his eightieth birthday next year. He would have written a very different book, I am sure, both less schematic and more elegant (without, of course, turning narrator). His work was a decisive influence on me when I first started to write, particularly his *Grosse Depression und Bismarckzeit* (1967). Intellectually I am deeply indebted to him and personally I feel privileged to have gained his friendship.

Munich, December 1983   *Jürgen Kocka*

Preface to the German edition

My interest in the economic and social history of Germany in the First World War goes back to a seminar on the German war economy, 1914 to 1918, which Professor Gerhard A. Ritter organised at the Free University, Berlin, in the summer of 1964. The manuscript of a talk I gave in December 1968 at St Antony's College, Oxford, on the social outcomes of the First World War in Germany was the first draft of the present study, which was reworked and extended during a stay at Harvard University in the winter of 1969/70. The manuscript which resulted contained the main results and structure of the present work. Other projects, and the since-relinquished intention to turn it into a broader and more detailed archival study, delayed the completion of a final, publishable version. Talks based on parts of that manuscript were given in 1970 at Professor Richard Tilly's seminar in Madison, Wisconsin, and at Professor Gerald D. Feldman's seminar at Berkeley, California, to the Heidelberg Worskshop for modern social history, the German-French Historical Colloquium on the First World War in Mannheim and a colloquium of the Historical Seminar in Münster in 1971, and at Professor Rudolf Braun's seminar in Zurich in 1972. In 1968 and 1971 I held seminars on the theme 'Germany in the First World War'. I am indebted to all these organisations and to the participants in the discussions for their criticism and encouragement. Earlier versions of the section on the Mittelstand (Chap. 3 here) appeared in the *Journal of Contemporary History*, 8, 1973, and in *Francia*, 2, 1974. For their criticism and encouragement I thank above all: Gerald D. Feldman, Hartmut Kaelble, Alf Lüdtke, Hans-Jürgen Puhle, Gerhard A. Ritter, Gustav Schmidt and Hans-Ulrich Wehler, who took the trouble to read the manuscript in its early form.

Münster, March 1973   *Jürgen Kocka*

1 Questions and Concepts

For the last three decades West German historical research on the First World War has concentrated, in the main, on two major themes; firstly, the work of Fritz Fischer, the controversy thus unleashed, and other resultant monographs have advanced our knowledge on the question of responsibility for that war and on Germany's war aims.[1] Secondly, there has been intensive research into the history of constitutional developments and party politics during the War; much has been done to clarify the issues by unearthing new materials and by bringing to bear the methods of political science; this type of work centred around the problem of the gradual parliamentarisation of the German political system.[2] Questions which the social and economic historian would raise were not entirely absent from these researches. Discussions of party politics often included the impact of pressure groups and the role of economic and social issues in the political debate. In the literature on the causes and circumstances leading to the War and on war aims, phenomena of external policy were frequently explained in terms of constellations of internal political and socio-economic interests. However, socio-economic interests were mainly considered through the political activity of interest groups, especially as revealed by studying the files of these groups. This was done largely with the help of traditional methods of textual analysis through the interpretation of the attitudes and actions of leading political and economic actors. Much of this work was marked by a concentration on the decision-making process and its determinants, rather than on the socio-economic structures and processes of change as such. Usually, political developments remained at the centre of this type of research and socio-economic changes were used to explain them, mostly with an almost exclusive emphasis on the way in which socio-economically determined interests sought or gained access to the political decision-making process.[3] For a long time the social and economic history of the

First World War remained a stepchild of West German historical research.[4]

The situation has changed in recent years. Research on the Revolution of 1918/19 has developed strong interests in economic and social history.[5] Gerald D. Feldman and others have made a thorough study of the relationship between economic change, social groups and the government.[6] East German historians have contributed much to this type of research; due to their Marxist framework they were always inclined to give a central place to socio-economic structures and processes, even if in an often one-sided manner.[7] Specialised monographs and broad surveys have been published about the German economy during the First World War.[8] The history of the labour movement has received some attention,[9] as have other social-historical topics.[10]

Much still remains to be done. There are many blank spaces on the map – in the fields of family and women's history, among others. Also, works of synthesis stressing the social-historical dimensions do not yet exist.[11] The history of German society during the First World War remains to be written.

The author cannot claim to achieve this task in the following chapters, although he does begin to move in this direction. Little attention has been paid to the attitudes and actions of the period's important decision makers (whereas in a broad, fully-fledged synthesis they would have to be covered more thoroughly). Individual institutions (such as trade unions or government agencies) and individual decision-making processes (such as the discussions and manoeuvring leading to the important Auxiliary Service Law of December 1916) will not be regarded as of so much interest *per se*; rather they will be studied with regard to the indications they provide about the structures and processes manifested in them. The author will be concerned above all with the inner structure and reciprocal relationships between social classes and social strata in their economic, social, socio-psychological and political dimensions, particularly with regard to their changes throughout the period of the War. Questions will be asked about socially relevant changes in the production and distribution process; about changing determinants of class, status and group formation; about alterations in collective class- and strata-specific attitudes, expectations, self-perception, hopes and protest potentials; about changing alliances and conflicts, struggles and compromises between social classes and groups; and, not least, about changes in the position of the state within the tension area of social classes and groups, and of changes in the relationship of society and state under wartime conditions.

As to the problems of continuity and discontinuity, interesting questions remain to be answered; do the wartime changes signify reversals, or ruptures, when compared with the years before 1914, or are they accelerated or retarded continuations of pre-war developments? The question of how far these processes continued after the War is also of interest. In this regard, it cannot be overlooked that a revolution, albeit a very incomplete one, occurred at the end of the period under discussion, so that the years before November 1918 may be regarded as a pre-revolutionary period. It is for this reason that this enquiry is particularly interested in tensions and conflicts, the uses of power and the forms of domination and protest.

The book is concerned with changing domestic conditions; international relations, battles and diplomacy, blockade and foreign trade, war aims and peace feelers are of interest only in so far as they influenced internal changes. But the reverse relationship will also be touched upon: the influence of domestic conditions on the foreign and military policy of the Reich.

The approach of this study is defined by these aims, as well as by its origins. It grew out of a short lecture which gave an overview of German social history between 1914 and 1918. The author's intention is still to offer a relatively short work, based mainly on published sources, and concentrating on essential structures and changes. On the one hand the book should offer quick access to basic information. On the other, by posing clear questions and hypotheses, it should stimulate more intensive comparative research into the social history of the War period.

If, in a short historical presentation of this kind, the selection of the relevant material is not to be arbitrary and merely additive, a clear but not too rigid conceptual framework is required. This may well be a general problem in historical research, applying equally to other themes. But such a framework is all the more vital, the more complex and comprehensive the material and the more compressed and selective the analysis. Writing the history of a whole society one can hardly just 'reconstruct' given structures (apparent in the sources), even less so if one concentrates on a narrative of motives, actions and events.[12] The need for social-scientific concepts, hypotheses, models and theories which can be used to select and connect data and sources in a way appropriate for historical knowledge and approaches is therefore particularly clear in work of this type.[13]

What follows is a social class model, derived from Marxian class theory, but removed from the context of a Marxian philosophy of history, and complemented by new findings in conflict research. It will be used in a Weberian way.

What are the elements of this model and what does it look like?[14]

A basic assumption is that the class position of individuals, families and groups, is defined by their place in capitalistically[15] organised social production – whether or not they participate in the (private) ownership of, and control over, the means of production.[16] Thus defined, class position is the decisive factor for the objective (or 'latent') interest position[17] of class members, which is not necessarily conscious. Because of the characteristics of work organisation in the capitalist system (which cannot be further discussed here), the two class-specific interest positions oppose each other, thereby engendering *class opposition* between the owners of the means of production and wage earners; this opposition is rooted in the socio-economic structure and is latently present even if those involved are not necessarily aware of it in such terms. One could also define class opposition as the main structural condition of class tension (see below). Thus, class opposition not only marks work relations but permeates social reality in all its dimensions, since the class position of the members tends to determine their life chances; for example, income, consumption, education and political power. This is why the state – in this model – tends to be an instrument of domination for the economically dominant class.[18]

At a second level, class position and class opposition increasingly determine the subjective (or 'manifest') interests, expectations and intentions, behaviour, attitudes and self-image of class members. Here class opposition is manifested as *class tension*. Unlike class opposition, class tension can be discovered in the consciousness and utterances of class members reflecting their dissatisfactions, hopes, resentments, protests, demands etc;[19] it can thus be understood to be the main psychological condition of class conflict.[20] The transformation of class opposition into class tension means, for the members of the dependent, dominated class, that they perceive a discrepancy arising between their actual life chances (as experienced and understood) and what they regard as legitimate expectations and claims, and that this discrepancy is interpreted with regard to the common class position.

One needs to ascertain in each case under what conditions and forms this by no means automatic transformation takes place. It should be borne in mind that the discrepancy between experienced life chances and legitimate expectations and claims can widen as a consequence of markedly reduced life chances, or of rising expectations, or of both.[21] Questions about what gives rise to such a discrepancy follow from these preliminary deliberations.[22]

At a third level class position and class opposition also determine the – ultimately political – organisation of class interests and the various measures and actions undertaken to promote or defend them. Thus class tension becomes *class conflict* in which – according to our model – the state is engaged in the service of the economically dominant class to the detriment of the dominated majority of the population. To what degree and in what form this crystallisation process takes place depends on empirically ascertainable and by no means automatically given conditions. It can be impeded, distorted or prevented through a lack of communication and contact between class members, through the non-availability of leadership groups and conflict-legitimating ideologies or through intensive political repression.[23] The tendency towards ever clearer class oppositions, increasing class tensions and stronger class conflict sharpens the situation in an increasingly revolutionary manner. In Marx's words: 'Society as a whole is more and more splitting up into two great hostile camps, into two great classes directly facing each other . . .'.[24] Ever greater and more concentrated wealth and ever more available power in the hands of ever less cooperative entrepreneurs on the one hand corresponds with an increase in '. . . the mass of misery, oppression, slavery, degradation, exploitation; but with this grows too the revolt of the working class, a class always increasing in numbers, and disciplined, united, organised by the very mechanism of the process of capitalist production itself'.[25]

If, for analytical purposes, a distinction is made between three levels or dimensions of class or class formation, this may easily be misunderstood as being mechanistic or teleological. It should be emphasised, therefore, that we are ascribing neither a causal unilinearity nor a strict chronology to our model of the relationship between the three levels. Rather, the way in which class conflict (third level) is acted out influences the forms of class tension and the development of class consciousness (second level). It would be wrong to suppose that class consciousness and tension (second level) should be fully developed before the emergence of class organisation and conflict (third level). The characteristics of class opposition (first level) are also influenced by the manner in which class tensions (second level) and conflicts (third level) are manifested. Such retrospective and reciprocal influences will need empirical substantiation, even if one considers this three-level order of the above dimensions as logically and historically dominant and even if their sharp analytical separation is indispensable for the sake of clarity and verifiability.[26]

If this model[27] is now used for the analysis of German reality between 1914 and 1918, this does not imply that the model covers that reality *in toto*. Notice must be taken of the fact that oppositions, tensions and conflicts occurred which were not of a class character – such as those between religious denominations, regions, generations, town and country, large-scale agricultural and industrial enterprises, different branches of industry, and so forth. Such social divisions cut across social class lines as sketched out in our model. Other forms of differentation such as income levels, consumption patterns, levels of education, traditional status differences and functional/occupational differences no doubt constituted layers and groups which were not identical with the classes according to the dichotomous model but were bisecting or fragmenting them. In no way does our model negate the existence of these lines of differentiation.

However, the model does imply the expectation (which needs to be substantiated) that the criterion of 'class' (as defined above) within the research period increasingly pushed other differentiations into the background. To put it another way: the model posits that the lines of differentiation which ran straight through those of class diminished in their objective and subjective significance; they were thus tendentially levelled out and blurred; classes hence became more homogeneous; the dichotomous class structure therefore became clearer and more dominant during the war.[28]

The model is therefore used in the sense of an hypothetical trend and used like an ideal type. The main interest is in describing and explaining the changing distance between reality (as manifested in the sources) and the model,[29] we are not concerned with its falsification or verification. Historical reality is compared with it in order to establish to what degree and in what regard it accorded with reality and whether and in what way and why reality approximated to the model (confirming its hypotheses) or became more removed from it (thus contradicting its hypotheses). We will return to the possibilities and limitations of this approach in the last chapter.

2 Workers and Employers in Industry

1. The situation in 1914

Before 1914 the numbers of those engaged in industry and craft production grew both absolutely and relatively. In 1882, 1895 and 1907, 34 per cent and 40 per cent respectively of those economically active were engaged in mining, industry and craft production. In these areas of the economy, the proportion of self-employed declined continuously, with the proportion of employees increasing to the same extent. More and more employees were working in large-scale enterprises – whether one defines these as enterprises with more than 50, 100 or 1,000 workers.[1] If one tries to confine the enquiry solely to industrial entrepreneurs and workers, leaving out artisan's ('Handwerk') workshops and white-collar industrial employees, one encounters problems of definition and statistics which are difficult to resolve. In Germany the social language, the law and (sometimes) statistics differentiate between craft production ('Handwerk') and industry ('Industrie'). But this distinction is inexact, open to dispute, multi-dimensional and ideologically charged. Following contemporary practice, all enterprises with more than ten workers are to be subsumed, in what follows, as *industrial* undertakings (Industrie), all those with ten employees and less as artisan's enterprises (Handwerk).[2] This schematic approach produces no more than approximate values, but it does allow one to use the Reichs-Gewerbe-Statistik, the official business statistics of the German Reich. According to these there were, in 1907:[3]

Size according to number of employees	Industrial enterprises	Total number employed
11 – 50	89,645	1,985,295
51 – 200	23,493	2,176,053
201 – 1000	4,993	1,875,628
Over 1000	478	879,305
Total	118,609	6,916,281

Thus, in 1907, nearly 120,000 manufacturers – of whom about one-quarter were owners or directors of enterprises with more than fifty employees – were ranged against about 6.2 million industrial workers (excluding white-collar workers), of whom nearly three-quarters worked in enterprises with more than fifty employees. The relationship between these two industrial classes changed in the two decades before the First World War in a manner which cannot be easily compressed into a neat formula.

Socio-economic differentiation within both classes was great. The unskilled worker in a small-town brickworks and the highly qualified mechanic in a Berlin electrical engineering firm differed widely in income, work conditions and life chances, while the owner of a small rural saw-mill differed even more from an industrialist like Krupp. However, under the conditions of progressive industrialisation, socio-economic differentiation between wage earners (but not between entrepreneurs) probably decreased rather than increased. The irreversible growth of the factory system with its machines, division of labour and tight discipline, slowly reduced the lingering effects of craft traditions. Certainly, with the advance of technology and production, new activity- and branch-specific differences, as well as new demands and qualifications arose; the large wage and salary differentials between branches of industry tended to increase rather than decrease between 1895 and 1913.[4] But it is noteworthy that the average earnings differential between skilled and unskilled workers had diminished since the 1890s and that, between 1895 and 1907 (taking the inexact figures of the occupational statistics), the number of unskilled industrial workers had grown more quickly than that of the skilled.[5] The situation of increasingly widespread large-scale enterprises in which workers from different trades worked together under similar circumstances produced a relative retreat of the craft component in the work situation of such industrial workers. Such a displacement found socio-psychological expression in a growing stress on a commonly experienced employee – or class – consiousness, despite the con-. tinuation of occupational earnings-related, attitudinal or regional differences; organisationally, it found expression in the rise of industrial unions, side by side with the traditional craft unions.[6]

The increasing, if limited, tendency towards homogeneity within the working class did not run parallel with its socio-economic emiseration. In many respects the wage earners of 1914 had more to lose than their chains, more than in 1870 or 1895. In contrast to the conclusions of previous research, it should be noted that from 1880 the average annual earnings of industrial workers rose continually, not only nominally, but also – despite a rising cost of living – in real terms. Although their real growth between 1900 and 1913 was admittedly slower than from 1890 to 1900, earnings did not stagnate or decline before 1913.[7] In the last years of peace, the average industrial worker still needed four-fifths of his annual income for food, clothes, housing and heating; he could, nevertheless, spend 4 per cent of his income on 'psychic and social needs' and could save 1 per cent.[8] In the decades before 1914 the average time spent at work decreased and the frequency of fatal work accidents fell (as did workers' mortality rates generally). The hesitant advance of workers' protection legislation and the social insurance schemes developed after the 1880s, together with the welfare provisions within some firms, embodied modest gains in economic and social security.[9]

However, these tendencies remained very limited: a redistribution of the per capita income of the population in favour of dependent workers at the expense of entrepreneurial activity and wealth did not occur, in spite of the slow growth in workers' real income. On the contrary: while the share of wages – that is, the proportion of the national income allotted to dependent workers – grew, it grew less (approximately) after 1890 than did the size of the dependent sector in relation to the economically active whole.[10] In other words, the growth of the German economy was fast enough to bring about a moderate real growth in buying power among the employed, while at the same time allowing entrepreneurial profits and investment income to rise even more quickly. The structure of taxable incomes changed accordingly. In Prussia, for example, the proportion, out of all income recipients, of those drawing small incomes (under 900M) declined very clearly from the middle of the 1890s. The small absolute number of those drawing very high incomes (over 100,000M per annum) seems, however, to have increased even more rapidly in the same period than did the number drawing medium-sized incomes.[11] Other limitations to the economic rise of the industrial labour force before 1914 must not be overlooked, even if it worked towards a degree of integration of the working class into the society of the German Reich: in particular, when there were several children to be fed the working-class family could not do without the wife's labour; such a double burden often had oppressive consequences for family life and the upbringing of children. In addition, accidents and illness could herald economic disaster. Old age continued to be an impoverished phase for most workers who survived long enough.[12] Parallel with the shortening of working hours went a not easily measurable intensification of work.[13] Little was changed in the basic determination of the worker's existence by others and by his dependence on the market.

Such limited improvements in the economic situation of the workers were only very partially transformed into improvements in their general life chances and chances of political influence. The sharpness of the difference between proletariat and bourgeoisie in Germany, which arose from the continuing effect of older traditions and the peculiarities of German nation-state formation, also marked the whole spectrum of social relations both inside and outside firms. The lack of parliamentarism in the political system and the incomplete democratisation of voting rights blocked the workers' chances of political influence. In 1914, on the eve of the War, the workers formed a quite clearly identifiable, excluded and underprivileged group.[14]

Despite economic improvements, the scarcely diminishing class opposition manifested itself in class tensions and conflicts, whose intensity and forms were influenced by the social and political systems at large. Mainly as a result of discrimination and exclusion, the Social Democratic labour movement, fast-growing since the 1890s, became a largely self-encapsulated, protective community concerned with the economic chances, political rights and the culture and life of its members. It combined concrete reformist endeavours (above all in the unions but then increasingly politically, first in local government, later on the level of the single states and finally, to a limited degree, in the Reich) with a socialist class-conflict type rhetoric and with revolutionary, internationalist programmes. This had little to do with its political praxis and the consciousness of most of its members, but it served both as a justification and pretext for the wide-spread anti-proletarian resentments and anti-Socialist heretications in Wilhelmine society. Defensive anti-proletarian attitudes and militant anti-Socialism certainly did not decrease before the First World War, but found – in close connection with nationalist-imperialist ideologies – their organisational form in new mass associations (for example, the Pan-German League of 1893, the German Navy League of 1898 and the Reich Association against Social Democracy of 1904).[15] These served as ideological cement for the otherwise differing ruling groups and were used, partly consciously and manipulatively as in certain forms of 'Mittelstand politics', as an effective means of integration to safeguard the status quo.[16]

The fast growth of the unions, particularly the Social Democratic ones,[17] and the rapid increase in the number of SPD votes in the Reichstag elections (mostly stemming from the working class)[18] reflected the growing significance of class position and class consciousness for the organisational and political behaviour of the workers. In the development of the unions, and in the subsequent extension, consolidation and finally fusion of the employers' associations,[19] one factor which increasingly influenced the transformation of class tension into class conflict before 1914 became evident: organisation.[20]

Class tension did not primarily manifest itself in an increase in spontaneous outbreaks of unrest, of collective protests or of violence.[21] Instead it showed itself in union-organised strike movements and in the increasing confrontation, at the level of the political decision-making process, between emancipatory forces and those defending the status quo. There are some indications that the organisation of class tensions and conflicts contributed to their domestication even before 1914. This could be seen in the advance of the principle of collective wage agreements (usually outside large-scale enterprises)[22] as well as in the careful, reformist, organisation-conscious politics of the union leadership, who were able to bring an increasing proportion of agitations for improved wages and working conditions to a successful conclusion without strike action. On the other hand, the *intensity* of conflicts would appear to have increased and the balance of power to have shifted noticeably in favour of the employers. The frequency and length of labour disputes reached a peak in 1906 and again in 1910 to 1911; in these the number of lockouts increased both absolutely and in relation to the number of strikes.[23] In large-scale enterprises the employers replied to union demands with new techniques of integration and domination – above all with the successful nurturing of 'yellow' works associations.[24] Laws which restricted the right of association and strike continued to be effective.[25] Welfare legislation, which was intended to reduce tensions and conflicts, was brought to a standstill after 1911.[26]

The widespread political and social efforts for emancipation and reform in the labour movement, which found partial but increasing support in left-wing middle-class circles, called forth in the last decade before the War (and especially after the great SPD success in the Reichstag elections of 1912) an increasingly organised and vigorous counter-movement from large sections of industrial and agrarian big business. These groups had a limited success, by relying on nationalism, anti-socialism, opposition to reform and fear of revolution, in pushing their differences into the background; their aim was to strengthen their mass base among the small farmers and lower middle class and to form a reactionary block against the forces pressing against them.[27]

This heterogeneous defensive alliance of socio-economically dominant groups[28] did not, however, include all entrepreneurs and it had only a limited influence on the state bureaucracy. It was not strong enough to bring about the dismantling of the degree of democratisation and parliamentarism which had been achieved by then; programmes of this sort – including the idea of a 'Staatsstreich' – had, it would seem, no real chance of being realised up to the beginning of the War. The alliance was, however, influential enough to block further emancipation, such as the reform of Prussian voting rights, the strengthening of parliaments in the Reich and in individual states, social policies, greater union recognition, and so on. Curtailment of the government's freedom of action and a socio-political stagnation which stood in sharp contrast to the socio-economic modernisation of Germany were the result.[29] But this situation of simultaneous tension and stagnation was not a pre-revolutionary one. Whether it could have been overcome without revolution and without war is a difficult and unsolved problem. But the present question is different – how did the relationship of the two industrial classes change in the course of, and under the influence of, the First World War?

2. Impoverishment and deprivation of the workers

The size and composition of the German labour force changed

considerably during the War. In industrial enterprises (including mining) with ten or more employees there were approximately the following number of workers:[30]

	1913 (in 1000)	1918 (in 1000)	Change 1913–18 (per cent)
Men			
Adults	5410	4046	–25
Under 16	384	421	+10
Total	5794	4467	–23
Women			
Adults	1406	2139	+52
Under 16	187	181	– 3
Total	1593	2320	+46
Men and women			
Adults	6816	6185	– 9
Under 16	571	602	+ 6
Total	7387	6787	– 8

Overall, the number of industrial workers only declined by about 8 per cent during the War. This loss apparently took place in the first two years: between 1916 and 1918 the total number of industrial workers probably increased again slightly, since it was only then that the number of female industrial workers grew rapidly above the prewar level without resulting in a further reduction of male industrial workers.[31] Indeed the number of adult male industrial workers had, at the end of the War, declined by only one-quarter from the prewar level. This was even though half of all self-employed craftsmen had been called up for military service or work (under the Auxiliary Service Law) by 1917 and nearly half of *all* German men between the ages of 15 and 60 had been conscripted by 1918;[32] furthermore the number of people insured by craft associations (Berufsgenossenschaften) decreased by a full 30 per cent between 1913 and 1918.[33] This relative numerical stability of the male industrial workforce was the result of a low call-up rate in comparison with other areas of the economy; of deferments and exemptions for work in the war industries;[34] of the recruitment of people previously working in less important areas outside industry (particularly craft and trade) who were redeployed, especially after the end of 1916; of the use of older men who were no longer eligible for military service; and of the employment of foreign workers and prisoners of war.[35] The reduction in the industrial male workforce which nevertheless took place was largely compensated for by the sudden rise in female labour after 1916. In 1913 the proportion of females in industry (in enterprises with more than ten people) had hardly reached 22 per cent; by 1918 it was 34 per cent. At the end of the War, there were, on occasion, more women than men working in the large armaments factories.[36] By comparison, the growth of juvenile labour was much less important.

The distribution of the workforce throughout industry changed radically, with the yardstick of change being the military importance of the goods produced. One may divide the various industries into three groups: *war industries,* producing primarily for military needs (metal manufacture, machine construction, including the electrical industry, and the chemical, petroleum and oil industries); *peace industries,* producing primarily for civilian needs (food production, textiles and printing); and an *intermediate group* which included mining, the building trade, quarrying, wood, leather and paper industries and the cleaning trade as well as 'other trades'. There was accordingly the following redistribution of the workforce:[37]

| | Numbers employed (in 1000) | | Change 1913–18 |
	1913	1918	(per cent)
War industries	2116	3050	+44
Intermediate group	2970	2359	–21
Peace industries	2301	1380	–40

Thus while the number of those employed in the peace industries was almost halved, numbers working in war industries rose by 44 per cent. Uneven recruitment for military service, stoppages and the redistribution of raw materials and contracts following the 1916 Auxiliary Service Law[38] brought about this profound restructuring, which was largely carried out during the second half of the War[39] and resulted in a hitherto unparalleled degree of mobility among employees. In the middle of 1917 the firm of Siemens-Schuckert, which had gone over from automobile to armaments production, stated that 'since the beginning of the War our workforce has renewed itself eight times'.[40] Two large iron works in the Düsseldorf area noted a labour turn-over during the War (up to 1 October 1918) which was four to five times as high as the average size of their labour force. *On arithmetical average*, therefore, each worker in these firms stayed scarcely a year at his workplace.[41]

This restructuring also implies that at the end of the War a higher proportion of necessary work than before was carried out by rapidly trained labour[42] (previously unoccupied women and juveniles and those previously working in other areas of the economy). Traditional occupational differences within the labour force were thereby further reduced and the proportion of minimally qualified workers increased sharply during the War.

Overall, the nominal earnings of workers were, roughly speaking, doubled and trebled during the course of the War, although the rate of development of the various branches of industry varied considerably, according to their importance for the war effort and the manpower needs of the respective sectors. The Reich Statistical Department kept track of the enhancement of earnings in 370 enterprises, as the Table overleaf (p.20) shows (these results were corroborated by other investigations carried out at regional and urban level).[43] Reference to this Table reveals that between March 1914 and September 1918 the average increase in annual earnings in the 370 selected enterprises was:[44]

	Men	Women
War industries	+ 152%	+ 186%
Intermediate group	+ 109%	+ 132%
Peace industries	+ 81%	+ 102%

The conspicuous advance of earnings in essential war industries (all of them production goods industries) points to the war-specific distortions of demand and deployment. Men working in food production (+ 50 per cent), benefited the least, women in metal manufacture (+ 324 per cent) and men in the electrical industry (+ 298 per cent) benefited the most. From the start of the War until 1916–17 earnings differentials between branches of industry increased significantly. This development was in contrast to the postwar trend and had already begun to be reversed in the last year of the War, probably because wage increases had to be granted to poorly paid workers on social and political grounds and because the labour

Average annual earnings in 370 enterprises 1914–18
(March 1914 = 100)   (nominal earnings)

Industry	1914 Mar.	Sept.	1915 Mar.	Sept.	1916 Mar.	Sept.	1917 Mar.	Sept.	1918 Mar.	Sept.
					Male workers					
Metal manufacture	100	102	114	125	135	145	178	213	217	234
Machine construction	100	98	120	132	139	149	173	202	243	245
Chemicals	100	96	104	118	125	134	157	194	203	232
Electrical industry	100	89	110	117	127	165	205	242	267	298
4 war industries	100.0	96.2	112.0	123.0	131.5	148.2	178.2	212.8	232.5	252.2
Quarrying	100	85	88	100	106	116	132	151	166	188
Wood	100	102	108	109	123	133	147	185	184	236
Leather & rubber	100	98	97	114	115	126	144	154	162	173
Paper	100	106	114	124	129	141	160	188	210	240
Intermediate group	100.0	97.8	101.8	111.8	118.2	129.0	145.8	169.5	180.5	209.2
Food production	100	102	104	105	103	108	114	132	137	150
Textiles	100	88	101	111	110	115	122	142	159	178
Clothing	100	72	94	98	106	97	130	155	180	216
Printing trades	100	92	104	111	116	118	142	140	148	179
4 peace industries	100.0	88.5	100.8	106.2	108.8	109.5	127.0	142.2	156.0	180.8
Average total	100.0	94.2	104.8	113.7	119.5	128.9	150.3	174.8	189.7	214.1

Industry	1914 Mar.	Sept.	1915 Mar.	Sept.	1916 Mar.	Sept.	1917 Mar.	Sept.	1918 Mar.	Sept.
					Female workers					
Metal manufacture	100	81	108	147	169	200	228	277	287	324
Machine construction	100	86	126	140	159	170	189	214	264	275
Chemicals	100	81	100	111	131	150	174	221	239	280
Electrical industry	100	76	109	124	142	175	191	225	239	267
4 war industries	100.0	81.0	110.8	130.5	150.2	173.8	195.5	234.2	255.7	286.5
Quarrying	100	89	97	112	117	131	154	172	186	232
Wood	100	89	116	98	111	130	159	191	219	274
Leather & rubber	100	84	88	98	108	113	134	147	148	171
Paper	100	104	107	118	123	133	170	190	213	250
Intermediate group	100.0	91.5	102	106.5	114.8	126.8	154.2	175.0	191.5	231.8
Food production	100	90	100	110	114	138	135	177	192	202
Textiles	100	89	97	101	105	101	112	144	170	187
Clothing	100	67	95	80	100	95	125	156	175	219
Printing trades	100	90	89	103	110	114	126	147	167	199
4 peace industries	100.0	84.0	95.2	98.5	107.2	112.0	124.5	156.0	176.0	201.8
Average total	100.0	85.5	102.7	111.8	124.1	137.5	158.1	188.4	207.7	240.0

shortages now hit the peace industries with renewed force.[45] If one looks at the nominal earnings and cost of living for separate categories of workers with regard to regional divergences, which tended to increase during the War, the differences become even greater. While a highly specialised setter in a Berlin armaments factory could earn more than before the War, perhaps 25M per day (7500M per annum), an unskilled worker in a small-town weaving mill received possibly only 3.50M per day, or 1200–1300M per annum – that is to say, one-sixth of that sum.[46]

Workers' earnings, however, became more uniform in other respects. The average earnings differential between skilled and the unskilled declined, with the exception of some particularly scarce categories of skilled labour in armaments production (such as toolmakers), which made particularly large gains. Such levelling was effected by an observable tendency towards a 'social wage' achieved by not allowing wages which lagged behind the cost of living to sink too far below subsistence level and by determining wages according to need, not simply according to market forces. Other levelling factors included the payment of lump-sum bonuses, rather than those calculated as a percentage of the wage; a tendency towards 'dilution', owing to the massive influx of labour which needed to be quickly trained; also perhaps the increased use of mechanisation, whose introduction in Germany, in sharp contrast to England, did not generally arouse the opposition of skilled workers.[47] In general, earnings differentials between men and women declined in the second half of the War, as female labour also became scarce and many women moved into better skilled, more highly valued occupations formerly reserved for men. The earnings of juvenile and adult labour also became somewhat more equal during the War.[48]

A number of reasons can be given for the devaluation,[49] at first slight but increasing rapidly from 1916. These include the destruction of assets due to the War and the great scarcity of goods; the financing of the War, primarily, by printing money; generous price policies adopted by a diminishing number of military and government agencies; the inability or lack of desire to effect a thorough-going reduction in purchasing power and a negative balance of trade. The actual degree of devaluation is estimated variously according to different methods of calculation. The following table shows average annual values (1913 = 100):[50]

	(1)	(2)	(3)	(4)
Year	$ rate	Food index (Calwer)	Wholesale trade prices	Standard of living index (Reich Statistical Dept/G.Bry)
1913	100	100	100	100
1914	102	101	105	103
1915	116	143	142	129
1916	132	198	152	170
1917	157	213	179	253
1918	143	229	217	313
1919	470	326	415	415
1920	1500	953	1486	1020

When calculated on the basis of the most reliable standard of living index (column 4) and the nominal annual earnings in the 370 selected enterprises referred to above, the annual earnings of the average male worker in the war industries fell, in real terms, by almost 23 per cent between 1914 and 1919, in the peace industries by a full 44 per cent and in the intermediate group by 36 per cent. The losses were somewhat less for women: 12 per cent in the war industries, 39 per cent in the peace industries and 29 per cent in the intermediate group. Even on the basis of the less reliable and incomplete Quante Index,[51] which probably somewhat underestimated the price rises of the War, many average male nominal earnings (outside the electrical industry) and female nominal earnings (outside the wood industry) fell behind the rising cost of living. Contemporary stories, based on the conspicuous but numerically few high-income earners amongst armaments workers, and historical interpretations of current opinion that workers achieved 'considerable material advantages' through the War[52] cannot, therefore, be accepted.[53] Rather, the prewar trend of slowly rising real earnings was suddenly and noticeably reversed during the War for most (though not all) wage labourers. The impoverishment of the labour force continued during the postwar inflation and was only made good after 1923.

German workers suffered a steeper decline in real earnings during the War than did their British colleagues (whose real average earnings, however, had probably already stagnated before 1914). In Germany between 1914 and 1918 both the standard of living index and the average nominal wage rose higher than they did in either Great Britain or the USA during the same period, while the ratio between the two was less favourable for the workers in the Anglo-Saxon countries than in the Reich.[54] This feature illustrates the particular difficulties faced by the Reich which, as an import-dependent country, was transformed by the blockade into a 'besieged fortress', suffering acutely from war-induced shortages. To a lesser degree, it points to a specific policy of financing the War which avoided, to an even greater extent than in Great Britain, financing it through taxes but rather through an inflationary increase in the money supply;[55] perhaps it points also to a weakness of workers' organisations *vis-à-vis* employers' interests and to a relative lack of state control and organisation within the economy. We shall be returning to these points below.

The following table presents a more detailed picture:[56]

Average annual earnings of workers in 370 enterprises, 1914–18 (March 1914 = 100)   (real earnings)

	1914		1915		1916		1917		1918	
	Mar.	Sept.	Mar.	Sept.	Mar.	Sept.	Mar.	Sept.	Mar.	Sept.
Male workers										
War industries	100	90.8	91.8	89.8	88.9	78.4	76.2	78.8	77.8	77.4
Intermediate group	100	92.3	83.4	81.6	79.9	68.3	62.3	62.8	60.4	64.2
Peace industries	100	83.5	82.6	77.5	73.5	57.9	54.3	52.7	52.2	55.5
Average total	100	88.9	85.9	83.0	80.8	68.2	64.3	64.8	63.4	65.7
	1914		1915		1916		1917		1918	
	Mar.	Sept.	Mar.	Sept.	Mar.	Sept.	Mar.	Sept.	Mar.	Sept.
Female workers										
War industries	100	76.4	90.8	95.3	101.5	92.0	83.5	86.7	86.0	87.9
Intermediate group	100	86.3	83.6	77.7	77.6	67.1	65.9	64.8	64.0	71.1
Peace industries	100	79.2	78.0	71.9	72.4	59.3	53.2	57.8	58.9	61.9
Average total	100	80.6	84.1	81.6	83.8	72.8	67.5	69.8	69.6	73.6

These figures demonstrate that, during the crisis of economic adaptation at the beginning of the War (high temporary unemployment and declining nominal earnings), real earnings fell by between 10 and 20 per cent;[57] that prices as well as nominal earnings rose only slowly in the second phase (to about the middle of 1916) and real earnings declined only a little; that the third phase (from the middle of 1916 to the spring of 1917) saw a sharp increase in prices with nominal earnings lagging behind; and, finally, that in a fourth phase (from the spring of 1917 to the end of the War) earnings kept pace with continued fast-rising prices and no further loss of real earnings took place; on the contrary, a slight recovery became possible.

The significance of such figures is nevertheless limited, even if one accepts their statistical basis as adequate and the methods of calculation as acceptable. In the first place, the absolute shortage of food and consumer goods increased, leading from February 1915 (with the introduction of bread and flour ration cards) to the rationing of all important foodstuffs. In this Germany differed noticeably from England and the USA, due to the success of the English blockade, to its long-standing dependence on agricultural imports[58] and to its concentration on war production at the expense of consumer goods. Shortages reached such a level that even the slight rise in real earnings in the last year of the War brought few real improvements; even with more money, one could not buy much in shops with empty shelves. Only a great deal of money, good connections and, increasingly, the barter of hoarded goods and valuables could help here. About one-third of the civilian foodstuffs consumed was said to have been distributed on the black market towards the end of the War.[59] Statements about the cost of living and about real earnings deviate from reality to the degree in which provisions were actually acquired through the black market and by direct exchange.[60]

In this situation – and this is the second limitation to be placed on the significance of the real earnings figures – the direct supply of free, subsidised or at least accessible foodstuffs which the large armaments factories offered their labour force (or sections of it) became an important factor in the living standards of the minority of workers who profited from this.[61] Finally, one must take into account the fact that the development of real earnings had a very varied effect on workers and their families, according to how many members of the family were able to earn. According to an official survey, the earnings of wife and children before the War affected the income of a worker's family by an average of 6 to 10 per cent;[62] while this may be an underestimate, the percentage will certainly have increased owing to the rising number of women and children at work. The income (on which, of course, their buying power depended) of the family of a skilled worker who had escaped call-up and who had a working wife and growing children, some of whom might also be earning, differed quite considerably from that of other families where the father had been called up and the mother could support neither herself nor small children on the meagre public assistance offered, and was therefore forced to take badly paid part-time or temporary work to the detriment of the care of her children.[63]

It is certain that, for the great majority of workers, deprivation increased. In 1918 the official food ration for each individual, generally only incompletely supplemented on the black market, covered only 57 to 70 per cent of the calories needed for light work and 47 to 54 per cent of those needed for medium-heavy work. Official food rations, expressed as a percentage of peace-time consumption levels,[64] were:

	1916/17	1917/18	1.7–28.12. 1918
Meat	31.2	19.8	11.8
Eggs	18.3	12.5	13.3
Lard	13.9	10.5	6.7
Butter	22.0	21.3	28.1
Sugar	48.5	55.7–66.7	82.1
Potatoes	70.8	94.2	94.3
Vegetable oils	39.0	40.5	16.6

Undernourishment and deficiency diseases increased.[65] In August 1918 the 'Zentralverband der Dachdecker Deutschlands' (Central Association of German Roof-workers) petitioned the Reich Office of the Interior: 'It cannot go on like this. Our colleagues are perishing physically. For the last two years the prices of goods have risen in an altogether shameless manner. Goods which are produced in Germany have become 300 to 400 per cent dearer. In order to buy a pair of working trousers, which formerly cost 4 or 5M, one now needs a week's earnings. In 4 years, we received 50 per cent rise in wages. But it is not the War, but the greed for war profits which is to blame! Despite the 50 per cent wage increase, our colleagues suffer want. They cannot afford black market prices, and rationed goods cannot fill their stomachs. They no longer have anything to wear. It gets worse every week. Various articles have increased twenty times in price, earnings by only a half. We can no longer go on. We have come to the end. . . . Our cupboards, our boxes are empty, our savings lie in the money bags of the usurers. Our children are starving, they lack all necessities. Other things decay, because we can no longer clean them . . . it is simply beyond our strength . . .'.[66]

Apart from an elite group of armaments workers there was a levelling down of the workers' standard of living. In the face of increasing shortages of foodstuffs, clothes, coal and – in the industrial conurbations – housing,[67] this standard often fell below subsistence level. After the high level of unemployment that obtained at the beginning of the War (22.9 per cent in July, 22.4 per cent in August 1914) had eased by the spring of 1915,[68] average worktime, against the pre-1914 trend, was increased, until protests in the summer of 1918 forced a new reduction; the number of accidents at work and of illness among workers increased significantly.[69] At the beginning of the War certain welfare protection laws (for example, on overtime and night work) were set aside.[70] The transfer of large parts of the labour force to different branches of industry and to other housing areas led, for many, to great difficulties of adjustment in work and daily life. A tool grinder reported from a Berlin armaments firm in 1917: 'Work conditions were such as they must have been under early capitalism. Something was always the matter. Particularly during the night shift. There was no night without the collapse of one or more women at the machines, because of exhaustion, hunger, illness. Rows of machines were stopped for hour after hour because transmission belts had snapped; sometimes material was lacking, sometimes tools. On some days in winter there was no heating, the workers stood around in groups, they could not and would not work. The canteen served turnips twelve times a week, turnips at midday and at midnight; sometimes, mostly without, potatoes. In the canteen, women had almost daily screaming fits, and sometimes depressing fights amongst themselves, because they alleged "the ladle was not full"'.[71]

The shortage of foodstuffs and of labour, the demands of a war which sought to mobilise all economic and human reserves and which was increasingly decided not only by particular economic and socio-political decisions but by the economic strength of the warring states, created for the working class a situation of shortage, deprivation and exploitation such as had not existed since the beginning of industrialisation.[72]

3. Changes in the socio-economic situation of entrepreneurs in the war economy

In order to arrive at an estimate of the changes induced by the War in the socio-economic situation of industrial entrepreneurs, one must first accept that the War represented an impoverishment of the whole national economy. According to Wagenführ's estimates, total industrial production during the period of the War and the Revolution declined by at least 40 per cent, though with large differences from industry to industry, and in spite of inducements and subsidies from the Reich.[73]

Production in important industrial branches (1913 = 100)

	1913	1914	1915	1916	1917	1918
NE-metal	100	89	72	113	155	234
Mining industry	100	84	78	86	90	83
Iron and steel	100	78	68	61	83	53
Merchant shipping	100	73	65	75	61	42
Building material	100	88	69	59	58	35
Textiles	100	87	65	27	22	17
Housing	100	68	30	10	4	4

Initially the recession, already evident in 1913, was intensified during the critical period of economic adaptation to the outbreak of war; this led to a decline in production. The far-reaching stabilisation of total production that took place during 1916 and 1917 may have begun in mid-1915 and certainly continued well into 1918. Its results were growth in those branches of industry necessary for the War effort, with a simultaneous decrease in non-essential sectors. Finally, defeat, collapse and revolution meant a sharp overall industrial and economic decline.

The chief causes of this loss of production were lack of raw materials and fuel,[74] shortage of labour and the decline in productivity that occurred in 1917–18 (at the latest).[75] This decline was the result of the war-induced changes discussed earlier, in which women, juveniles and rapidly-trained semi-skilled and unskilled workers formed an increasing percentage of the labour force, where their performance deteriorated owing to under-nourishment and overwork and, most probably, as their inner doubts as to the utility and purpose of their exertions grew. In addition, the machinery used suffered from lack of proper maintenance, inappropriate usage and the use of ersatz raw materials and lubricating oils.[76] Thus the wearing out of the overworked apparatus of production and the changing centre of gravity of industrial production to countries not centrally involved in the War, especially outside Europe,[77] already apparent before 1914 but now accelerated, were prominent among the long-term disadvantages that industrial entrepreneurs suffered as a consequence of the War. Against such losses, however, should be set their positional gains, very noticeable in comparison with those of other social groups and, historically, of greater weight.

It is widely recognised that, during the War, it was the military and civilian authorities who influenced and organised production and distribution processes to a degree unknown in peacetime, although by no means total. Their aim, under the extreme conditions of a war which increasingly depended on the economic strength of those engaged, was to maximise the Reich's chances of victory, expansion and, ultimately, of self-preservation. As the most important customer, and as entrepreneur, the state more and more replaced, or worked in conjunction with, private entrepreneurs in production which was increasingly adapted to meet wartime needs. With the aid of traditional but greatly expanded economic and financial policies, it *partially* suspended the previous private economic market mechanism, to a constantly greater degree and with successively increasing intensity. Admittedly, industrial production did not come under such strong public control as did trade and agriculture. But the state administration wielded a strong influence on industry by its growing public control of raw materials, which soon became almost total; by the allocation of contracts; by influencing the labour market through call-up and deferment; by such intervention in welfare and wages as the direct re-distribution of the labour force under the terms of the Hilfsdienstgesetz (Auxiliary Service Act) of December 1916; by investment legislation; and by the founding of new enterprises and the selective closure of existing ones. Conversely industrialists, for their part, found they had gained new incentives and opportunities to exert an influence on interventionalist public authorities.[78] At the same time, the organisation of economy and society through the state had for individual authorities and officials the function and, for many interested parties, the additional purpose of re-distributing or securing economic and social opportunities and power. The use of public money in the form of credits and subsidies, for instance, as well as state participation in the private sector of essential war industries operated both to further the national war economy *and* to the advantage of individual groups of entrepreneurs. This was particularly the case where there was rapid new development (for instance, in aircraft construction, aluminium smelting and nitrogen manufacture), where existing plants were converted for armaments production and where the investment returns for private entrepreneurs appeared to them to be too low. In such cases it was the public sector who largely took on the risks while the profit remained with private entrepreneurs.[79] While actual production declined, some productive capacity was enlarged with the help of public funds, thereby propelling an (admittedly war-distorted) industrial expansion.[80]

The requirements for an effective war economy also favoured entrepreneurs in other respects. As industry's main customer and on the basis of its interest in the most rational distribution of factors of production in short supply, the state encouraged, strengthened, demanded and occasionally enforced the organisation of the producers who came under its supervision. State officials wished to have dealings with only one negotiating partner in each branch of industry; it was this individual to whom raw materials, contracts and directions could be given, prices and conditions negotiated, and further contracts, materials and to some extent labour be apportioned and to whom certain supervisory and executive functions (the receipt of supplies, requisitions, decisions over stoppages, prevention of competition, control of exports etc.) could be handed over. The 200 War Associations and War Boards which gradually emerged, each specialising in a particular branch of industry and employing a total of some 33,000 by 1918,[81] served this purpose first and foremost. By the purchase of shares, any enterprise could affiliate itself to one of these organisations, which were often founded as either 'Aktiengesellschaften' (AGs, or joint-stock companies) or 'Gesellschaften mit beschränkter Haftung' (GmbH – a special type of company with limited liability), using both public and private funds, and which were prohibited from making profits over a certain percentage of return on capital. A firm was well-advised to join, since through affiliation it gained contracts, factors of production and information. Such self-administrative organisations – for example, the 'Kriegs-Metall AG' or the 'Kriegsausschuss für Baumwollindustrie' – undertook, in changing forms, tasks which had arisen partly from the war but most of which had previously been left to individual enterprises; for the more effective functioning of these tasks, the state delegated some of its authority. On the other hand, they were subject to varied forms of government supervision and under increasing[82] state control and influence. The close financial, staff, functional and spatial links between the industrial self-administrative organisations and the public authorities responsible for them make it difficult to assess the degree of influence and dependence between entrepreneurs and the authorities, between the private pressure group official or industrialist and the civil servant.[83] We shall return to this point. At all events, the decision-making process within bureaucratically organised institutions, that is, the negotiations and compromises between various directors of enterprises on the one hand, and between them and the state's representatives on the other, replaced the regulatory function of the capitalist market to a previously unknown degree. Competition and risk were thereby largely eliminated for the entrepreneurs, only the gains remained theirs![84]

The tendency towards a limitation of competition, already apparent before 1914 in an increase in the number of industrial agreements, associations, cartels and mergers, was thus enormously accelerated during the War; this led not only to the founding of the War Associations and Boards discussed above, but which disappeared after the War, but also to a long-term strengthening of industrial associations and an absolute increase in cartels and syndicates. With both an expanded role and state guarantees, these became a necessary part of the war economy, either as War Associations, or their subsections; in many cases they survived into the postwar period. By 1922 there were 1,500 cartels, three times as many as in 1906 – in the machine-processing industry alone there were 150 industrial associations as against twenty-five before the War. The members of the Association of German Machine-tool Factories numbered 89 in 1914, 200 in 1916, 299 in 1918 and 395 in 1921, while the business interests of the Association broadened out in a cartel-like manner. In other industries the centralisation of existing local industrial associations and syndicates was an after-effect of the War.[85]

Newly emerging wartime influences speeded up prewar long-term tendencies in this respect. Intensive support by the state for economic combinations and mergers, even to the extent of forcing through the creation of cartels and syndicates in areas such as the soap and shoe industries that had not been thoroughly organised by until then, and the prevention of the dissolution of existing cartels in spite of entrepreneurial opposition (as in potash, coal and steel), was a phenomenon which had not existed prior to 1914. This subsided after the end of the War. We will be returning to his point later on.

If a study of the development of wages can provide us with a certain amount of information about the condition of workers during the War, then the same may be expected from information on the profits made by entrepreneurs. Although the discussion about war profits had already begun in the first year of the War, and has been continued in the literature ever since, one must regard any questions about actual profits as still insoluble.[86] This is because entrepreneurs were able, during the War, to thwart[87] all official attempts to compel them to disclose their internal accounts and because the joint-stock companies, in the face of increasingly critical public opinion and the tardy, slight but growing tax on war profits, concealed their profits more completely than hitherto.[88] Declared profits must therefore be regarded as providing a minimal base-line for the computation of actual profits. These remained, as did dividends, far below the threefold increase in the cost of living and the doubling of wholesale prices. According to the published figures, changes in net profits and dividends in German joint-stock companies were as follows:[89]

Profits and dividends in German joint-stock companies (AGs)

Year	No. of AGs	No. of AGs with declared net profits	Total net profits in billion Marks	Net Profits as % of total comp- any capital	Dividends as % of total comp- any capital
1911/12	4,712	3,936	1,470	10.1	8.4
1912/13	4,773	3,979	1,656	10.9	8.7
1913/14	4,798	3,944	1,575	10.0	8.1
1914/15	4,748	3,600	1,230	7.9	6.6
1915/16	4,761	3,686	1,748	11.0	8.1
1916/17	4,710	3,858	2,049	13.0	9.3
1917/18	4,723	4,081	2,213	13.7	10.1
1918/19	4,553	3,822	1,425	8.7	8.1

A compilation by the *Frankfurter Zeitung* gave more precise results for the first two years of the War by examing the depreciation reserves, net profits and dividends (including super-dividends and other payments to shareholders) in a selected cross-section of German joint-stock companies on the basis of published accounts. These companies, with a total capital of some four billion Marks (about a quarter of all German share capital) realised very much higher gross profits in 1915 (1915/16) than in 1913 (1913/14). The breakdown and differentiation between different branches is shown in the table below. Nearly all the concerns examined adhered assiduously to a stringent financial policy and, apart from the cement, paper and rubber industries, bituminous

Accounts of selected joint-stock companies[90] for 1913 (1913/14) and (1915 (1915/16)

Branch of industry	Capital base (in Mill. Mk) 1915 or 1915/16	Depreciation (in 1000 Mk)		Net profit (in 1000 Mk)		Dividends & bonus (in Mk)		Dividends & bonus (in %)		Reserves (in 1000 Mk)	
		1913 or 1913/14	1915 or 1915/16	1913 or 1913/14	1915 or 1915/16	1913 or 1913/14	1915 or 1915/16	1913 or 1913/14	1915 or 1915/16	1913 or 1913/14	1915 or 1915/16
Chemicals	345.0	36,223	50,378	85,516	90,920	60,165	61,240	20.9	17.7	12,179	16,639
Munitions	91.7	5,656	12,361	10,598	44,980	8,716	20,870	14.2	22.7	632	17,831
Steel works, metal foundries and metal processing	180.5	14,326	37,392	26,347	85,368	17,756	37,400	9.8	20.7	5,604	42,225
Automobiles	87.3	7,319	18,933	11,154	38,023	5,976	15,355	7.7	18.4	3,455	18,711
Cement	77.1	6,530	627	10,514	−35	7,248	1,452	9.4	1.9	1,608	−1,298
Cellulose and paper	69.1	7,383	6,936	10,201	3,024	7,362	3,229	10.6	4.6	1,300	300
Rubber	5.2	7,822	9,082	10,824	2,192	9,067	3,882	16.1	14.8	2,055	3,474
Mills	36.3	2,276	3,957	3,771	5,992	2,554	3,915	7.0	10.8	879	1,171
Machines	252.2	21,874	34,049	33,287	46,809	20,687	31,101	8.6	12.3	8,936	8,174
Iron and steel	233.3	30,013	48,495	26,956	57,458	19,867	37,834	8.5	16.2	4,773	16,857
Mixed mining and foundry works	718.5	82,814	127,093	101,661	186,774	68,112	92,949	10.7	12.9	32,077	83,665
Coal	267.5	27,912	27,779	41,220	36,245	34,270	32,625	12.8	12.2	3,848	1,804
Leather	47.6	2,300	21,056	6,331	21,243	3,176	9,103	6.0	19.0	1,162	9,120
Electrical industry	727.8	27,864	49,000	77,465	103,627	60,064	74,146	9.1	10.4	9,290	16,425
Textiles	169.8	11,341	17,344	20,061	33,095	14,803	19,089	8.7	11.2	2,214	8,598
Shipbuilding	77.6	10,947	17,217	3,696	10,344	2,986	6,024	3.9	7.8	995	3,323
Lignite industry	231.9	21,992	25,895	29,819	29,830	24,039	24,972	10.4	10.8	2,969	2,479
Sugar	67.8	3,024	4,445	10,784	18,096	7,698	12,479	15.9	26.7	899	2,803
Hotels	42.2	3,727	2,744	1,187	−1,290	1,972	290	4.7	0.01	1,835	177
Breweries	107.6	10,453	11,795	16,616	17,743	8,952	10,238	8.4	9.5	4,951	4,165
Shoe manufacture	28.8	1,932	3,863	2,820	5,051	1,955	3,100	7.0	13.0	464	1,939

coal mining and the hotel trade, achieved high net profits, which usually more than made good their losses through inflation. For most of the large joint-stock companies in the iron and steel industry and (predictably) for the armaments and munitions factories, a large increase in gross profits can also be established for 1917.[91]

These figures can be regarded as more informative than the carefully laundered net profit figures in the Table on p.32. In addition the number of active German joint-stock companies fell slightly, from 4,773 (1913) to 4,723 (1918), while the number of companies with limited liability grew from 26,790 (1913) to 29,763 (1918).[92] Taken together with the fact that from the reopening of the stock exchange in 1917 to the late summer of 1918 the average share price stood clearly above the prewar level,[93] it would seem that, apart from the early adaptation crisis and the months of collapse in 1918, the War was not unprofitable for the large industrial enterprises generally. (It is more difficult to make statements about the profits of family firms, but later we shall have more to say about small businesses and about variations between branches of industry.) Nevertheless the favourable overall picture remains, even if we concede the loss of industrial capital (lack of maintenance, little or no replacement, running down of reserves) and the unsatisfactory nature of the available statistics, especially for the second half of the War.

Finally, German industry also reaped long-term benefits from certain positive consequences of the wartime shortage of labour and raw materials. The labour shortage speeded up the introduction of modern machine tools which could be used by the semi-skilled, by women and juveniles. Such gains through rationalisation partly account for the high profits; for example, the mining of lignite, whose use as a source of energy was first exploited during the War, became mechanised and in many industries mechanised handling of materials and products was introduced in order to redeploy scarce human labour.[94] An arms factory reported towards the end of 1917 on advances in rationalisation thanks to the introduction of preformed base plates; this change had enabled them to engage cheap, semi-skilled female labour: 'The previous manufacturing process required 6 skilled men and 1 woman to produce 42 pieces per day. Under the present one only 1 man and 3 women are needed to produce the same number of pieces in the same amount of time; labour costs have been reduced by 50 per cent.'[95]

The modernising effects of the War were indirectly strengthened by state intervention. In order to satisfy the enormous demand for armaments and munitions, the authorities dealing with supplies distributed their contracts among various firms; to guarantee the necessary uniformity of the components they successfully enforced standardisation between firms – a procedure sought by some entrepreneurs before the War but never implemented – thus contributing to the general advance of mass production in Germany.[96] The massive demand induced by the War aided the introduction of mass production methods in the optical industry and in steel manufacture. Thus in many cases the War laid the foundation for many post-war rationalisation policies;[97] for example, the development of the Haber-Bosch and Franck-Caro processes of nitrogen fixation was stimulated by the disappearance of imported saltpetre; advances in aluminium production were stimulated by the lack of copper and other imported metals. Among the many ersatz textile materials which were developed to alleviate the shortage of raw materials artificial silk, at least, survived the War. In response to the widespread shortage of coal, certain advances in heating technology were made, even though there were inadequate supplies of liquid heating material. Attempts to replace imported rubber by the production of synthetic could not meet the Army's need for tyres, although it did serve as the basis for later developments. State subsidies and state participation encouraged these innovations, which had long-term value and in which research played an ever more central role.[98]

But the fruits of war benefited some industrialists more than others. On the one hand, the far-reaching replacement of market forces by decision-making processes in formal organisations such as the War Associations (compulsory), cartels and associations often worked to the disadvantage of the smaller entrepreneur. Many medium and small enterprises were, for instance, reluctant to put capital into the War Associations and at first remained outside them. But even if they joined, their financial contribution and therefore their influence in the decision-making process remained slight. The large firms could easily second one or more employees as permanent representatives to these powerful administrative agencies, the small ones could not. The former had a better chance than the latter of placing their own people into the executive committees of the War Associations and similar groups, and thus of gaining privileged information and of influencing the decision-making process to their own advantage. The partial replacement of a market economy by a political-bureaucratic decision-making process in formal organisations tended to strengthen the already-existing superiority of the large over the small.[99] Stoppages, largely due to shortages of raw material and labour and, in 1917 and 1918, to closures decreed by the authorities, no doubt affected more strongly the medium- and small-sized firms, which were regarded as less efficient and which were not as capable of asserting themselves during negotiations as the large firms. We have already established that the number of joint-stock companies declined by a mere 1.5 per cent during the War, the number of limited liability companies even rising by 10 per cent. Thus the larger enterprises, constituted as shareholding companies, did not decline. It is estimated that in all 8 to 10 per cent of all factories were closed by the end of the War, either by the authorities or of their own 'free will' (that is, because of shortages of fuel, raw material, transport or orders) or were amalgamated with other firms.[100] These reductions must therefore have taken place largely at the expense of family firms and of other privately owned firms. Accelerating prewar tendencies, industrial concentration increased during the War, not only horizontally through the reduction in the number of competitors in individual branches of industry, but also vertically. Heavy industry in particular strove to participate in manufacturing industry and shipping through board-room influence and the acquisition of shares. The tendency towards vertical integration also gained impetus from the efforts of producers to avoid certain new taxes introduced during the War, especially the 'Warenumsatzstempel', a form of turnover tax.[101]

On the other hand, the redeployment of industrial workers and the uneven development of output in different branches of industry[102] indicates that industries producing armaments and war materials profited very much more from the wartime boom than did those producing for civilian needs. The following profited from the wartime redeployment of labour – chemicals (+ 170 per cent), engineering (including electrical engineering) (+ 49 per cent), timber (+ 13 per cent); metal fabrication (+ 8 per cent) and mining (+ 5 per cent).[103] These industries were – with the exception of timber – those which had exhibited a rapid growth in numbers employed (or at least a less than average decline)[104] during the period 1875 to 1913. The quarrying industry (–59 per cent), textiles (–58 per cent), the building trade (–57 per cent), the clothing industry (–32 per cent), the printing trade (–31 per cent), the food industry (–24 per cent), paper (–20 per cent) and the leather industry (–17 per cent) lost an above-average number of employees during the War. This signified a break with the prewar growth period for the building and printing trades and the paper industry. For most sectors, however, the War did not signify a reversal but rather an enhanced continuation of long term prewar developments. If one looks at the three industries in which a break occurred with the prewar development, it emerges that only in the case of paper manufacture did this discontinuity constitute a turning point which continued after the War. In the other instances, the prewar trend was resumed after the War.

At first glance, then, it would appear that the War had no substantial long-term effects on the pattern of industrial growth, other than to emphasise the existing superior growth of capital goods over consumer goods industries. But a more precise analysis of the prewar period presents a different picture. Between *ca.* 1890 and 1913 there was a distinct tendency for differentials in the growth rate between capital goods and consumer goods industries to diminish. This heralded a slow but perceptible shift of emphasis from capital to consumer goods. It would seem that this was interrupted by the War and the resultant long-term disruption of mass consumer demand. The War thus helped to preserve the proportionately greater part which production goods industries (especially in the heavy sector) contributed to total production – and with this probably also a greater degree of social and political power – for longer than would have been the case under continued peacetime conditions.[105]

Calculations as to the volume of production from individual companies during the War should provide clearer evidence as to trends than those relating to numbers of employees, since workers in some peace industries worked fewer hours per week throughout the War than did their colleagues in the armaments industries.[106] Firms were closed down under the terms of the 'Hindenburg Programme' for the speedier production of war materials, which was largely initiated by heavy industry and carried through by the Third Supreme Military Command ('Oberste Heeresleitung' – OHL) under Hindenburg and Ludendorff. This policy rarely affected those who had changed to producing for wartime needs in good time, but rather the so-called peace industries. In some non-essential sectors of production such as cotton, glass, shoe manufacture and the soap industry, closures and amalgamations reduced the number of independent firms to well below 50 per cent of their prewar number.[107] Entrepreneurs in the vital war industries usually profited more from the War than did their colleagues in non-essential industries. This may be initially deduced from dividend payments; according to Wagenführ's calculations (which exclude price changes and confirm the general picture outlined above as to the pattern of entrepreneurial gains and losses) dividends differed sharply – in percentage of share capital – between the *overall* industrial average and two war industries selected as examples:[108]

Year	Industry total	Iron and steel	Chemicals
1913/14	7.96	8.33	5.94
1914/15	5.00	5.69	5.43
1915/16	5.90	10.00	9.69
1916/17	6.52	14.58	11.81
1917/18	5.41	9.60	10.88

These industry- and company-related trends towards differentiation no doubt countered the progressive homogenisation of the entrepreneurial class in relation to socio-economic status and objective interests. In particular the loss of ground by small- and medium-sized entrepreneurs during the War continued the profound and accelerating prewar developments, which were barely reversed after the War. One should not, however, exaggerate the tendencies of different sectors of industry towards differentiation.

Mergers certainly meant a considerable loss of independence for the owners; they did not signify impoverishment or even any loss of status and power if a continuing leading position in the merged enterprises was guaranteed. Official and 'voluntary' closures were very limited (less than 10 per cent). 'At whatever cost those firms designated for closure have procured orders, raw materials and coal by the back door.' Local authorities often lacked the power to enforce or supervise closures.[109] In addition, most entrepreneurs affected by closure received fairly high compensation. Closures were also confined to the War period. Those affected were assured that they would be given preferential treatment and supplies in the transitional postwar economy;[110] in the long term the number of the self-employed in industry and craft between 1907 and 1925 fell more slowly than between 1895 and 1907 and between 1882 and 1895.[111] Constitutional and interest-based resistance to closures was strong;[112] even within the peace industries the number of larger enterprises set up as joint-stock companies hardly declined.[113]

Number of active joint-stock companies 1911/12 and 1917/18

Industry	1911/12	1917/18
Food and drink	816	800
Commerce	688	694
Machine, instrument and equipment industries	555	634
Transport	472	466
Textiles	348	341
Quarrying	342	328
Mining, foundry and salt works	209	203
Metal manufacturing	164	175
Chemicals	155	168
Paper industry	103	99
Leather/leather-type material industries	56	67

The (mostly small) enterprises affected by closures may have been counted as losses in a particular sector of industry while in actual fact temporarily changing over to another sector in the readjustment of production. The clear differences in profits need to be seen in proportion and must not be exaggerated; even the joint-stock companies in the textile industry – which can certainly not be counted as a war industry and which is commonly included among the declining sectors[114] – succeeded, despite all the loss in production and number of employees, in more than doubling their net profits between 1913 and 1917.[115] Even if these results were far below those usually achieved in, say, the armaments industry, they were nevertheless remarkable enough in a period of a general impoverishment of the masses. Their misery and poverty, it seems, were not a direct consequence of the relative decrease in profits in the peace industries.

The relevant sources often refer to the deprivation of the lower strata in town and country, of the industrial workers and of the 'Mittelstand', about which we shall have more to say later. They do not refer to the deprivation of the entrepreneurs, even if individual instances may have occurred, since there were scarcely any groups which survived the War without some suffering. But even the directors of firms which had been closed down had good prospects of continuing to avoid conscription, since they could allegedly not be spared from supervising the maintenance of the closed-down works. In addition they received as a rule regular, usually high, compensation payments from the active 'high efficiency enterprises' in their sector of industry – an equalisation of burdens that shielded them from poverty, deprivation and perhaps even loss of social status and which was financed from the high prices which restricted sectors (textiles, shoe and soap manufacture) were allowed to charge, to the increasing bitterness of the consumers.[116]

Certainly, the rich had to accept only very few reductions in their living standards up to the end of the War. 'Everything is still available in any amount at a high price.'[117] And these high prices were paid. It is noticeable that the production of luxury foodstuffs in the War declined less than industrial production in general.[118] Even in the last months of the War, the visible luxury of the few stood in sharp contrast to the increasingly critical hardship of the masses. Those who had money could still provide for themselves on the black market 'not only well, but amply' as late as August 1918.[119] In any case, the price mechanism, in so far as it escaped legal controls or avoided these via the black market, operated anti-socially and to the disadvantage of the less well-off. The concentrated demands of an increasingly impoverished population for the most basic necessities resulted in 'prices for the least valuable type of basic goods' tending to increase more sharply. In relation to their prewar incomes,[120] also, the higher income groups experienced a lesser curtailment of their buying power than did the great mass of consumers. The Regional Army Command for Berlin ('Stellvertretendes Generalkommando') reported in 1918 that '. . . places of entertainment of all types are overcrowded; above all the best seats have been booked for days in advance. Several times during the day there are long queues in front of the booking offices. Trains to the Baltic coast seaside resorts are fully booked, despite higher fares'.[121] In other holiday resorts and spas in Germany 'noisy parties make themselves conspicuous by debauchery, undignified behaviour on the beaches and in the swimming pools and by the extravagant make-up of more or less easy women'.[122]

Industrialists and their top employees from private firms and in the War Associations were probably only one part of this privileged minority, next to businessmen and black marketeers, farmers and rich *rentiers*, the wealthy and war profiteers of all types. There were also many wealthy and well-to-do people who refrained from such conspicuous consumption. However, given the income and growth in profits outlined above, it is probable that most entrepreneurs could afford the expensive but ample and only slightly reduced standard of living to which a minority had always had access, but which was unavailable to the great mass of workers.[123]

4. Dissatisfaction and protest in the labour force

(a) Factors causing stress

From the above analysis, and with reference to the categories of the analytical model presented in Chapter 1, it is possible to draw the qualified conclusion that the social-structural changes during the War tended towards a polarisation and a sharpening of class opposition, rather than towards its diminution. The general impoverishment which the War produced affected workers more sharply than entrepreneurs; there was no levelling in the socio-economic situation and objective life chances between the two classes. Internal differentiations within the working class diminished somewhat, it is true. Nonetheless its deprivation and exploitation increased, its dependent position remained unchanged, its common class situation became more marked. The entrepreneurs increased their wealth, on average, relative to the working class; in many, though not all, respects the War was advantageous to them. There were undoubtedly counter-tendencies on both sides, as shown by high-earning armaments workers' families or declining small entrepreneurs and by a new vertical and socially significant division of industrial sectors according to their importance for the War which ran at right angles to the dividing-line between the classes. All these factors worked against a further homogenisation within classes and hence against a sharper formation of class opposition.

The question is how far social-structural changes corresponded with social-psychological and organisational-political changes; how far, in the categories of our model, did changes in class opposition lead to corresponding changes in class tensions and class conflicts? One needs first to look for factors which hindered or facilitated the processes by which workers and employees became aware of the increasing opposition between them and, also, to investigate the specific forms by which this opposition was expressed on both sides. Five war-determined factors will be selected as promoting and marking the process of transformation of latent opposition into manifest tensions in a special way.

Firstly, even if actual differences in the distribution of economic and social opportunities had not increased objectively, they would nevertheless have become more apparent and noticeable to those affected by the general restrictions and sacrifices of the War. Deprivation in the First World War worked to expose differences: even a minor degree of reduction in life chances (the standard of living, affordable leisure, gratification from social contacts) hit those who were less privileged from the start, who had fewer alternatives and whose 'store' of opportunities for gratification was more quickly used up, given the same absolute level of reduction, than was the more diverse and richer 'store' of the privileged.[124] Poorer people had suffered the growing shortages from early on in the War, more than the wealthy, since the latter had 'stocked up earlier and for a longer period (especially with potatoes) or had made use of their contacts, or were given preferential treatment as valued customers by tradesmen, and could buy expensive foodstuffs whose purchase ordinary people could not even contemplate'.[125] The intermittent closing of cinemas in some towns during the coal shortage in the winter of 1916/17[126] would have affected the porter in an engineering firm, who would not have many other evening entertainments open to him, more than it would the director of the firm, who had access to a variety of social entertainments.

Under these conditions, the economic and social differences between himself and his employer must have struck the worker more directly than hitherto. The monthly reports of the Home Front Regional Army Commands were strongly focused on these aspects. From the spring of 1916 until shortly before the end of the War, secret information about the mood of the population was systematically sent to the Prussian War Ministry or to the War Office and then passed on to other interested military or civilian authorities.[127] They repeatedly stressed that the uneven distribution of goods in short supply was more noticeable and caused more dissatisfaction among the population than the shortage of goods in itself. At the height of the 'turnip' winter of 1916/17, the representative of the Regional Army Command in Münster wrote: 'It is strange that the people will put up with any privation, but that they cannot stand it if others have a bit more than themselves. If one would be able to reassure everyone that inconveniences resulting from food shortages were evenly distributed, dissatisfaction would disappear at once'.[128] Annoyance at the uneven distribution of scarce consumer goods showed itself above all in a growing resentment against war profiteers and against the visibly ample and luxurious life of the rich. We shall return to this point. But annoyance over the lack of fair shares also arose within the working class in 1916/17 when certain groups of workers, chiefly heavy labourers in the armaments industry, were granted special additional food rations which other workers did not receive.[129]

Secondly, it was not the experience of hardship but the experience of reduction and decline after a period of relative and increasing prosperity which was responsible for the fact that the growing and more visible economic and social differences were not accepted with resignation, but were attacked as injustices. If massive revolutionary dissatisfaction is fostered by a lengthy period of improving conditions and rising expectations followed by an abrupt turn for the worse in which expectations are no longer met,[130] then this was precisely the case, as we have shown, for Germany in 1914 to 1918. Because of the War, the slow but constant prewar improvement in living standards and conditions of work which occurred for the majority was suddenly halted and reversed. Awareness of the discrepancy between expectations and demands, on the one hand, and the possibility of meeting these, on the other, must have come sharply to the fore in the feelings and consciousness of those affected.

Thirdly, the experience of massive horizontal mobility at greater than prewar levels (above all towards large towns with armaments industries) and the observation of rapid vertical mobility, not infrequent during wartime, are likely to have had the effect that the unequal distribution of economic and social opportunities was no longer regarded as unchangeable and determined by fate, but as changeable and hence called into question. These social-psychological dimensions of the war-determined mobilisation of the masses are an important precondition for the emergence of dissatisfaction and readiness to protest and must be kept in mind as a major condition for the translation of class opposition into class tensions.[131]

Fourthly, one must point to the ambivalent role of the so-called 'Burgfrieden' ('internal truce') in the early war years for the heightening of class tensions. The community spirit and feelings of solidarity of the first months of the War,[132] fostered by skilful government policies and press propaganda during the July crisis, led to much spontaneous cooperation between previously hostile groups and often to a pledge to abstain from conflict.[133] The experience of the outbreak of the War, the summoning of all forces for the good of a national effort which was overwhelmingly regarded as just,[134] the coming together of the German nation, dampened down tensions and conflicts and pushed them into the background behind the one big external conflict and the one great common effort. The great majority of workers had, prior to 1914, a degree of identification with the German Reich,[135] despite all economic, social and political discrimination and traditional opposition. For many of them, national solidarity was an enthusiastic-ally carried out duty, a social-psychological reality of the highest order. As will be shown, this solidarity became hollow and was pushed into the background in the course of the War, but it never, so it would seem, disappeared entirely among the majority of workers.

The experience of August 1914 and the Burgfrieden contained, in the view of many who had experienced the privileges of others, the promise of an actual practical reconciliation of class tensions. The Kaiser's words, 'I recognise no more parties; I know only Germans', seemed to offer the possibility of equality, whose realisation required reforms – initially at the end of the War, which everyone expected to be short. It was precisely this expectation which was central to the experience of August 1914[136] for SPD politicians and middle-class professors like Naumann, Meinecke and Troeltsch. But in the view of Conservative circles, which hoped for a strengthening of the status quo from the War, the Volksstaat had already been attained[137] by the 'spirit of 1914', by the still very limited cooperation between previously hostile groups and, in particular, by the patriotic behaviour of the labour movement. In the understanding of the Army High Command, the Burgfrieden signified 'upholding the spirit of steadfastness and devotion to the great national objectives, obviating all threats to the unity of the German people, and preventing any impression that the firm will to victory was wavering'.[138] In this ever more prevalent interpretation, the Burgfrieden did not serve as a promise or even as a vehicle for emancipatory reform, but – together with the doctored War reports of a strict wartime political control and censorship – as a means of suppressing controversial and unpopular views and open discussion.[139] The Burgfrieden became increasingly hollow, first through discussions and attacks on food policy and distribution, then on war aims and military policy and finally, from the spring of 1917, through increasing internal political controversy. But censorship and the State of Siege Law, the prohibition of gatherings and the persecution of left-wing Social Democrats under martial law, which fluctuated widely from month to month and Regional Army Command to Regional Army Command down to October 1918, were preserved and formed a major target for Social Democratic and socialist attacks.[140] So long and in so far as the Burgfrieden was adhered to, it contributed to the emergence and thickening of the general 'fog of unreality' and facilitated the formation of rumours and illusions, thus laying the foundations for the emergence of the later legend of the 'stab in the back'.[141] It served as an excuse to throttle discussions and initiatives directed towards change and so helped to secure the status quo.[142] Together with the intensified government repression of radical opponents (as compared with the prewar period) it prevented open debate of the tensions and conflicts which piled up under the surface of the Burgfrieden. This made the tensions and conflicts only more acute, since a regulated, institutionalised and clearly organised debate was made difficult.[143]

Fifthly, and most importantly, the war-determined increase in burdens and duties which were demanded of each person on behalf of the nation (and certainly not less was demanded from the mass of the underprivileged than from the wealthy and powerful) led to a sharpening of class tensions, since these increasing demands were not really accompanied by compensatory reforms. The people had to suffer, fight and die for their country, to lose friends and relatives, be on their own, work more and put up with all kinds of deprivations. This democratisation of duties was bound to awaken or reinforce feelings of bitterness among the underprivileged, so long as this was not paralleled or followed by a democratisation of rights and opportunities. The War was egalitarian regarding the duties and the related claims, expectations and demands of the masses.[144] 'Everyone seeks equality today. The individual's whole attention is directed towards whether others are doing better than they are. Inequalities which one took for granted in peacetime and accepted as unalterable, in that one came to terms with the existing social order, are no longer acceptable today.' This is how the local branch of the War Office at Frankfurt described the mood in the labour force in their region in June 1917.[145] The head of the War Office, General Groener, had the same changes in mass expectations in mind when he observed that the First World War signified the largest democratic upsurge which had ever occurred among the nations.[146] As early as August 1914 the Social Democrat Eduard David noted in his diary: 'Next to the military-nationalistic wave (there is) a strong surge of democratic feelings'.[147]

This connection between growing wartime burdens and reinforced demands for equality and emancipation entered into the arguments of contemporary reformers as well as into the fears of anti-reformist Conservatives and reactionaries. Reference to the 'national commonwealth, for which the blood of all fellow beings, classes and parties is being shed',[148] had played a large role since the beginning of the War in demands for the abolition of undemocratic privileges, especially the Prussian 'Dreiklassenwahlrecht' (three-class voting system). With a different emphasis (giving superior voting powers to those who paid higher taxes) and growing insistence, marked especially since February 1917 by a fear of revolution, reformist Social Democrats, left or Conservative-Liberal middle-class reformers as well as influential members of government demanded either immediate or postwar compensations for the masses by granting them political and to some extent social equality, or advocated at least a few steps in this direction.[149]

The moderate SPD deputy David stated that 'we expect a democratic reform of voting rights as the price for the workers' war effort' and that the 'democratic demands will be a strong force in the consciousness of the homecoming defenders of the Fatherland.... Having taken on all duties for the country, we also want full equal rights in the army'. In other words the claim was that Social Democrats, in contrast to the prewar period, should now also be able to become officers.[150] The chairman of the SPD parliamentary party, Philipp Scheidemann, referred to the altogether logical connection between equal duties and sacrifices, on the one hand, and the demand for equal rights, on the other. This was after the Russian Revolution of February 1917 when, in reaction to the increasingly radical mood of the working class, he openly, if very indirectly, held out the threat of a 'German revolution'.[151] Nor were speakers from among the Independent Socialists (USPD) unaware of the connection between the enforced sacrifices and the thereby justified demands for equality.[152] Middle-class professors like Max Weber and Friedrich Meinecke pleaded that the connection between the general duty of all to serve and equal voting rights be made.[153] The Imperial Chancellor Bethmann Hollweg also made use of this argument in his futile plea for a speedy reform of the Prussian voting system shortly before his fall in July 1917.[154]

Although Conservatives did not overlook the connection between the burdens of war and emancipatory tendencies, they underestimated it just as they overestimated the national enthusiasm among the working class,[155] or they brushed aside the demands arising from this war.[156] They set the 'energetic and unyielding resistance of State authority' against the rising wave of democratisation and would not shrink, in the words of the Conservative Party leader von Westarp from 'the most extreme consequence', by which he probably meant a military dictatorship.[157] Many of them hoped that military annexations would save them from the, for them fatal, consequences of the demands for democratisation which had been unleashed.[158]

The revolutionary left around the Spartakus League, on the other hand, rejected the practical consequences of the connection between war burdens and emancipatory demands, where they were drawn by members of the executive, as nothing but a counter-revolutionary concession by the ruling class. In advancing this argument they demonstrated their correct sense of where the real threat to the revolution for which they were hoping came from. When the Kaiser announced in his Easter Message of 1917 a reform of the Prussian voting system, in order to stem the growing discontent, quench the effects of the Russian Revolution on the German working class and keep the masses in their place and under the influence of the Majority Socialists (MSPD), this was rejected by the Spartakus League as a 'diversion of Social Democratic voters' and as a 'voting rights ballyhoo'. The typical reformist reference to the necessity of enlarged and democratised rights and opportunities in the face of universal sacrifices and duties was also highly peripheral to the increasingly revolutionary agitation of the groups to the left of the Independent Socialists.[159]

Certainly the War brought reforms, but considering the huge deprivations and burdens these were slight and came too late. After the identification by the overwhelming majority of members of the labour movement with German nation and Imperial state in August 1914, there did not follow, as in France, the appointment of one of their representatives to a high post, but only a visit by some high-ranking Prussian ministers and Imperial secretaries of state to trade union headquarters and to the offices of the Association of Wood and Metal Workers.[160] There is no doubt that the power of the trade unions increased during the course of the War. Recognising them for the first time as legitimate representatives of the workers, civilian and military authorities cooperated with them to an extent which would have been unthinkable before 1914, in the hope of retaining the loyalty of the workforce necessary for the War, and in order to use the workers' organisations to control budding resistance and radical protests.[161] In order to solve war-determined problems concerning the provision of foodstuffs, employment and welfare, and (especially since the Auxiliary Service Law) with regard to wage or employment policies, contact and a limited degree of collaboration took place between the unions and those enterprises which were otherwise hostile to the recognition of the unions. In the primarily small-scale industries, where wage agreements had already been developed before 1914, these earlier ties were strengthened and extended during the War.[162] But workers' associations urgently demanding parity, recognition and equality of rights received a short answer in most large-scale enterprises, where an attitude of 'I am the master in the house' persisted, particularly in the heavy industries of Upper Silesia and the Ruhr. This lasted until the autumn of 1918 when collapse was imminent and cooperation with the trade unions appeared to be the last remaining defence of the entrepreneurs against revolution and state interventionism.[163]

One paragraph in the industrial code, long under attack by the labour movement, was rescinded. This paragraph had outlawed all measures of direct and indirect compulsion during labour disputes. It had gone beyond the general criminal law, had protected strike breakers in particular and had always been regarded by the unions as severely discriminatory. It was rescinded in March 1918 after several unsuccessful attempts. The Labour Law demanded by the workers' representatives failed to materialise.[164] Supplements to the Association Law in 1916 and 1917 eased the work of the trade unions. It was a concession which the Imperial Chancellor explained was necessary in order to strengthen the SPD revisionists against the SPD radicals.[165] A certain improvement in the system of labour exchanges, the engagement of welfare workers in factories, new regulations for the wages of out-workers, but above all the Auxiliary Service Law of December 1916 and the establishment of a Reich Labour Office signified advances in social policies which had stagnated before 1914 and had suffered a slight reversal at the beginning of the War.[166] On the other hand, there were no effective controls on war profits through price restrictions or taxation – a shortcoming which contributed very considerably in the last months of the War to the inflamed mood and bitterness of the rest of the population not engaged in these activities.[167] The Reichstag and the parties of the centre (including the Majority Socialists) certainly increased their influence considerably in 1916/17 and again from the summer of 1918; steps towards parliamentarism were taken before constitutional parliamentarisation was completed[168] in response to pressure from the Army High Command and the political parties and in the face of the threatened defeat in October 1918. But the Prussian three-class voting system, widely regarded as discriminatory, especially by labour, remained in force until October 1918.[169] The changes actually implemented in the direction of greater equality of rights and fewer privileges clearly fell below the expectations and demands of large sections of the population. The democratisation of opportunities and rights did not keep pace with the democratisation of duties.

(b) Economic hardship and the longing for peace
The transformation of objectively growing class differences into clearly visible class tensions was facilitated by the role which deprivation played in revealing the reactionary character of existing differences; by increasing mobility; by the concealing and aggravating function of the Burgfrieden in maintaining the status quo; and by the strongly felt discrepancy between increasing duties and sacrifices, on the one hand, and improved but still very unequal opportunities and rights on the other. Within the labour force this was expressed by an increasing sense of grievance, discontent and readiness to protest, by mistrust and rumours, by bitterness and anger whose target was far from uniform and often remained unclear. It took shape as visible but scarcely organised conflict in the form of demonstrations, strikes, the disruption of opponents' meetings (for instance, of the right-wing Fatherland Party)[170] and acts of violence against town halls and shops, well before the outbreak of the Revolution in 1919. The inseparable though often unclear connection between bitterness over the economic situation, longing for peace, social protest and political demands in the statements and demonstrations of workers and others makes the analysis of the content and trend of these collective attitudes and actions difficult.

Grievances were most clearly the result of the economic factors which slowly quenched the enthusiasm of August 1914.[171] General economic difficulties, sacrifices and starvation remained dominant concerns and were on the increase, with growing hardships, to the end of the War.[172] Their intensity depended on the food situation and, therefore, on the time of year. In the late summer and early autumn the new harvest tended to ease the food shortages, and thereby the popular mood, a little.[173] Demonstrations against food shortages, profiteers and low wages, hunger riots and attacks on shops took place, probably with increasing frequency, from 1915 onwards.[174] It was mainly women and juveniles who took part in these actions; unionised workers and skilled men in the armaments industries were apparently only peripherally involved. As the commander of the Mainz fortress wrote in the middle of 1917: 'It is almost always women, whether from the lower or better classes, who express their dissatisfaction [with the supply and distribution of food stuffs] in bitter scolding. The men are quieter and more restrained. The women's behaviour is understandable. They are supposed to cook and cater for their hungry families and see that they are powerless to do so'.[175] But there were also strikes by workers in essential war industries from the summer of 1916 onwards; in view of the labour shortages in these industries the better-paid munitions workers could more easily afford to strike than the less well-off workers in the non-essential peace industries. Such strikes were usually concerned with questions of food supplies, the failure of incomes to match constant price increases and, towards the end of the War, with the demand by overworked people for shorter working hours.[176]

In March 1916 the food situation – the increasing shortages, the consequent worsening of mood and the problems of food policy[177] – became the subject of extensive internal discussion within the SPD parliamentary party.[178] The widespread call for a 'food provisions dictator' was only temporarily lulled by the founding in May 1916 of the War Food Provisions Office.[179] During the 'turnip winter' of 1916/17 fury over the extreme scarcity of provisions, especially fats and potatoes, and over the lack of fuel, reached its height; the reduction in the bread ration, including that for heavy manual workers, in April 1917 contributed decisively to the eruption of the April strikes, in which in Berlin alone some 200,000 workers in about 300 enterprises (particularly munitions factories) took part.[180]

In June and July 1917 the massive discontent over food shortages was the central issue in the monthly military reports. The War Office branch at Danzig reported to Berlin in July in altogether typical and graphic fashion: 'Last season's potatoes are no longer available since last month and substitute deliveries of bread and flour are in no way sufficient, especially not for the working population. Demand for new potatoes and vegetables is therefore unusually strong. The very small supply which comes to market is seized by excited housewives. If the police protection on hand is insufficient, the wares are brutally snatched from the farmers' and retailers's stalls. In order not to expose themselves to such treatment in the future, the farmers stay away from the market and sell their products on their farms. The townspeople flock to the country in their hundreds in order to stock up with potatoes and vegetables. Apart from the fact that considerable damage to cultivated areas occurs as a result of these mass wanderings through potato and vegetable fields and that farmers are distracted from their sometimes very urgent work, these potato and vegetable pilgrims are also not deterred from thieving from the fields. This leads to very ugly scenes here as well as in the markets. The agitated women return home in an embittered mood and pass this on in an inciting manner to the members of their family on their return home from work, who in turn carry it back to their factories'.[181] Reports about hoarding expeditions and peasants' complaints about reckless 'self-provisioning' by the invading hordes of townspeople continued from this period until the end of the War.

Nevertheless, in the winter of 1916/17, judging by the monthly reports of the Regional Army Commanders, the food shortage receded somewhat in people's consciousness in the face of the oppressive coal shortage and growing bitterness over watches and shoes which they could no longer afford. The Frankfurt War Office branch observed that 'the dance after provisions has stopped [and thus the inconvenient queues in front of certain shops, also disliked by the authorities for fear of riotous assemblies] but in their place the dance after shoes has begun in various cities'.[182] In the large strike movement of January/February 1918 the economic motive clearly receded behind the political.[183] It was only in June 1918 that reports on the general mood once again stressed the mounting dejection and bitterness of wide sections of the population about the high cost and shortages of food and clothing. Economic anxieties weighed heavily in people's growing fear of a fifth wartime winter.[184]

Although strongly dependent on the outcome of battles at the front, war-weariness and the longing for peace became increasingly linked, as the War drew on, with discontent and bitterness over economic hardship. After the winter of 1915/16, these feelings characterised the mood of the less well-off and particularly the working class.[185] On 1 May 1916 Karl Liebknecht called for peace and revolution in front of thousands of demonstrators. After he had been arrested and sentenced for this, there were strikes in Berlin and other towns in which demands for peace and freedom for Liebknecht became primary concerns.[186] In September 1916 the Prussian War Ministry declared that 'among some sections of the population as, for example, the lower classes, who live in constrained circumstances and who hardly expect their situation to change, whatever the outcome of the War, there exists a depressing indifference. Without being a pessimist one can say that for the most part the people are war-weary'.[187] The commanding officer wrote from Koblenz in January 1917: 'Among these [poorer] sections of the population one can hardly find any who still believe that the old standard of living can be re-established in the foreseeable future after the War.... The word 'peace' in the understanding of the masses has become dissociated from ideas of victory'. His colleague in Strasburg reported 'not only a longing for peace, but in some places demands even for peace at any price'.[188] In May 1917 the report from Frankfurt confirmed the strong desire for an 'honorable peace. But on the other hand one does not want to see the War continued in order to achieve exaggerated War aims. The lower orders up to and including much of the middle class particularly reject War aims of this sort'.[189] Descriptions by those on leave from the front about the horrors of war (and also about the unequal provision for, and treatment of, officers and men at the front) fanned the anti-War mood at home.[190]

On the other hand, major military successes or events promising success – such as the introduction of unlimited submarine warfare in February 1917, the Isonzo victory against the Italians in October 1917 and the western offensive from March to June/July 1918 which was initially successful and well publicised and bound up with high hopes – temporarily drove out war-weariness and indifference and awoke, even within the working class, widespread new annexationist hopes.[191] Karl Retzlaw, a member of the Spartakus League, reported on the difficulties he faced in political discussions with workmates who had been sent back from the front to the Berlin turbine factory of AEG in 1917: '"We know what the War is, you go to the front" they said to me. But it only needed the announcement of some victory and the atmosphere changed at once. In such conditions[192] revolutionary agitation was as difficult as sawing through a steel chain with a nail file'.[193]

In the last months of the War, hopes of victory melted; from the end of June the high level of optimism of the preceding months began to evaporate under the impact of the failure of the Austrian offensive in Italy and the halting of the German spring offensive in the west.[194] In July the loss of morale, discouragement and the 'demobilisation of the mind'[195] accelerated and could no longer be stopped. The commanding general at Koblenz declared that 'the impulse of the patriotic spirit had died and that there existed the greatest apathy among the masses'.[196] At about the same time the Social Democrat

Noske found a widespread and 'absolute indifference regarding the fate of the Reich and the nation. In the factories even Social Democratic workers [now] said in discussions that we had no interest in warding off the British; they would know how to protect our valuable labour, so why should we still fight on'.[197] In the face of the threat of a fifth winter of war and the collapse of the high hopes of June, the disillusionment was more extreme than at any time during the War. The desire for peace without annexation, even (increasingly) peace at any price, tiredness, disillusionment and despair 'now marked the mood in the towns, in the working class and among large sections of the middle class'.[198]

(c) Social criticism and political protest
Complaints about economic deprivation and expressions of a longing for peace and of war-weariness were combined in the working class with resentment against the privileged and powerful.[199] To begin with, given the ever-more-widely discussed profits of many manufacturers and traders, discontent about shortages turned into protest against the wealth of the few; the impoverishment of the majority was seen less as a consequence of war than as a consequence of enrichment by a minority. The first monthly reports of the military administration already noted that profits in the war industry and in wholesale trade were objects of massive unease.[200] In 1918 they were still reporting on increasing bitterness against manufacturers and traders; war profits were increasingly held responsible for the oppressive inflation and hence became an ever-stronger target for resentment and hate.[201]

Secondly, the extensive failure of food production and distribution and the booming of the black market ensured that growing differences in income and wealth were translated more clearly than hitherto into provocative differences in patterns of consumption.[202] It is true that it was in no way only the rich who made use of the black market; in 1918 no one in the towns could survive on the official rations and there was 'hardly anybody . . . who did not rely to some extent on the black market or on occasional "personal hoarding" for their provisions'.[203] Once established, as the result of shortages and the absence of effective controls, the black market was hard to put down, precisely because its effective abolition would have led to even greater difficulties in food provision and, especially in the case of the black market supplements for armaments workers often offered by individual firms, would have led to the threat of a social explosion.[204] It must be recorded, nevertheless, that the black market illegally withdrew about a third of the available[205] provisions from the public distribution system which made an attempt at social equity, and distributed this third according to the criteria of income, wealth and general economic power. In this way it contributed to turning the protest against hardship into a protest against inequality. 'The little man and the middle class see with bitterness that official measures concerning requisitioning etc. fail. Everything is still available for money in large quantities.' Publication in July 1917 of the fact that in the better restaurants of Karlsruhe 'not only did champagne and expensive wine flow in streams, but food was available in abundance', proved provocative. A bill of 76M for a dinner for two was presented side-by-side with the statement that wartime public social security for a woman with two children was 65M per month.[206]

In March 1917 the Chief of the Frankfurt Army Corps cited the *Hessischer Volksfreund* in his report: 'Nothing contributes more to the excitement of the population than an unfair distribution of food. The possibility that those who are well off financially can provide for themselves as well, and sometimes even better, than in peacetime is a sad fact which destroys our faith in a common, just purpose to hold out.... Constant reference is also made to profiteering and black marketeering and it is stressed that these manifestations constitute a considerable danger on the home front of our country. The following list of complaints made in a letter to the editor of the *Mainzer Volksstimme* accorded with many people's views. The correspondent wrote: "I am indignant (1) Because last year, despite ample depreciation, 22 coal mining companies distributed an average dividend of 19 per cent and now they raised the price of coal by 40 to 50 pfennigs per fifty kilos. (2) Because I had to pay 25 Marks for a pair of shoes for a ten-year-old boy, although the leather companies paid a 65 per cent dividend last year. (3) Because the larders of farmers and the well-to-do are filled with bacon, ham and sausages, while my family's food consists mainly of potatoes and turnips"'.[207]

In July 1918 the Regional Army Command at Magdeburg passed the following report on to Berlin: 'The previous large gulf between rich and poor, which had largely been closed in the early days of enthusiasm for the War, now continues to widen, the more the longer. Among the poorer sections of the population a pernicious hatred against the rich and the so-called war profiteers has built up, which one can only hope will not lead to a terrible explosion. This hatred is occasioned less by the ownership of wealth as such than by the fact that certain groups with almost unlimited financial means are in a position to provide for themselves not only sufficiently, but very well, and to surround themselves with nearly every luxury, while the greater part of the population suffers actual deprivation and hunger. Nearly all decrees by the authorities are now regarded critically, and are seen as only helping the rich and harming the poor'.[208]

War profits, black market successes, the visible pleasures of the rich seemed to show clearly that these did not share in the general deprivation, but indeed often exploited and grew fat on it. During the War, wild rumours soon exaggerated this real connection, as when the tale went round among the labour force of an AEG factory in Berlin in the winter of 1916/17, 'that the Crown Princess bathed in milk, while infants were not given any'.[209] Thus partly in justified, partly in unjustified ways, many shortages were regarded as a betrayal; deprivation was regarded as an injustice and not as a war-related misfortune; for this, the privileged and the powerful appeared to be responsible.[210] Discontent about economic shortcomings merged with social resentments and protest; it was in this way that they became politicised and turned into an important precondition of the Revolution.

War-weariness and longing for peace were similarly transformed into social criticism. Given the high war profits of manufacturers and traders, the view became prevalent in the second half of the War 'that this was why one could not yet expect the War to end, because many people had an interest in prolonging it for as long as possible'.[211] The Spartakus League, the clearest and most explicit advocate of this class interpretation of the War, which consequently tried to ally rejection of the War with demands for a social revolution, added to the mostly unformulated mistrust. 'The notion is skilfully spread amongst the workers that the continuation of the War is only in the interest of big business and that nationality is of little concern to the worker, since in England they are paid exactly the same as in Germany.'[212] Even if the Spartakists did not succeed in producing a revolutionary class-consciousness in significantly large sections of the workers,[213] a diffused feeling about the War as 'a matter concerning the rich, in whose capitalist interests it is being conducted' was by no means confined to the Spartakists. Leaflets appeared such as: 'The War is a swindle: down with the big heads, up the Revolution...' (Munich, January 1916). There was also a handwritten text on the lavatory walls of a third-class compartment on a train which read: 'There are real idiots, who take pleasure in this horrible War'.[214] These documents point, not to agitation by ideologically-trained revolutionaries, but to fairly spontaneous outbursts which were also directed against 'those up there'. At any rate it was also assumed by unpolitical workers that the ample life of the powerful and rich, who (besides) were not fighting at the front, would not entice the decision-makers towards a quicker ending of the hated War. 'The politically indifferent wrote and pasted up [in the winter 1916/17] in all sorts of places [in a Berlin armaments factory] the slogan: "Equal wages and equal grub, in which case the War would be long forgotten!"'[215]

Such vague interpretations of the War, though basically seen in terms of social class, were re-emphasised by discussions over war aims and the dispute about whether peace was to be achieved through victory or through negotiation. Against the principles of the Burgfrieden of 1914 and against the wishes of the Reich government, the War aims discussion was first made public by annexationists after the middle of 1916 and conducted practically unrestrictedly in public from the end of 1916. It reached a first climax with the peace resolution of the Reichstag majority in July and the founding of the annexationist anti-reformist Fatherland Party in September 1917. Its course and domestic ramifications cannot be dealt with here in detail. In the context of our argument, it is the following which matters: the dividing line (which in any case shifted constantly with the changing War situation) between the various champions of an annexationist peace through victory and the champions of a negotiated peace did not coincide exactly with the dividing line between social classes. By no means all workers were definitely anti-annexationist, particularly not in early 1918 when the Treaty of Brest-Litovsk was imposed on the defeated Russians and the German troops were successful on the Western Front.[216] On the other hand, some major entrepreneurs, particularly from the banking sector, supported the ephemeral 'Volksbund für Freiheit und Vaterland' which saw itself as a moderate, essentially anti-annexationist opposition to the Fatherland Party. Bourgeois parties – the Left Liberals, the Centre and some of the National Liberals – supported the Reichstag's anti-annexationist peace resolution, whose social basis was by no means restricted to the working class.[217]

It is noticeable, nevertheless, that the political discussion of war aims, especially during the second half of the War, had the tendency to be structured along class lines. Decisive support for the Fatherland Party came from large industrial, agricultural and Mittelstand associations of entrepreneurs. Apart from two small nationalist workers' organisations, no purely labour organisations were associated with this party.[218] Conversely, no employers' organisations, but most of the important labour organisations, responded to the call of the Volksbund für Freiheit und Vaterland.[219]

The class basis of the War aims discussion becomes even clearer, if one considers the internal programmes and functions of the two camps: on the one hand, the Fatherland Party sought an anti-reformist and anti-revolutionary preservation of the status quo or even the restoration of the earlier power balance while, on the other hand, the Volksbund called for 'an immediate reordering of the domestic political order'.[220] On both sides the War aims demands were partly used deliberately to block or further a political re-orientation.[221] It is this interconnection between War aims and domestic policies which essentially corroborates the vague and often all-too-simplistic suspicions of the working class and other sections of the population that the War was to be seen as primarily an affair of the rich and powerful. The annexationist propaganda of the Fatherland Party, at least, can be shown to have contributed to the phenomenon that the longing for peace among most workers was increasingly merged with a socially critical attitude towards 'those up there'.[222]

In addition to their economic, socially critical and anti-War components, the disturbances, resentments and protests had an explicitly domestic dimension from as early as 1916. The Prussian War Minister wrote on 2 March of that year: 'It is not only questions about war aims but also domestic policy questions about voting rights, taxation, increased prices etc. which cannot be totally excluded in the long run and which threaten this unity [of the nation]'.[223] In the sympathy strikes for Liebknecht, the imprisoned Social Democrat deputy, the call for peace was already confused with protests against internal repression under martial law.[224] In the monthly reports by the Regional Army Commands, however, it was only from the spring of 1917 that domestic factors were accorded any great significance in explaining the mood of dissatisfaction among the people.[225] The Russian Revolution of February 1917 had not only revived the hopes for peace; it had also politicised the workers in other ways. 'It is unmistakable', read a report from the Württemberg War Ministry at the end of March 1917, 'that news about the role which industrial workers have played in the movement in Russia has affected German workers so that they believe that they can considerably extend their influence both on their own employers as well as on the political leadership. Quite often the employers hear that the Russian example should be imitated.'[226]

In point of fact the political events of March and April 1917 formed the basis for a kind of politicisation which was surprising in intensity and quality in a people who had been worn down by the 'turnip winter'. The Revolution in Russia in February undoubtedly had far-reaching effects. The Prussian government's Fideikommissgesetz (Entailed Estate Act, an attempt to change inheritance laws in favour of the landed classes) added to the Reichstag debate on the domestic situation (29 March), the founding of the Indepdendent Socialist Party (USPD) in April and the Kaiser's Easter promise to reform the Prussian voting system, all contributed to an increasing politicisation of the dissatisfied majority. External and domestic political aims (for peace and for democracy) also played a substantial, though not yet primary role in the strike of April 1917.[227]

It was only in the large strike movement at the end of January and beginning of February 1918 that economic motives clearly receded behind political ones. The main strike aims were a quick peace settlement without annexations or reparations, consultation of workers' representatives in the peace negotiations with Russia at Brest-Litovsk, an increased supply of foodstuffs, an end to the 'state of siege' and to the 'militarisation of firms', the release of all political prisoners, the democratisation of the state and a reform on voting rights in Prussia. These demands, however, still remained totally within a framework that was compatible with a bourgeois parliamentary democracy, even if great sympathy was shown in the course of the strike for the Soviet system. Workers' councils were formed twice during the strike movement, in April 1917 and January 1918. The January strikes, with more than a million participants in different cities, signified the increasing radicalisation and politi-cisation of the working class. Indignation at Germany's conduct at Brest-Litovsk, which was rightly blamed for the continuation of the War in the East despite the Soviet government's readiness for peace; the annexationist efforts of the anti-reformist Fatherland Party which had gathered momentum; and disappointment over the lack of progress in the voting rights questions in Prussia, which had been discussed with increasingly high expectations since the spring of 1917, were the chief factors in this process. Widespread dissatisfaction was increasingly converted into political demands; a wish for democratisation, propagated by Bolshevik and western politicians and publicised in Germany also seems to have had some influence.[228]

In the last months of the War, the reports of the Regional Army Commanders took constant account of how domestic policy issues affected the mood of the population, according them more importance than in previous years. The rejection of the bill to reform the voting system by the Prussian Chamber of Deputies was accepted relatively quietly only because 'one had not expected a different decision from the Chamber of Deputies and was counting on the dissolution of the Chamber'. It was a firmly-held belief that a democratic suffrage would soon become a reality. The Regional Army Commander in Frankfurt added a warning that 'if the population was ultimately disappointed in this belief, dangerous shocks to our political life would be unavoidable'.[229] Tax legislation was more frequently discussed among the population at large when Tax Bills came before the Reichstag; the war profits issue attracted attention.[230] Parliamentarism in general was also being discussed.[231] These issues and particularly the problem of the reform of voting rights (and its rejection by the Conservatives) remained important points of attack for the workers' representatives in July, August and September 1918, even prior to President Wilson's Fourteen Points of October (when he demanded internal democratisation as a precondition of peace) and even before the question of the abdication of the Kaiser became acute.[232]

Increasingly, it would appear, economic grievances and warweariness were subsumed into political protest. A mass meeting of workers at Riesa in Saxony demanded in September 'that at last all the citizens of the Reich . . . receive the same political rights and that the constitution be built up on a completley democratic basis, since it is the existing unequal rights which have led above all to the present indefensible position regarding the food situation'. The Regional Army Commander in Dresden commented that ' . . . the Social Democrats have succeeded, through extremely active and skilful agitation, in conveying this conviction to the masses; in many gatherings in other parts of the region similar views are being expressed'.[233] The Regional Army Command at Koblenz stated: 'It is noticeable that the political movement at home has come to the forefront of discussion despite the mighty events on the battlefields. The clamour for a settlement of the Prussian voting rights Bill is to be heard as much from the organised and trade-union trained worker as from the ranks of the middle class, and even from wide groups of people without particular political convictions who in their heart of hearts actually care nothing for a reform of voting rights. But even if the call for a reform is therefore based merely on the result of successful agitation rather than on people's inner conviction, one has nevertheless to speak of a general mass movement in the region which it would be disastrous to oppose . . . '.[234]

(d) The causes of protest

Bitterness over economic misery, longing for peace, social protest and frustrated expectations of reform have been analysed as the chief components of the discontent and bitterness which more and more came to characterise the mood of the urban masses. These four motivational elements were linked in various degrees and with increasing intensity to a diffuse and unfocused mixture of apathy, discontent, disappointment, resentment and indignation. These pushed the hopes of 1914 for victory ever more into the background (though not in a linear progression) and weakened national solidarity. A more precise analysis of strikes, their motives and aims, however difficult a task, would reveal the close and varied inter-relationships of these four motivational complexes.

The outlines of these four closely-linked components of unrest remained unclear and fluid; each could merge with or reciprocally influence another. Yet the possibility of substituting one form of discontent for another was limited, as is illustrated by the attempt of the Leipzig branch of the War Office which, during the strike of April 1917, granted economic concessions and urged 'that the reason for the strike be deflected from the political to the economic arena and thereby deflated'.[235] The opposite case of transposing economic discontent, which could no longer be met by economic means, into political resentments and protests, also occurred.[236] The internal connections between these four areas of tension were clearly shown when the high hopes for peace generated by the success of the spring offensive in 1918 drove complaints about shortages and disappointment about continuing social inequality and lack of reforms into the background, only for them to return strongly to the fore when the summer showed the prospects for victory to be illusory and a deep war-weariness set in. It is precisely the *possibility* of this substituting one area of discontent for another which allows us to recognise how greatly the success or failure of a protest movement was dependent on outside events or on decisive leadership groups.

All the same this mixture of discontent, apathy, bitterness, resentment and indignation contained, as has been shown, an increasing if not completely resolved, general current feeling against 'those up there' – the propertied and powerful, the manufacturers and traders, war profiteers and the wealthy and, particularly, against 'the authorities', a subject to which we shall return in a later analysis of the relationship between society and state. The growing class opposition hence corresponded with an increase in class tension, long before the panic-stricken parliamentarisation of October 1918 or the collapse of the monarchy in November of that year and the subsequent outbreak of revolution. But in its diffuseness working-class consciousness remained a far from clearly-defined, solidaristic or even revolutionary consciousness directed against the capitalists and their means of domination; the national solidarity of the majority of workers, overwhelmingly strong as it had been at the beginning of the War and rooted in a long prewar tradition, had been by no means totally eroded by Germany's wartime preoccupations. It had only been weakened by the tensions described above.

We do not know enough to relate different categories of workers to differing forms of protest or to decide how far socio-economic differences within the working class hindered the development of solidarity. While there was some direct connection between the degree of economic deprivation and a manifest willingness to protest, there were exceptions to the rule.[237] The leading role played by highly-paid armaments workers in the USPD in the great strikes of April 1917 and January 1918, in the rise of the Council movement and in preparations for the Revolution[238] contradicts such a simplistic assumption. The fact that it was precisely the better-paid workers who formed the radical core of the protest movement needs further investigation,[239] but it would seem to indicate that existing differences in income and standard of living within the working class impaired class solidarity less than might at first be assumed.[240]

Certainly most of the traumas, disappointments and sacrifices were not the result of the class structure but of shortages and the horrors of the War itself. These were underlined and strengthened in the context of social class through the privations and disappointments which stemmed from the unequal distribution of opportunities in Wilhelmine society. Even deprivations caused directly by the War were thus transmitted on a class basis and experienced by those concerned in a class context. In the areas described and with many variations, the complaints about deprivation and the War became accusations against those in power and finally, as will be shown, against the political system itself.

In accordance with the model developed at the beginning of this book, it might be expected that the growing, though still diffuse, class tensions manifested themselves through more radical organisations and were expressed in ever sharper conflicts. But this was only partly the case.

(e) Frustrated protest: workers' parties and the unions

The number of strikes, which had declined abruptly at the beginning of the War under the influence of the Burgfrieden and high unemployment rates, grew (as far as may be judged from the unreliable wartime statistics) from 137 in 1915 to 240 in 1916 and 561 in 1917. In 1918 only 531 strikes were recorded but in 1919 and 1920, by contrast, there were 3,700 and 3,800 respectively.[241] (In 1912 and 1913 the numbers had been between 2,500 and 2,100.) Despite certain inaccuracies, the real growth in the number of strikes during 1914–18 is likely to have been correctly recorded, as is their lower frequency relative to the pre- and postwar periods. Undoubtedly unrest, demonstrations, riots and looting increased rather than decreased during the War, but no figures are available for this.

In addition, the radicalisation of the workers showed itself in the growing membership numbers, both in absolute terms and relative to the SPD,[242] of the USPD, which became an independent party in April 1917. (During 1916–17, roughly the same group of left-wing Social Democrats and Socialists had formed a 'working party' within the SPD, the 'Sozialdemokratische Arbeitsgemeinschaft'.) This new party differentiated itself from the more moderate SPD of Ebert and Scheidemann by a more emphatic anti-War policy, by rejecting cooperation with the Government, by a stronger emphasis on mass activity, as against party bureacracy and 'hierarchies' and, finally, by a growing emphasis on a Socialist class standpoint instead of one based on patriotic solidarity.[243] The membership of the SPD fell from 1,086,000 in 1914 to 586,000 in 1915, 433,000 in 1916 and 243,000 in 1917 – a low point which remained unchanged up to the Revolution.[244] The USPD estimated that they had gained about 100,000 members by the beginning of the Revolution.[245] The SPD attributed their losses not only to the high rate of conscription among their members, but also to the appeal of the more radical USPD. 'In the switch of our numbers to the Independent Party our membership figures suffered considerable losses, which were increased by disillusionment with the party engendered by the unrestrained criticism of the Opposition which unfortunately became the occasion for some former Party members to turn their backs on political activity altogether . . . '.[246] Even the leaders of the SPD accepted that they had to attribute the decline in their membership to a radicalisation of the working class to which their Party had not responded. This happened, despite the fact that the SPD's social and general political demands for reform certainly became firmer, more insistent and in part more threatening during the course of the War, and despite the fact that some SPD local branches went through a radicalisation process during the War, which made them appear closer to Haase's USPD than to Ebert's and Scheidemann's Social Democracy, the retention of the old party name notwithstanding.[247] Whether certain categories of workers, such as the poorer ones from the peace industries, were more likely than other categories to move over to the USPD, cannot generally be established.[248]

In addition, incipient moves towards creating new organisations pointed to a certain radicalisation of the working class. In distancing themselves from the trade unions, sometimes even in opposition to them, these embryonic organisations became the channels for radical action, falling to some extent under the influence of the very small Spartakus group. This group, on the left wing of the USPD but with few roots in the labour force, was the forerunner of the Communist Party (KDP), to be founded officially at the end of the War. The development of groups of 'revolutionary shop stewards', especially in Berlin in the large-scale metal-processing industry, and the formation of workers' councils in April 1917 and January 1918 indicate an increasing potential for protest within the working class, which was not activated by the traditional organisations, by the trade unions or by the Majority SPD.[249] Increasingly, the militant activities of 1917–18, which reached their peak in the January strike of 1918, were initiated outside the trade unions, without their support and sometimes even against union opposition; this makes clear that the widespread lack of radicalisation in the trade unions and SPD must not be taken to indicate a similar lack of radicalisation amongst the majority of workers.[250]

That increasing class tensions were not more clearly translated into organised class conflict was due partly to the suppression and persecution of the radicals through martial law. The surveillance, even prohibition of unapproved gatherings, censorship of inflammatory literature, military control of key enterprises, the conscription of prominent ring-leaders, detention for 'reasons of security' and quick sentencing under martial laws were the most effective means which the authorities had at their disposal. The limited effectiveness of Spartakists was certainly connected with the fact that their leaders and many of their members soon found themselves in prison or in the trenches.[251] Heavy penalties for strike leaders, printers and distributors of leaflets, agitators and 'rabble-rousers' of all kinds and, above all, the threat of the trenches (particularly to those in reserved occupations, but also to trade union and party officials who had been granted deferment) meant a risk in open conflict for other activists, especially for left-wing Social Democrats and Socialists inside the SPD, and, later, in the USPD, which was closely watched by the military and the police.[252]

That increasing class tensions were not more clearly transformed into correspondingly vehement and organised class conflicts was, above all, due to the role of the most powerful working-class organisations – the trade unions and the SPD – which seem, in theory, to have been best able to effect such a transformation but which renounced such action.[253] In particular, the top officials of the trade unions, who usually supported the right wing of the Majority SPD, reflected the piling-up class tensions in a very distorted and watered-down form. It is true that strong minorities of USPD sympathisers and supporters were formed among the membership of some industrial associations, such as the Metal Workers' Association, and in some smaller central associations (furriers, clerks and shoemakers) and local unions which supported the USPD.[254] It must also not be overlooked that the policies of the three large federations of unions (Social Democrats, Christian and Liberal) whose policy differences were reduced somewhat in the War and whose cooperation increased,[255] experienced a significant broadening of outlook; although social policy remained their central concern, general and economic policy received more of their attention than hitherto.

The public statements of the General Commission, the central organisation of the Social Democratic trade union movement, reflected the increasing politicisation of the working class from the spring of 1917. Urgent statements on the question of voting rights and a new orientation of domestic policy in general appeared in the official trade union publications; more clearly than before, the top ranks of the Social Democratic unions made a stand against annexationist War aims propaganda. They supported the Volksbund für Freiheit und Vaterland.[256] From 1916 they were involved with problems concerning the establishment of state-supervised monopolies for mining, for large parts of the energy sector and for the wholesale trade; they also demanded state control for these enterprises together with trade union participation in the social and economic field. The unions put forward their demands with increasing self-confidence and insistence. Their central demands were for both state and employers to accord them full recognition as representatives of the labour force and for co-determination in a variety of fields, especially in the courts of arbitration, conciliation boards, Reich offices, regional labour boards and councils and employment exchanges.[257] As will be discussed in more detail below, social and political reforms in the interest of, and under pressure from, the trade unions were instituted long before the collapse of the monarchy, leading to the unions' widespread recognition by the government and to the increase of their power at the expense of the employers.[258] In addition their bread-and-butter policies achieved a great deal for individual workers on the everyday level, in order, as the trade union leader Carl Legien put it, 'to mitigate the horrendous effects of the War as much as possible for the workforce'.[259] They thus made their influence felt across the whole field of welfare and food provision.[260] Even though the number of trade union-led strikes remained far below the prewar average, the number of trade union 'agitations' for increased wages, shorter working hours and other improvements in working conditions continued to grow and to achieve results without stoppages. This tendency was a continuation from prewar times but – after a setback in the first two years of the War – was one which reached a level far beyond the prewar average. The Table opposite is based on figures from the General Commission.[261]

But these efforts did not prevent the emiseration of the masses, who discredited the unions for this reason; they appeared too weak and half-hearted, especially since it was deliberate policy to avoid the use of the sharper-edged weapon of the strike. All the social and political reforms could not eliminate the increasing discriminations made against the lower classes, which contributed greatly to making their

	Trade union-led movements overall totals		Movements not ending in work stoppages	
	Instances	Nos involved	Instances	Nos involved
1910	9,690	1,025,542	6,496	656,531
1913	9,972	1,214,523	7,372	965,537
1914	4,866	363,040	3,457	266,359
1915	3,749	818,467	3,683	816,246
1916	6,991	1,464,833	6,849	1,450,194
1917	10,529	2,798,975	10,336	2,732,341
1918	10,859	2,439,657	10,696	2,417,924

experience of hardship one of relatively 'losing out'. By abstaining from the more radical policies of class conflict, the trade unions paid for their undeniable but limited successes by supporting the War effort and by thus being identified with the warring State. Since support for the War effort was the reason for their limited successes, they were hindered from giving a more open, radical expression to the mounting tensions. Even before the War the unions had never closely supported class conflict; now they moved even further away from such a position.[262] Thus they failed to respond to the social and psychological changes which had taken place at grass-roots level.[263]

The much-discussed and contentious patriotic war reformism of the trade unions, which was the principal determinant of union policy in all the great industrial combatants, had many causes.[264] We have already referred to the strong anti-revolutionary tradition in the German labour movement, which existed under the cover of a rhetorical radicalism and which was more pronounced in the unions than in the Party even before 1914. This remained the case during the War, despite heightened class opposition and tension, because of the national danger and of new opportunities for cooperation with the Government. The motives of the union leaders were manifold. The well-founded fear of unemployment at the beginning of the War, with its enfeebling consequences for the unions, fear of repression, deep-seated patriotism, pleasure at the relative end of their 'outsider' existence and at recognition from (often secretly admired) officials and officers, the desire to relieve want and, finally, the hope that loyalty would be rewarded with equality and reforms – all played their part.

From a structural point of view, it is important to remember that there were good reasons why the relative estrangement of large complex organisations from their membership base, as well as their tendency towards self-preservation at whatever cost, became the theme of a classical enquiry – a study which took its empirical material from the organisational history of the German working class.[265] Within the organisation, the world of the managerial staff differed from the world of the worker more strikingly during than before the War. From the start of the War up to 1916, the trade unions lost more than half of their members, chiefly because these were recruited into the War. In September 1914, 28 per cent of union members were at the front, in July 1915 43 per cent and, at the end of 1916, 64 per cent. Thereafter – probably because of a growing number of exemptions and reclamations – the percentage decreased, falling to 58 per cent at the end of June 1918.[266] The Socialist unions suffered the biggest loss of membership.

Trade union members[267] *(in 1000)*

	Social Democratic unions	Liberal unions	Christian unions
1913	2,574	107	343
1914 (1st half)	2,511	} 78	} 283
(2nd half)	1,664		
1915	1,159	61	176
1916	967	58	174
1917	1,107	79	244
1918	1,665	114	393
1919	5,479	190	858

The renewed growth in numbers, starting in 1917 (although the Social Democrats at least never regained their prewar level), was due to the unions' new role in the war economy following the enactment of the Auxiliary Service Law and, possibly, of the revised Association Law (1916) which allowed the trade unions to recruit juveniles under eighteen. Many of these now took the place of conscripted men who had been union members for many years. The new recruits, most of whom had never belonged to a union, were semi-skilled workers from other branches of the economy, mostly juveniles and women. In the Social Democratic unions, 230,000 female members were enrolled in 1913. Their number rose to 423,000 in 1918.[268]

The proportion of women thus grew from 8 per cent to about 25 per cent. It is likely that similar changes occurred in the proportion of juveniles and semi-skilled workers. In other words, the membership in

1918 was no longer that of 1913. The prewar members were mostly of long standing but were in no way more radical; they were responsive to trade union indoctrination, which had as its priority the preservation, extension and recognition of the union. The unprecedented shifts and the new experiences of the War altered the composition of the unions' base, but not that of their traditional bureaucracy which, together with the Party, retained more authority over the working class than did any other organisation.[269] Herein lay the structural basis for the growing split between the membership and the 'grass roots'.[270]

But more momentous changes than these were actually taking place. With the tendency, however limited, towards radicalisation and mobilisation in the working class, the union bureaucracy not only remained firmly rooted in its prewar traditions, but exhibited more strongly than ever before its integrationist, revisionist and anti-class-war approach to problems. This change of emphasis, which ran counter to the development at the base, can only be explained, within the model adopted here, if light is thrown on the tensions between society and state. This will be attempted in Chapter 4 below.[271]

5. Attitudes and alliances among employers

At this point we have established that there was an intensification of industrial class opposition and have tried to show how and to what degree this found socio-psychological expression among the working class and led to organisational changes and open conflict. We must now examine how far there was a corresponding development on the side of the employers. How did changes in their own class position and changes in the working class influence the attitudes and behaviour, the organisations and reactions of the industrialists? Did the criterion of class membership enter into the attitudes and behaviour of entrepreneurs, did the dividing line with the proletariat consequently become more pronounced and did other dividing lines within the entrepreneurial class recede into the background; was there, alternatively, a move in the opposite direction?

As discussed at the beginning of this study, the competitive nature of the German economy up to 1914, all monopolistic prewar tendencies notwithstanding, prevented the formation of unified opinions and attitudes throughout industry.[272] Divergent branches of industry had very varied interests, frequently standing in a producer-consumer relationship towards each other; there was also the opposition between export- and home-market-orientated sectors and differing attitudes in large and small firms. Most importantly, no clear consensus of attitudes towards agrarian interests or towards social policy had been achieved prior to 1914.[273] Entrepreneurs were, however, agreed in principle that the socialist challenge was to be resisted in so far as it was aimed at the radical reform of the power structures within industry or in society at large or even at revolution. With the perceived growth of the socialist-proletarian challenge, this common anti-proletarian, anti-socialist base among the entrepreneurs came to the fore in the last decade before the War, although individual differences were not entirely obliterated.[274]

The outbreak of the War signified a break in continuity; the Burgfrieden policy of both Social Democracy and the unions and the patriotic spirit evinced by so many of the working class (which came as a surprise to many entrepreneurs) seemed to resolve the long period of increasing confrontation, which the employers had done little to prevent. 'The dictatorship of revolutionary slogans has been broken', a major employers' association newspaper (*Deutsche Arbeitgeber-Zeitung*) stated at the beginning of August 1914, 'not through the intervention of the State but through the vicissitudes of world history.'[275]

It seems that most entrepreneurs had failed to recognise and did not experience the increasing discontent and readiness to protest of the majority of workers as either a threat or a challenge,[276] at least not until 1917, at the earliest. Leading entrepreneurs and organisations long maintained 'that the patriotic spirit amongst the labour force is unquestionable. . . . Workers called upon to join up responded to this call with enthusiasm. . . . In such a labour force the patriotic spirit will always remain alive'.[277] Some entrepreneurs believed that this opened up an opportunity to activate the nationalism of the working class as a launching pad for a new anti-international, anti-Socialist workers' organisation and thus to destroy the basis of the independent unions once and for all. They blamed the government for working with the trade unions and 'for failing to take advantage of the magnificent and mighty patriotic upsurge amongst the mass of workers for the good of the State and the economy'.[278] The vast discontent and bitterness of the working class was regarded by them primarily as the temporary consequence of hardship and shortages, and was not seen as a protest directed against continuing economic, social and political inequality.[279]

Above all, where entrepreneurs recognised that the mobilisation of the masses and their demands were direct consequences of the War, they were confident for the most part that patriotic belief in victory and the final victory itself would check the discontent and divert the demands for radical change.[280] Where the politicising, critical developments of the spring and summer of 1917 increasingly brought the loyalty of the masses into question, it was this 'social-imperialist' solution on which the large entrepreneurial groups placed reliance. All the important entrepreneurial organisations supported and financed the Fatherland Party, that right-wing mass movement whose nationalistic and anti-reformist propaganda was directed, amongst others, at activist workers who had begun to be mobilised.[281]

It is only if one keeps in mind the increasingly unrealistic belief (propped up as it was by 'social-imperialist' hopes) of most entrepreneurs in the patriotic 'reliability' and harmlessness of the working class that one can understand the repulsive policy of their organisations towards the unions. However, this policy was not a uniform one; particularly in those sectors which had implemented wage agreements before the War, cooperation between entrepreneurs and unions was strengthened during the War. In the building, wood, decorating, brewing, tailoring and printing trades, in community enterprises, health insurances and cooperative societies – i.e., chiefly in small businesses not favoured by the War – there were, in 1914 and 1915, voluntary equal partnerships formed, without visible pressure from the authorities, which concerned themselves with problems of welfare and the provision of labour and which also partly regulated hours of work and wages in a cooperative fashion.[282] There were also industrialists, chiefly in the manufacturing branches, who regarded the limited cooperation with the unions enforced by the authorities with less critical eyes than did the western German and Silesian industrialists.[283] However, as far as can be deduced from statements about voluntary cooperation in welfare and food distribution, in general the German industrial employers and their representative organisation, the 'Vereinigung Deutscher Arbeitgeberverbände', flatly rejected the completely non-revolutionary offers of cooperation and demands for co-determination by the unions. Where a cooperative equality of the two classes prevailed in large-scale industry during the War, this usually occurred through the insistence of the unions, against the will of the entrepreneurs and under pressure from the military and civilian authorities, as will be discussed further below.[284]

Most entrepreneurs interpreted union demands as power-seeking by union officials, just as they ascribed the increasing radicalism of demands for reform by the workers' parties, gatherings and publications, to certain radical agitators, ringleaders, party politicians and 'rabble-rousers'. In this way they were able to preserve their view of an ultimately patriotic and dutiful German working class, whose chief sufferings were caused by the deprivations of war, increasing indications to the contrary notwithstanding.[285] Because they did not as a rule view union and Social Democratic demands in relation to the sharpening moods of the masses, they were also highly critical of the relative indulgence shown by the government towards the unions,[286] and stubbornly fought the demands for equality, recognition and reform.[287] On grounds of principle the Vereingung Deutscher Arbeitgeberverbände warned their members against arbitration tribunals with equal representation; these would only help the union leadership to bring about a fundamental shift of power, especially 'taking into account that questions of basic significance were not to be broached out of regard for the current Burgfrieden'.[288] Up to the autumn of 1918, they rejected offers from the General Commission to cooperate in a central joint committee ('Zentralarbeitsgemein-schaft').[289] As a rule they were very unwilling to allow welfare laws and measures designed to strengthen the power and the co-determination of the unions to be foisted on them and stressed that their validity applied only to wartime. In the autumn of 1916 the Vereinigung der Deutschen Arbeitgeberverbände explicitly defended the point of view of 'master-in-the-house'.[290] In a memorandum on the period of postwar transition and the peacetime economy, dated March 1918, it rejected equal co-partnership with the unions and demanded the speedy abolition of the existing arrangements for equal representation instituted by the Auxiliary Service Law and other regulations.[291] German employers obviously felt strong and secure; so little of their power had been lost through trade union influence that they did not consider it necessary to make voluntary concessions in order to prevent worse from happening.

An important, but ultimately ineffective anti-trade union device of the employers' organisations was their support of the co-operative non-confrontationist and employer-dependent 'yellow' workers' unions which now collaborated increasingly on an inter-firm basis.[292] The employers tried, through an increasing number of non-confrontationist employers' organisations, to counter not only the growing power of the trade unions and to exploit the still-patriotic mood of the working class, but also to bolster their own dominant position within their organisation.

It is true that many employers acquired new modes of discipline which had not been at their disposal in peacetime, such as their right to distribute foodstuffs in essential factories and their influence over the deployment of workers designated as indispensable, deferred or absent on leave, who were liable for military service.[293] The employers in essential industries could also be sure that too radical a challenge by the labour force would lead to intervention of the military and to the military control of working conditions, even though they themselves preferred to avoid such interventions, which curtailed their own freedom of manoeuvre.[294] To the extent to which personnel were mobile, the work-force was able to elude employer control to some extent in firms where this had rested on long-established and traditional feelings of loyalty to the company, skilfully fostered by the firm's welfare schemes. In the years before 1914 German big business had laid increasing stress on indirect techniques of integration and discipline which had enabled it to avoid direct confrontations with labour. Through company pension funds, bonuses, works' magazines, anniversary celebrations, lectures and other welfare benefits, employers had tried to generate employee loyalty and dependence and in this way reduce the opportunities for trade union influence.[295] How far this 'secondary paternalism' gave rise to a real loyalty which strengthened the legitimacy of employer-dominance in the firm remains an open question. However, in so far as it had ever succeeded it was to be largely negated by wartime changes in the labour force.[296] These changes, detrimental to the employer, in the system of labour exchanges[297] and the establishment of blue-and white-collar workers' committees, following the Auxiliary Service Law, were an additional help in undermining the employers' power base and strengthening the unions within the firms.

The intensive promotion of the 'yellow' union movement after 1915 was intended to counteract those tendencies which were clearly not in the employers' interest. It seems that employers took less notice of the 'yellow' unions in the first year of the War and the relatively calm atmosphere of the Burgfrieden than they had done in the immediate prewar period. In any case, as far as can be established, the membership of these unions fell from 280,000 (1913) to 133,000 (1915), thus they initially suffered greater losses than did the other trade unions.[298] But from October 1915 at the latest the most important employers' associations cooperated when it came to giving financial and propagandist support to the 'Wirtschaftsfriedlichen'.[299] Their membership did in fact increase between 1915 and 1916 whereas the numerical decline in the various 'confrontationist' unions continued in this period.[300] Given the increasingly critical mood of the labour force in many firms, these attempts by employers met with little ultimate success, since the Auxiliary Service Law and other official measures which the other unions had been promoting were proved disadvantageous to the 'yellow' unions.[301] Whereas the confrontationist unions began to make good the decline in their membership after 1916, membership of the 'yellow' unions declined between 1916 and 1918.[302] Often members of these unions showed their true colours in secret ballots and in other situations free from control by the employer, indicating that they had only joined the 'yellow' movement for opportunistic reasons but had secretly remained loyal to their trade union convictions. When in March 1917 there was a secret ballot in accordance with the Auxiliary Service Law at Krupp, a centre of the 'yellow' movement, to elect a workers' committee, only 4,000 out of 40,000 workers voted for the Wirtschaftsfriedlichen.[303]

For the greater part of the War it was less the growing radical potential of the working class as such than the less radical reformist demands of the trade unions which were identified as a danger in the employers' press and rejected by their associations.[304] This negative attitude to trade union demands was rooted, on the one hand, in a certain under-estimation of the discontent and willingness to protest among the working class; on the other, it was based on the hope that any possible radicalisation of the masses could be diverted with the help of 'social imperialism', victory and annexationism. It was only in the late summer of 1918 that employers altered their assessment of the situation in the face of the defeat which was threatening. They had to acknowledge that nationalist, annexationist propaganda and 'yellow' works' unions had not taken permanent root among their workers and that these could be expected to lose their raison d'être in the coming defeat. The danger of revolution now became all too clear.[305] In this situation the employers united to accept as the lesser evil demands for recognition and co-determination by unions which were still prepared to cooperate. They did so in order to protect themselves as far as possible from the gathering protest among the masses, now recognised as explosive, and the interventions of the State which had begun to democratise itself.[306] The 'Zentralarbeitsgemeinschaft der industriellen und gewerblichen Arbeitgeber und Arbeitnehmer Deutschlands' (ZAG) which was established in October/November of that year on a basis of equal representation of labour and capital, was primarily a product of the threatening, then ensuing, collapse. It resulted from a reversal of attitudes amongst employers, who revised their prewar and wartime policies towards their workers and the trade unions in the face of the imminent revolution.[307]

Thus the common interest of the entrepreneurs in resisting the proletarian challenge, first in its moderate trade union, then in its revolutionary, form became more marked during the War. But this class-based unity, which has been very roughly sketched out here, was undermined by economic interests which continued to divide the various entrepreneurial groups, even if the Allied blockade and general excess of demand over supply which soon became noticeable removed some of the central points of dispute (such as customs policy), between different industries.[308] The previously described distortions and redistributions resulting from the peculiar growth of the wartime economy led to new divisions of interest between the war industries and the peace industries, and generated resentments against the expansion of a prosperous heavy industry into new fields. It reinforced some of the discrepancies between large- and small-scale firms and created tensions between the regions, above all between the industries in south Germany and those in Prussia to whom the wartime policies of the Berlin government gave preference.[309] The methods of dispute changed. Market competition between individual firms or industrial groups partly ceased. Conflicts within formal organisations (associations, cartels, war associations) and the struggle for influence on the distributive departments of the government greatly increased in significance, even though there had been a discernible trend in the prewar years. Representation on certain decision-making bodies, contact with important officials (or the placing of informants in official positions) and political and bureaucratic methods now became more important than business acumen or technical competence.[310] If a firm was forced to close, it was no longer primarily because its production or sales were deficient, nor because of the market and old-style capitalist competition; what was decisive was the degree of influence which could be exerted on a key man in the War Raw Materials Department or (from the end of 1917) on the Reich Economic Office. The composition of the Standing Committee for the Consolidation of

Firms or of an advisory council attached to a federal state's agency could also be of significance. The advance of 'bureaucrats' within the firms' management at the cost of 'entrepreneurial personalities' was a side-effect of these changes which speeded up the inexorable process of industrial bureaucratisation.[311]

Despite the many traditional and war-determined divergences of interest, employers drew ever more closely together during the War. The founding of the War Committee of German Industry, on 8 August 1914, by representatives of the two largest industrial federations – heavy industry's 'Centralverband Deutscher Industrieller' (CVDI) and the 'Bund der Industriellen' (BdI), representing the manufacturing and export industries – in the presence of the Secretary of State for the Interior, reflected the growing need for co-operation among industrialists under the new organisational conditions of the wartime economy. The War Committee wished to take over the systematic distribution and placement of labour, the support of ailing branches of industry and the distribution of state contracts and to be able to inform its members about the growing flood of laws and decrees.[312] Industrialists preferred to keep the coordination necessitated by the War in their own hands and thereby to render an Economic General Staff, of the kind already under discussion before the War, superfluous. From the start, all this furthered the interest of most industrialists.[313]

It is not possible at this point to investigate how far the different interests represented on this War Committee led to internal tension and rivalries,[314] or to what extent – and no doubt increasingly – important decisions were taken by other war committees, war associations for single industries and through informal decision-making channels. How under-represented some groups felt is shown *inter alia* by the founding of the independent 'Ausschuss der Deutschen Friedensindustrien' at Leipzig at the end of 1916; this body hoped to be able to obtain a few compensations, chiefly at the War Office, against the influence of 'the War industries favoured by the present situation and the Auxiliary Service Law'. The War Committee simply called for a boycott of this new body.[315] Nevertheless it cannot be denied that, with the founding of the War Committee, an organisation with the interests of nearly the whole of German industry was realised. It was the result of a development which had already led, in the last years before the War, to a rapprochement at various levels between the two big industrial pressure groups, the CVDI and the BdI.[316]

Step by step and in parallel with the labour movement's tendencies towards unification after 1914, the entrepreneurs moved towards unification, thereby manifesting the further growth in common interests. On 25 October 1916, the BdI and the CVDI, together with the independent Verein zur Wahrung der Interessen der chemischen Industrie Deutschlands, established the new federation Deutscher Industrierat. This federation was intended to bring the interests of the individual associations into line, while protecting their independence, and with the problems of the postwar period in mind. The aim was to provide the whole of industry with more bargaining power *vis-à-vis* both government and Parliament, as well as in the 'difficult battle against enthusiasts and champions of state-socialist ideas' during the changeover to a peacetime economy and during the period of reconstruction.[317] Apparently the federation did not become active before the beginning of 1918,[318] but then quickly intensified its activities until, early in 1919, it became the much more compact Reichsverband der deutschen Industrie. The functions of the original Industrierat, were extended and broadened, particularly through negotiations with the unions as well as through the fight against the 'demagogic slogans of Socialism' and the 'madness of the socialisation experiments'.[319]

The causes for this growing unification in the employers' camp have been partly analysed above: it occurred in the defence against the proletarian challenge, at first in its revisionist trade union form and then in its revolutionary guise. At the same time, the organisational unification of the entrepreneurs took place on the basis of their common, ever more dominant, wish for defence against state intervention, which drove their differences of opinion into the background. Within certain limits, the state increasingly freed itself from its class basis. Through its attempted organisation of both the economy and society at large, as well as through its eventual failure, it stimulated important interests to mobilise against itself. Before dealing with this aspect more thoroughly in Chapter 4, it will be necessary to discuss briefly the changes that took place in class relations relevant to those social groups which we have not so far considered.

3 The Polarisation of the Mittelstand

1. The situation in 1914

If an attempt is made to analyse German society before 1914 in terms of a class structure whose primary criterion was the ownership and control of the means of production, it is difficult to place skilled craftsmen and small tradesmen, on the one hand, and salaried employees on the other, within such a framework. These two groups were frequently lumped together by contemporary writers – jointly with the majority of small farmers and the self-employed – into the Mittelstand, separated off from those 'above' and those 'below', from capital and wage labour, from the ruling classes and the proletariat. This chapter deals with the socio-economic characteristics, the ideologies and social alliances of these middle groups, with their wartime development and the resulting changes.

According to the 1907 occupational census, the last before the War, there were about 2 million white-collar workers as compared with 13.7 million wage labourers in Germany; in other words there were approximately seventy wage labourers to ten white-collar workers.[1] Most of these (1.1 million) were engaged in the service sector of the economy, where they had been active (admittedly in much lower numbers) long before industrialisation. They were mainly clerks; barely 700,000 of them worked as technicians, traders, supervisors and office personnel in industry and mining, forming a group which had in essence come into being with industrialisation and which had quickly proliferated, especially after 1890, with the bureaucratisation and commercialisation of the secondary sector. The rest were employed in agriculture (100,000) and with professionals (*ca.* 50,000) in lawyers' offices, pharmacies, etc. About three-quarters of the total were engaged either in trade or general office work, about one-quarter as technical or supervisory staff.[2]

There was little which bound this heterogeneous group together in terms of activity, function, education, income, legal status or other objective criteria, apart from their class position. They belonged to the category of the employed, the dependent workers, and not with the owners of the means of production. This was not, of course, specific to them; they shared their class position, as well as an increasing degree of division of labour and of collective behaviour with the manual workers. However, they were distinguished from the latter by at least one, although more often several of the following characteristics: white-collar workers earned more, on average, than manual workers, even if there were many overlaps; their income was almost exclusively in the form of a salary rather than a wage; many of them still worked in closer proximity to and had more actual contact with their 'principal' (the entrepreneur) (particularly in the commercial sector); they did no manual work, or at least not exclusively; as a rule they enjoyed greater security of employment as well as other privileges within the firm; and they differentiated themselves from manual workers in life style, patterns of consumption and career expectations. They did not consider themselves in general as employees, let alone proletarians, but as business people, technicians or 'private civil servants', and were accepted as such by most people. The concepts 'Privatbeamter' and 'Angestellter' denote much more emphatically and clearly than the Anglo-Saxon concept of 'white-collar employee' or the French 'employé salarié', a distinct social stratum with a specific status and rights which embraced a large variety of occupations, but which was clearly separate from the manual workers on the one hand and on the other from those of independent standing such as employers.

The organisational and political behaviour of white-collar employees was generally very different from that of manual workers. Although in 1907 about one in three of white-collar employees belonged to an Employees' Association, most of the quite numerous associations (53 in 1913) were open to the self-employed as well, thereby demonstrating that they were not orientated towards pure unionism.[3] Many were local associations, others were only interested in purely professional matters, most served as a focus of social life. Only a few of them, such as the 'Bund der technisch-industriellen Beamten', who had 23,000 members in 1913, the socialist 'Zentral-verband der Handlungsgehilfen', with 18,000 members in the same year, and the 'Verband der Bureauangestellten Deutschlands' with 8,000 members in 1913 and which was also affiliated to the General

Commission, accepted the concept of the strike as a means of achieving their aims. A powerful right wing of the organised white-collar employees, under the leadership of the nationalist, antisemitic 'Deutschnationaler Handlungsgehilfen-Verband' (DHV) with 123,000 members in 1913 combined a militantly anti-Socialist and illiberal ideology, full of resentments, with a readiness for a tough policy of self-interest – 'Standespolitik' as they called it. The greater majority of white-collar workers appear to have divided their support more or less equally between the Liberals, the Conservatives and the Catholic Centre Party. Only a small minority voted Social Democrat.

The gap between manual and white-collar workers was more of a social reality in Germany than in other comparable industrialised countries. The bureaucratic traditions of Prusso-German society served the quickly growing middle strata of employees, the Privatbeamten (!), as a model for collective self-identification and thereby as the basis for the claiming of privileges and a separation from manual workers. Confronted with a radical socialist protest movement, with a proletariat which appeared to be revolutionary and which was incompletely integrated into society, most white-collar employees stressed that they belonged to the middle class, to the non-proletarian and to the anti-Socialist camp. The more the working conditions and the economic situation of most white-collar and manual workers came to look alike, with continuing industrialisation, the more actively and determinedly white-collar workers defended their traditional privileges, their increasingly out-moded status advantages, and their consciousness of being 'different' from manual workers. Only a small minority, particularly those in the 'Bund der technisch-industriellen Beamten' which was founded in 1904, showed a readiness for limited cooperation with workers' trade unions. Since 1900 most white-collar associations had been agitating for privileged treatment in insurance matters and later for privileges in general labour and social legislation. In this connection it became customary to refer to them as the 'new Mittelstand'. Their efforts to distance themselves from the proletariat chimed in well with the anti-Socialist integration policies of both the middle-class parties and the Reich government, which wished to prevent the further growth of the socialist camp through social legislation. From 1911 a series of Reich laws, at first concerned with social insurance, but soon with other areas as well, separated white-collar from manual workers by awarding privileges to the former and, unlike England and the USA, by cementing a socio-economic differentiation whose functional basis was increasingly being eroded by the advance of economic modernisation. In the last years before the War, however, the growing demands of some white-collar employees' associations and the brusque response of their employers indicated that this middle-class integration policy would not, in the long run, be sufficient to shield all white-collar employees from a further radicalisation of their demands and from drawing closer to Social Democracy.[4]

As a rule the middle and lower strata of the civil service were also included in the 'new Mittelstand', whose number before 1914 was reckoned to be between 1.5 and 2 million.[5]

The peculiarities of the German civil service were reflected in advantages and disadvantages which extended through the various categories of an 'occupational group that ranged from Reich Chancellor to postman' in very varying degrees.[6] These included a particular relationship of loyalty towards the State, which was laid down by public law and which went beyond the ordinary usages of a civil law employment contract: recruitment according to general ability rather than specific qualifications; absolute security of tenure; pension rights; salaries, partly according to the principle of adequacy; an indefinite distinction between work and the private sphere as far as the rights of the employer were concerned; social security; relatively high prestige and a specific self-esteem. These conditions of service ensured that civil servants constituted an identifiable group, separate from other white-collar employees – although distinctions between them and white-collar workers in the public sector were somewhat blurred, with the latter striving to achieve civil service status, though gaining it but slowly.[7] Civil servants felt little sense of identity with other white-collar groups, while trade union representation was ruled out not only by law but also by their consciousness of their own status. And yet, even within this group there were, before 1914, a few weak indications of a movement of growing resentment and protest.

One reason for this may have been that their traditionally very limited income, which increased only slowly with age, appears to have fallen behind rising prices; but it also remained below the earnings of comparable white-collar groups in the private sector – as civil service spokesmen complained. Demands were voiced for the lifting of the civil service regulations which severely restricted civil servants' right to join clubs, associations and unions, thus keeping them under the tight control of the authorities. Out of the very scattered multiplicity of small civil service organisations, a general political interest group, the 'Bund der Festbesoldeten', emerged in 1909; it was not, however, very successful. Its demands included: higher taxation of large incomes and assets, rejection of the Prussian three-class voting system and the strengthening of self-government in the Reich, the federal states and the municipalities. The 'civil servants' question' had thus become a theme of German politics, albeit a subordinate one, well before 1914.[8]

In Germany the distinction between 'Handwerk' (skilled craftsmen, often self-employed) and 'Industrie' (manufacturing firms of medium to large scale) has played a much larger role than in the English-speaking countries, both as a semantic and as a social reality. Even today this distinction is legally enforced; there are laws pertaining to Handwerker only and there are semi-public craft boards (Handwerkskammern) in which all Handwerker have to become members. Other businesses are registered in different, obligatory, self-administrative bodies which have semi-public functions – Industrie-und Handelskammern. The size of the firm is one of the criteria by which Handwerk units are distinguished from Industrie, but this is not a very exact yardstick and other factors influence the distinction – for example, tradition, the degree of mechanisation and the decisions of those most concerned.[9] The number of master craftsmen (Handwerker) and small retailers (Kleinhändler) in the period before the outbreak of war is hard to determine. Trade statistics for 1907 show 3 million units with ten or less workers, but this number is unnaturally high since it refers to 'technical units', not units of ownership or firms; that is, it included sub-units of larger enterprises as well as independent small firms.[10] Estimates to be found in the literature draw on qualitative criteria – such as prevalence of craft work, degree of division of labour and production to order or for the local market – and arrive at the lower figures of around 1.5 million Handwerker and 500,000 Kleinhändler in the last years of the Wilhelmine period.[11] These two million Handwerker and Kleinhändler found themselves – seen in terms of their class position as independent owners of the means of production and, frequently, as small employers – in the same category as industrialists and other larger entrepreneurs. However, they differed from these not only in their life-style, but also in their socio-economic and political orientation. Frequently, Handwerker tended towards traditional values and life-styles; their continuous demands were directed partly openly, partly implicitly, against the capitalist market economy, against the principle of unrestricted competitiveness and against large firms with their competitive advantages. From 1848 until the 1860s, many Handwerker had supported both Liberal-Democratic political aims and semi-reactionary anti-capitalist socio-economic programmes, of which only the latter survived. From the 1870s and 1880s they organised themselves into numerous associations, many partly competing with each other. They demanded the revival of a guild-like regulation of competition (including the power to fix prices), of compulsory guilds and of special certificates of qualification, stipulating that applicants be admitted only on the basis of a test set by them. Behind the struggle against 'unfair competition', which they often carried on in the name of 'decency and morality', there was hidden the resentment of traditional small-scale enterprises against the extremely competitive behaviour and business acumen of successful large firms with their marketing techniques, their sales and special offers. Handwerker frequently turned towards the state with their social-protectionist demands, presenting themselves as a stratum between the classes, as a 'factor of order'; ultimately, they demanded something very like a guarantee of their economic and social status from the state, to protect them from the effects of progressive industrialisation. They were successful to a limited degree. Thus, the guilds were slowly reinstated to their former position; in 1897 the 'fakultative Zwangsinnung' was instituted, giving the authorities the power to declare guilds obligatory where this was proposed by a majority of craft firms in a town or district; in 1908, special certificates of qualification were required from those who set up in business as Handwerker; in 1909 the 'law against unfair competition' was passed and preferential consideration was given to master craftsmen in the allocation of state contracts.[12]

Their opposition to unrestricted competition and big business united the Handwerker to a certain extent at least, with the originally more liberal Kleinhändler who, in pushing for a restoration of their status, had also turned for help towards the state. The retailers' demands were anti-liberal and anti-capitalist; their struggle was also directed against the market economy, large-scale enterprises (especially department stores) and unfair competition, as well as against itinerant trade and – increasingly – cooperative societies.[13] Associations which sought to unite the two groups were founded, especially after the 1890s. Organised Handwerker and Kleinhändler frequently depicted themselves as being the losers in the industrialisation process;[14] they found a common ideology in 'mittelständische' ideas and slogans which stressed their 'reliability' against 'revolution', their significance for a 'healthy' state and their worthiness of and need for protection against big business. All in all, this Mittelstand movement was both unstable and heterogeneous. While 36 per cent of the master craftsmen belonged to guilds in 1907, only a small proportion of them were members of voluntary associations. The right wing of the Handwerker movement, where chief support was in Saxony and Lower Saxony and whose best-known organisation (founded in 1911) was the 'Reichsdeutsche Mittelstandsverband', harked back in reactionary style to *ancien régime* forms of organisation and ideologies, professing an aggressive anti-Socialist, antisemitic, nationalistic world view. Other craft associations, such as the south German Gewerbevereine, remained closer to Liberal orientations. Guilds ('Innungen') and particularly Handwerkskammern, were more or less obligatory institutions, under state supervision and with a semi-public character; they were more restrained and less 'political' than the voluntary associations.[15]

Making use of the vagueness and positive emotional connotations of the concept, these two groupings – of Handwerker and Kleinhändler and of white-collar employees – were lumped together from the end of the century as the 'old' and the 'new' Mittelstand[16] and, increasingly, there was a political purpose behind this conceptual combination. It concealed the deeply opposed interests which resulted from the divergent class positions which white-collar employees and the petty bourgeois Mittelstand occupied. Indeed, the tensions between the 'old' and the 'new', between the self-employed and the employed Mittelstand repeatedly rose to the surface as tensions within organisations such as the Reichsdeutsche Mittelstandsverband or the 'Hansa-Bund' which tried to unite both groups. The talk about a Mittelstand and policies derived from this notion belied the tension and played an integrating role in a society in which increasing class conflict would otherwise have required quite different, more radical and, for the ruling classes, more costly solutions.

The quest for Mittelstand protection and appeal to Mittelstand interests was both vague and emotional enough to be useful to the ruling groups in the promotion of their interests. The agrarian Bund der Landwirte proclaimed an illusionary common interest between large-scale agriculture and the 'Mittelstand in town and country'. Agrarians and big business paid the Mittelstand at least verbal respect when they sought to win the support of as large a proportion as possible in order to mount an anti-Socialist and anti-democratic counter-movement; this coalesced in 1913 into an unstable organisation, known as the 'Kartell der schaffende Stände'. The anti-agrarians who clustered around the more liberal Hansa-Bund and who were supported by the big banks and some sections of industry also tried to draw Kleinhändler and white-collar employees into their camp; they, too, did so by including Mittelstand demands in their programme.[17]

But apart from its political and ideological functions, talk of the 'old' and the 'new Mittelstand' underlined an important reality: the existence of two groups, similar by virtue of their separation from the groups 'below' (working class) and 'above' (big business), who perceived themselves as the worthy, threatened 'sound core' that needed to be preserved. Consequently, their objective class position was not the defining condition for the life-styles, expectations, organisation and political behaviour of either white-collar employees or of Handwerker and Kleinhändler. Both groups organised themselves predominantly against those whose class position they shared; the Kleinhändler dissociated themselves from large-scale capital and industry, white-collar employees from the working class.[18] Together they formed a significant factor by which Wilhelmine society was distinguished from a clearly marked, dichotomous class society. Encouraged by the State, they acted as a sort of padding, which somewhat muffled the growing class conflict. During the War, this padding was ripped apart.

2. The proletarianisation of the 'new Mittelstand'

Immediately following the outbreak of the War, temporary stoppages and unemployment – quickly exploited by some entrepreneurs – led to drastic wage cuts among many white-collar employees, sometimes in breach of contract. A clerks' association in Hamburg discovered that out of 2,288 of its employed members, 1,018 had suffered wage reductions, mostly between 25 per cent and 50 per cent, in November 1914.[19] The wartime boom which set in shortly afterwards did not enable most white-collar workers to make good this loss even at the level of nominal wages, although the cost of living rose by 30 per cent up to the end of 1915. The Reich Insurance Office gave the average annual income of white-collar workers earning up to 5,000M (and therefore liable to pay insurance contributions) as 1,941M for men and 997M for women in 1914, but as only 1,871M for men and 955M for women in 1915.[20] This decline in the nominal value of white-collar incomes contrasted with the average annual income of blue-collar workers in the same period which, while also remaining well below the rise in prices, did not decline nominally. In the first eighteen months of the War the average white-collar employee had already lost more purchasing power than the average blue-collar worker.[21] Between 1916 and the end of the War the nominal earnings of most white-collar workers rose, on average, to above the prewar level. This was not, for the most part, due to an increase in basic salaries, but to special allowances, temporary increases designed to cover inflation, child benefit payments and the like. Among poorly-paid white-collar workers at Siemens, for example, these amounted to 10 per cent of their salary in October 1915, rising to between 50 per cent and 60 per cent in July 1918.[22] Entrepreneurs hoped to achieve thereby greater flexibility in labour costs for the period after the end of the War or in case of falling profits; they feared that it would be more difficult to reverse salary increases than War allowances or wage increases for workers.[23]

Despite these allowances and limited salary increases, white-collar incomes remained well below the rising cost of living index and below manual workers' wage increases as well, between 1916 and 1918. A survey by the Deutschnationaler Handlungsgehilfen-Verband among its members showed that their nominal earnings between 1 August 1914 and 31 December 1917 had risen by 18.2 per cent, from 2,393M to 2,829M; on the other hand the cost of living index had risen by 185 per cent in this period, while workers had recorded average increases of over 40 per cent in the 'peace' industries and of more than 100 per cent in the War industries.[24] It was not only in the often very hard-hit trade sector, but also in the high-earning War industries that white-collar employees lost ground financially compared with manual workers. In July 1917 the 'Meistervereinigung der Siemens-Schuckertwerke' protested to the management that their members earned too little in comparison to the workers. Including all allowances and the thirteenth-month salary, the average monthly earnings of a foreman had increased from 238M to 390M (66 per cent) since the beginning of the War, whereas the wage of a skilled worker had risen from 172M to 306M (that is, by 87 per cent); this was without taking into account overtime payments, which were accorded to all workers but not to all foremen.[25] It is true that some lower-level white-collar employees had always earned less than well-placed skilled workers. Nevertheless, before the War average white-collar earnings had been approximately 15 per cent above those of manual workers,[26] even though the trend towards a levelling was clearly recognisable. In some industries, such as mining, the promotion of a worker to the lower ranks of the firms' white-collar staff 'mostly meant a reduction in income'.[27] In armaments factories many manual workers earned more towards the end of the War – often by a significant amount – than many white-collar workers.[28]

It was not only manual and white-collar earnings which came to approximate each other during the War, but the differentials in earnings within the white-collar group were also reduced, partly because a certain minimal existence level had to be maintained. Moreover, the traditional ranks reached according to length of service became less important; in general younger workers caught up with longer-serving older ones during the War.

Annual average earnings at Siemens (in Mk)[29]

Before tax	1914	1921	Multiplication factor
Male manual workers	1,800	19,000	10.6
Male white-collar workers	2,700	25,200	9.3
Senior white-collar workers (Normalbeteiligte)	6,000	58,400	9.7
Deputies	10,400	86,900	8.4
Senior clerks	20,400	140,500	6.9
Workshop etc. directors	—	141,300	—
Deputy board directors	32,000	195,000	6.1
Board directors	91,000	350,000	3.8
After tax			
Male manual workers	1,750	17,100	9.8
Male white-collar workers	2,600	22,600	8.6
Senior white-collar workers (Normalbeteiligte)	5,700	47,000	8.2
Deputies	9,800	84,700	6.6
Senior clerks	19,100	96,100	5.0
Workshop etc. directors	20,600	116,200	5.6
Deputy board directors	30,000	143,400	4.8
Board directors	83,000	238,150	2.9

Take Siemens as an example: although differentials between income categories had been re-emphasised in this firm in October 1921 through staggered increases, the income gradations between the various categories of employees were less at the end of 1921 than they had been before the beginning of the War.

These levelling tendencies continued in the 1920s, particularly during the 1923 inflation. If one compares nominal incomes in terms of annual averages for 1913 and 1928, the average workers' income increased by two-thirds in those fifteen years, but that of white-collar employees by only one-third. At the beginning of the great slump of 1929–33, both semi-skilled and skilled workers had on average exceeded their pre-1914 real incomes; in contrast, the real incomes of most white-collar workers were still lagging behind those of 1913, as late as the end of 1929. The long-term levelling of wages and salaries expressed in these figures corresponded with a similar change which occurred in other highly industrialised countries, such as the USA (even if it was less drastic there and was not accompanied by a long-term stagnation in per capita real incomes).[30]

A similar process took place among civil servants. As the Table below makes clear,[31] the War signified a sharp reduction in purchasing power for all categories of civil servants; but the senior civil servants lost more than the middle and lower ranks, as salary increases after 1917 were awarded on the basis of social criteria in order to mitigate the worst hardships.

Civil servants, with their fixed salaries, came to the notice of the Regional Army Command earlier than white-collar employees, appearing as 'needy and impoverished' in their regular reports made to Berlin on the condition of the population. In August 1916, the Regional Army Command detected signs of 'dissatisfaction and bitterness' among civil servants and municipal officials in Berlin, since they were now earning less than many industrial workers.[32] In October of that year the Command reiterated, with the support of other Rear Army Corps, that 'we must once again refer to the predicament of those on fixed salaries, namely the civil servants, whose incomes have not risen during the War as have those of manual workers. The Chief of Police in Berlin quite rightly points out that rising prices (about which no more need be said) prevent many civil servants from feeding and clothing themselves and their families in any way adequately. Quick and effective help is required here; it must be possible for the State and the Reich to find the necessary funds for this. Among the

The decline in civil service salaries

	Higher civil servants			Middle-grade civil servants			Lower-grade civil servants		
	Monthly income (in Mk)			Monthly income (in Mk)			Monthly income (In Mk)		
	Nominal	Real	Index	Nominal	Real	Index	Nominal	Real	Index
1913	608	608	100.0	342	342	100.0	157	157	100.0
1914	608	591	97.2	342	332	97.2	157	153	97.2
1915	608	470	77.3	342	264	77.3	157	121	77.3
1916	608	358	58.9	342	202	58.9	157	93	58.9
1917	660	261	42.9	420	166	48.6	213	84	53.6
1918	891	284	46.8	589	188	55.0	342	109	69.6
1919	1,015	245	40.2	778	187	54.8	582	140	89.3
Dec. 1920	2,325	201	33.0	1,813	157	45.8	1,344	116	73.9
Dec. 1921	4,900	254	41.8	3,320	172	50.4	2,285	119	75.5
Dec. 1922	138,487	202	33.3	103,945	152	44.4	70,766	103	65.8
Dec. 1923	309.50	251	41.3	210.75	170	49.8	115.25	92	58.6

many pressing reasons which necessitate this, one only needs to consider that justified discontent among civil servants can have serious political consequences in the long run; it must also have a considerable effect on popular morale, which would be losing a strong prop'.[33] Such warnings run through the monthly reports with increasing urgency.[34] Towards the end of the War a representative of the Civil Servants' Association complained: 'The civil servants' economic attire was threadbare and worn out long before the War began. . . . Civil servants fought a constant battle for their social existence. And during the War they lost this battle. Broad sections of the population overtook them; their decline could no longer be halted'.[35]

The causes for these unfavourable developments of salaries in the public and private sectors were manifold: all inflations hit salaries (less flexible, less market-dependent) harder than wages; for the time being private and public employers had no need to fear any radical opposition from their white-collar employees who had no strong, aggressive associations at their command, while the non-unionised civil servants generally supported the state. Employers knew how to exploit this. The military authorities, however, after much prodding by the associations, did advocate better pay for white-collar workers as well as (though less eagerly) for manual workers; they did not, after all, expect massive strikes detrimental to the economic management of the War from the white-collar Privatbeamten. More importantly, given the wartime labour shortage, employers could more easily manage with fewer white-collar employees than with fewer wage labourers. Thus Siemens-Schuckert in Berlin increased its labour force by one-third during the War, but its white-collar personnel by only one-tenth.[36] The labour market favoured manual workers over white-collar employees or civil servants, especially since independent or self-employed persons from those branches which contracted during the War evidently preferred to apply for office posts after the enactment of the Auxiliary Service Law (HDG), in order to escape compulsory transfer to manual work or to the Front.[37]

This absolute and relative impoverishment weighed heavily upon the social status and self-image of the 'new Mittelstand', whose members had after all defined themselves in terms of their difference from wage labourers; this was their main grievance and the main reason for their discontent. Other deprivations and shocks were added to their loss of earnings. The short period of mass unemployment at the beginning of the War[38] brought the reality of their position, with its insecurity and dependence on market forces, clearly home to white-collar employees.[39] Until then their 'Privatbeamten' consciousness had deceived them about this. Worse, those who had been re-employed, were newly employed or had been promoted during the War had reason to fear for their jobs once the War was over and conscripted white-collar workers returned to claim their posts. Similarly, with the abolition of the principle of seniority in salary agreements and of certain specifically white-collar privileges within firms, this group increasingly felt that its 'Beamten' self-image was being called into question.[40] More women were employed during the War, especially in commercial and general offices, in the technical professions and in the civil service. The 'women's question' and 'wage-reducing female labour' was an irritant to many civil servants and white-collar employees.[41] Rising rents and exorbitant prices for clothes were predominant among Mittelstand complaints, particularly in the last year of the War. The regulation promulgated in the summer of 1918 that all spare clothing should be given to armaments workers angered white-collar employees, civil servants, craftsmen and Kleinhändler.[42] This denial of what they saw as basic democratic rights and the simultaneous imposition of further wartime directives angered manual workers and anti-socialist white-collar employees alike. In August 1916 the right-wing Deutschnationale Handlungs-gehilfen-Verband even demanded a democratisation ('volkstümliche Gestaltung') of the plutocratic Prussian voting system.[43]

Finally, it must have been annoying to activist white-collar employees that the entrepreneurs treated their associations in a manner even less respectful and more dismissively hostile than they did the strong and aggressive blue-collar trade unions; the latter even received limited support from the military authorities, who feared to lose War production. Members of the very moderate technicians' and clerks' associations were even placed on 'black lists' as a disciplinary measure, the employers refusing throughout to enter into any collective bargaining with white-collar associations. They stuck rigidly to the notion that the relationship between the entrepreneur and his Privatbeamten must be an individual one, scenting an 'atmosphere of class war'[44] in every collective action by white-collar workers. The authorities were very suspicious of the growing activity of the many small civil service associations and used their power of control to prevent, for as long as possible, the rise of independent associations with avowed welfare and incomes-policy aims.[45]

3. The leftward drift of white-collar employees

Of course, the ideological reactions of white-collar employees to these changes in their situation were not uniform. Many of them extolled their Mittelstand status the more it was threatened. This was particularly true of many commercial employees, who tended to work in smaller firms and in closer contact with their employers than did most technicians, who tended to be employed in large-scale enterprises. A spokesman for a commercial employees' association confirmed this as late as the end of 1917: 'We are well aware that there exist attitudes and conditions among the lower ranks which incline them towards the workers . . . [but] 'we are not the masses and cannot have a mass impact like manual workers. Our working day is individual . . . we have a different relationship with the entre-preneur. . . . We adhere to the special character of our relationships and demand free rein for a pure "white-collar employee policy" [Angestelltenpolitik]'.[46]

At the same time, and in marked contrast to such verbal affirmations, there emerged a bitter feeling and the gradual recognition that, as employees, it would be necessary to behave as did the wage labourers.[47] Even so old-fashioned an association as the Hamburg Verein für Handlungs-Commis, founded in 1858, which always stressed the individualistic nature of white-collar employment, resorted to collective demands. They demanded basic salaries, graded according to function and age – although they did not yet promote collective agreements.[48] The Deutschnationale Handlungsgehilfen-Verband, in common with nearly all other associations, for a while had categorically rejected the strike. In July 1917, however, the association's chairman reported that many members wished to follow the example of manual workers and use 'the most radical means'; he made it fairly clear that 'in the end even the mass of white-collar employees would be ready for wage struggles on a proletarian basis'; indeed it was this association that was to lead a number of successful strikes in the spring of 1919.[49] In the autumn of 1917 white-collar workers at AEG, the large Berlin electrical engineering firm, went on strike for better salaries.[50] In January 1918 the foremen of factories in Nuremberg indirectly promoted a mass strike.[51] What, with few exceptions, had been sharply rejected by white-collar employees before the War as 'beneath their status' or even immoral, became acceptable during the War and a reality during the Revolution.[52] In many large firms the white-collar workers' committees, which (together with manual workers' committees) had been made obligatory by the Auxiliary Service Law of 1916, became the starting point for many a strike threat and for the radicalisation of white-collar employees, as of manual workers, within the firm. Junghein, a director of Siemens, stated at the beginning of 1918 that 'since the establishment of a white-collar workers' committee, white-collar office workers have fallen victim to agitation and political poison; it is getting worse all the time and the firm has to resist this with all its might'.[53]

Apart from disciplinary measures and the dismissal of white-collar employees who had joined an association, the entrepreneurs responded by speeding up the creation of 'yellow' collaborationist white-collar associations which they apparently hoped to use as counter-measures, especially during elections to works' committees. The small privileges which these 'works' associations' offered to underpaid white-collar workers must have been particularly attractive in the years of hardship. These 'yellow' white-collar organisations appear to have been started in 1908 by the Nuremberg firm of MAN. At Krupp's, in Essen, they obtained nearly 50 per cent of the white-collar vote in the elections for the works' committees in 1917. The growth of 'yellow' white-collar associations during the war points to the counter-offensive mounted by the employers against their radicalised white-collar employees, who increasingly came to disbelieve in the Beamten mentality fostered by the entrepreneurs.[54]

These counter-measures of the employers against the 'radical aspirations of the large commercial and technical white-collar associations' reached their climax at the beginning of 1918 with the founding of the inter-regional non-confrontationist newspaper *Die Hanse*. Supported by advertisements and donations from all branches of trade and industry, this journal was distributed free to many white-collar workers; it advocated the 'protection of capital and the productive estates through the promotion of entrepreneurial activity' and a 'middle-of-the-road conciliation of interests' between capital and labour 'to the exclusion of the Government, state Socialism and association terrorism'. It urged the founding of an 'Association of non-confrontationist white-collar workers modelled on the patriotic workers' associations, but having regard for the particular circumstances' of white-collar workers.[55] As in the case of the 'yellow' workers' associations, these attempts never got very far; they were confronted by the increasingly embittered and critical attitude of white-collar employees, by the determined and, for this purpose, joint opposition of manual and white-collar workers' unions, and by the ever clearer disapproval on the part of the Government, which had the unionised labour movement looking over its shoulder.[56] In the face of the ever more marked leftward shift of white-collar workers, the non-confrontationist alternative to the increasingly unionist orientation of the 'new Mittelstand' met with only limited success.

This (limited) leftward movement of white-collar workers under the influence of the wartime crisis was reflected among a minority by a radical political commitment. The relatively small, socialist Zentralverband der Handlungsgehilfen, which organised chiefly the worst paid (mostly female) office clerks, belonged to the left opposition within the general Commission of Free Unions and supported the USPD.[57] It was not unusual for white-collar workers to be represented in local USPD groups, particularly in southern Germany,[58] and the leader of a Berlin Spartakus cell worked as a chief engineer at Siemens,[59] although these were certainly exceptions. All the same, in August 1918 the Regional Army Command at Leipzig spoke, without differentiating, of 'the great multitude of workers, white-collar employees etc., whose incomes in no way correspond with constantly increasing prices. The full weight of official influence is required here, if serious unrest is to be avoided in the long run . . . '.[60]

A slightly more representative picture may be gained from an analysis of the changes that occurred in the white-collar associations during the War. The organisations which were most strongly orientated towards the manual labour unions had already decided, as early as 1913, to cooperate with them on a supra-occupational basis. In 1917 they formed the 'Arbeitsgemeinschaft freier Angestelltenver-bände'. Two further federations of separate associations were created during the War: the moderate 'Arbeitsgemeinschaft technischer Verbände' and the emphatically middle-class 'Arbeitsgemeinschaft kaufmännischer Verbände'.[61] In July 1917 these three white-collar federations concluded an agreement to intensify cooperation over questions of common interest. This coming together of white-collar associations during the War was a reaction to hardship and to new sorts of work. The associations presented joint petitions for improvements in food supplies and distribution, and in matters concerned with the execution of the Auxiliary Service Law; in firms which had strong non-confrontationist associations, the union-orientated associations frequently joined to put up alternative candidates at elections, in order to break the influence of the 'yellows' on white-collar committees; cooperative approaches were also made to the management when asking for price increase allowances for salaried employees. These concerted actions by the associations were much helped by the fact that labour exchanges became increasingly centralised during the War, thus removing an important reason for the competition which had divided the associations while the allocations of jobs was still partly under their control.[62] Beyond these concrete instances, cooperation between white-collar associations also reflected the increasing importance of the 'employee' status, which was common to all of them, at the cost of more specific professional identifications, which had served hitherto as the basis for the formation of divergent white-collar associations. However, these changes were only clearly apparent during the War among a minority of those organisations; others no more than hinted at changes among a welter of more traditional ideological self-definitions. It was not until after the Revolution that these trends became fully assertive.[63]

The increasing significance of the employee component in the consciousness of white-collar workers, which was at the cost of the traditional professional and/or Privatbeamten self-image, also facilitated awareness of their common interest with other paid labour, particularly with manual workers. A clear majority of white-collar associations continued to have strong reservations on this point. Despite increasing cooperation between all white-collar and manual workers' organisations, the commercial associations in particular emphasised their special position as an estate and refused, for example, to become organised jointly with manual workers in the obligatory works' chambers which were being planned in 1918.[64] On the other hand, a growing minority of white-collar associations stressed their pro-union orientation and their broad range of common interests with the blue-collar trade unions, which were reciprocally seeking cooperation with the white-collar workers.[65] Repeatedly, they turned jointly to the civil or military authorities in order to influence the implementation of the Auxiliary Service Law or to protest against the government's food policies or against agricultural profits and to demand stronger control by the War Office.[66] Manual as well as white-collar unions supported the anti-annexationist Volksbund für Freiheit und Vaterland; neither manual nor white-collar unions – not even the 'völkisch' DHV – belonged to the grass-roots of the Fatherland

Party.[67] The strength of the new rapprochement between manual workers and white-collar employees is shown by the fact that, at the end of 1917, some 50 per cent of the organised white-collar workers were in favour of being included in the obligatory Works' Chambers then being planned; in other words, they refrained from demanding separate white-collar-employees' Chambers.[68]

This reorientation is also reflected in shifts in the relative strength of the associations. All white-collar associations, it is true, suffered a great decline in their membership, caused chiefly by conscription; it is possible that a lesser degree of organisational loyalty among white-collar employees explains this reduction, which was even more marked than in the case of the labour unions. Conversely, the white-collar organisations never achieved the degree of significance and recognition in the eyes of the authorities which, from the end of 1916, enabled the blue-collar unions to attract new members.[69] Financial difficulties added to the problem. All this makes changes in the membership figures (not always correctly recorded in the statistics) into a not entirely reliable indicator. Yet it does seem remarkable that the Arbeitsgemeinschaft freier Angestelltenverbände (AfA), a clearly union-orientated group, was the only one which began to make good its loss of membership as early as 1917, whereas the other two, the middle-class Arbeitsgemeinschaft kaufmännischer Verbände with its Mittelstand orientation and the moderate Arbeitsgemeinschaft technischer Verbände, continued to lose members, until the Revolution brought about a general influx into all organisations (see the Table below). The faster growth of the more radical associations during the war reversed the trend of the period immediately prior to 1914, in which the more conservative Mittelstand associations had increased their membership more rapidly than the more union-orientated ones.

Despite these clearly recognisable leftward tendencies amongst white-collar workers, the majority probably did not develop a definite 'employee' consciousness, let alone a proletarian class-consciousness. The better paid, higher grade white-collar workers, who were generally not enrolled in the associations discussed here, remained particularly reserved and mistrustful, rejecting the attitudes mentioned above. Even the members of the increasing socialistically-orientated Arbeitsgemeinschaft freier Angestelltenverbände (AfA), which increasingly advocated the notion of class struggle, continued to emphasise their relative separateness from blue-collar workers; no

Membership figures for employees' associations 1913–18[70] (without self-employed members)

	1913	1915	1916	1917	1918
Deutscher Verband Kaufmännischer Vereine, Frankfurt/M. (1889)	43,000	29,686	28,914	25,731	45,483
Verein für Handlungskommis von 1858, Hamburg	113,723	47,423	36,902	31,924	107,302
Verband Deutscher Handlungsgehilfen, Leipzig (1881)	96,516	38,214	30,619	25,004	88,622
Deutschnationaler Handlungsgehilfen-Verband, Hamburg (1893)	140,392	72,619	17,985	13,323	140,593
Verein der Deutschen Kaufleute, Berlin (1873)	21,809	13,680	9,923	10,032	21,459
Verband katholischer kaufmänn. Vereinigungen Deutschlands, Essen (1877)	24,250	13,250	11,250	10,250	[24,250][74]
Verband Reisender Kaufleute	7,900	5,500	5,000	3,700	7,700
Verband junger Drogisten Deutschlands, Berlin (1902)	2,483	567	461	270	[2,483][74]
Arbeitsgemeinschaft Kaufmännischer Verbände (AKV) (8.10.1916)[71]	450,073	220,939	141,054	120,234	437,892
Deutscher Werkmeister-Verband, Düsseldorf (1884)	62,373	51,651	49,600	51,428	65,674
Deutscher Techniker-Verband, Berlin (1884)	26,519	16,000	16,000	8,518	—[75]
Deutscher Faktoren-Bund, Berlin (1896)	2,229	1,665	1,636	1,619	2,244
Arbeitsgemeinschaft technischer Verbände (27.12.1915)	91,121	69,316	67,236	61,565	67,918
Zentralverband der Handlungsgehilfen, Berlin (1897)	24,809	19,372	19,216	22,775	61,860
Bund der technisch-industriellen Beamten, Berlin (1904)	23,386	6,913	5,690	7,188	30,143
Werkmeister-Verband f. d. dt. Buchbindergewerbe, Berlin (1907)	317	198	255	306	517
Deutscher Zuschneider-Verband, Berlin (1888)	3,045	1,255	1,079	1,030	2,687
Verband der Büroangestellten, Berlin (1893)	8,414	5,798	5,683	9,265	26,520
Deutscher Polier-Bund, Braunschweig (1902)	3,500	1,415	1,281	1,425	3,000[76]
Genossenschaft Deutscher Bühnenangehöriger, Berlin (1871)	12,036	11,821	10,823	11,095	14,978
Deutscher Chorsänger- und Ballett-Verband, Mannheim (1884)[72]	2,599	2,183	2,176	2,839	4,101
Internationale Artistenloge, Berlin (1901)	2,473	2,138	1,475	1,436	[2,473][74]
Arbeitsgemeinschaft zur Herbeiführung eines einheitl. Angestellenrechts (1913), from the autumn of 1917 known as Arbeitsgemeinschaft freier Angestelltenverbände (Afa), Berlin[73]	80,579	51,093	47,678	57,359	146,279

organisational fusion between AfA and the Social Democratic manual workers' unions took place.[77] Other white-collar workers saw themselves more explicitly as employees and joined in with radical demands for reforming social policy, even while combining this with an anti-socialist, nationalistic consciousness and the policies which followed from this.[78] This attitude was still muted in 1918 but became more pronounced later.

Within the limits described, it is clear that wartime conditions had dealt the 'harmonious Mittelstand' image of white-collar employees a severe blow, both objectively and subjectively. Wartime changes in the economy and in society had accelerated a process whereby the socio-economic expectations and social attitudes of white-collar and manual workers were levelling out. Among white-collar employees – particularly in the lower and middle ranks – resentment against 'those up there' (particularly employers) also grew.[79] How far the upper strata of white-collar workers moved in the opposite direction must here remain an open question. Cooperation between manual and white-collar organisations increased; employers' resistance became more inflexible and their tactics differentiated less and less between manual and white-collar workers. The tendency towards a levelling out of the differences between manual and the lower strata of white-collar workers which had been significant, even if limited, before 1914, threw class structures into sharper relief. Class opposition became more marked, class tensions increased, the beginnings of conflict along class lines became clearer.

The November Revolution of 1918 removed certain legal, political and emotional obstacles among white-collar groups which had stood in the way of a clear manifestation of the discontent which had been building up during the War. All white-collar associations now adopted a clearly union-like point of view which accepted the strike and also excluded the self-employed, the more so since this was a prerequisite of their inclusion in the newly-founded Zentrale Arbeitsgemeinschaft of employee and employers' organisations. It was precisely the more radical white-collar associations which gained most in membership during the Revolution. Most of them took part in the major strikes during the winter of 1918/19. The left wing of the organised white-collar workers, especially those in the Socialist Zentralverband der Handlungsgehilfen, later claimed to have taken an active and leading role in the development of the Revolution.[80] Among the majority of white-collar workers, the effect of inflammatory, partly radicalising wartime experiences and rapid adaptation to changing conditions appears to have been a relatively passive but basically tolerant and affirmative attitude towards the Revolution. While this was a far cry from a proletarian class consciousness and a radical-democratic commitment, it was equally remote from being a defence of the previous system or of the ruling groups who were under attack.

4. The reaction of the civil servants

It appears that lower- and middle-grade civil servants (Beamten) went through a similar development, although modified by their specific legal position and their ideological traditions. The Regional Army Commands issued frequent warnings in their monthly reports about the bitterness of civil servants who felt themselves neglected by the State; they warned of the 'drift of many of them to the left... all the more so, the more the moderate Social Democratic Party is gently edging towards the right in its outlook'.[81] Some elements of the traditional civil service ethos collapsed during the War, together with the limited but highly valued socio-economic advantages of civil service tenure and the high esteem accorded to the State, in which the State's servants tended to participate. In June 1918 the Regional Commander of the Second Army Corps at Stettin complained about the general collapse of respect for the law and about the disintegration of public morality in the face of uncontrollable destitution. 'Things are stolen and taken wherever possible. Whole trains are plundered by the [railway] employees, including Beamten, as a daily occurrence. The sale of government property for private use increases to a horrendous degree. It is impossible to detail sufficient watchmen and sentries to protect property since one finds time and again that the watchmen participate in the thefts. The most sophisticated safety measures are taken to send goods of all sorts with some degree of security; but all this is in vain; there is no security anymore'.[82]

The reports of the Regional Army Command leave no doubt about the despair of these minor state functionaries on fixed salaries.[83] These lower-middle-class groups not only suffered badly from the almost intolerable economic situation, but also from the collapse of their hard-won social position and from the corresponding challenge to their status.[84] War and its concomitant deprivations resulted in much more profound psychic shocks to their group than to the workers. The result was a disorientation which could be exploited in many ways. When the Reich Chancellor's advisor Kurt Riezler wrote during the War that 'the people are now a fluid mass',[85] this certainly included the 'small man' on a fixed salary who could easily be mobilised.

The better-paid, higher-grade civil servants lost relatively more income during the War than the lower and middle grades and were likewise faced with economic ruin if they did not have large savings and assets to draw on.[86] Concerning illegal dealings in the black market, which civil servants took part in, a local authority report from Posen, dated September 1918, includes the following passage: 'The undersigned, a higher secretary of a Reich government authority, is nothing but a proletarian today and will be one after the War. There is nothing on hand, neither food nor money nor clothes nor linen, and everything and anything is running out'.[87] The Königsberg Regional Army Commander gave expression to a widespread feeling when he wrote in the spring of 1918, with particular reference to the better situated civil servants, 'that the Mittelstand is becoming increasingly squeezed between newly-formed capital on the one hand and the growing might of the working class on the other.... Several professions, whose members devote themselves to public and cultural tasks, watch with concern how the provision of the simplest means of subsistence makes such heavy demands on all their resources that they are forced down to a lower social level'.[88]

Neither a shift to the left nor a far-reaching disorientation among higher-grade civil servants may be blamed on to the rapid deterioration of their position during the War. At the end of the war few belonged to the civil servants' associations which were becoming active in the field of income and welfare policies,[89] while their widely *déclassé* position after the collapse of the monarchy did not prevent them from proving themselves to be an important bulwark against the Revolution.[90] In 1917-18 they were most probably among the adherents of the Fatherland Party, in company with many other people with a university education. This party exhibited many of the traits of a right-wing, nationalist, anti-socialist and anti-democratic protest movement without, however, those dynamic egalitarian, pseudo-democratic and anti-conservative components of the National Socialist movement of subsequent years.[91] It was chiefly judges, together with parsons, teachers, university professors, businessmen and large-scale industrialists, who predominated in the local group of the Fatherland Party at Nuremberg, which has been analysed in detail elsewhere.[92]

The 'Beamten movement', to which mainly lower- and middle-grade civil servants belonged, did not acquire a clearly defined political profile during the War. Several hundred organisations, differentiated according to trade, public authority and rank and totalling nearly a million members, existed at the end of the War in a variety of forms and degrees of fragmentation.[93] It is possible, nevertheless, to discern several distinct tendencies. Firstly, their common plight during the War brought the civil servants' associations a step nearer to each other. Despite resistance within their own ranks, an increasing number of them came together after February 1916 in a loose Interessengemeinschaft Deutscher Reichs- und Staatsbeamtenverbände. By the beginning of 1918 about half a million members belonged to this Interessengemeinschaft, from which, in December 1918, there emerged the Deutsche Beamtenbund with some 1.5 million members.[94] Secondly, economic themes came more strongly to the fore in the associations' policies than previously. A number of civil service organisations had attached themselves to the 'Kriegsausschuß für Konsumenteninteressen' (War Committee for Consumer Interests) as early as December 1914; manual and white-collar unions were also members.[95] The 'extension of the system of salaries and allowances on a uniform socially just basis, applying equally to all grades of the higher, middle and lower civil service and bearing in mind the respective economic and price conditions', as well as the extension of Beamten consumer cooperative societies, in close connection with other cooperative associations, were the main policies of the Interessengemeinschaft. At the same time they favoured unified, 'up-to-date' civil service laws, the standardisation of conditions of entry into the higher, middle and lower ranks of the Service and improved chances for promotion, which should be according to qualification and proven practical ability (these latter policies being chiefly of benefit to the lower- and middle-grade Beamten).[96]

Finally, the change of emphasis that occurred in the general political attitudes of civil servants during the War may be indirectly analysed by looking at the visible aims and means of the organisations which represented their interests. Civil servants increasingly pointed to the inadequacy of the welfare provided for them by the State. What had been supported by no more than a small minority of the prewar period (namely the collective representation of their interests in systematically-organised and public attempts to influence the political decision-making process) now began to be practised by their largest association. Mass rallies were planned, publicity was strengthened and, although they observed neutrality with regard to party politics, a 'parliamentary committee' was created from among those civil servants who held parliamentary seats. 'The best will in the world [of his superior] is of no use to the civil servant, if he does not rouse himself and prepare the ground in which better conditions are to grow. Parliament is, after all, the second factor in legislation, and the civil servant is just as dependent on its goodwill as he is on the goodwill of his authority.'[97] This change in strategy implied a certain rejection of the authoritarian traditions of the state and of the specific civil service restrictions on freedom of expression, of assembly and of associations. It also implied a looking towards greater 'self-administration' – 'co-determination' as it came to be called in the Revolution – by civil servants and was therefore an acceptance of at least some aspects of the 'new orientation'. From 1916/17 a number of spokesmen of the civil servants movement called for the political activation of the civil servants for their entry into political parties and for the 'self-administration of the people' in place of the existing 'authoritarian government'. In 1917 the Interessengemeinschaft supported the anti-annexationist, moderately reformist Volksbund für Freiheit und Vaterland, rather than the reactionary annexationist Fatherland Party.[98]

The politicisation of the civil servants undoubtedly remained limited. Old traditions did not change overnight during the War and many civil servants certainly remained nationalist, state-orientated, anti-socialist and anti-democratic in outlook. The trend, however, is clear. More and more lower- and middle-grade civil servants moved closer to parliamentary, democratic and Social Democratic notions during the course of the World War.[99] After the collapse of the monarchy the great majority of them were, at the least, tolerant of the Revolution[100] and did not defend the old authorities. Their associations quickly came to terms with the new reality and soon adopted the rhetoric of democracy. In a confused but opportunistic fashion the lesser Beamten supported the new 'People's State' and accepted the newly-created possibilities for exerting democratic influence (which included civil servants' councils) – not least in the fight for a 'professional civil service' and thus for the old 'well-earned rights'. By clinging to these specific demands, their moderate move to the left proved to be limited; this was ultimately the reason for their rejection of the political principle of councils. It was also the reason for their renunciation of the right to strike and hence of a strictly union-type orientation, although this came about only after prolonged and controversial debate.[101]

5. Handwerker and Kleinhändler

The precise influence of the War on the economic situation of Handwerker and Kleinhändler is hard to determine. Only a few incomplete observations can be offered here. If one tries to assess how the situation of small workshops differed from medium- and large-scale industrial enterprises, it must first be emphasised that small firms were more strongly represented in those branches which were not essential to the war effort; they were also less profitable or even suffered losses. Small enterprises with from one to ten employees comprised 25.2 per cent of the iron and steel industries, 65.3 per cent of engineering, 70 per cent of chemical and 73 per cent of electrical industries. Things were different in the 'peace' industries, whose order books suffered severely from the changed situation. In the printing trade 80.3 per cent, in the building trade 88.5 per cent, in the toy industry 92.9 per cent and in textiles 98.9 per cent of firms had ten or fewer employees.[102] For this reason alone, the average Handwerker took a smaller share in wartime profits than the average industrialist. He was also more liable to have his employees taken away by conscription; such staff losses were more likely to lead to closure in the case of a small company than in the case of medium- or large-scale enterprises. At a rough estimate, about 500,000 (about 50 per cent) of all Handwerker had been called up by the end of 1917 and about 33 per cent of their workshops had been closed down.[103] Many of those that survived were carried on by wives or journeymen. To make things worse, the average Handwerker had greater difficulty in obtaining the necessary raw materials, either from the relevant public authorities or their own trade sources – one reason for this latter difficulty was that trade suppliers came under the influence of the large industrial associations or other groups in which small enterprises wielded little power.[104] As the War Office stated at the beginning of 1917: 'Middle-grade civil servants, skilled craftsmen and small retailers suffer particularly severely under the present food supply difficulties. The civil servant, whose fixed salary has not been raised, in contrast to the disproportionate increase in food prices, cannot feed a largish family on his limited income even with the supplementary allowances for inflation. The same holds good for small retailers and skilled craftsmen whose activity has become more and more restricted since most goods have become subject to public distribution'.[105]

After the proclamation of the 'Hindenburg Programme' at the end of 1916, a measure which drastically increased state intervention in manufacturing in order to secure a more effective management of the war effort, small enterprises were in still greater danger of compulsory closure. Shortly after the beginning of the coal crisis General Groener, the War Office chief, explained in July 1917, shortly before his downfall: 'All enterprises without work must be closed down, regardless of the consequences. In the same way, all small enterprises must be removed, because they make uneconomic use of coal and manpower'.[106] Even if the artisans' representatives were able to intervene, apparently effectively, in the processes of amalgamation and closure,[107] the Kriegsausschuss der Deutschen Industrie (War Committee of German Industry) was so dominated by large-scale industry that its great influence over the decision-making process ensured that small craft enterprises suffered much more than large-scale industrial concerns.[108] The pressure brought to bear on the small- and medium-size branches of industry (breweries, bakeries, soap, shoes and textiles), and the measures taken by both the 1917 Ständiger Ausschuss für Zusammenlegungen (Standing Committee for Amalgamations) and the later Reichswirtschaftsamt (Reich Economic Office) will have had the same effect.

Complaints by Handwerker about runaway apprentices, who were able to earn more in wartime industries, were common. In the area covered by the Berlin Craft Association the number of apprentices fell from 41,000 in 1914 to 7,800 in 1918.[109] At the beginning of the War, the military procurement offices favoured large enterprises with their orders, since small-scale workshops were thought to be less productive and did not, unlike heavy industry, have central supply offices at their disposal.[110] Kleinhändler also suffered as mass consumption contracted and state offices, municipalities and large-scale industry looked after distribution to the consumer themselves. The distribution network became far more rigorously regulated by the fixing of price ceilings, coupons and other rules than the productive sector ever was.[111]

Even before the War the Handwerker had complained frequently about their lot and had evinced a somewhat unrealistic pessimism as to their future. One should not, therefore, take the complaints of their representatives during the War entirely at face value.[112] While the numerous enforced closures undoubtedly led to loss of income and general deprivation, they should not be seen as signifying the general 'degradation of independent owners of enterprises to the position of day labourers'.[113] There is no evidence that the erstwhile Handwerker earned less than other war-workers, while most of them appear to have started in business again when able to do so. According to the informed estimate of W. Wernet, the number of Handwerker enterprises was reduced by barely 8 per cent between 1907 and 1919.[114] In the long term the proportion of small (1 to 10 persons) enterprises in the economy decreased steadily between 1882 and 1907 and continued to do so, with a slight acceleration, between 1907 and 1925; the proportion of self-employed actually declined less during the latter period than it had in the previous twelve years, from 1895 to 1907.[115] Indeed, despite the disadvantages of self-employment we find that the number of self-employed enterprises rose by about 2 per cent between 1914 and the end of the War.[116]

Moreover, the situation of Handwerker differed greatly in different branches and regions. Thus the Regional Army Commander of the Twentieth District (Allenstein in East Prussia) wrote in July 1917: 'The position of the families of skilled craftsmen who have been at the front since the start of the War is particularly unfavourable. In the border areas these families have suffered greatly from incursions by the Russians. Even when they have been released from military service, craftsmen will often lack all opportunities of working their way up again. In general skilled craftsmen in the towns suffer especially from unavoidable wartime regulations. Although the bakeries in East Prussia have sufficient flour, they cannot develop properly because their activity is confined to producing rye-bread. Earning possibilities in the butchery trade are slight because of the host of regulations. The shops are limited to distributing the amounts allowed to them to a list of customers. Sausages are produced only in limited quantities. In other trades morale is low because the acquisition of raw materials is very difficult, if not impossible – as among tailors, shoemakers and cap-makers. In contrast, plumbers, painters, smiths, locksmiths and carpenters are in a favourable position because of the brisk building activity in the destroyed areas. In the building trade complaints can be heard that outside competitors are brought in in place of local craftsmen who are doing military service, and that these leave the area again as soon as they have lined their pockets. In contrast to craftsmen, and despite the numerous wartime legal restrictions, there is a certain level of prosperity amongst the retailers in East Prussia which stems mainly from the first two years of the War'.[117] In October 1917 the Württemberg War Ministry reported on the situation of the Mittelstand in their area: 'Many people's existence is threatened in situations where the breadwinner has been taken away from his profession for three years of War, while a large number of medium- and small-scale craftsmen who have not been called up for military service have taken advantage, as have most workers, of wartime economic conditions'.[118]

Small workshops which did not have to close down did reasonably well, especially those who worked for the military such as saddlers, mechanics, locksmiths, joiners, cartwrights, shoemakers and tailors. Despite the sympathies which the staff of the military Supreme Command (OHL) felt for large-scale businesses,[119] the military procurement offices gave early preference, for social-protectionist reasons, to orders placed with Handwerker enterprises.[120] In July 1917, after enforced closures had been going on for six months and had begun to slow down again, General Groener stated, at an internal War Office conference: 'In the first War years we spread ourselves [with orders and the distribution of materials] in order to allow all groups to participate. We quite rightly sought to sustain small enterprises as well as the Mittelstand, not least for reasons of internal policy'.[121] It seems that a policy towards the Mittelstand, which took into consideration this 'section of the population which was so important for the State',[122] was never completely suspended during the War. Thus certain aspects of the 1918 turnover tax favoured the Mittelstand.[123] Even some Handwerker representatives admitted at the end of 1917 that the trade associations had accumulated so much money that they no longer knew where to invest it.[124]

Above all, the long-term effects of the War were to strengthen both the capacity and the means of the Handwerker to achieve cooperation and self-help beyond the confines of their enterprises. Since the authorities rarely dealt with single firms, the craft associations and guilds (after some initial confusion, because they were not authorised to deal with such matters) took over the function of negotiating and distributing orders for their members. The summer of 1915 saw the development of a system of centralised organisations which undertook the distribution of both orders and raw materials to the workshops.

Thus, working in close cooperation with the military and civilian authorities, Handwerker were able to develop a system which, while relieving individual enterprises of certain entrepreneurial tasks, strengthened their position.[125] Whereas a mere 36 per cent of Handwerker had been organised in guilds in 1907, by 1919 this proportion had grown to 51 per cent. It is probable that the number of cooperative societies (979 at the beginning of 1914) almost doubled during the War.[126] These developments brought to fruition the old and hitherto unsuccessful proposals of Liberal Handwerker spokesmen – that is, self-organisation on a cooperative basis instead of demanding compulsory guilds and state aid.[127] This organisational strengthening and emphasis on collective self-help formed the basis for a new type of corporate self-administration after the War.[128]

The effect of the War on the Handwerker was thus far more complicated and ambivalent than is commony supposed.[129] Under the influence of these wartime socio-economic changes, there occurred shifts in self-perception, interest-formulation, socio-political orientation and a readiness to cooperate with other groups which did not conform to a uniform pattern. Put simply, it is possible to distinguish two forms of response, both of which breached the traditional middle-class orientation of Handwerker.

Embittered by their socio-economic decline and disappointment over the lack of state assistance, a minority of Handwerker turned to supporting left-wing oppositional groups. More than once the reports of the Regional Army Commander recommended the strengthening of Mittelstand protection on political grounds: 'The situation of the Mittelstand, of small-time civil servants, retailers and craftsmen becomes more and more difficult. It is precisely in this section of the population, hardest hit by the War, that one frequently encounters despondency and a resigned bitterness. The conviction is widespread among the Mittelstand that they lack all support by the State. There is a great danger that out of this basic mood of resignation, wide sections of the Mittelstand will turn in their discontent towards the Social Democratic Party, the more so, since, in contrast to the old days, no "odium" is attached to the majority wing of this party';[130] and again: 'The urban Mittelstand, particularly the partly-idle craftsmen, present a dismal picture because of the losses suffered by the War and the threat of bankruptcy. Nevertheless they have shown themselves to be a factor for stability even now; they hope for a speedy end to the War and for state aid through legislative action, for which preparations are being made in Baden at the instigation of the dynamic Federation of Craftsmens and Retailers' Associations. As among the workers, bitterness against those people who make enormous profits from the War is increasingly noticeable among the Mittelstand'.[131] In January 1918 the Second Army Corps at Stettin asserted that, next to the workers, Handwerker who had been very hard hit by the War 'were pushing for revolution'.[132] The right-wing *Nordwest-deutsche Handwerkszeitung* thought it appropriate to issue a warning in May 1918 against a 'merger with Social Democracy because of a momentary vexation'.[133]

Traditionally, poorer Handwerker – mostly journeymen but also master-craftsmen – have played a large role in the German labour movement. Small masters, with little capital and unable to employ others, shoemakers, weavers, saddlers, turners, tailors, printers and cigar makers, together with inn keepers and small tradesmen, made up the core of the petty-bourgeois minority in the pre-1914 SPD.[134] Their number probably grew rather than declined during the War. Self-employed *déclassé* by the War, Handwerker in the 'peace' industries and some Kleinhändler appear to have become radicalised under a left-wing banner. In the recent analysis of local groups of the Munich and Nuremberg USPD we find large numbers of Handwerker, especially among those trades which were being disadvantaged by the War.[135]

It is not yet clear, however, whether these Handwerker were the independent owners of small firms, their journeymen or even, on occasion, skilled factory workers, who, as is well-known, at times still continued to describe themselves as 'Handwerker'. In any case, the number of owners of independent workshops or small businesses among the SPD and USDP in the National Assembly in 1919 and the Reichstag in 1920 was fewer than their number in the SPD in the Reichstag of 1912. In contrast, the leftward shift among white-collar employees and civil servants was reflected in a definite increase of these groups among the members of the Parliamentary SPD from 1912 to 1919 and in 1920.[136] More detailed research has still to be done; but it is very unlikely that many additional small-scale self-employed people found their way to one of the workers' parties or even became 'passive followers of the November Revolution'.[137] A growing sympathy during the War for radical slogans as well as for the labour movement and a parliamentary democratic 'new orientation' is not to be found among those Handwerker who employed journeymen and who, as owners of well-established, more capital-intensive firms, must have largely determined the policies of their guilds, associations and free political unions. Among the small, poorer Handwerker who suffered from the War, a longing for peace and an indifference towards the annexations and reparations associated with this, may have been particularly strong towards the end of the War.[138] Nevertheless, their organisations largely gave their support, in contrast to the white-collar associations and blue-collar unions, to the Conservative annexationist Fatherland Party rather than to the Volksbund für Freiheit und Vaterland.[139] Discontent and bitterness towards the State which had neglected them did not lead the associations of the self-employed middle-class either to formulate demands for democratic reform or, even, to seriously question the existing system. Representatives of craftsmen's associations as well as house-owners' and landowners' associations fought against the introduction of the universal suffrage in Prussia.[140] Nothing is known of any statements in favour of electoral reform from among these groups.

Surprisingly the Handwerker and Kleinhändler's organisations did not intensify their traditional Mittelstand criticism of those who wielded economic power. Instead, there appeared a growing feeling among them that all entrepreneurs were in the same boat. There were, it is true, some points of conflict between the two sides. Anger over the desertion of apprentices to better pay in large-scale industry, the preferential treatment of industrial workers with regard to military deferment, competition for military orders and fear that the Hindenburg Programme and the Auxiliary Service Law would both work to their disadvantage is reflected in their newspapers;[141] but even a cursory reading of these, particularly of the right-wing *Nordwestdeutsche Handwerks-Zeitung*, published in Hanover, and the moderate Berlin *Handwerks-Zeitung* leaves the clear impression that attacks on 'capitalism' and 'large-scale industry', on 'economic freedom' and 'cut-throat competition' diminished considerably during the course of the War even, in certain circumstances, disappearing completely. Instead, two other areas increasingly claimed the attention of the Handwerker.

Firstly, the attacks against organised labour and its demands, which had decreased during the first half of the War, probably under the influence of the Burgfrieden, were revived from 1917 in an intensified form by certain categories of Handwerker. As early as May 1915 the *Nordwestdeutsche Handwerks-Zeitung* had commented, critically and with concern, on the increasing growth and power of the unions; the paper directed that the employers' associations draw the appropriate conclusions.[142] Anti-union and anti-Social-Democratic rhetoric intensified in the following years, focusing upon union demands on co-determination, apprentices, social policies and strikes as well as their general call for equal representation.[143] There were, it is true, a few branches where owners worked in partnership with their employees;[144] but even in the building trade, which belonged to this flexible sector, the unions interpreted the growing organisational links between employers, forged in 1917, as a threat to workers' interests.[145] Towards the end of the War and during the Revolution, the organised Handwerker showed just as much distaste for Socialist demands and the threat of revolution as did their industrial 'class-comrades', the owners and managers of larger enterprises.[146]

Secondly, the struggle against incursions by the state and 'state socialism', against the danger of bureaucratic 'over-organisation' and the new 'system of compulsion' came to occupy the centre of attention of small entrepreneurs in crafts and trade – whether they were moderate Liberals or middle-class Conservatives. Criticism of the 'bankruptcy of state socialism', of the bureaucratic institutions of the wartime economy and of extensive state intervention into economy and society was aroused initially by the Auxiliary Service Law of 1916, from which most artisans expected only disadvantages.[147] It was continued in their rejection of the War regulations, which were seen as being the product of those who had been influenced by 'armchair socialists' and who were thus presumed to be out of touch with reality; and it culminated in a polemic against the centralising tendencies of the War Associations.[148] Trade and commerce, it was argued, could never be replaced by bureaucratic institutions.[149] The more it looked as though regulation by the state would survive the War and become a permanent feature, the more vigorously was it criticised.[150]

Towards the end of the War there began to emerge a certain consensus among the Handwerker and also among the Kleinhändler. While they partially rejected the sharply anti-capitalist restorative demands of the pre-1914 period,[151] they still hoped for some limited state aid, such as the provision of credit and access to raw materials, but the call for self-help and professionalism now received greater emphasis. No longer was the cry for 'state welfare policies along the lines of workers' welfare policies. Artisans are in fact small entrepreneurs...'. The demand was for 'the free play of market forces' and 'the freedom of movement necessary for traders must be re-established as soon as possible'.[152]

This new tendency to oppose state intervention, which partly contradicted the authoritarian tradition and traditional protectionist demands of the 'old' Mittelstand, was a reaction to the unparalleled extension of state activity during the War and to the interpenetration of the state and socio-economic sectors which was so greatly accelerated by the War and to which we shall have to return. The decisive point here is that, by rejecting the encroachment of the state, Handwerker and Kleinhändler sided with large-scale industry, their enduring differences in other areas notwithstanding. We find that, with a few exceptions such as the frequently over-rated Walther Rathenau, nearly all those who represented entrepreneurial interests in industry, large-scale trade, banking and agriculture turned increasingly against the 'state-socialistic, bureaucratic leading strings from above', against intervention by the authorities, the control of which they were increasingly denied.[153] The more the defenders of the 'free initiative of entrepreneurs' against state intervention came to the fore, the more large and small entrepreneurs, Industrie and Handwerk, large- and small-scale retailers found themselves in the same boat.[154]

This tentative rapprochement between large and small entrepreneurs, however incomplete, was based on at least three developments: the growing challenges of organised labour, both before, but mostly after the War when there was a real possibility of socialist principles being put into practise, made apparent the common interests of employers and owners (in other words, the class interests) among the 'old' Mittelstand and big business.[155] This was expressed very clearly, in July 1918, by the *Deutsche Arbeitgeber-Zeitung*: 'In the face of the efforts which Social Democracy and the unions are making finally to take the reins into their hands, all employers, whether large or small, industrialists or artisans... must take care to safeguard their position...'.[156] Under the motto: 'The enemy is to the left, it is Socialism and Communism', large- and small-scale retailers who had already cooperated since 1917 in their joint defence against state regulation, now moved organisationally closer together.[157]

Secondly, consumer interests became increasingly articulated and organised, enabling Handwerk and Industrie to become more aware of the similarity of their interests as producers. The strength of the co-operative movement, which had detached itself, after a conflict, from the credit cooperatives in 1902 and which was rejected by Handwerker and Kleinhändler alike, doubled between 1903 and 1910.[158] The wartime shortages made many people aware of consumer interests. This was apparent as early as 1914, when the Kriegsausschuss für Konsumenteninteressen was founded and to which consumer cooperatives as well as manual workers', white-collar employees' and civil servants' organisations belonged. It is also reflected in the repeated appeals for a unified food policy which united white-collar and manual workers. By contrast, the organisations of the self-employed Mittelstand regarded the consumer organisations as an irritation and found support for their protests from the ranks of large-scale industry.[159]

Thirdly, Handwerker and Kleinhändler could more easily put to one side their anti-capitalist and anti-free-trade polemics than before 1914. The mechanisms of a market economy had to be largely suspended during the War and the corporatist, state-interventionist, post-Liberal structures of 'organised capitalism' became more strongly anchored in the economy and in society than they had been in previous decades. In reaction to these changes the owners of large and small firms formed a defensive union; common resistance to intervention by a state that was threatening to become increasingly democratic overruled all other differences.[160]

6. The separation of the 'old' and the 'new Mittelstand'

The paths of the 'old' and the 'new Mittelstand, began to diverge more clearly than ever before. Both had accepted alliances with groups whose class situation they shared, but against whom they had originally rebelled. Wartime conditions had dealt the 'mittelständische' character of white-collar workers a heavy blow, both objectively and subjectively. The employees' associations, initially a product of their strong desire for separation and differentiation from the manual workers came, during the War, to stress their general community of character and interest. They began to cooperate with workers' organisations, adopting a clearly anti-entrepreneurial stance. The other 'mittelständische' group of employees, the civil servants, also moved a step closer, in their demands, organisation and strategy, towards manual and white-collar workers, even if their legal position and ideological tradition delimited their reorientation. The organisations of the 'old' Mittelstand, which had been established on the basis of anti-capitalism and the call for state aid, now stressed the entrepreneurial character of Handwerker and aligned themselves with the industrialists against state intervention and the proletariat; a small proportion of less fortunate Handwerker, impoverished and *déclassé* by the War, sank to the level of the proletariat.

The trend towards this class-based polarisation of the Mittelstand during the War was not unexpected. It was rooted in tendencies, already apparent before 1914, which were accentuated by indications of a weak but growing pro-union attitude among white-collar employees in the immediate prewar period. Among Handwerker and Kleinhändler the first signs of cooperation with industrial and employers' associations, which could be discerned during the first decade of the century, became more apparent after 1910.[161] This admittedly limited drawing together of big business and self-employed Mittelstand had already manifested itself in attempts at Liberal and Conservative 'Sammlung': the Hansa-Bund (1909) and the Kartell der schaffenden Stände (1913). (The Hansa-Bund even included a section of white-collar employees.) By blurring the differences between Liberal and Conservative Sammlungen and by blocking the inclusion of the more strongly class-orientated white-collar employees, the wartime cooperation between big business and self-employed Mittelstand may be seen as a confirmation and an intensification of prewar tendencies.

On the other hand, there was no clear-cut line of development into the postwar period.[162] Closer cooperation between white-collar employee associations and the increasingly politicised inter-occupational organisations was in fact preserved and even strengthened. But the left-wing drift among white-collar workers which characterised the War years was only partially continued during the Weimar Republic. In 1920 the Social Democratic and union-orientated Allgemeine freie Angestelltenbund (AfA) was larger, with 690,000 members, than the politically more right-wing Gesamtverband Deutscher Angestelltengewerkschaften (Gedag) with 463,000 members and the moderate Liberal 'freiheitlich-nationale' white-collar associations (GdA) with 300,000 members. By 1930 the balance had clearly changed; the greatly enlarged Gedag, which included the right-wing Deutschnationale Handlungsgehilfen-Verband, was the undisputed front runner, whereas the AfA had lost nearly 30 per cent of its members.[163] In 1930 white-collar workers were the largest occupational group in the Nazi Parliamentary Party. By 1932 and 1933 white-collar workers, together with self-employed Handwerker and small farmers, were, in contrast to industrial workers, over-represented among NSDAP members. This was also true of Nazi Party voters. The perceptible leftward wartime drift among white-collar workers was partly reversed after 1918, a phenomenon which cannot be further discussed here.[164] The prevalent discontent among the white-collar middle strata benefited the Social Democrats and the unions less and less. By seeking to renew their distance from the working class, the majority of white-collar employees finally found themselves supporting radical right-wing protest movements which had not existed during the War, thus contributing to the destruction of the first German Republic.

After the immediate danger of 'state socialism' had passed and the Revolution had failed to bring the proletariat to power, opposing standpoints between Handwerk and Industrie once more came to the fore. Among their differences were the demands for occupational status and social protectionism with which the Handwerker – rather more than the Kleinhändler – attempted to renew prewar traditions, while big business, for a few years at least, preferred limited ties with the unions to an anti-proletarian, anti-socialist bourgeois block. Nevertheless, the basic pattern of rapprochement between small business and large-scale industry remained, to be reactivated in the crisis years of the early 1930s. As Joseph Schumpeter put it in 1929, '... small business had learnt to abandon its sharply anti-capitalist position which it had held into the twentieth century and to join up more and more with industry, which for its part understood, or began to understand, that consideration for a petty-bourgeois stratum could be more important for its own social prospects than the elimination of the latter might be for its economic prospects'.[165] This new orientation of the 'old' Mittelstand appeared, after some hesitant prewar attempts, during the War. This had prepared the way for that tension-filled alliance of small business and large-scale industry against the working class movement, against democracy and parliamentarism, which contributed so decisively, under the acute conditions of the great slump of 1929 and 1930, to the victory of fascism in Germany.[166]

4 Class-society and State

1. **Trends and counter-trends in the class system: relationships between town and country, the generations, religious denominations and minorities.**

So far, our analysis has shown that the dichotomous class structure of Wilhelmine society became more pronounced during the War, in spite of the presence of some factors that worked in the opposite direction. The common class interests of blue-collar workers and white-collar employees were revealed more clearly as differentials between wages and salaries were reduced and the polarisation of the income structure became more apparent. As they became more impoverished (both relatively and in real terms), the life prospects of wage and salary earners became closer in character. Access to consumer goods, entertainment, leisure, recreation and children's education was reduced in equal measure for both workers and employees. Their life-styles became more similar, as well as their conditions of employment; for example, the previous white-collar privileges of job security and automatic salary increments were much reduced during the War. The general dominance of material economic criteria in a period of great shortages weakened the significance of traditional, non-economic status characteristics in both self-appraisal and the ranking accorded by others. Increasingly, their economically-conditioned membership of a common class moved to the forefront of the consciousness of both wage and salary earners, facilitating the discovery of common interests, the emergence of common attitudes *vis-à-vis* the authorities and the possibility of common action. At the same time most entrepreneurs, together with their chief employees, avoided the general impoverishment which the greater number of dependent employees experienced. In the face of such shared challenges, the differences between various categories of entrepreneurs and employers also became less important. Increasingly, class position dominated their experiences, attitudes and politics.

But these were only trends. There was neither complete socio-economic uniformity in either camp, nor did all dependent workers share a common, let alone a revolutionary, consciousness. Traditional differences between strata never quite disappeared, while organisational fragmentation continued on both sides and the increasing class tensions were only very partially transformed into class conflict. There were even some counter-trends. Isolated examples of workers who earned particularly high wages and of Handwerker and Kleinhändler undergoing economic difficulties, the varied effects of wartime conditions on different trades according to their importance to the armaments industry, as well as the increase in regional tensions within the entrepreneurial camp – all these instances contradicted expectations derived from the class model presented at the beginning of this study. Nevertheless, and despite the fact that these trends and counter-trends cannot be quantitatively assessed against each other, German society between 1914 and 1918 did approach the ideal-typical model of a class society in which this study has its origins.

This result needs to be tested further regarding certain areas of economic and social concern which have so far been hardly touched upon; in particular, in the countryside. Did a polarisation according to class criteria take place here in the same way as in the industrial field and in the Mittelstand? One would also need to make a broad-based investigation as to whether, as would be expected on the basis of the original model and the results so far, other non-class contrasts and lines of possible conflict receded, relative to class; for example, between religious denominations, the generations and town and country. On these, only a few comments will be offered here.

An increasing emphasis on class structures in agricultural regions ought to have shown itself in two verifiable changes: firstly, in sharper differences and increased tensions between agricultural workers, on the one hand, and agricultural employers and landowners, on the other; secondly, in the reduction in the socio-economic differences, divergences of interest, tensions and conflicts within the group of agricultural proprietors of all kinds.

Class tensions and conflicts played a minor role in the monthly reports of the Regional Army Commanders and in the publications of the Bund der Landwirte, the powerful agricultural organisation dominated by large-scale agricultural interests. The departure of agricultural workers for better-paid jobs in industry and the lack of labour generally, which was not sufficiently replaced by the one million prisoners of war and about 500,000 other foreign workers, appear to have presented agrarian employers with greater problems than protests by workers. Such protests were not entirely lacking, however. In April 1917, the Second Army Corps at Stettin reported tense labour relations in agriculture because of a shortage of food and of overwork by those who were not self-supporting. In the first years of the War ' . . . harvesters were given additional barley, either in the form of barleymeal or in an increased bread ration. . . . Now this has finished. There is no more cabbage or beetroot. What barley allowances still existed have been taken away. Bread and potatoes are in short supply, so that now the harvesters actually go hungry. The consequences become clearer every day; there is great discontent amongst them, agricultural workers have gone on strike, and the military has had to intervene, although there have not yet been any serious disturbances'.[1] Spokesmen for agrarian associations repeatedly advocated the partial militarisation of agricultural work, aimed primarily at the exploitation of prisoners of war and at the abolition of workers' freedom of movement, which had been reduced but not yet made completely impossible by the Auxiliary Service Law.[2] For the agricultural labourer, increasing contact with town dwellers and with socialist ideas (both at the Front and through contact with additional labour from urban areas), declining real wages,[3] restrictions on freedom of movement, food shortages (even in rural areas) and the general burdens of the War period may also have increased the willingness of agricultural labourers to protest to their masters. These resentments and hostility surfaced during the last months of the War and during the Revolution.[4]

But it seems that these conflicts and the resulting willingness to protest remained very restricted in scope compared with what happened in the industrial field; this applies even to the large East Elbian estates which relied heavily on agricultural labour, as well as to the small- and medium-size farms which dominated in other areas, particularly in the south-west of Germany. Traditional aspects of agricultural labour conditions contributed to this; in 1907, 1.3 million out of 3.2 million agricultural workers belonged to the category of 'Gesinde' – a legal term for farm servants who were still under the strict control of their master, serving thus for the whole or a part of their life. Frequently, ownership of a smallholding was compatible with the status of an agricultural worker. Despite the continuing decline in paternalism, class differences were far less crystallised in rural areas than in trade or industry. Paternalistic regulations, the legalised withholding of the right to freedom of association until the end of the War and other legal measures favoured the landowners (especially those of East Elbia); the ignorance of the agricultural worker and the continued effect of long tradition on behaviour and attitudes also combined to support the power of agrarian employers and thus prevented Social Democratic and trade union ideas from spreading among agricultural labourers, at least until the Revolution. Finally, of course, it should be noted that agricultural workers, who were still paid largely in kind, were much less exposed to starvation and were better provided for in times of food shortage than were most town dwellers.[5]

Tensions and conflicts between different groups of land owners and agricultural entrepreneurs were not altogether lacking during 1914 to 1918. The holders of small- and medium-sized farms frequently entertained the suspicion that state controls, stock-taking and requisitions were used more strictly against themselves than against more influential estate owners and this mistrust partly merged with regional tensions.[6] Prewar differences between the large agrarian-dominated Bund der Landwirte and other, very much smaller, liberal or populist farmers' associations[7] also continued to manifest themselves in responses to social policy directives and other government initiatives during the second half of the War. An example is given by the Fideikommissgesetz, which was introduced in January 1917 in the Prussian Chamber of Deputies to secure the undivided maintenance of large-scale land ownership;[8] large-scale landowners and small-scale farmers also appear to have differed with regard to the issues of electoral reform, of parliamentarism, and even of war aims agitation.

The main complaints, however, of small- and medium-scale farmers were concerned with grievances that were also held by large landowners. The complaints about shortages of labour, owing to the above-average rate of conscription in rural areas, and increasing bitterness over growing interference on behalf of a fast-growing state-controlled economy, which was regarded as unjust and ineffective, occupied first place in all complaints and protests. Added to this was the shortage of materials and of animal fodder, overwork, jealousy of the supposed preference given to town dwellers and anger at the criticisms of agriculture made by urban consumers. The longer the War continued, the more clearly hatred against bureaucratic interventionism in the production and distribution of agricultural products became the focus of discontent among large and small producers. Small-scale farmers and the owners of small- and medium-sized estates were equally embittered by the controlled prices paid to producers, which they claimed were too low, given rising production costs and the non-controlled prices of industrial products; there was also bitterness against the prohibition of certain feeding practices, home slaughtering and other directives, which changed so quickly that not even the strictest police control could guarantee that they would be observed. Mention must also be made of requisitioning, a practice which brought in troops to search farmsteads for food in the winter of 1917/18; a flood of questionnaires and regulations; the closure of flour mills; rapid changes of delivery practices within a largely communalised or nationalised system of distribution; individual powerlessness when confronting public authorities, War Offices and War Associations, which repeatedly demonstrated incompetence in attempts to direct agriculture without reference to prevailing conditions; and, finally, local differences in delivery conditions dictated by the local authorities, resented because experienced as unfair, especially in the first half of the War. Such were the consequences of a war-orientated economy which attempted to control the prevailing market economy in agriculture through rigorous planning, requisitioning, and the use of force, but which was unable to prevent the market principle from reestablishing itself by the backdoor, that is, through the black market. Restrictions were applied very much more rigorously than to industry. All these factors embittered the small- and medium-sized farmers in the same way as they embittered the large landowners in the Bund der Landwirte.[9] In the face of state intervention, which they regarded increasingly as a common threat, the owners of large estates and the rural Mittelstand appear to have drawn closer together, despite other continuing differences; it was a development similar to that between Handwerk and Industrie in the commercial field.[10]

A variety of agricultural landowners therefore shared common aims and anxieties. Here, however, the question arises whether the complaints expressed by farmers about contrasts between town and country did not cut right across social class divisions, hence modifying and weakening them. Here it is necessary to differentiate between two levels.

At the level of major capitalists and entrepreneurs, the War reduced the divergences between the industrial-commercial and agrarian spheres; it enabled major industrialists and Junker to draw closer together than before the War. It is true that the exodus of the rural labour force to the towns kept alive an old conflict between industrial and agrarian interests. Firstly, however, the economic boom and the protectionist effect of the blockade enabled large-scale agricultural and industrial interests to put aside some central points of conflict, in particular the old bone of contention over tariffs. Secondly, large-scale industry and large-scale agriculture increasingly closed ranks against the challenge of organised labour in favour of a peace through victory and annexations, even if the details of these aims were controversial.[11] Finally, and with ever-increasing clarity and insistence, they united in the battle against 'state-socialist' interference and in support of 'freedom of the economy' from state intervention and of free enterprise. It is true that the agrarians, influenced by the concept of 'self-government', had argued until the beginning of the War for the fixing of price ceilings, the requisitioning of stocks and centralised distribution agencies; they had supported criticism of the free market and of capitalism and had demanded a protectionist policy. Now they changed their views and joined hands with the spokesmen of heavy industry.[12] Roesicke, the chairman of the Bund der Landwirte which as a body had previously been rather critical of some aspects of the existing market economy, stated in May 1917 that it was wrong to put 'a centralised bureaucracy in place of decentralised trade . . .; there was something wrong, if businessmen became bureaucrats, and bureaucrats became businessmen'. The battle against 'restrictions on the freedom of movement of farmers, the restraints and formal abolition of their independence in economic management' became a central theme in agrarian propaganda from 1917.[13]

The promotion of 'Siegfrieden' ('peace through victory') and growing readiness for 'Verhandlungsfrieden' (a negotiated peace) by a state which was slowly developing features of parliamentary government, brought to fruition the much-vaunted 'solidarity of the productive classes, as Bismarck had advocated';[14] it was the solidarity of large-scale entrepreneurs, both urban and rural, and, since it included both the BdI and the Hansa-Bund, was more broadly based than the 'Kartell der schaffenden Stände' (Cartel of the Producing Classes) of 1913. After 1917 the greater majority of entrepreneurs (agrarian, industrial and commercial) condemned state intervention and the 'new orientation' of constitutional and political matters – which included the slow increase in union power, the plans for the democratisation of the Prussian voting system and the gradual increase in the effective influence of the Reichstag.[15] There were exceptions; smaller, more conciliatory and reformist groups were to be found among the smaller farmers and in certain areas of manufacturing industry, banking and the wholesale trade (BdI, Deutscher Bauernbund).

In terms of the conceptual framework adopted here the increasing cooperation between agrarian and industrial capitalists signifies a further, more intensive emphasis on class than had been true of the earlier coalition of 'Eisen und Roggen' ('iron and rye'). Shifts in the balance of power between the two partners, which probably led to a stronger emphasis on the industrial elements during the War, need to be analysed separately.[16]

However, this movement towards a rapprochement between urban and rural capitalism and towards the emergence of a stronger class structure was countered by long-established tensions between town and country which influenced attitudes and viewpoints, particularly in the lower and middle strata. This town/country antagonism was undoubtedly reinforced by a series of factors: the general shortages of food and the unequal availability of what there was; the widely-publicised selfishness of farmers, such as hoarding and the reduction of production because of low financial incentives; the forays by town dwellers into the countryside in an affort to obtain food directly, which resulted in many incidents and conflicts and, finally, the obtrusive wartime state controls – all these cut, to some extent, across the existing lines of class conflict. The monthly reports of the Regional Army Commands placed more and more emphasis on the anti-town resentments of the farmers and the anti-country animosities of the urban population. Thus the Second Army Corps reported in the autumn of 1916 on the growing mistrust of the Pomeranian farmers against townspeople. The General concerned wrote: 'What I was told a few days ago by a countrywoman whose husband is a soldier, is typical. She said: "For the past year I have been working alone on the farm with the help of a prisoner. When I come home tired at night, I have to clean out the stables and have to get up again early to milk the cows. If my butter is now taken away from me, I will sell my cows, which will fetch a good price. I will keep only one for myself, no one can take that animal away from me, and I will have less work to do. I am at the end of my tether; I am not going to flog myself for the people of Berlin; *they* are not going to come and clean out my stables" '.[17]

The Regional Army Commander at Kassel reported a little later: 'Unfortunately, the differences between town and country are becoming sharper. The whole town population, whether rich or poor, looks with envy at conditions in the countryside where the products the townspeople particularly miss, such as butter, milk, eggs and pork, are still said to be available in quantities which are perhaps exaggeratedly large, and where living standards are not supposed to have changed much since before the War. Many attempts are made to impart an understanding of the deprivation of the urban industrial population to agricultural circles'. A highly-placed official from Thuringia added in the same report: 'Large and small landlords as well as farmers all behave not according to national, but according to narrow, egotistical motives. In comparison with life in the towns, I have found good living not only in Mecklenburg, Oldenburg and Holstein, as everywhere else in Thuringia, but also in the provinces of Saxony, Franconia, Posen and Silesia – even if restrictions and great difficulties naturally exist in comparison with conditions before the War. Milk, eggs, butter, in short all the necessities of life, are available in more than sufficient quantities. It is only exceptionally, particularly among peasants, that I come across the notion that it is necessary to help by willingly handing over surpluses; instead there is a malicious pleasure in the fact that townspeople have to come and beg. Insight into the seriousness of the situation is still lacking; a certain amount of indifference is still widespread. Is it believable that the owner of a fairly large estate keeps no more than three pigs, solely because it is inconvenient to keep more?' The Regional Army Commander at Karlsruhe reported in a similar vein: 'There is a firm opinion among the urban population that potatoes are being withheld in the hope of higher prices in the spring, which adds to the heightening tensions between town and country. The contrast between the two is altogether one of the most remarkable and depressing manifestations of the War'.[18]

Similar quotations could be provided in any number. They refer to the envy felt by agricultural workers and by some farmers against the better-earning industrial worker and the wartime profits made by industrialists and tradesmen; they tell of the farmers' bitterness when, towards the end of the War, the grocers in the towns would only sell them their wares in exchange for farm produce, whereas townspeople still paid cash; they talk of the mutual animosity between farmers and town dwellers, which came increasingly into the open over what became a mass movement of people journeying to the farms to buy food directly. Finally, there was the farmers' anger over the runaway prices for non-agricultural goods and the town dwellers' suspicion that shortages and high food prices had something to do with declining productivity and the farmers' refusal to hand over their produce.[19]

Real conflicts of interest, which were not subsumed into class differences, underlay these tensions. It must be noted, however, that since this was chiefly to do with tensions between producers and consumers and since the majority of consumers were employees and the producers were as a rule owners, tensions were largely incorporated into clearly-emerging class divisions, even if they were not experienced in terms of class. The farmers, in particular, neither felt nor behaved primarily as owners of the means of production and as employers in their dislike of town dwellers. 'The town' appears instead to have been the symbol or to some extent the locus of a barely-understood, but nevertheless oppressively experienced regime in which 'those up there' made all the decisions which imposed such heavy burdens on the rural population.[20]

There were in wartime Germany other lines of tension and conflict, apart from those between town and country, which did not coincide with the more clearly emerging class line. Regional resentments surfaced; there were anti-Prussian feelings in some south German regions[21] and German/Polish tensions which increased in the eastern provinces of Prussia after the German government's proclamation of an autonomous Kingdom of Poland in 1916.[22] Moreover, there arose an ever-more-virulent antisemitism, especially after the end of 1915. The integration and partial assimilation of the German-Jewish population had made considerable advances up to the outbreak of war in 1914. As in previous crises, though, the tensions resulting from the remaining elements of 'otherness' were channelled into misunderstood, sadly distorted protests and aggressions that contained, as their source, elements not in the least related to the Jews, the actual targets of attack.[23] For example, a Landrat (regional civilian administrator) from the area of the Twenty-first Army Corps wrote that 'the population clearly expresses its displeasure at the fact that Jews are given preferential treatment, especially in the institutions of the war economy, and the War is frequently described as a "Geldkrieg" ["money war"]. Comments such as: "The Jews have not yet earned enough, that is why the War has not yet ended", are not uncommon. The most absurd statements are gullibly believed to be true. What the regional Kommandantura at Posen has to say on this point is not without interest. It states that there is no mistaking the ever stronger antisemitic movement in town as well as country. In the towns, the Jews make money from all foodstuffs and daily necessities, in the country it is nearly always a Jew who acts as the agent for stock dealers' associations or the numerous War Associations when purchasing animals, straw, potatoes, grain, etc. and who without effort and without risk pockets the very high commission payments'.[24] Once the effect of the Burgfrieden had worn off, the Jews were accused, quite openly but completely unfairly, of shirking military service as well as of usury and war profiteering. In October 1916 the War Office conducted a count of Jews amongst soldiers and officers. The results of this 'greatest statistical monstrosity that a public authority had [hitherto] been guilty of', as Franz Oppenheimer put it, were not in the end published.[25] Finally, and particularly in the second half of the War, Liberal, populist and Social Democratic demands for peace and reform were denounced as 'Jewish poison'; the population's diminishing powers were ascribed to 'Jewish subversion'.[26]

However deeply this antisemitism was rooted in prewar traditions, particularly amongst the urban and rural Mittelstand, it must be stressed that its potential force needed the stimulus of demagogic persuasion. Here there was a decisive expansion in comparison with prewar times; under the brutalising effect of the War and out of fear of the 'flood of democracy', antisemitism became acceptable to those sections of the educated and propertied upper classes which up to now had tolerated rather than actively supported the more aggressive antisemitism of the petty bourgeoisie or the farmers. A small section among these ruling groups, seeing their power threatened, now tried more openly to manipulate antisemitism as an anti-socialist and anti-democratic instrument; this was particularly the case during the autumn of 1918, when hopes of a social-imperialist resolution of internal conflicts through external expansion broke down and a military dictatorship no longer stood a chance against the mobilisation of the masses. Among the leadership of the Pan-German League, which collaborated with the most powerful entrepreneurial associations within the framework of the Fatherland Party and which spearheaded the right-wing opposition's propaganda war against government policy, antisemitism was stirred up cold-bloodedly and used as a weapon against parliamentarism, democracy and Socialism.[27] Anticipating certain fascist techniques, the right wing attempted to ride the tiger – that is, they accepted the arousal of the masses, but hoped, with the help of antisemitism, to direct the forces thus unleashed in an anti-socialist, anti-Liberal and anti-democratic direction. In 1918, such an attempt was not successful;[28] during the following decades further attempts met with more success and, finally, with uncontrollable consequences for the ruling groups themselves.

After 1918, the transformation into a class society and, in particular, the limited move to the left of sections of the 'new Mittelstand' did not continue but became increasingly distorted by the rise of the National Socialist movement.

Thus the wartime experience foreshadowed later developments. It is also clear that growing antisemitism, which at first sight seems to cut across class conflict, can be understood partly as an incitement of class conflict from above and partly as a means of deflecting and taming this conflict in the interest of the dominant classes. A 'scapegoat' mechanism thus distracted attention from the deprivations and inequalities suffered by sections of the population by generating antisemitic resentments and protests. Antisemitism may therefore be seen as contributing to the fact that there was no clear crystallisation of class solidarity on the basis of class membership. In this respect, antisemitism resembled regional tensions and other phobias against national or ethnic minorities, with the result that the class structure did not fully emerge but remained partially overshadowed by a confusion of other criss-crossing polarities.

In other respects, peacetime differences and conflicts diminished during the War. Traditional differences between the old and the young were reduced not only with regard to earnings, but also in the less tangible areas of social relations. Where military virtues, such as strength and energy, were upgraded as a result of the War and family cohesion was loosened, the dependence of the young on the old decreased and traditional, often ritualised forms of respect changed.[29] The weakening of differences between the generations, although of course limited, manifested itself in a corresponding diminution in the cohesion and homogeneity of youth sub-culture; thus it was the general social and above all political lines of division that increasingly structured and divided the youth movement.[30] The same probably holds good for religious affiliations. The War strengthened conflicts, at least in the Protestant Church, which reflected those within the wider society.[31] For the Catholic Church the relative decline of confessional characteristics signified a stronger integration into society in general.[32] Non-class differences underlay the frequently discussed tensions between the Front and Home.[33] But even in the army, despite the much-vaunted and no doubt often effective 'community of the trenches', and despite opportunities for upward mobility due to the high casualty figures, class tensions emerged which clearly corresponded to those at home.[34] The inequitable treatment of and provision of food for privileged officers and other ranks fighting at the Front were reported to those at home by soldiers on leave or wounded; this unfavourably influenced morale on the 'home front'.[35]

2. Structural and functional changes of the State

So far we have been trying to show that, certain qualifications notwithstanding, the reality of the social structure in Germany between 1914 and 1918 approached the class model presented at the beginning. However, the discussion of the groups which we have dealt with so far – mainly industrial workers, entrepreneurs, the self-employed and employed Mittelstand, farmers and estate-owners – remained incomplete and left certain themes unfinished which we shall now have to take up. The increasing gap between the working class and the unions, as well as the attitudes and alliances between various categories of entrepreneurs, cannot be explained without reference to their altered relationship with the State.[36] As in all previous periods of modern German history, changes in class relations during the First World War cannot be understood without taking the changing economic and social functions of political institutions into account.[37] The connection between the intensification of class structures and conflicts in Germany between 1914 and 1918 and during the Revolution of 1918/19 can also be understood if one includes the socio-economic conditions of the state-dominated political process. This analysis is briefly attempted below.

The term 'state', as used here, describes a system of institutions, processes and effects which contributes centrally, through the legislature, the administration and the courts, to both the formation and implementation of the political will of a society; which lays claim, as a means of domination, to the highest political authority and to a monopoly of legitimate physical force within a defined geographical area; and which depends in many respects on non-state societal structures and relations (especially interests), on which it has an organising, formative, dominating and allocative effect.[38] Because of the close, but varying, connection between state and society, a definitive, precise demarcation between state and non-state and societal structures and processes is extremely problematic; such a definition will vary with the purposes of the analysis and, in any case, needs to be approached differently for different countries and for different periods. In the case of wartime Germany, and for the purposes of this enquiry, it will be necessary to take into account, next to the monarchs, the civilian and military administrations, parliaments, parties and law courts in the Reich, the individual states and the municipalities. The powerful interest groups which, even in prewar times, had been hardly distinguishable from the political parties in their degree of influence on the decision-making and executive process should also be included, to a certain extent at least.[39] The relationship between state and society, in respect of certain of its sections, groups and classes, will be the central concern of the ensuing chapter. How far was there a correlation between, on the one hand, state power and, on the other hand, control over the means of production and the social power that derives from it? Did the War, as predicted by our initial model, strengthen the instrumentality of the state to the advantage of the socio-economically dominant classes, the owners of the means of production and the entrepreneurs, whose internal disagreements decreased, as we have shown, and whose relationship with the mass of dependent workers became more tense?

It would be wrong to describe the pre-1914 German State purely as an instrument of the ruling class or as an agency of the capitalists. There was a long tradition, stemming from Absolutism, of a strong and relatively autonomous bureaucracy which had not been subordinated to parliamentary institutions; there was also a powerful and continuing tradition of 'revolution from above'; finally, there was the rivalry between pre-industrial and industrial-commercial power élites who temporarily set aside their deep-seated differences in an unstable cooperative alliance against the democratic and socialist challenges. These and other factors ensured that political reality in Germany never corresponded with the clichés of the nineteenth-century Liberal-capitalist state which some writers have used as a background to explain present-day relations between the state and the social classes.[40] In addition the constitutionality and rule of law of the Wilhelmine system, which existed in principle even though threatened and even, on occasion, violated by thoughts of a 'Staatsstreich' (coup d'état) further reduced the state's class character. The same was true of the post-1871 univeral manhood suffrage in the Reich.

On the other hand, the class character of the pre-1914 political system showed itself quite clearly, such qualifications not-withstanding, in the three-class voting system of the Prussian State. Prussia was of central importance for the decision-making process in the Reich and its restricted suffrage system directly translated the economic and social superiority of proprietors into political power advantages; the class character of the political system was also reflected in the weakness of the parliaments, both in the Reich and in individual states. This weakness disadvantaged especially those strata which had no privileged access to the political decision-making process through the Court, the bureaucracy or the administration. Of course, these strata chiefly comprised the mass of workers and employees.

Other reflections of the state's class character may be found in the power of the second chamber, on whose composition the great majority had no influence; in the disposition of voting constituencies, which disadvantaged the urban areas in which the great majority of workers resided; and in the generally deficient development of a democratic parliamentarianism.[41] The lower strata were largely exluded from recruitment and composition of the political élites.[42] Finally, although there were many individual exceptions, the essentially class-orientated structure of German society at this time was apparent in that those who were socially and economically dominant identified themselves with the government and policies of the Kaiserreich – policies which (again with exceptions) were greeted with scepticism by the great majority of the workers.[43]

What of this ambivalent situation during the War? Did the incomplete but noticeable class character of the German political system become more marked between 1914 and 1918, as the War revealed more clearly the importance of class in social relations? Four aspects of this question will be discussed here, that is, constitutional structure, state employees, certain results of the political decision-making process and the attitude of key social groups to the state and its functions.

Recent research has shown that a remarkable, if incomplete, parliamentarisation of the processes of government at national level occurred between 1916 and October 1918. This in turn accelerated the development of certain processes which had been scarcely discernible up to the outbreak of war in 1914.[44] In order to deflect criticism from its food policy, the government agreed to the setting up of a parliamentary 'Beirat für Volksernährung' (People's Food Advisory Board), thereby reversing the earlier parliamentary retrenchment as codified in the Enabling Act of 4 August 1914.[45] The many varied sources of discontent with government policy within the political parties to the left of the Conservatives gave rise, from the start of 1916, to pressure for stronger Reichstag influence. In October 1916 this pressure led to a transformation of the Budget Committee into the permanent 'Hauptausschuss' (Main Standing Committee) of the Reichstag; since the powers of this Committee were not restricted to financial matters, the power of the Reichstag was thereby increased.[46] The parliamentary debate on the Auxiliary Service Law in November 1916 demonstrated the enhanced powers of the Reichstag against the bureaucracy which was intervening more and more in social and economic affairs. The codification of these new powers may be seen in the establishment of the Committee of Fifteen, set up to help control the application of the Auxiliary Service Law by participating in the formulation of its executive regulations; the Committee strengthened the cooperation which had been developing between the two large parliamentary centre groups who were between the Conservatives and the left-wing SPD. This cooperation promoted the development of a parliamentary majority which was a vital precondition for the functioning of a parliamentary system.[47]

In March 1917 the political atmosphere was made more tense by the debate on war aims, the 'turnip winter', the entry of the United States into the War, the inflexibility of the Prussian Conservatives (over the Fideikommissgesetz and also their refusal to support allowances for deputies) and the Russian Revolution. The Prussian three-class voting system became once again the topic of intensive discussion and this time the Reichstag forced the setting up of a constitutional committee.[48] This was primarily at the behest of the Social Democratic majority which was worried about the discontent among its members and was itself under pressure from its left wing. In his Easter Message of 1917, the Kaiser promised the reform of the Prussian voting system; on 11 July, under pressure from Reich Chancellor Bethmann Hollweg, this promise was defined as meaning universal suffrage.

Parliamentarisation reached its peak during the first half of July and at the same time its limitations were made clear. The majority parties institutionalised their cooperation in a permanent 'Interfraktioneller Ausschuss' (inter-party committee), comprising the SPD, FVP, Centre and, to some exent, the National Liberals. They asserted the influence of the Reichstag on foreign policy with their 'Friedens-resolution' (Peace Resolution) and, in cooperation with Hindenburg and Ludendorff, effected the downfall of Bethmann Hollweg who, for his part, would have been willing to take representatives of the majority parties into the Government. In October 1917 the majority parties proved strong enough to bring about the fall of the new Chancellor, Michaelis, to commit his successor Hertling to the minimal programme they had agreed on between themselves [49] and to push the FVP deputy Payer and the National Liberal deputy Friedberg into the Government, as vice-chancellor and vice-president respectively, of the Prussian State Ministry. But the Reichstag and its majority were too weak to be able to designate the new chancellor or even to select him from their own ranks; they were also too weak and disunited to enforce the implementation of their programme.

In the first half of 1918 the Reichstag relapsed into general political impotence. Only when the hope of victory, raised by the Brest-Litovsk peace settlement in the east and the initially successful spring offensive in the west, faded in the summer of 1918 and a fifth difficult winter approached did the Reichstag majority close ranks. They renewed their demands for reform, put through, under Hertling, a revision of the Reichstag constituency boundaries which somewhat reduced the advantage of the rural areas,[50] and pressed for a government reshuffle, further parliamentarisation and a negotiated peace. However, this was not successful until 28 September when the OHL, in the face of defeat, changed direction very sharply, demanding the speedy installation of a parliamentary government which would take over responsibility for the lost War. With the entry of SPD, FVP and Centre politicians into the Cabinet of the last Imperial Chancellor, Prince Max von Baden, and with their commitment to the new programme of the majority parties, a degree of parliamentarisation was instituted which was codified by the constitutional reforms of October 1918. Although the new constitution still differed from the Western parliamentary model and was not seen as a far-reaching change by the German public, a certain parliamentarisation of the German system of government had been effected which was directly connected with the changes of 1916 and 1917.[51] These changes in political structure took place in spite of the opposition of the dominant classes and of most capitalists and entrepreneurs, while increasing the influence of the majority working class.[52] On the other hand, this shift, which reduced the dependence of the state on the socio-economically dominant classes, was very limited in its scope.

The limits of Reichstag power and of parliamentarisation, which had only been achieved in the face of defeat and with the consent of the now greatly weakened OHL, were drawn from a specific pre-parliamentary tradition in the German party system which prevented the majority parties from making a determined bid for power.[53] Furthermore, the heterogeneity of the majority parties, in terms of their interests and programmes, caused them more and more frequently to use their power as a negative veto against the government; they were unable to arrive at a consensus which would have made possible a consistent policy on any important issue.[54] Inside the parties to the left of the Conservatives (mainly the Centre and National Liberals) were those whose affiliations with entrepreneurial circles were also very strong. They worked against any fundamentally new orientation so long as internal political crises and/or external political pressure did not force them to tolerate or even support reformist strategies. These anti-democratic and anti-parliamentary forces, which were most strongly represented in the Conservative parties, were still powerful enough in Prussia to block the introduction of universal suffrage, a measure advocated by the Reich government from July 1917 until October 1918; they thus successfully defended one of the main bastions of the class state, keeping alive a point of conflict which antagonised the masses.[55]

Next to these traditional obstacles to parliamentarism, to which must be added the problems naturally resulting from the federal structure of the Reich, the War stimulated a new type of anti-parliamentary mass movement that pushed Hindenburg and Ludendorff in the direction of plebiscitarian military dictatorship. The War also saw a reduction in the power of the Reichstag and the political parties by the extent to which the OHL was able to influence the civilian authorities. This quasi-democratisation of the system of government continued prewar trends under wartime conditions[56] and ran parallel, following the take-over in August 1916 of the Supreme Command by the popular Third OHL of Hindenburg and Ludendorff, with the above-mentioned move to partial parliamentarisation.[57] The founding of the Fatherland Party in August/September 1917, a direct response to the growing strength of parliament and the political parties, reinforced this process. Fired by new hopes of victory, the Fatherland Party temporarily rolled back the pressure for parliamentarisation in the first half of 1918, but foundered with the coming defeat. The power of the OHL, which depended directly on military successes, was first shattered by the failure of the unlimited submarine warfare waged in the early summer of 1917. Having regained its strength, it collapsed finally after July 1918. The OHL was never sufficiently powerful to assert itself in dictatorial fashion. The means by which it consciously sought to cultivate its popular base, for example through a programme of patriotic indoctrination in the Army, were on the whole unsuccessful. From the spring of 1917 to the midsummer of 1918 the OHL was the most important opponent of the increasing strength of the Reichstag. It was able to block the reorientation of domestic policy and the move towards parliamentarisation; it did this through the exercise of its power (over which parliament had no control) which was based on its anti-parliamentary populist stance, its identification with the interests of heavy industry and its continuing support of anti-reformist interests concerned to maintain the status quo – especially over the suffrage question.[58]

Summing up, therefore, we may say that during the War the state became less dependent upon the class structure of society in terms of its constitutional structure. The second question then arises, as to whether it is possible to establish a parallel trend concerning the social background of political decision-makers. The low proportion of businessmen or members of their families among the personnel of the political institutions of the Kaiserreich (civil and military authorities, the legislature, political parties), unlike the relatively high proportion of people with agrarian backgrounds, no doubt pinpoints certain weaknesses in the position of the bourgeoisie in a political system still largely dominated by pre-industrial groups (Junkers, civil servants).[59] It is true that the numerically low personal representation of industrialists in politics and in the bureaucracy does not necessarily imply that their political influence was slight. The study of élites is not necessarily the study of the process of decision formation. Particularly in the last two decades of the Kaiserreich, the safeguarding of interests ceased to be a concern of entrepreneurs as individuals. Large companies, which did not primarily seek to influence the political process through federations and chambers of trade, set up offices and departments to represent them *vis-à-vis* the authorities; they also engaged in public relations in order to safeguard their social and political interests. These tasks were assigned to specialists, most frequently lawyers.[60] Neither the degree nor the success of industrial lobbying in the social and political fields can be established at all reliably for this period, since the available research is based on mobility studies or on business biographies.

Nevertheless, the fact that so many higher civil servants came from neither the landed aristocracy nor the industrial capitalist class but were recruited mainly from within their own ranks,[61] shows clearly how difficult it was to transform social or economic pre-eminence into political domination in the Kaiserreich. At the same time there is no doubt that the proportion of workers (including the lower ranks of white-collar employees) and their families was also very small, well below the number recruited from either business or academic backgrounds.[62]

There are no quantitative surveys available concerned with changes in the social composition of the key political groups during the War and this is a gap that cannot be filled here. A preliminary survey indicates that the War led to an increase of the number of industrial entrepreneurs and their delegates on bodies with political influence, especially in the areas of economic and domestic policy. In particular, top managers of large firms, businessmen, and business association officials all increased their influence at the expense of traditional officialdom[63] and, probably, of groups with landowning backgrounds or connections. This process occurred in the degree to which administrative functions proliferated due to the demands of a wartime economy, which required an expertise and influence which the traditional higher civil servants usually lacked. Karl Helfferich, Walther Rathenau, Wichard von Moellendorff, Richard Merton and Kurt Sorge are the best-known examples of former entrepreneurs and managers who played a significant role in high administrative positions during the War. A large number of managers worked in the War Associations and War Offices and hence in a sphere where the private economy and the state sector were closely intertwined. On a great number of boards, such as the 'Reichskommissariat für Übergangswirtschaft' of 1917 or its successor, the 'Reichswirtschaftsamt', founded in the summer of that year, there sat powerful representatives of large-scale industry or of entrepreneurial associations. They maintained a direct influence on the decision-making processes, particularly on economic policies, since they were now affected by these much more deeply and directly than before the War.

For many of these managers their administrative activity was a transitional career limited to wartime, similar to those American entrepreneurs, known as 'one-dollar-a-year-men', who worked for a nominal salary between 1917 and 1918 in wartime Washington. But further research may well show that not all returned to their businesses and that the contacts, widened range of functions and experiences established between 1914 and 1918 were strong enough to maintain, in the peacetime administration, some of the commercial attitudes, practices and interests which had penetrated the political institutions during the War.[64]

The War brought similar far-reaching changes in the military leadership, traditionally dominated by aristocratic groups. The demands of an increasingly technological War and of a wartime economy, the ever greater dependence for success on the mobilisation of all economic and social resources at home and the consequent many-sided demands on the military leadership, the plebiscitary aspects of a modern people's War and the huge growing demand for qualified personnel, promoted the rise of a new type of military leader. He was of middle-class background; technically, politically and organisationally more capable than the former Prussian conservative type of officer, he found his best-known embodiment in Ludendorff, Groener and Bauer. Kurt Riezler, adviser to the Chancellor, noted this point in his diary: 'The rising talents in the War, such as Ludendorff, Groener: immense energy, gross philistinism..., ultimately an Americanised type... Hindenburg (by contrast)... completely a representative of Prussian particularism'.[65]

The strengthening of middle-class elements among the civilian and military leadership and the greater penetration of the entrepreneurial spirit and of technical intelligence into the traditional bureaucracy (which until then had been composed mainly of individuals with a legal training), corresponded to the inclusion of representatives of the lower classes in the political leadership. This latter development had started, in a limited fashion, even before 1918. August Müller, a right-wing trade unionist and Social Democrat, and Adam Stegerwald, leader of the Christian trade unions, belonged, from 1916 onwards, to the executive board of the War Food Office. Müller became Under-Secretary of State, first in the War Food Office and later in the Reich Economic Office. Alexander Schlicke, president of the Metal Workers' Association, was given a leading post in the War Office at the end of 1916.[66] Social Democrats and trade union representatives sat on numerous central, state and municipal administrative councils concerned with food supply and the wartime economy, with the amalgamation of firms, the Auxiliary Service Law, welfare measures and so on. Workers' representatives who gained a limited political influence through such cooperation and who thus broadened the social base of political leadership, often had to defend their collaboration from the criticism of ordinary trade union members, who saw in this activity a deviation from the traditional positions of class struggle.[67] Such criticism may well have reduced the interest of workers' representatives in taking up the influential positions which the government, urgently requiring the cooperation of the working class and against the opposition of the Conservatives, was grudgingly, and within narrow limits, prepared to offer them.

These wartime changes in the social structure of the leadership point to the retreat of those bureaucratic and aristocratic elements among the political élite, who had hitherto limited the transformation of economic and social power into political domination. The shift that occurred was chiefly in the direction of an increase in middle-class, entrepreneurial and technocratic power and less to the advantage of the working class. As regards its constituent members, the class character of the German state apparatus tended to become more marked. This whole question would certainly repay further detailed research.

The picture that emerges if one considers, thirdly, the activity of the political authorities and the results of the political decision-making process as class function is undoubtedly ambiguous. Many political decisions certainly favoured, although in a very erratic manner, the interests of industrial and agrarian entrepreneurs at the expense of dependent workers. Governmental decisions in favour of entre-preneurs have been discussed above, in relation to wartime economic policies, and could be supplemented with many examples of the opportunities provided for industry in the occupied territories, in general taxation policy and in many other issues. But against this there are important aspects of the political decision-making process which were directed *against* the interests of the economically dominant classes as a whole – and not just, as so often, against some part of them. The most important example is the Auxiliary Service Law of 5 December 1916[68] – a law that affected the structure of German society as did no other piece of wartime legislation. It marked the State's most intense wartime attempt to intervene in the spheres of social and economic policy. Those involved in its ratification were conscious of its great significance. The existing social and political power relationships and configurations are clearly revealed in its preparation and implementation and in the reactions it triggered among different social groups.[69]

In its original form, as envisaged by the newly installed Third OHL and by representatives of heavy industry, the bill sought to ensure the maximum mobilisation, redistribution and utilisation of all available labour in the interests of wartime economy and of the conduct of the War. It was aimed at the limitation of the growing mobility of labour, which pushed up wages and reduced productivity. It provided for the 'militarisation' of work conditions; this would be at the workers' expense, although undoubtedly of benefit to those responsible for the conduct of the War and of wartime industrialists, no further curtailment of whose freedom of management was envisaged. At the same time, however, the decision to create a 'Patriotic Auxiliary Service' was intended to be a powerful declaration to the outside world, an impressive manifestation of the will to victory and a demonstration of the greatest possible mobilisation of the entire German people; it was for these reasons that the bill was to be ratified by the Reichstag.[70] In the discussions within the government certain members – above all Helfferich, Sydow and Bethmann Hollweg, who represented a more flexible line and who tried to anticipate some of the criticisms of the Reichstag parties – introduced various modifications into the bill to provide it with a chance of success in the Reichstag. The most important of these modifications involved both employers and employees' representatives in the implementation of this radically interventionist measure. 'The task is extraordinarily difficult', General Groener stated. 'It can only be solved in the closest understanding with industry and labour. The War could in any case not be won against the opposition of the workers.'[71]

The preparation of the bill placed the Reichstag in a key position; to the civilian and military leadership it appeared indispensable as the legitimating authority for state intervention on such a scale.[72] As has already been discussed above, the Reichstag majority which collaborated on the preparation of the Auxiliary Service Law, at the same time expanded the constitutional position of the Reichstag and its majority parties. During the legislative process the unions and the SPD, with the support of the other parties to the left of the Conservatives, succeeded in implementing changes in the Law which the entrepreneurs were forced to accept, although very unwillingly and on certain conditions.

One of these conditions was the restriction of the Law to the period of the War only. The Conservative majority of the Prussian Ministry of State agreed to the changes with bad grace and only because they could not afford to allow the failure of a law which was so urgently desired by the OHL[73] and which the Liberal sections of the government (for example, Bethmann Hollweg) praised as a step towards a 'new orientation'. Among the changes accepted by the Reichstag were, in particular,[74] the establishment of workers' and employees' committees in the larger firms covered by the Auxiliary Service Law which, despite their limited powers, signified the end of 'entrepreneurial absolutism';[75] the development of a system of official arbitration committees with equal representation of both management and labour, which both sides could appeal to not only over questions concerning the application of the Auxiliary Service Law but also over any disputes over wages and working conditions; the effective continuation of the possibility of workers, including so-called indispensable workers, being able to change their place of work when seeking 'improvements in work conditions' and, finally, a significant strengthening of the unions through their participation in the implementation of the law, which is likely to have contributed to the growth of their membership as well as to their increasing integration into the mechanics of the wartime economy over the following two years.[76]

Without doubt, the law entailed a restriction of the workers' freedom of movement and bound the unions more tightly to the war effort. It was also hotly disputed among the SPD parliamentary party, particularly in the early stages of the debate.[77] The SPD was unable to get all its demands accepted,[78] such as full coalition rights for railway men and the control of profits. The left wing of the SPD (later the USPD) and the Spartakus group (later the Communist Party) criticised the Auxiliary Service Law as a curtailment of workers' freedom and as an instrument for integration;[79] the unions and the majority SPD, on the other hand, came to accept it more and more unequivocally. Criticism of the Law increased quite significantly, however, among businessmen and the more conservative parties in the Reichstag and among the bureaucracy in the course of the last two years of the War. The Law did almost nothing to control fluctuations among the labour force or the rise in wages, whereas it considerably increased the power of the trade unions and the Reichstag.[80] By making concessions to the Reichstag and the labour movement which worked against the interests of the entrepreneurs, the Law achieved acceptance by the trade unions of a limited compulsory labour service. The role of the government, which was in no way united in engineering this compromise, was rather that of a very weak mediator seeking to balance divergent interests than that of an instrument of the economically dominant class.

Fourthly, and finally, one has to consider the growing animosity amongst small and large businessmen and the agrarian entrepreneurs, to the activities of the public authorities. Even if certain tensions had existed between the government and some entrepreneurs before 1914 (mainly in the area of agrarian protectionist policy and social legislation, which was too extreme for many industrialists) one can nevertheless describe the businessmen's attitude before 1914 as predominantly 'uncritically at one with the State'[81] – given the State's general restraint over interference in the economy and its willingness to defend the existing order against 'the Revolution'. Despite verbal protestations to the contrary, there were indications by the first year of the War of the later anti-state polemic of the entrepreneurs. They emerged in the doubts of the industrial War Committees over the too strongly centralised organisation of the wartime economy and the too detailed regulation of the labour market.[82] Attempts by the military procurement authorities to control production as well as to persuade employers to make certain wage- and welfare-concessions for the sake of greater productivity and loyalty by the workers was an early cause of vexation for the mangers of War industries.[83] As early as October 1915, the liberal *Vossische Zeitung* and the newspaper representing the amalgamated employers' associations gave space to Gustav Stresemann, who issued a warning against increasing 'compulsion by the State any further than was necessary'.[84] Those entrepreneurs who were outside heavy industry similarly had very mixed feelings about the Hindenburg Programme.[85] The Auxiliary Service Law, with its disruption of the traditional patterns of industrial management, also came up against considerable opposition from heavy industry on the Rhine and the Ruhr.[86]

In 1917 resistance to state intervention in the economy became the chief issue relating to domestic policies among entrepreneurs. The *Arbeitgeber* now not only openly and frequently attacked the Reich Chancellor's promise of a future 'new orientation', which he had given to an increasingly restive working class, but also stood against the 'illusion of state socialism'. Apart from annexations and reparations, it demanded a return to 'the economic policy of the previous era which has so amply proved itself during the War'; it also advocated a 'release from all the shackles brought about by the War' and a return to the 'free play of all forces'.[87] The great majority of entrepreneurs rejected the planning policies of Walther Rathenau and his collaborators.[88]

Gustav Krupp rejected the moves to 'nationalise firms'.[89] The Association of Saxon Industrialists, dominated by medium-sized manufacturing industry, objected in the name of the 'free initiative of each entrepreneur' to state plans for the setting up of compulsory syndicates; they were not able to prevent them from being partially instituted.[90] The Hansa-Bund held a demonstration in favour of 'freedom for industry, trade and craft'.[91] In September 1917 representatives of Rhenish industry made a stand against what they called the 'Communist form of economy', 'which in their opinion had shown itself during the War to be useless or harmful in its state-socialist impact'.[92]

We have already established that businessmen, Kleinhändler, agricultural producers and other capitalists were in complete agreement with their industrial colleagues in resisting excessive state intervention.[93] Most entrepreneurs agreed – despite the large profits and competitive advantages that many had derived from the wartime economy – as to the necessity (as they saw it) of resistance to the comprehensive reorganisation of economy and society by the State. Within the entrepreneurial camp there were naturally significant differences of opinion on the question of state control and also over the form of the postwar economy, although the exact nature of these differences needs clarifying by further research.[94] This generally defensive attitude, common to many entrepreneurs, was many-layered: fear that wartime planning controls would continue into the postwar period; resentment at the imposition of controls on, for example, the formation of new joint-stock companies (AGs) and on prices, although the latter were never implemented; resistance to state-enforced mergers and, finally, resentment against those authorities who went 'too far' towards meeting the increasing demands of the labour force, thus often over-reaching their administrative capacity – few individual entrepreneurs (Walter Rathenau was a notable exception) felt other than threatened. During the second half of 1918 the democratisation of the German State appeared more and more probable. The majority of entrepreneurs voiced their fears, combining this with resistance to the demands of labour, and began to make their own specific demands for the 'Übergangswirtschaft' ('transitional economy').[95] Unless we take into account this anti-state attitude of the industrialists we cannot understand their decision, taken in October 1918, to cooperate with the trade unions, not only in order to resist the Revolution 'from below' but also to reject 'state-socialist, bureaucratic manipulation from above'.[96] There had, of course, been anti-bureaucratic statements by German industrialists even before 1914; they had also rejected the trend towards state intervention, complained about unnecessarily comprehensive social policies and the fainthearted repression of the proletariat, while the possibility that employers and trade unions could become allies against bureaucracy and parliament had appeared as early as 1908.[97] The clear predominance and strength of anti-interventionism among entrepreneurs was, however, a product of the War.[98]

With the exception of the wartime changes in the composition of the leading groups within the state apparatus, the conclusions reached in this chapter contradict the expectations derived from our introductory model. All our analyses – of the structural constitutional changes that occurred and of the widespread reaction of the socio-economically dominant class to state intervention (both threatened and real) – as well as our discussion of the results of the political decision-making process, indicate that the state apparatus functioned less as an instrument of power of the dominant class during the War then it had done before 1914. Thus the class element in the relationship of society and state became less rather than more pronounced during the course of the War. This was in contrast to the intensification of class confrontation in social relations and in contradiction to the hypothesis derived from our initial model; this model served as a starting point, but does not adequately explain the state of affairs which has been diagnosed in this chapter.

3. State monopoly capitalism?

Neither can our findings be explained satisfactorily with the help of the theory of 'state monopoly capitalism', advanced by Marxist-Leninist historians to interpret German history since the early 1900s and in particular, to analyse developments during the First World War. According to this theory, both the purpose and the function of the bourgeois imperialist state consist in safeguarding capitalist conditions of production and in the advancement of monopolistic tendencies; the state is also considered to guarantee and increase monopolistic profits as well as to stabilise the hegemony of the monopolistic sectors of the bourgeoisie over the great majority of the population. The development of state monopoly capitalism, which is thought to have begun long before 1914, was presumably speeded up by and during the War; it is supposed to have culminated, even if racked by occasional 'contradictions', in 'the fusion of the power of monopoly, with the power of the state' into a 'single mechanism'. The State apparatus functioned as an instrument of political control by the economically dominant class (or parts of it) at the expense of society as a whole. It particularly facilitated the more intensive exploitation of the working class. The underlying assumption is that class tensions rose, conflicts within the bourgeoisie intensified and instability within the whole system increased. 'The history of state monopoly capitalism is the history of the development of the control mechanism of monopoly capital.'[99]

In the relatively flexible form in which this theory is being used by contemporary East German historians, it is conceded that the War economy was not only a vehicle for the enrichment of the ruling class, but also a war-determined necessity, an unavoidable economic back-up to the conduct of the War.[100] The theory also allows for the consideration of conflicts between entrepreneurs and hence provides an explanation of those state decisions which favoured only certain parts of the 'monopoly bourgeoisie' and which had to be carried through against the protests of other groups within the business community.[101] It finally demonstrated its value by analysing such phenomena as the growing centralisation and concentration of industry, the close cooperation and intermeshing between state authorities and industrial management and the preferential treatment of heavy industry by the State. Furthermore, through its concepts the focus of research was almost immediately directed on to questions of economic and social change in wartime, a field long neglected by West German historiography.[102]

However, this theory[103] falls down – and this is one of its limitations – when trying to explain those decisions taken by the state which went against entrepreneurial interests in general, while going some way towards meeting the interests of the workers, in the face of protests from industry. It leads to a neglect of important aspects of social history and furthermore results in an unpalatable and inappropriate distortion of historical issues. For example, the analysis of the Auxiliary Service Law by Marxist-Leninist historians remains inadequate and distorted.[104] It is part of an interpretation that presents the state, particularly during the War, as the 'instrument of power of the dominant class'[105] and that therefore falsely interprets the

Auxiliary Service Law as the most important measure whereby 'a *military prison* was created for workers (and to some extent for peasants), but a *paradise* was created for bankers and capitalists'.[106] An interpretation in closer accordance with the facts, i.e. that the Auxiliary Service Law was a decision by the state which *also* took interests of the workers into account and which, under the influence of organised labour, required far-reaching concessions from entrepreneurs, would not only be difficult to reconcile with certain one-sided political interpretations of German labour history, but also with the view which this theory takes of the relationship between society and state.

Similarly, the theory of state monopoly capitalism cannot succeed in explaining the striking increase in the animosity that the entrepreneurs showed to state interference in the private economy, because it interprets the undeniably close connection between the private economic sphere and that of the state in far too undifferentiated a manner, as 'amalgamation'. But how does this latter theory reconcile the entrepreneurs' animosity to state interference in the private economy with the view that the state is an instrument of monopoly bourgeois domination? To some extent East German historians simply ignore those anti-state protests which do not fit their hypothesis.[107] The majority argue, however, that state intervention aroused the protest of only *one* section of industry but found support amongst other sectors which profited from those policies or thought them necessary for a variety of other reasons.[108] This type of explanation, appropriate in many cases,[109] cannot be applied to the growing opposition of more or less all entrepreneurial groups against increasing state intervention in what was previously the private economic sphere. In order to uphold such an interpretation, the breadth of the anti-state, anti-interventionist opposition is denied and falsely limited to one section of industrialists. Accordingly the few exceptions in the entrepreneurial camp who supported state interventionism – such as Walter Rathenau – are inflated into a large 'liberalising wing' of the German monopoly bourgeoisie.[110] The theory of state monopoly capitalism with its assumptions about the instrumentality of the state and about the 'amalgamation of monopolies and state', under the domination of monopolies, thus blocks insight into one of the central social changes of the First World War. Confrontation with facts and sources which contradict the theory leads to a distortion of the former rather than to a re-examination of the latter.

Criticism of this theory does not imply that the state is seen here as

being independent of class. Rather, an explanation is required which
does not neglect the intensifying class tensions nor the relative
estrangement of the socio-economically dominant class from the state.

4. Tendencies making for the autonomy of the state and their restrictive conditions

Even for a state whose main function in peacetime would consist of the
protection and realisation of the interests of the socio-economically
dominant class and the maintenance of the internal status quo, the
assumption seems to be justified that, in times of war, when aggression
is directed externally and self-preservation is a prime concern, policies
derived from considerations of system stabilisation may to some extent
contradict the ruling socio-economic interests. The state increasingly
attempts to organise divergent social forces in such a way as to enhance
its fighting capacity. In considering the overriding importance of this
military aim, the civil and military authorities will, if necessary, injure
particularist class interests; this may even include the interests of the
privileged, if this is seen as unavoidable for the effective management
of the war. In wartime and thus in the interests of an aggressive
expansionism and of self-preservation, the political system appears to
gain a degree of autonomy and to loosen its dependence on the ruling
classes.[111]

Not *all* state measures for the organisation of an economy and a
society can be taken as indirect evidence of a significant growth of state
autonomy during times of war. Some of them merely indicate the rapid
growth and qualitative change in state administration generally.[112] In
1918 there were more than twice as many civil servants working on
labour problems in the old Reich Office of the Interior than in 1914.[113]
The period of the First World War may well have been the decisive
phase in the transformation of the old and limited 'Ordnungs-
verwaltung', even if it never existed in pure form, into the quickly
growing 'Leistungsverwaltung' of the modern welfare state.[114] This
question needs further detailed investigation, particularly with regard
to internal bureaucratic changes (new structures, categories of
officials, techniques, attitudes and modes of behaviour). If, as Max
Weber maintained,[115] the First World War signified the triumphant
advance of bureaucracy, it also signified its metamorphosis.

Evidence of the increasing relative autonomy of the state may be found in those government measures that came up against the resistance of the majority of the socio-economically dominant class. To these belonged those state interventions into aspects of the private economic order which those affected regarded as basic to that order.[116] Such measures threatened the owners of the means of production the more they lost their purely temporary, wartime character and became permanent 'state-socialist' changes in an economic system which had been structured until then largely along private capitalistic lines. Entrepreneurial fears of a partial cementation of administrative interventions which were occurring on a haphazard *ad hoc* basis during the War were not entirely groundless. Even in the case of a German victory, a quick return to prewar practices would have been impossible in the confusion of the change-over from a wartime to a peacetime economy. In addition, 'state-socialist' reformist attitudes came to play a greater role within the increasingly powerful labour movement and in parts of the administrative apparatus as indicated by the ideas of Delbrück, Riezler or Moellendorff.[117] Amongst those government measures not acceptable to the business groups were those interventions and decisions which, like the introduction of company committees with equal representation and of collective agreements, as well as certain aspects of the Auxiliary Service Law, decisively changed the balance of power between employer and employee in favour of the latter. Despite many assurances to the contrary, it was quite clear to those involved that these changes were also largely irreversible. The first set of these interventionist measures was in reaction to a growing awareness of the inadequacies of the private economy under wartime conditions, without the intervening authorities being able to offer any convincing alternative; the second set of such measures emphasised the connection, also recognised by some contemporaries, between social integration and the resolution of conflict on the one hand, and military power, on the other.

Under the conditions of a modern war the warring states are dependent, by virtue of their economic requirements and the burdens they impose on everyone, upon the mobilisation and loyalty of the population; in view of this, social tensions and conflicts are tantamount to a weakening of military strength. Internal social pacification becomes a precondition for the successful conduct of war.[118] As soon as this pacification can no longer be achieved through ideological pseudo-integration (the 'Spirit of 1914') or demagogic manipulation (for example, the rather unsuccessful attempt to create an annexationist mass movement through the Fatherland Party), other means must be sought. Under a continuing war situation within a class society which is perceived as unjust, and whose injustices become more acute if no conscious counter-measures are taken, there remains only the possibility of internal reforms; these are designed to establish mechanisms of the regulation of conflict and to fulfil at least some of the demands of the underprivileged, in order to retain their loyalty and to secure a minimum of social cohesion. As is well known, conservative reformers like General Groener and 'Liberal imperialists' like Max Weber, Gustav Stresemann and Friedrich Naumann justified the need for limited social reforms, both before and after 1914, in these terms.[119]

At the same time, social-imperialist orientated annexationists – again, both before and after 1914 – regarded external expansion and success as the means of achieving internal integration and the deflection of social tensions towards the outside world; with the help of these policies the position of the ruling circles – threatened by reform and revolution – would be secured.[120] But their strategy also confronted them with an objective dilemma, which had existed before 1914 but which loomed larger as the wartime emergency progressed: the sought-for military victory that was to secure the internal status quo, increasingly required a very thorough change in that same status quo without, of course, being guaranteed by such change. Given this conflict of goals, the tendency of the political system to counteract heightening class tensions with the help of many, if hesitant, reforms and concessions, indicated the primacy of foreign policy and called into question the social-imperialist calculation.

This analysis needs certain qualification but would still stand even if it were convincingly argued that a German victory suited the interests of the socio-economically dominant class and even if it could be shown that the state, in pursuing these goals, no matter whether it acted against other of their class interests, remained an instrument of that dominant class and promoted their objective interests against their manifest attitudes and actions. If such an argument is not merely a tautology immunised against empirical tests, it must imply that both victory and the absence of defeat were *not* in the 'objective' interests of the socio-economically dependent class. The great majority of that class, however, and despite the growth of class tensions, hoped fervently until the middle of 1918, if not for annexations, then for victory in the sense of the prevention of defeat.

These are not sufficient grounds for repudiating this argument. It is not as absurd as it may at first appear, at least as far as the situation during the First World War is concerned, providing that we are prepared to concede (as we are) that the parliamentarisation of the constitution, the democratisation of state and society and the emancipation of the lower strata constituted central interests of the working class, and that these had been held in check by the structure of prewar Germany. A victorious peace was a goal both desired and pursued by powerful ruling groups as a means of strengthening the threatened status quo and, to some extent, as a vehicle for the restoration of prewar conditions. Indeed, the experience of the first half of 1918 shows how obstructive the improved prospect of victory was to the process of parliamentarisation and democratisation which was by then under way; it is not difficult to visualise how obstructive a glorious victory would have been to this process!

It would nevertheless be difficult, if not impossible, to make out a case that a German military defeat in these years was in the interest of the masses, even if the opposite view predominated among them. After all, the alternatives had less and less to do with a choice between peace on the basis of the status-quo-ante and a continuing war but, in view of the stalemate at the Front, the sacrifices and the hate generated on all sides, the choice was increasingly between a disastrous defeat or some sort of victory.[121] It is by no means clear, despite the social-imperialist annexationist hopes of Hugenberg, Class and others and despite the experience of the spring of 1918, what a German victory would have meant for the inner structure of the Reich and the individual states; it is clear that it would not have meant revolution; but it is less clear whether the fundamental democratisation of the War and the tensions arising from this could, in reality, have been checked and reversed; nor is it certain that the by no means secure and effective power of the military, its plebiscitary support notwithstanding, could have been maintained for long after the War. The postwar experiences of the victors would seem to justify such doubts. At all events, while some groups engaged in social-imperialist annexationist speculations and hopes, there existed in German society hopes that a far reaching 'new orientation' could be achieved even in the event of a German victory.[122]

If, furthermore, one takes into account the dire consequences, for all classes, of a defeat after four years of nearly total war, it becomes very difficult to establish that prevention of defeat was in the interest of a dominant minority *only*. Given that no regime of terror, such as occurred in the Second World War, existed in Germany at the time, the chance of a democratisation of the political system without military defeat was by no means out of the question. In the face of the stubborn blocking of suffrage reform by the Prussian Conservatives up to the moment of defeat and the fact that large business interests maintained their strong position, even in exceptional wartime conditions, some scepticism over the notion that democratic change would occur sooner or later is understandable. On the other hand, long-term structural changes such as the shift to the left, begun before 1914 and strengthened during the War, among the rapidly growing white-collar group, would probably have continued even if there had been no defeat and the consequential rise of fascism. Together with the workers, who would not easily have been pushed back into the ghetto of discrimination and of a pseudo-revolutionary subculture after the War, the white-collar employees could have effected a great strengthening of the forces of reform.

Such questions in such a complex field are necessarily speculative and cannot admit unambiguous answers. This applies even more to the assertion that a successful war was, objectively, solely in the interest of the dominant class. The German State, so the argument continues, while fighting for victory and the prevention of defeat, was an instrument of the socio-economically dominant class, although the majority of its members were as little aware of this as the great majority of the population. Our comments should have questioned this type of argument sufficiently to allow for the further development of our hypothesis that the relative autonomy of the State increased during the War.

Mention of 'the State', in this context, must not be allowed to obscure the fact that the constituent political institutions were rarely in agreement with each other. In 1916/17 heavy industry exerted a strong influence in the Third OHL, other entrepreneurial interests in the Reich Office of the Interior. The Prussian Minister of Agriculture, who was the chief representative of agrarian interests inside the Government, opposed all concessions. Various social groups sought the support of different parts of the political system; these parts emancipated themselves in various ways from their entanglements with interest groups, at the same time remaining closely involved with one another through the all-embracing organisational structure of government.[123] Further research would be needed to bring out the heterogeneity of the State apparatus but is unnecessary for the purposes of this analysis.

The War Office and the Reich Chancellory belonged to those parts of the governmental system which were most prepared to promote limited reforms and measures of integration and to initiate interventionist measures. It was to some extent thanks to these policies that the underprivileged (and above all their leaders) continued to support the government until the autumn of 1918. This support was less than whole-hearted but at least served to maintain the government's management of the war effort. The associations and other interest groups, especially the trade unions, were important instruments of integration within the economy and society. They operated under a pre- or crypto-parliamentary system, which had no strong political parties to act as intermediaries. The direct cooperation between interest groups and administration over such matters as the regulation of war production, the provision of work, welfare and aid, and the channelling of protest, as well as the retreat of the political parties from political mediation, in a way served to throw into sharp relief the corporatist principles upon which the Wilhelmine Reich was built.[124]

On the other hand the War, with its need for the organisation of economy and society by the state, changed the relationship between the administration and the various interest groups, particularly in the case of the trade unions. Associations, whose prime purpose was to represent the interests of their members against management and the state (but who also had other, chiefly educational and social functions) developed into organisations which adapted their peacetime purposes to wartime conditions while increasingly functioning as instruments for the official organisation of their members. This shift of emphasis in union functions during the War, the double role they played between state and working class and their relative alienation from the mass of the workers have already been discussed. We have argued that the reformist and integrationist policies of the unions were inadequate reflections of the growing class tensions at the grass roots. Many explanations for this lack of rapport have been put forward, [125] but the historical structural meaning of this shift of emphasis in trade union functions is only now becoming clear; it was the result of successful integrationist efforts by the state, forced into these policies by the War and into making concessions in a political system in which the associations acted like political parties in a parliamentary system. As a result of the success of the integrationist policies of the state, the cleavage between the leadership of the labour movement and the mass of workers, between trade unions and working class, which had always existed in principle, grew wider. The effect of this was that class tensions built up, were insufficiently manifested in the behaviour of the workers' organisations and, as a rule, could only find expression as conflict outside the union organisations.

Understanding of the pacificatory function and relative autonomy of the state during the War explains not only the integration of the unions, but also the increasing mistrust shown by the socio-economically dominant class towards the political system and the bureaucratic and military authorities, which we have demonstrated above. Mistrust and rejection of the state, which at crucial moments acted against entrepreneurial interests, and discontent with an administration which often proved inadequate in dealing with its wartime tasks, led to growing criticism of the bureaucracy.[126] The ruling groups became increasingly mistrustful of a state whose members were far less subservient than they had ever been; when the state's lack of success and its weakness became apparent it was easy for these groups to withdraw their support.[127] However, while state controls and measures of reform and equalisation went too far for the entrepreneurs, they were not far-reaching enough to appease the growing discontent of the great majority of the population.

Increasing price and production controls angered farmers and tradesmen while leaving the demands of the consumers unsatisfied; nor did the controls escape criticism by employees' associations and the labour unions, prevent hunger or stifle the growth of the black market with its criminalising aspects and its social injustices. Plans for the systematic amalgamation of firms not important to the War effort provided a focus for anti-state resentments among artisans and entrepreneurs in the so-called 'peace industries', yet their real impact on the war effort was minimal, partly because of the successful resistance of those affected and their organisations. Despite several attempts, it did not prove possible to tax war profits effectively or to organise the tax system on a more egalitarian basis. Towards the end of the War, feelings against the unjust tax system may have been the cause of as much general discontent as the lack of suffrage reform in Prussia.[128] The attempts to control entrepreneurial profits, which were a cause of anger to many people, through direct supervision also failed.[129] Despite the Auxiliary Service Law, which served the Left as an issue for agitation, it did not prove possible to reduce fluctuations in the labour force although this would have strengthened war production. The level of wages was basically determined by market forces, which functioned particularly unfairly owing to the wartime distortions of the economy. More far-reaching constitutional reforms, including the democratisation of the Prussian voting system, which might have succeeded in cushioning the increasing class tensions, failed to materialise before the defeat and foundered even in the modest and hesitant form in which they were finally proposed by the government. The necessary wartime reorganisation and integration of economy and society was probably less successful in Germany, that apparent model of national organisation,[130] than in Great Britain.[131] Why was this so?

It would only be possible to answer this question with the aid of a detailed comparative enquiry; no such research has yet been undertaken. Here we can only formulate hypotheses.

As a 'beleaguered fortress', isolated and blockaded, Germany no doubt suffered from problems of shortages much more acute than those of the members of the Entente. From this arose corresponding heavy burdens on the German social and constitutional structure – a difference which can only add to the difficulty of any future comparative research. In addition, and despite wartime centralising tendencies in the federal character of the Reich, the particularism of the various military organisations, the power of the regional army commands, which only began to be reduced in 1916/17, and the continuing dualism of military and civilian authorities hindered the effective application of controls and coordination.[132] The failure of the Reich government to carry through the reforms necessary for social integration points both to the weakness of a government which was without firm parliamentary support and perhaps also – this might be tested through a comparison with Great Britain – to the inferiority of a non-parliamentary system of government; for this system showed itself, when faced with the stresses of the First World War, to be both less efficient and less dynamic, partly because it was also less democratic.[133] Although the Third OHL was more powerful than the civilian government, its lack of success in foreign policy and, to some extent, in domestic policy – where its attempt to intensify its hold on the economy justifies references to a 'Ludendorff dictatorship' – points to the limits set on internal military repression during a total war, which cannot be won without a degree of support from the whole population.[134]

In the final analysis, however, the continuing class character of the State (all tendencies towards autonomy notwithstanding) may well be at the root of both constitutional problems (which cannot be discussed in detail here) and the government's insufficient willingness or ability to deal effectively with social tensions or to establish any internal control over particularist interests for the sake of the war effort.[135] There were certain sensitive areas where the mobilisation of all economic and social resources for optimum war efficiency would have so injured the core of the existing economic system that the base on which the political power of the owners depended would have undergone considerable revision. The dependence of the holders of civil and military power on the most important groups in the socio-economically dominant class turned out to be so close as to make impossible the fundamental reforms which would have been necessary for an improved military capability and strength. This dependence manifested itself particularly forcefully in the failure of every attempt to introduce price and profit controls in industry; this in turn prevented the imposition of more rigid controls on the mobility of labour and on wages. Both measures would have aided the internal consolidation and thus the strengthening of the Reich; both were promoted by powerful authorities and both were prevented, not by workers' representatives, but by industrialists.[136]

The attempt to legislate on the investment activity of industry brought loud protests from the entrepreneurial camp, but in fact remained very half-hearted.[137] The military supply authorities were forced to respect the profit motive, one of the main principles of the existing economic system, if they did not want to risk reducing the efficiency of that system. 'The spirit of enterprise must be preserved in industry, otherwise it will not be possible for the War Administration to meet those needs which it is duty-bound to meet if we want to continue the War.'[138] In the case of the agricultural producers, whose goods were much more directly related to the daily needs of the masses and hence to attempts at social pacification than were industrial goods, the authorities, who were under pressure from both employers' and consumers' organisations, intervened increasingly against the profit motive and actually achieved its partial abolition. This happened to the accompaniment of vehement protests from the agrarians, who openly and provocatively insisted on the necessity for material incentives as a precondition of adequate production.[139] Because they could offer no real alternative incentive and did not have sufficient powers of control at their command, the authorities to a large extent failed in their frequently incompetent, confused and technically inappropriate agricultural and food policies. The patriotism which the workers were expected to show proved to be no substitute for the profit motive among the farmers either. In the final analysis, the authorities were frustrated by the market and profit principles, for whose controlling functions they found no adequate replacement. Producers and tradesman remained so fixated on these basic capitalist principles and so opposed to the State's attempts at control that they began to restrict output if the gains were too small.[140] They also saw to it that the market and profit principles were re-established as an incentive for production and as a criterion of distribution for most foodstuffs via the black market. The clear limits to any war- or state-socialism were indicated by the success of this industrial and agricultural profit orientation, which was directed against state intervention in the interest of an optimum mobilisation of all economic and social resources for the war effort. The same connection could be established between attempts at constitutional and political reform and the entrenched opposition by particularist interests, above all by Conservative forces in Prussia, which continued to be strong enough to block the government's proposals for the democratisation of the Prussian voting system until October 1918. Further examples could be added.

Several mechanisms limited both the autonomy and the reforming capacity of the State. There were those contained in the constitution which protected established privileges (especially the three-class voting system) and which could not be altered without great difficulty; there were close personal relationships, social contacts and the possibility of exerting personal influence on decision-makers in the War Associations and War Offices (although personal contact does not necessarily indicate the direction in which influence would work) and, finally, there existed a readiness, if need be, to obstruct government orders.[141] The Government evidently pulled back when it was a question of taking vigorous action against the declared positions of strong industrial groups. The fact that a technically and economically untrained army and bureaucracy were dependent on the knowledge and skill of entrepreneurs and managers from the private sector, and the risk of a boycott if administrative decisions were enforced, made any radical curtailment of industrial power during the War appear inadvisable. In addition to being confronted by an entrepreneurial group which was resolved to preserve its privileges and power at almost any price, the dangers of a drop in production and of an entrepreneurial boycott that could have jeopardised the paramount objective of victory prevented civil servants and the military from attempting to push through fundamental reforms in the economic and social system, even if some of them toyed with such ideas. The strategic position of the entrepreneurs was strong enough to prevent far-reaching concessions to the working class, even though the latter's power was growing; such concessions would have facilitated a more effective conduct of the War, besides being actually desired by influential authorities. However, plans for really radical change seem to have had little influence on the civil and military bureaucracy. The chances for the authorities to initiate and implement decisive and anti-capitalistic structural reforms were reduced by the presence of a certain sense of solidarity among the ruling strata, a feeling of confronting the masses together as well as sharing deep-rooted anti-socialist and anti-democratic convictions. These feelings countered the prevalent conflicts and tendencies towards a relative autonomy by the state; they also limited a consistent parliamentarisation and democratisation 'from above', except in a situation of extreme crisis, such as occurred in September 1918.[142]

It is true that a slow modification of the system to an extent regarded as extremely threatening by the entrepreneurs was a possibility; even in the period of the First World War, however, the autonomy of the political system was circumscribed by 'restrictive conditions', which may be paraphrased as the pressure not to abandon certain basic characteristics of a private capitalistic economic system. What these 'basic characteristics' consisted of and where the limits of what could be imposed against the interests of the entrepreneurs lay, was decided by changes in the distribution of power in specific situations. Even for such a limited time period as that of the First World War, the 'restrictive conditions' on the autonomisation of the state elude a general and at the same time reasonably precise definition.[143]

We have shown that restrictive conditions based on the organisation of the relationships of production and on the distribution of social and political power that limited the scope of the political system, prevented the full mobilisation of existing resources for the effective application of military force. This finding points to a basic problem in the interpretation of the connection between class structure, domestic politics and foreign policy in German history in the late nineteenth and early twentieth centuries. This connection has frequently been written about, primarily under the label 'social imperialism'.[144] Looked at from this viewpoint economic crises, social tensions and internal conflicts are conceived of as the crucial pre-conditions and causes of externally-directed aggression, of imperialist-expansionist tendencies and of international tensions. The manner in which these occur stresses the internal function and, in part, the conscious domestic manipulation of such externally-directed force; it is argued that the preservation of the social and political status quo at home may be achieved through the deflection of the forces pressing for internal change onto external objectives. This approach has long proved its usefulness for the analysis of concrete historical situations and developments, but it needs to be supplemented.

As Germany's pre-1914 armaments policy, and the connection between class structure and war effort from 1914 to 1918, show, internal inequalities, tensions and conflicts within the state not only promoted aggression, which was then directed towards the outside, but also restricted and limited it. However useful a 'rattling of sabres' may have been for the stabilisation of the position of the dominant classes, it could become dysfunctional for the maintenance of the internal distribution of power and privilege as soon as it built up, through intensive rearmament or war, to an extreme display of national power. As Eckart Kehr has shown, even before 1914 efforts to rearm were retarded by a lack of internal consolidation within a Reich which was racked by sharp internal conflicts.[145] Institutionalised inequalities and internal conflicts prevented Germany's mobilisation for a 'total war' from being really successful between 1914 and 1918.[146] Conversely, this explains why social-imperialist techniques amount to a playing with fire for those who apply them. If the line between 'sabre-rattling' and real war is over-stepped, and it is very difficult to control this, then the escape into external conflict, taken to ensure internal stabilisation, disrupts the structures of internal power and privilege in a way which that escape was originally designed to prevent. To some extent, this is what happened during the First World War.

5. Social-historical pre-conditions of the Revolution of 1918

We have now reached the point at which the connection between class structure, the War and the Revolution must at least be outlined. The restrictive conditions, rooted as they were in the organisation of productive relations and the distribution of social and political power which limited the State's room for manoeuvre to mobilise the economy and society for War, prevented the machinery of the State from being able to deal adequately with the growing class tensions. Among the great majority of the population, therefore, the State lost prestige, support and legitimacy. In contrast to the entrepreneurs, the workers were demanding more, and more effective, intervention by the State – naturally for their own advantage.[147] To the extent that the State and the administration did not fulfil either expectations or demands – partly because there were contrary interests which outweighed them, but partly also because the administration was simply overburdened with the new problems and tasks caused by the sheer volume of shortages and hardships – they became the focus of feeling of disappointment, mistrust and bitterness. Thus the class tensions diagnosed in Chapters 2 and 3 above were largely transformed by workers and farmers into protests against the State, the bureaucracy and the 'system' instead of being transmuted into aggression and protest against their class opponents.

The Regional Army Commands had been concerned with this topic since they began to report on the mood of the population in the spring of 1916. There were few problems whose causes were not laid at the door of the bureaucracy. Agricultural producers blamed the authorities for intervening in ways that were both too far-reaching and too clumsy, for price ceilings that were set too low, for too much requisitioning, for the rapid changes in delivery regulations and for prohibitions on animal fodder and slaughtering.[148] 'Bitterness is usually very unjustly directed against the lower level authorities, which are held responsible for every official intervention even though they are only carrying out measures ordered by the central authorities which are strictly necessary in order to feed the whole population. The unavoidable result is severe injury to the authority of the State in the countryside.'[149]

Consumers directed their anger not only against producers and private tradesmen, but also against the authorities. In their opinion the latter did not sufficiently control the former, did not fight hard enough

against inflation and the black market and did not use the courts
sufficiently to punish profiteers and those withholding goods; in short,
they railed at authorities who did not prevent hardship, but merely
papered over the cracks, and this was reflected in many military
reports.[150] 'The population's confidence in official measures and
statements is disappearing.' 'Confidence in the military authorities is
high; it is by contrast altogether minimal as far as the civilian
authorities are concerned, especially those responsible for problems to
do with food.' Price policies produced 'great bitterness in the towns
and no sympathy in the countryside', the Frankfurt Army Corps
stated in 1917. The urban population thought that economic policy
was geared too much 'to the pressure of producers and traders'.[151] But
in the same report the Army Corps at Stettin wrote of the situation in
the rural and provincial areas of Pomerania: 'A pretty embittered
mood has gradually developed in the economic sphere. It is directed
against the enormous profits from the creation of trusts and of the War
economy.... The result of this economic grievance is a growing
disobedience of the law, a decline in the authority of the state and the
openly expressed conviction that after all no one can survive in a
communist economy ...'.[152] What was too little state regulation for one
person, appeared as too much to another.

On the political level the authorities received criticism from two
sides, at least if one follows the reports by the Regional Army
Commands which were, of course, highly coloured by the attitude of
the reporter. In August 1918 it was reported from Frankfurt that
'confidence in the government among the workers and large sections of
the Mittelstand is fast disappearing'. The majority of the population
was said to be in favour of a negotiated peace, but there were fears of
'the influence of irresponsible Conservative forces upon the top
Liberal politicians'.[153] At the same time, however, the report from
Stettin described the growing mistrust felt by the rural areas and the
'educated classes': 'The State and its agents only have contact with [the
greater part of the population] when carrying through measures of a
state-socialist economy of compulsion with all its embittering and
demoralising consequences. The ground is thereby being prepared
that favours an overthrow and the rural areas will no longer offer the
existing political order the support in any coming storm which would
previously have been customary. So far only the victories and
successes of German arms and their unlimited confidence in the
Supreme Command have kept the people going. The deep discontent

over the state-socialist economy of compulsion, over the weakness of foreign policy and over the complete break in domestic policies with the Prussian tradition, which is very deeply rooted in this area, has been regretfully and quietly accepted; but this has been done in the hope that the army would make it all good again'.[154]

The more deeply and intensively the State authorities intervened in most people's lives, the more they became identified with the increasing hardship and difficulties of all sorts; it is possible that a more skilful, less over-burdened and less under-staffed administration would not have been able to prevent these developments either. Here are a few examples: the special food rations for heavy labour were distributed in the summer of 1916 sometimes at the place of work, sometimes at the place of residence of those eligible, because there was no central control. 'Consequently, miners who lived for example in Herne and worked in Recklinghausen got no additional rations, whereas those who lived in Recklinghausen and worked in Herne received double rations.' The resulting discontent was directed against the authorities.[155] In the summer of 1918 the Mittelstand (especially house owners) were angered at the regulations concerning the collection of clothing for armaments workers, the incomplete beginnings of a communal and regional rent control and the order to hand over all dispensable metal objects; again this anger was directed particularly against the State. [156] Both the official measures against the growing black market and the ineffectiveness of these measures helped to dissipate a good part of the traditionally high regard in which the bureaucracy was held. When the urban housewife returned from a moderately successful journey to forage food in the countryside and the policeman on the train, searching through her bags, took away the eggs she had collected with such difficulty, she felt very bitter; the more so, since everybody knew that the professional wholesale black market was tolerated, nor could anyone be sure any longer that the hungry official who had confiscated the eggs would not cook them for himself.[157]

Above all, the authorities revealed themselves as less and less capable of carrying out their own strongly-worded decrees in the face of resistance; this undermined their authority even more. The second Army Corps reported in July 1917:[158] 'One abuse which the shortage of food has created is to be found in the daily plundering expeditions by train to the country, where food has been carted off in great quantities either through persuasion or through force. The

Greifenhagen district has so far delivered around 36,000 hundred-weight of potatoes and estimates that a further 10,000 hundred-weight have been taken out of the area in illegal ways. The rural police have been strengthened by thirty-six men, petty officers and sergeants, from the garrison at Stettin. The transport of potatoes is prohibited on the train and on river boats, but the illegal trade has still not quite been stamped out. Potatoes and vegetables are carted away in cars and in small boats that come down, not on the River Oder, but on the River Reglitz. At times, complete anarchy reigned on the railways. The railway personnel, consisting chiefly of conductresses, were completely powerless; nor could the military at the railway stations prevail over the masses. At the moment, things have improved considerably. But this has more to do with the rainy weather and the more plentiful supply of potatoes and vegetables than with the relevant regulations, which are not being carried out because of staff shortages. At times, the authority of the State is put in jeopardy. The situation has gone so far that soon no respectable person will be able to travel by train. Class distinctions no longer exist, and the railway staff are simply powerless'.

Two months before the Revolution the Württemberg War Ministry described the collapse of laws and regulations as follows: 'If on top of this these have the mark of bureaucratic pettiness or practical inapplicability, then keeping such regulations is not only not guaranteed, but people everywhere are all the more inclined, and increasingly so, to regard all regulations with indifference'. It was the inflated prices of things in daily use that gradually brought 'wide sections, particularly the Mittelstand and the poorer working population, to despair; but above all it was the fact . . . that no effective steps to counter these extremely morally damaging influences were taken by those responsible. Sooner or later this will lead to an explosion, if no remedial measures are launched at the last minute'.[159] 'The small man and the Mittelstand watch with exasperation the failure of official policies.'[160] And in September 1918 an assembly of workers at Stuttgart observed the complete 'helplessness of the government'.[161]

The bureaucracy and the civil servants (whose economic handicaps became more visible during the War) lost much of their traditionally high prestige.[162] In contrast, up until the end of the War there was a widespread and often irrational admiration for the military, particularly for the General Staff. In contrast with Great Britain, where the disaffected called for a government run by industrialists and business-men,[163] there was a belief, held also by manual and white-collar workers, that an 'economic dictator' and the direction of economic and food policy by a military leader, would improve the situation.[164] But this admiration, which formed the plebiscitary basis on which rested the power of the Third OHL, declined when the War came to an end.[165] The expansion of state activity and the growing recognition of state responsibility contrasted with continuing hardship and increasing burdens and pressures; these were accordingly laid at the door of the State and thus undermined the prestige and validity of both law and state.[166] There was also the State's lack of success at home and over the longed-for ending of the War; it proved incapable of putting through certain reforms; finally, there was the prevalence of illegal behaviour (such as the black market, which had become a necessity in the face of want) and a war-conditioned 'moratorium on economic morality' (Baumgarten) in general. In May 1918 the Regional Army Command at Breslau complained that: 'Love of justice, loyalty and faith as well as respect for the law is fast disappearing. Violations of the wartime laws are not infrequent, even in better class circles. Thefts and burglaries, usually by teenagers, as well as brutalities of all sorts are becoming frighteningly prevalent'.[167] There was a rapid increase of collective thieving from farmland: 'In the neighbourhood of the cities troops of 50 to 100 persons descend on the fields, and the farmers are powerless against them'.[168] In September it was reported from Frankfurt that half the fruit harvest had been stolen.[169] The Seventh Army Corps in Münster reported that the use of firearms during thefts and robberies had increased. The state was powerless against this. Two months before the Revolution the Regional Army Command in Hanover, faced with the unavoidable shortage of rural police, recommended 'self-help' to leading farmers who complained about break-ins and thefts.[170] The Koblenz Army Commander reported that in the towns in the Ruhr soldiers overstayed their leave, and in some cases did not return to their units at all. 'Allusions to the coming reversal in power relations' were 'insolently' expressed in public and hardly any other citizens objected to this.[171] Authority had begun to disintegrate in Germany before the Revolution; by 1918 the State had lost a great deal of support and respect amongst owners and amongst dependent workers. The collapse merely made manifest this loss of legitimacy.[172]

It is only when one begins to understand the role of the state during the War that a connection can be made between the growing class tensions and conflicts of wartime and the Revolution of 1918–19 which, at least in its early stages, cannot be described primarily as an attack by the working class on the owners of capital and industry. It was at least as much an attack – unleashed by the military revolt – against a bureaucracy that was no longer defended by anyone; against a weakened and paralysed state. Because of the wartime organisation and integration of economy and society by the State, the latter increasingly lost the support of the socio-economically dominant class. In the limitations, which were chiefly those provided by the class structure, of such attempts to organise and integrate economy and society, the State forfeited much of its legitimacy among the masses. The unprecedented deprivations resulting from the War and the blockade, which overtaxed the State's powers and made failure almost inevitable, increased the tensions in this three-cornered relationship. Disillusionment with the State and criticism of the administration grew on both sides, amongst the owners and amongst dependent workers, although for very different motives. A negative anti-bureaucratic coalition was formed. The State, despite all its efforts, could neither bridge nor mediate the increasingly divergent expectations of both sides; in the end, it was crushed between them. This is why the class tensions analysed above were in large part expressed as anti-state resentments and anti-bureaucratic protest.

Heightening class tensions as well as the State's tendency to organise and integrate economy and society, and the limits of its ability to do so, are among the most important determining factors of the German Revolution of 1918–19. This Revolution cannot be explained by war-weariness, longing for peace and defeat alone. The crucial question is why this strong mass feeling turned against the rulers, against the State and against the system as a whole. Class tensions, heightened by the War, and the State's half-hearted attempts at integration that foundered in the face of the strength and intensity of those tensions and thereby lost the support of both sides, were the structural and historical preconditions of the Revolution. In it, long pent-up tensions were discharged in clear and increasingly predetermined directions. Arthur Rosenberg's hypothesis that this 'strangest of all Revolutions' ultimately rested on a misunderstanding – in the sense that what the great majority of the working class wanted had already been granted in the October parliamentarisation and in the coming armistice at the beginning of November – has rightly been modified from a number of different perspectives.[173] Within the structural-historical framework used here the Revolution does not appear as a misunderstanding, but as the logical consequence of the course of German social history during the First World War.

It may be argued, on the other hand, that it was the relative success of the State's wartime attempts at organisation and integration, which was reflected in the change in function of the trade unions and their partial alienation from the masses as well as in defensive anti-state attitudes in the entrepreneurial camp, that caused the Revolution to fail. In October 1918, the new role of the unions made possible the 'Zentralarbeitsgemeinschaft der industriellen und gewerblichen Arbeitgeber und Arbeitnehmer Deutschlands' (ZAG). The motivation for this agreement between employers and unions was provided by the new anti-state stance of the entrepreneurs; ZAG served to distance both sides from the extensive demands of the revolutionary movement as well as from the weakened, increasingly democratised state and what the entrepreneurs had fought as 'state socialism' during the War.

Both sides of this alliance continued, on the one hand, with those policies that they had advocated and adopted during the War years while, on the other hand, they made an abrupt U-turn. Under the threat of defeat and revolution, the entrepreneurial organisations, in September/October 1918, suddenly accepted the unions as equal partners, in marked contrast to their attitude during the War. They also fulfilled some of the union's political demands which they had completely rejected until then. Continuity with the preceding years was preserved for the entrepreneurs in their defensive anti-statism; for the trade unions it lay in their abandonment of the class war and their willingness to cooperate with the employers on equal terms. This had been their aim throughout the War and to some extent even before that. A rather more novel aspect of union policy was their support for the defensive move away from the democratising State which the existence of the ZAG implied.[174]

The ZAG, which had been the subject of negotiation even before the Revolution, constituted an acceptance of the changes in the domestic front lines which resulted from the War; these were the relative estrangement of the state from the social classes and of the trade unions from their base. The ZAG, this settlement between organised business and organised labour, was probably the strongest bulwark against extreme revolutionary change, and it rested as much on the social changes resulting from the War as did the Revolution itself.

5 Methodological Epilogue

This book has been an experiment in theory-orientated history. In it an attempt has been made to present an historical-sociological analysis of Germany during the First World War. The idea was to establish what an ideal-typical model, elaborated on theoretical grounds and modified with regard to the object to be researched, could contribute to the analysis of an entire society and its short-term changes and, conversely, to see what it could not do. While the application of social scientific theories and models to historical research has clearly been on the increase in Germany, a theory-orientated 'history of society' has not yet been tried very frequently.[1] It may be appropriate here to briefly review the methodological opportunities, limits and problems of this approach.

The dichotomous social-class model mainly developed from Marxian ideas which was presented at the beginning of this book was not intended to be 'tested' in the later chapters. This means that we were not primarily concerned to check the hypotheses and expectations derived from the model against the empirical evidence and thereby falsify and refute or reformulate or confirm and so ultimately substantiate the initial theory.[2] The model served much more as an instrument of analytical identification, of making explanatory connections and of providing plausible representations of elements and factors within a particular historical reality. Was it important to use such a model? What difference did it make? If this model (or a similar one) had not been used, certain parts of historical reality would probably have escaped the attention of the researcher altogether. An example of this is the question of the Mittelstand, which has hardly been researched to date and which was made accessible only through the category system used here. Without such a model, this historical reality would, because of the apparent diversity of its elements, have been difficult to synthesise and put into words that could be retraced. Our model provided the tools for the delineation and selection of the facts and helped in reconstructing their inter-connectedness. It allowed us to analyse German social history between 1914 and 1918 from the point of view of its continuity and discontinuity in relation to the pre- and postwar periods. It could also have been used as the conceptual framework for a comparison of German development with that of other countries during wartime, had this been our purpose.

The model fulfilled these functions chiefly in that it allowed and even encouraged us to 'measure' the changing distance between the model itself and historical reality, and to perceive that both the character and variations of this distance required explanation. However, the questions and attempted answers which this approach gave rise to could frequently no longer be discussed with the help of categories of the model; rather they forced us, in an *ad hoc* manner, to resort to supplementary explanations and interpretative statements, partial models and theories.[3]   In this respect it was precisely the 'explosion' of the model that proved its fruitfulness.

At this point too, however, some problematical aspects of the method applied here become apparent. Firstly, in determining the gap between model and reality it was not always possible to go beyond a juxtaposition of tendencies and counter-tendencies of the 'on-the-one-hand, on-the-other-hand' type, followed by a judgement (which it was difficult to substantiate) to the effect that this or that counter-tendency not withstanding, those changes prevailed through which reality came closer to the model (or vice versa).[4] One could perhaps go beyond such rather subjective conclusions, if one systematically modified the initial model because of its no more than partial concordance with reality, and began to improve and reformulate it. Probably it is impossible to bring tendency and counter-tendency on to *one* common denominator in order to weigh the one up against the other.

Secondly, it cannot be overlooked that at many points our enquiry included reflections, concepts and attempts at explanation that were not covered by the initial model. 'Non-correspondences' between model and reality were not only not ignored; neither were they regarded merely as deviations from the model (that is to say, negatively, in terms of its categories); rather we made an attempt to understand them with the help of supplementary and *ad hoc* concepts and hypotheses. The initial model thereby served as the skeleton and engine but not as a corset or brake for guiding a train of thought which was constantly straining to go beyond the initial limits. The enquiry thus gained a high degree of flexibility; but in exchange it had to accept a certain amount of eclecticism and hence possesses no complete defence against the charge of arbitrariness. Whether this not entirely satisfactory situation can be fully overcome in research open to criticism is a fundamental question that cannot be discussed here. In so far as it could be overcome, we would need a comprehensive, differentiated model – in effect, a comprehensive historical theory of society – which is not now available, and probably never will be. For the present, Historical Materialism may be the only attempt to offer such a theory, although in its contemporary Marxist-Leninist form it creates more problems than it solves.[5] At the same time it may be assumed that one could get much further in reducing eclecticism with the aid of more comprehensive and differentiated models and theories than has been attempted here.

The third objection is closely connected with this point. Since, as has been stated, we were not primarily concerned with the falsification, revision or strengthening of our initial model, and since this model was to be deployed in an ideal-typical function to determine the distance between reality and the model, it did not necessarily lose its utility and explanatory capacity if the expectations and hypotheses derived from it were not confirmed when held against the documentary evidence. Effectively, the expectations and hypotheses formulated at the start have only been partly confirmed; they did not hold up, for example, with regard to the transformation of class tensions into class conflict, nor with regard to the relation of society and the state. It was precisely in this non-correspondence between model and reality that there lay the stimulus and possibility for an expansion of our knowledge and it was at least as great as in cases where the model and reality were in agreement. In other words: even if most tendencies relating to the reality which we investigated had gone against the expectations of the model, that is, if they had contradicted the notion of class polarisation, the model would not therefore have had to be discarded; it would not have lost its instrumental function. Whether the hypotheses were confirmed or refuted, in either case the model was able to fulfil its expected unlocking and structuring tasks. However, if the model used in this way cannot so easily be defeated by reality, what are the criteria and tests which can or must make it preferable to competing models and what are the criteria by which it is selected, or rejected?

These questions cannot be answered without reference to cognitive interests and research practice. It is not the fact that reality evolved in a direction *counter* to the model's hypotheses which reduces its usefulness and forces one, should this happen with any frequency, to abandon it; rather it is the 'demonstration' that certain traits of reality which are important by our cognitive interest criteria cannot be manifested in the model at all, traits which fall through its meshes and, by not fitting the model in either a positive or negative sense, get overlooked. For example, the model used here did steer the analysis towards the finding of a relative decline in class tensions in favour of a town-country dichotomy, even if this contradicted its hypotheses. A relative shift in the weight of the tensions between town and country on the one hand and denominational tensions on the other lay outside its identifying capacity and hence could neither be identified nor problematised by it. Clearly the model used here would not have been the best for the regional or ecclesiastical historian.

The 'demonstration' of the applicability or otherwise of a model in this sense (which, as we have said, has little to do with the falsification of the hypotheses derived from it) is, usually under conditions of unlimited freedom of discussion and open scrutiny by an expert public, a complex, slow-moving process of argumentation and persuasion in which the previous results of the discipline's tradition, changing needs and interests outside that tradition, experiences and forms of thought but also decisionist factors play a part. In principle, two authoritative tests can be applied in this process when making the case for the superiority of a particular model or a particular interpretation, though none of these tests ensures the selection of *the* one correct model; they are merely effective in reducing the arbitrariness of the choice. Firstly, the subject under consideration itself limits the choice of model best suited to it; for although a particular subject does not clearly prescribe certain concepts, questions and models, not all of these are appropriate to the structure of the subject matter. Secondly, changing cognitive interests, partly determined by cultural social and economic factors, represent points of reference of which account can be taken when choosing and justifying particular research strategies and models. However, these reference points do not provide one, under the conditions of free scholarly and public discussion, with clear-cut deductions. This is because heterogeneous and competing research interests tend to arise if there is no enforced homogenisation; because interpretations of what is most relevant tend to vary and, lastly, because very broadly formulated research interests, for example an 'interest in a reasonably organised future society' (Max Horkheimer) can legitimate several competing research aims and interests. This is the situation in which controversial debate is both possible and necessary and in which scholarly progress can be made. It provides the basis for the legitimacy, necessity and limits of a plurality of models and interpretative attempts; it indicates the impossibility of aiming at more than a limited, constantly queried and changing consensus over preferred interpretations, questions and models; and of the unrelinquishable function of open discussion, both in the professional forum and by the general public.[6]

In such a discussion, our decision to use the Marxist model chosen – a decision in favour of one option among many – could be substantiated on various grounds, of which only three need to be mentioned here.

Firstly, a Marxist-orientated conceptual system is in a better position than most others to structure an extensive spectrum of reality. It facilitates the study of the mutual relations between economy, society, politics and ideology, while hypothetically assigning the socio-economic dimension a certain dominance, although no mono-causal emphasis, over the others that is likely to be the equivalent to its real importance, at least in the industrial society of the nineteenth and early twentieth centuries.[7] A Marxist-orientated model applied to research within this period has the advantage of being commensurate with the subject, in contrast with attempts which steer away from the decisiveness of the socio-economic dimension and also with others which deal only with one narrow aspect of reality, such as enquiries which look at the internal development of Germany in the First World War primarily from the viewpoint of progressive or restricted parliamentarisation. This latter viewpoint is incorporated within the inclusive model used here.

Secondly, one cannot ignore the fact that, however incomplete it may have been, a revolution did actually occur at the end of the research period, which presented and largely justified itself in Socialist terms. An enquiry into German society during the First World War is therefore also an enquiry into the pre-conditions of the Revolution and will be able to derive some of its guiding principles from this. A dichotomous model geared to enquiring into fundamental conflicts which, moreover, emphasises the dynamic character of oppositions, tensions and conflicts hence appears to offer better prospects for good results than the stratification models which have dominated sociology for so long. These tend to emphasise the functionality of individual strata rather than the conflicts between them; they also emphasise the static rather than the dynamic aspects and they tend to apply criteria which facilitate the identification of stratification phenomena in the form of continuities and hierarchies; they do *not* help us with an analysis of dichotomous structures.[8]

Thirdly, it should be remembered that books are written to be read. Their key concepts should be relevant to the intellectual climate of the audience they hope to reach and to the major issues presently under discussion. This does not mean simply adapting to and confirming current fashions; on the contrary, it can and should mean the picking up of predominant paradigms in order to evaluate them in the light of new evidence, to question them if necessary and, perhaps, to broaden them and to develop them further. For this reason the historical arguments should be framed in a way which does not render them too alien to current debates or too unrelated to present concerns. For some time elements of Marxist thought have played an important role in the intellectual life of Western Europe. In numerous forms, including simplifications, these elements have pervaded large areas of contemporary attempts at self-understanding and intellectual debate, often in such a manner that they are no longer to be identified as Marxist but are taken as self-evident. We have been both impressed by and convinced of the historical strength of socio-economic structures, processes and conflicts, in contrast to the limited impact of the actions of individuals or of ideas. By organising its subject matter in the way that it has, this book has attempted a relationship with the intellectual debate and its many controversies.[9] It may be that such an attempt exacts a price; intellectual moods change and what catches the intellectual imagination in one decade may not necessarily do so in the next. In 1984 this book may be further removed from the prevailing intellectual climate than it was when it was written in the late 1960s and early 1970s.

In this book Marxist theories have been used in a Weberian way.[10] They aided the construction of a model which then served as an instrument for historical understanding by permitting the description and explanation of the variable 'distance' between model and reality. There are certainly other ways of applying theory to history.[11] Maybe one could and should go a step further by trying to reformulate the model in the light of its non-congruence with reality. The aim then would be to achieve a more systematic reformulation ('theory') of the inter-relationship of economy, society and state in Germany during the First World War. In so far as long-term tendencies towards change, identified as existing before 1914 and continuing after 1918, came to the fore with particular clarity during the First World War, such a theory would have to include the basic characteristics of both pre- and postwar development. On the other hand, it could also serve to emphasise the war-specific changes that occurred during the years from 1914 to 1918 and which receded again after the War; on the basis of such a theory one could try to compare the German development with that of other industrial societies at war.[12] It may still prove worthwhile to undertake this task within the framework of the recently debated concept of 'organised capitalism'.[13] But this would require separate examination and another book.

Afterword

Since this book was conceived as a methodological experiment and was thus particularly amenable to professional scientific discussion, it may make sense to use this new edition to respond selectively to the wide reaction which the book brought about.[1] Here I shall concentrate on objections which appear to me to be particularly important, either because they go to the centre of my argument or because they lead beyond it. I take into account neither the predominantly positive reactions nor criticism which is the result of misunderstanding or is completely wrong (as that of W. Stump); nor is there space to deal with a series of detailed objections.

1. The application of theory as practised above was criticised from three different angles:

(a) On the one hand, critics questioned whether 'the display of method and theory was not somewhat exaggerated and whether the results could not have been derived without them' (thus A. Hillgruber, similarly Conze). Against this one must stress that a socio-historical[2] synthesis, as attempted in the book, is not possible without a guiding theory, unless one regards an associative adding together as synthesis.[3] One cannot do without a minimum presentation and justification of the selected theory or theories if one wishes to meet the demand, central to every discipline, for maximum clarity and self-enlightenment and if one wants to offer others the possibility to test, discuss, accept or reject and determine the advantages and limitations of one's own theoretical starting point. This is after all what happened in much of the criticism and it would not have been possible without such an explicit 'display of method and theory'. Finally, my experience during this work has convinced me that the explicit introduction of theory in the manner used here allows for the possibility of being directed towards subjects and questions which one would otherwise

171

not have considered in the context; in this case, for example, the treatment of the 'old' Mittelstand and the 'new Mittelstand' – regarded by many critics as a new and definite advance on our level of knowledge – was the result of such a use of theory.

(b) On the other hand, the so far unfortunately scanty[4] Marxist-Leninist criticism objected to the purely instrumental use of Marxist theory – 'separated from his conception of history and detached from its revolutionary consequences', as B. Kaulisch put it. I have indeed applied Marxist thoughts in a Max Weber-like manner and made use of sharpsighted insights by Marx selectively and for a particular purpose, rather than reverentially reproducing them or regarding them as infallible. That this instrumentally distanced attitude towards theories is appropriate and legitimate – that they cannot be arbitrarily taken up as out of a tool-box, but need to be selected for a reason and then modified for historical work – follows from my theory of knowledge premises and methodological considerations, which cannot be repeated here.[5]

(c) The most weighty of the doubts expressed by critics such as C. Maier, M. Stürmer, W. J. Mommsen, H. Haumann, K. Jarausch, E. Hanisch and others, appears to me to be that which asks whether, after the model developed at the start was partly confirmed but also partly 'refuted', one should not in the end have formulated a model which applied more closely to reality. Alterntively, since one knows about the non-congruence between model and reality before the book goes into print, or even before one begins to write it, should one not have introduced a more realistic model from the start? Here I would defend myself with reference to the nature of the ideal-typical method, which depends precisely on the non-identity between model and reality.[6] I find it attractive and appropriate, given the process-like character of scientific thought, to argue in these three steps: model; representation; partial demolition of the initial model. Three things must be conceded here, however: firstly, this form of presentation is not generally accepted. Some critics talked about their 'surprise' (D. Hertz-Eichenrode) at the 'change' at the end of the book, and who knows how many readers were able to read only single chapters without getting lost? A lack of understanding of the mode of argument used was shown by some critics when they regarded the non-correspondence of reality and model as a negative 'test' outcome for the model (W. J. Mommsen) or when they well-meaningly reassured the author that seldom had anyone 'reported his own expectations and preconceptions . . . so honestly and discerningly' as he had at the end of his book (W. Conze); as if this were the admission of a previous mistake, as if one had only noticed the non-correspondence of model and reality at the end and had simply been too 'honest' to quickly incorporate the relevant corrections into the early section! In future one will have to take account of this not always totally available readiness to re-design the pattern of argument; the chosen form of presentation is supposed not to increase but to diminish the danger of misunderstanding. Of course, one must concede that the model used here *can* easily lead to paralysis over selecting a particular theory. If the chosen model may not be faulted for its contradiction of reality, how should one proceed? How slight must the similarity between model and reality actually become in order to persuade the author to alter or exchange it? I have given my reply to this question on page 165. It is perhaps not entirely satisfactory. On the other hand I am convinced that in most historical work, concepts, models, theorems and theories are not immediately set aside or replaced if they do not fully coincide with reality (in that they continue to serve as an aid to its comprehension). Perhaps further discussion here would be in the interest of greater clarity. Finally, one must concede that the first (model) and second (presentation) steps of the mode of argument under discussion here could be retained while the third step could consist of a positive reformulation of the initial model, as several critics have suggested.[7] Such a reformulation as a consequence of the study of just *one* case (the First World War) could only take place with reference to this case and should not be taken as a falsification of the theory underlying the intial model *in genere*; for this, one would need more than one 'test case'. Thus, even with the desired reformulation of the initial model, in the end the use of historical theory would remain clearly distant from the use of theory in the sense of analytical scientific theory.[8]

2. Several critics (C. Maier, H.-A. Winkler) questioned whether the unequal time period between that of the study, which was four years plus previous history, and the longer time period of the related theory of Marxist conceptions of long-term changes in class relationships, did not constitute a methodological burden for the present undertaking, the more so – thus Winkler – since the First World War development had in many respects to be regarded as untypical. It seems to me that the incongruous time periods would only be a problem – and a very

difficult one – if the work was aimed at *testing* such a long-period theory on the basis of a short-term development. As frequently stressed, this is precisely *not* the case. In addition one can easily exaggerate the untypicality of the war period. Of course the War signified an extreme situation, which existed neither before 1914 nor after 1918; one thinks of the mobilisation, of mass deaths, the 'state of siege', massive impoverishment, war-orientated production and much more. In the present study, however, important continuities with the prewar period are determined, in pre-1914 developments which were speeded up, sometimes abruptly, or were particularly accentuated. These include a trend towards organised capitalism as well as increasing state intervention; increasing economic concentration and organisation of interests at Reich level; a gradual, weak 'turn to the left' by white-collar workers; the gradual levelling out of the gap between large entrepreneurs and the small self-employed; and a change of emphasis from status to merit in the hierarchy of administration. One may even regard the sharper development of class lines, in the sense of this study, as a very long-term process, which reached a certain high point in the First World War but did not continue to develop in the Weimar Republic and after, being obscured by the superimposition of other differences and lines of conflict. Conversely, it is indisputable that important processes of change during the war period continued after 1918, if perhaps not with the intensity of the years from 1914 to 1918. One thinks of the long-term trend for state intervention in the economy and in society, the organisation of groups, the tendency to settle a firm's internal conflicts at an external level, social policy, the restructuring of the administration. This is also true for some less visible continuities. The limited 'move to the left' by white-collar workers, observable before 1914 and during the War, was not simply reversed in the Weimar period. It did, however, take on a new form,[9] given the rise of National Socialism, above all, which appeared to add to the alternative political voting possibilities by offering a 'third way' between a status quo and a left-wing opposition. Finally, the most recent literature on National Socialist social and wartime economic policies is occupied with assessing how strongly the problems of 1933–45 resembled those of 1914–18.[10]

3. One central objection is formulated most clearly by G. Schramm (pp. 250–1).[11] Is it sufficient to use one conflict model or should it not be supplemented by a second one 'which brings out the common

patterns of feeling and behaviour that exist in the nation right across the board'? Here one can see the connection between intellecutal purpose and choice of model. If one is primarily concerned with the causes of the Revolution of 1918/19[12] and bears the less disruptive pre-1914 period in mind for comparison, then one will stress description and analysis of the growing conflicts and introduce the opposing forces (a sense of togetherness, solidarity, the sense of 'the nation', common interest in the prevention of defeat) to a certain extent negatively, as the limit of the central tendencies to conflict. This was the procedure followed in this book, which in no way denies this mutuality. If one applies an unfortunately mistaken international-comparative perspective, introducing the much earlier conflict-torn and disintegrating Russia of the First World War as a comparison then one really will have to ask, as does Schramm, why the outbreak of class and other conflicts did not occur earlier in Germany; from where did the system derive its relatively high stability, to be able to resist the internal and external pressures for so long? Here one will probably not be able to make do with one conflict model *alone*. Even apart from this comparative point of view, there would seem to be something in favour (for example, Schramm, pp. 251-2) of conceptually grasping the cohesive forces of this system more clearly and placing them more centrally in the model than was done here, and thus view them as more than 'secondary integration' and the result of ideological manipulation, political concession and 'bribery'. That would entail going beyond a Marxist conflict model and would clearly change the conception of this study. In any case, at this point a limit to the present study has to be conceded.

4. It also has to be conceded that the interpretation of the state's function from 1914 to 1918 – in the sense of its integration into overall theories of the 'state monopolitic capitalism' type – was not fully argued through to the end in this study. Several critics addressed themselves to this point (H. Haumann, G. Schramm, G. Stollberg and others). It may be that the representation and evaluation offered here is more in keeping with an undogmatic state monopoly capitalism premise than has been assumed above. But it makes one suspicious when, as shown on pp. 137-40 above, work which is based on this theory either overlooks or denies (perhaps has to) such central (and undervalued, Schramm, pp. 258-9) attitudes and utterances critical of the state from nearly all entrepreneurs. This leads to fundamentally

mistaken interpretations of important state processes, such as the carrying through of the Auxiliary Service Law.[13] Furthermore, I think it unlikely that one could adequately interpret the attempts by the state apparatus to prevent a defeat of the Reich in the First World War using only a class analysis, in which the state seeks to stabilise capitalist economic and social relations in an effort which is in contradiction to the interests of the dependent masses. Conversely this means that (as Karl Liebknecht thought) defeat had to be regarded as being in the interests of the dependent masses in Germany (on this, see pp. 144–7 above and the criticism by H. Haumann). But this is how one would have to argue, as Haumann so carefully does, if one consequently wishes to interpret the actual efforts and achievements of the state apparatus in the framework of the premise of a state monopoly capitalism or any other *purely* conflict-theoretical conception of the state.[14] Those who argue in this way must ask themselves two questions: firstly, are there not situations, and was not the defeat after the World War such a one, where the revolutionary abolition of capitalist relations of production signified little or no advantage for the mass of the population, relative to the undoubted burdens and sacrifices which defeat after such a war also meant for the great majority of the population? Secondly, are there not system functions of the state in capitalist-bourgeois systems that are not absorbed into the maintenance of *capitalistic* relations, but are at the same time very important for many people's lives? This second question leads to a discussion on the state which cannot be undertaken here. The first is naturally counter-factual and could well turn out to be so complex as to be empirically unanswerable (and so empirically irrefutable). But since its refutation lies (naturally, it seems) at the base of that purely class-analytical interpretation of victory and defeat, state and war, that is under debate here, this would already be a contribution towards rationalising the discussion. In any case it seems to me that the continuing discussion about the function of the state in the capitalist-bourgeois system could only gain by drawing in the role of the state in wartime more strongly – as an extreme case which revealed some otherwise hidden dimensions.

Abbreviations

AEG	Allgemeine Elektricitäts-Gesellschaft
AfA	Arbeitsgemeinschaft freier Angestelltenverbände
AfS	*Archiv für Sozialgeschichte*
AK, AKs	Armee-Korps
AKV	Arbeitsgemeinschaft Kaufmännischer Verbände
Annales E.S.C.	*Annales, Economie, Société, Civilisation*
Archiv	*Archiv für Sozialwissenschaft und Sozialpolitik*
ASG	*Archiv für Sozialgeschichte*
BdI	Bund der Industriellen
BdL	Bund der Landwirte
BHR	*Business History Review*
Butib	Bund der technisch-industriellen Beamten
Corr.bl.	*Correspondenzblatt der Generalkommission der Gewerkschaften Deutschlands*
CVDI	Centralverband Deutscher Industrieller
DAAP	Deutsche Arbeiter- und Angestellten-Partei
DAZ	*Deutsche Arbeitgeber-Zeitung*
DHV	Deutschnationaler Handlungsgehilfen-Verband
DHW	*Deutsche Handels-Wacht*
DIBZ	*Deutsche Industriebeamten-Zeitung*
DIEW	*Deutschland im Ersten Weltkrieg*
DTV	Deutscher Technikerverband
EHR	*Economic History Review*
Fs.	Festschrift
FVP	Fortschrittliche Volkspartei
GdS	*Grundriß der Sozialökonomik*
Gedag	Gesamtverband deutscher Angestelltengewerkschaften
GG	*Geschichte und Gesellschaft*
GWU	*Geschichte in Wissenschaft und Unterricht*
HDG	Hilfsdienstgesetz
HSt	*Handwörterbuch der Staatswissenschaften*
HWZ	*Handwerks-Zeitung*
HZ	*Historische Zeitschrift*
IESS	*International Encyclopaedia of the Social Sciences*
IWK	*Internationale Korrespondenz zur Geschichte der deutschen Arbeiterbewegung*
Jb.	*Jahrbuch*

Jbb.	*Jahrbücher*
JbfWG	*Jahrbuch für Wirtschaftsgeschichte*
JContHist	*Journal of Contemporary History*
JMH	*Journal of Modern History*
JNS	*Jahrbücher für Nationalökonomie und Statistik*
Ka.	Kriegsamt
Ka.d.Dt.Ind	Kriegsausschuß der Deutschen Industrie
KM	Kriegministerium
KRA	Kriegsrohstoffabteilung
MB	Monats-Berichte ('Summaries of the monthly reports of the Regional Command')
MEW	Marx/Engels, *Werke*
MKdI	*Mitteilungen des Kriegsausschusses der deutschen Industrie*
MSPD	Mehrheits-SPD, resp. Mehrheitssozialdemokratie
NHWZ	*Nordwestdeutsche Handwerks-Zeitung*
NSDAP	Nationalsozialistische Deutsche Arbeiterpartei
NWB	*Neue Wissenschaftliche Bibliothek*
OHL	Oberste Heeresleitung
Prot.	Protokoll
PVS	*Politische Vierteljahrsschrift*
Quellen GPP	*Quellen zur Geschichte des Parlamentarismus und der politschen Parteien*
RGBl	*Reichsgesetzblatt*
RWA	Reichswirtschaftsamt
SAA	Siemens-Archiv-Akte (Akte des Werner-von-Siemens-Instituts, Munich)
SAZ	Ständiger Ausschuß für Zusammenlegung von Betrieben
SDG	*Sowjetsystem und Demokratische Gesellschaft. Eine vergleichende Enzyklopädie*
S&H	Siemens & Halske
SSW	Siemens-Schuckertwerke
StdDtR	*Statistik des Deutschen Reichs*
Sten.Ber. Reichstag	Stenographische Berichte über die Verhandlungen des Reichstags
USPD	Unabhängige Sozialdemokratishce Partei Deutschlands
VfZ	*Vierteljahrshefte für Zeitgeschichte*
Vst.	Vorstand
VSWG	*Vierteljahrschrift für Sozial- und Wirtschaftsgeschichte*
WUA	Das Werk des Untersuchungsausschusses
ZAG	Zentralarbeitsgemeinschaft der industriellen und gewerblichen Arbeitgeber und Arbeitnehmer Deutschlands
ZfG	*Zeitschrift für Geschichtswissenschaft*
ZfP	*Zeitschrift für Politik*
Zs.	*Zeitschrift*

Notes

Chapter 1. Problems and Concepts

1 Cf. F. Fischer, *Griff nach der Weltmacht: Die Kriegszielpolitik des Kaiserlichen Deutschland 1914-18*, Düsseldorf, 1961; *idem, Krieg der Illusionen: Die deutsche Politik von 1911 bis 1914*, Düsseldorf, 1969. Among the critics of Fischer is A. Hillgruber, *Deutschlands Rolle in der Vorgeschichte der beiden Weltkriege*, Düsseldorf, 1970; see also K.H. Jarausch, *The Enigmatic Chancellor: Bethmann Hollweg and the Hubris of Imperial Germany*, New Haven, 1973. An informative survey of the debate with references to the most important titles is contained in V.R. Berghahn, 'Die Fischerkontroverse: 15 Jahre danach', *Geschichte und Gesellschaft*, 6, 1980, pp. 403ff. There is a convincing interpretation in H.-U. Wehler, *The German Empire 1871-1918*, Leamington Spa, 1984, Chap. 8. The diaries of Karl Reizler, intimate adviser to Bethmann Hollweg, were one of the major pieces of evidence in this debate; they cast doubt on some of Fischer's views. See K. Reizler, *Tagebücher, Aufsätze, Dokumente*, ed. K.D. Erdmann, Göttingen, 1972. More recently the controversy has been partially revived by questioning both the validity of crucial parts of this source and the soundness of its editor's work. See F. Fischer, *Juli 1914: Wir sind nicht hineingeschlittert. Das Staatsgeheimnis um die Riezler-Tagebücher*, Reinbek, 1983; B. Sösemann, 'Die Tagebücher Kurt Riezlers. Untersuchungen in ihrer Echtheit und Edition', *HZ* 236, 1983, pp. 327-70; and the rebuttal: K.-D. Erdmann, 'Zur Echtheit der Tagebücher Kurt Riezlers. Eine Antikritik', *ibid.*, pp. 371-402.

2 Cf. the editions of source materials by E. Matthias and R. Morsey, E. Matthias and E. Pikart, W. Deist, K.-P. Reiss and R. Schiffers and M. Koch. Among the monographs and surveys the following are particularly useful: D. Grosser, *Vom monarchischen Konstitutionalismus zur parlamentarischen Demokratie: Die Verfassungspolitik der deutschen Parteien im letzten Jahrzehnt des Kaiserreichs*, The Hague, 1970; U. Bermbach, *Vorformen parlamentarischer Kabinettsbildung in Deutschland: Der Interfraktionelle Ausschuss 1917-18 und die Parlamentarisierung der Reichsregierung*, Cologne, 1967; E.R. Huber, *Deutsche Verfassungsgeschichte seit 1789*, 5, *Weltkrieg, Revolution und Reichserneuerung 1914-1919*, Stuttgart, 1978; R. Schiffers, *Der Hauptausschuss des Deutschen Reichstags 1915-1918: Formen und Bereiche der Kooperation zwischen Parlament und Regierung*, Düsseldorf, 1979; S. Miller, *Burgfrieden und Klassenkampf: Die deutsche Sozialdemokratie im Ersten Weltkrieg*, Düsseldorf, 1974; G.A. Ritter, *Arbeiterbewegung, Parteien und Parlamentarismus: Aufsätze zur deutschen Sozial- und Verfassungsgeschichte des 19. und 20. Jahrhunderts*, Göttingen, 1976, pp. 102-57.

3 A good example is D. Stegmann, 'Azischen Repression und Manipulation: Konservative Machteliten und Arbeiter- und Angestelltenbewegung 1910-1918', *Archiv für Sozialgeschichte*, 12, 1971, pp. 351-432; *idem, Die Erben Bismarcks,*

179

Cologne, 1970.

4 In earlier surveys of German history during the First World War, both social and economic history were relegated to the sidelines. Cf. P. Graf Kielmannsegg, *Deutschland und der erste Weltkrieg*, Frankfurt, 1968; H. Herzfeld, *Der Erste Weltkrieg*, Munich, 1968. That the same is still true may be seen in K.-D. Erdmann's overview in Gebhardt, *Handbuch der deutschen Geschichte*, 9th ed., Stuttgart, 1979, 4, pp. 3-144. In the 1920s and 1930s the Carnegie Foundation's *Economic and Social History of the World War (German series)* had gathered many insights and materials, which were hardly used or incorporated by later historians. A list of these volumes may be found in Kielmannsegg, p.719.

5 Cf. K. Bosl (ed.), *Bayern im Umbruch: Die Revolution von 1918, ihre Voraussetzungen, ihr Verlauf und ihre Folgen*, Munich, 1969; K.-L. Ay, *Die Entstehung einer Revolution: Die Volksstimmung in Bayern während des Ersten Weltkrieges*, Berlin, 1969; K.-D. Schwarz, *Weltkrieg und Revolution in Nürnberg. Ein Beitrag zur Geschichte der deutschen Arbeiterbewegung*, Stuttgart, 1971; see also the books by P.v. Oertzen, E. Kolb, R. Rürup and H.-A. Winkler in the bibliography below. Particularly important is the contribution by G.D. Feldman, E. Kolb and R. Rürup, 'Die Massenbewegungen der Arbeiterschaft in Deutschland am Ende des Ersten Weltkrieges (1917-1920)', in *Politische Vierteljahrsschrift*, 13, 1972, pp. 84-105.

6 G.D. Feldman, *Army, Industry and Labor in Germany 1914-1918*, Princeton, 1966; R.B. Armeson, *Total Warfare and Compulsory Labor: a Study of the Military-Industrial Complex in Germany during World War I*, The Hague, 1964. Feldman has continued his research on the War and the early Weimar period, concentrating on the effects of the inflation. Cf. Feldman and H. Homburg, *Industrie und Inflation. Studien und Dokumente zur Politik der deutschen Unternehmer 1916-1923*, Hamburg, 1977; G.D. Feldman, *Iron and Steel in the German Inflation 1916-1923*, Princeton, 1977; G.D. Feldman and O. Busch (eds.), *Historische Prozesse der deutschen Inflation 1914-1924. Ein Tagungsbericht*, Berlin, 1978. Further results will be published in English soon. See also n. 8 below.

7 See the representative three-volume work, *Deutschland im Ersten Weltkrieg*, 1, 3rd ed., 1971; 2-3, 2nd ed., 1970 [DIEW] (with bibliographical references); *Studien zur Geschichte des deutschen Imperialismus bis 1917*, Berlin, 1977; H. Nussbaum and D. Baudis, *Wirtschaft und Staat in Deutschland vom Ende des 19. Jahrhunderts bis 1918-19*, Vaduz, Liechtenstein, 1978. Further works of East German historians (Gutsche, Schröter, Richter, Kuczynski, A. Müller, H. Weber and others) are quoted below.

8 Cf. F. Zunkel, *Industrie und Staatssozialismus*, Düsseldorf, 1974; H.P. Schäfer, *Industrie und Wirtschaftspolitik während des Ersten Weltkriegs in Baden*, Stuttgart, 1980; G. Hardach, *Der Erste Weltkrieg 1914-18 (Geschichte der Weltwirtschaft im 20. Jahrhundert, 2)*, Munich, 1973.

9 See the works by J. Reulecke, S. Miller, H.-J. Bieber, D.W. Morgan and R. Wheeler in the bibliography below. Most recent is G. Mai, *Kriegswirtschaft und Arbeiterbewegung in Württemberg, 1914-1918*, Stuttgart, 1983, with a comprehensive and updated bibliography.

10 For example U. von Gersdorff, *Frauen im Kriegsdienst 1914-1945*, Stuttgart, 1969; W.E. Mosse (ed.), *Deutsches Judentum in Krieg und Revolution 1915-1923*, Tübingen, 1971; K. Hammer, *Deutsche Kriegstheologie 1870-1918*, Munich, 1971; H. Missalla, *Gott mit uns: Die deutsche katholische Kriegspredigt 1914-1918*. See also the contributions to a Franco-German historians' conference on the First World War in *Francia*, 2, 3, 1974, 1975. Many other works will be quoted later in this volume.

11 There is no work on Germany of a similar nature to A. Marwick, *The Deluge: British*

Society and the First World War, London, 1965. The First World War is poorly treated in the most recent synthesis of Imperial Germany: M. Stürmer, *Das ruhelose Reich: Deutschland 1866–1918,* Berlin, 1983. Nor is the social and economic history of the war sufficiently discussed in the companion volume, H. Schulze, *Weimar: Deutschland 1917–1933,* Berlin, 1982.

12 It is indisputable that the material of the subject being researched can never, by itself, structure the research process. Here I am simply pointing out the undeniable fact that the well-attested and pressing need for an explicit theoretical and conceptual tool is less strong when researching (for example) the attitudes and actions of the chief participants in the crisis of July 1914 than when researching (for example) changes in the German class structure between 1914 and 1918.

13 For the general conditions regarding the application of social science theories and models in social and economic historical research see also J. Kocka, *Sozialgeschichte*, pp. 83ff., 99ff.; *idem*, 'Gegenstandsbezogene Theorien in der Geschichtswissenschaft: Schwierigkeiten und Ergebnisse der Diskussion', in *idem* (ed.) *Theorien in der Praxis des Historikers, GG* (special issue), 3, Göttingen, 1977, pp. 178-88.

14 For the following see K. Marx and F. Engels, *Werke*, Berlin, 1957ff. [MEW]. *Ergänzungsband*, 1, pp. 471-97, 510-23, 533-46 (Ökonomisch-philosophische Manuskripte); 2, pp. 37f. (Die Heilige Familie); 3, pp. 20-46 (Die deutsche Ideologie); 4, pp. 140ff., 462ff. (Elend der Philosophie, Kommunistisches Manifest); 8, pp. 139ff., 153 (Der achtzehnte Brumaire des Lousie Bonaparte); 23 (Das Kapital 1) esp. pp. 328-9, 511-12, 675, 790-1; 25 (Das Kapital III), esp. pp. 51-2, 207-8, 632, 892-3. Marx and Engels used several concepts of class and distinguished many variations but arrived at no systematic definition. See E. Bernstein, *Klasse und Klassenkampf, Sozialistische Monatshefte*, 9, 1905, pp. 857-64; R. Aron, 'Social Structure and Ruling Class', *British Journal of Sociology*, 1, 1950, also in L.A. Coser (ed.), *Political Sociology*, New York, 1966, pp. 48-100 (esp. pp. 52-66); R. Bendix and S.M. Lipset, 'Marx's Theory of Social Classes' [1953] in *idem*, (ed.), *Class, Status and Power*, New York, 1966, pp. 3-35; R. Dahrendorf, *Class and Class Conflict in Industrial Society*, Stanford, 1959, Chap. II; H. Skrzypczak, *Marx, Engels, Revolution. Standortbestimmung des Marxismus in der Gegenwart*, Berlin, 1968, pp. 72-5; M. Mauke, *Die Klassentheorie von Marx und Engels*, Frankfurt, 1970).

15 Capitalism is to be understood as an economic system that is predominantly based on private ownership and private control of capital for the production and exchange of goods for profit. Modern industrial capitalism, with which we are exclusively concerned here, is additionally determined by industrial enterprise based on capital accounting and formally free, contractually regulated wage labour.

16 As the ownership and control of capital become separated, the question arises as to the class position of the growing group of entrepreneurial managers. This problem leads to certain difficulties within Marxist theory which are not entered into here. See Dahrendorf, *Class*, pp. 41ff., *passim*. For the purpose of this enquiry, this group is included under 'entrepreneur', along with owner-entrepreneurs and other owners of capital who have decision-making powers.

17 The problem with this concept is not solved by substituting 'latent' for 'objective' (Dahrendorf, *Class*, pp. 173ff.). Perhaps, without having to share all Marx's historical-philosophical premises, one could understand under 'objective interests' those interests that arise for a person or a group on the basis of their class position, provided that they are pursuing certain basic aims (such as the improvement of life chances, minimising imposed control, maximising their autonomy, etc.). These 'objective interests' need not be identical (because of counter-influences such as a lack of clarity and consistency of consciousness, ideological effects, traditions

emotional ties, etc), with conscious intentions and the actions derived from these.

18 This is undoubtedly the central idea of the Marxist concept of 'the state' and that which has academically and politically the greatest effect, Marx's varied, often contradictory and changing statements about the structure and function of 'the state' notwithstanding. For a useful overview, see R. Miliband, 'Marx and the State', *The Socialist Register*, 1, 1965, pp. 278–96.

19 This line of thought follows Dahrendorf's important representation of conflict theory. See particularly R. Dahrendorf, 'Elemente einer Theorie des sozialen Konflicts', in *idem, Gesellschaft und Freiheit. Zur soziologischen Analyse der Gegenwart*, Munich, 1961, pp. 197–235, esp. pp. 218–30. But we modify his approach in several respects.

20 The difference between 'class tension' and 'class conflict' corresponds with L.Coser's differentiation between 'hostility' and 'conflict'. See L.Coser, *The Functions of Social Conflict*, 2nd ed., Glencoe, 1964, pp. 35-8.

21 See, in clarification, T. Gurr, *Why Men Rebel*, Princeton, N.J., 1970, pp. 23-58.

22 It would not be difficult here, as in other places, to arrive at a much more differentiated model. One could set out the factors which probably facilitate or hinder the formation of such discrepancy in general, as, for instance, the ambivalent role of individual mobilitiy (see Coser, *Functions*, pp. 35ff.) and the advancing and then interrupted experience of improvements in life chances (see J.C. Davies, 'Toward a Theory of Revolution', *American Sociological Review*, 27, 1972, pp. 5–19). It is useful to have such hypotheses taken from the literature in mind.

23 See Dahrendorf, *Class*, pp. 182–8, 239.

24 K. Marx, *Manifesto of the Communist Party*, London, 1888, p.43

25 K. Marx, *Capital*, I, London, 1887, p. 789.

26 For further discussion of this model of class formation cf. J. Kocka, *Lohnarbeit und Klassenbildung. Arbeiter und Arbeiterbewegung in Deutschland 1800-1875*, Berlin/Bonn, 1983, pp. 21–30. This approach differs from both the Thompsonian and the East German brand of Marxist class history. For criticism of these modes of analysis see J. Kocka, 'Klassen oder Kultur? Durchbrüche und Sackgassen in der Arbeitergeschichte' in *Merkur. Deutsche Zeitschrift für europäisches Denken*, 36, 1982, pp. 955-65; *idem*, 'The study of social mobility and the formation of the working class in the 19th century' in *Mouvement social*, III, April/June 1980, pp. 97-117, esp. 98, 115.

27 There are differences between 'ideal type' and 'model', which make it appear appropriate to describe the conceptual system used here as 'model', although it is meant to be used in an ideal-typical function. See T. Schieder, 'Unterschiede zwischen historischer und sozialwissenchaftlicher Methode' [1970] in Wehler (ed.), *Geschichte u. Soziologie*, pp. 291ff.

28 See Coser, *Functions*, pp. 72-81; Dahrendorf, *Class*, p. 213.

29 A basic text for the concept of 'ideal-type' is M. Weber, 'Die "Objektivität" sozialwissenschaftlicher Erkenntnis', in *idem., Gesammelte Aufsätze zur Wissenschaftslehre*, 3rd ed., Tübingen, 1968, pp. 189ff. See also J. Janoska-Bende, *Methodologische Aspekte des Idealtypus. Max Weber und die Soziologie der Geschichte*, Berlin, 1965; J. Kocka, *Sozialgeschichte. Begriff, Entwicklung, Probleme*, Göttingen, 1977, pp. 86-8.

Chapter 2. Workers and Employers in Industry

1 The number of self-employed shown in the industry and craft division of the Reich statistics (including mining) were (1882) 2,201, (1895) 2,012 and (1907) 1,977 million. Of all those economically active in this division, this represented a

proportion of *ca*. (1882) 36.6 per cent, (1895) 25.7 per cent and (1907) 18.2 per cent. See *StdDtR*, 466, 1937, p. 194. Statistics on size of enterprises are in W.G. Hoffmann, *Das Wachstum der deutschen Wirtschaft seit der Mitte des 19. Jahrhunderts*, Berlin, 1965, p. 212.

2 For an introduction to this problem cf. J. Kocka, 'Craft traditions and the German labour movement in the 19th century', in G. Crossick *et al.* (eds.), *The Power of History. Essays for Eric Hobsbawm*, Cambridge, 1984. On the problem of definition, see J. Wernicke, *Kapitalismus u. Mittelstandspolitik*, 2nd ed., Jena, 1922, pp. 326ff.; A. Noll, 'Wirtschaftliche u. soziale Entwicklung des Handwerks in der zweiten Phase der Industrialisierung', in W. Rüegg and O. Neuloh (eds.), *Zur Soziologischen Theorie u. Analyse des 19. Jahrhunderts*, Göttingen, 1971, pp. 196-7; H.A. Winkler, *Mittelstand, Demokratie u. Nationalsozialismus. Die politische Entwicklung von Handwerk u. Kleinhandel in der Weimarer Republik*, Cologne 1972, pp. 25-6, 29. If the Reichs-Gewerbe-Statistik are used in the following, there is a further problem: the numbers refer to 'technical units' and thereby include offshoots (workshops, branches) of larger, not necessarily independent enterprises. They are therefore too high. This error may be ignored, however (especially for firms with more than ten workers), since it is more or less cancelled out by an inexactitude in the opposite direction. In larger enterprises, the 'entrepreneur' did not consist of a single individual, but of the many senior employees and supervisory councils who would also have to be included in the class of 'entrepreneur' in a socio-historical enquiry.

3 *StdDtR*, 466, 1937, pp. 188. The number of economically active also includes managers, white-collar employees and manual workers. In order to assess the number of manual workers, there are assumed to be *ca.* 120,000 managers and *ca.* 615,000 industrial white-collar employees in the economy in 1907. See *StdDtR*, 220, p. 105; G. Hartfiel, *Angestellte u. Angestelltengewerkschaften in Deutschland*, Berlin, 1961, pp. 15ff., 52ff.

4 Based on the figures in A.V. Desai, *Real Wages in Germany 1871-1913*, Oxford, 1968, pp. 109-10, the earnings in seventeen branches of industry in 1895, 1900, 1910 and 1913 were compared in such a way that earnings in the engineering industry were set at 100 and the other earnings expressed as a percentage of this value. This produced a range in 1895 from 39 to 100 per cent, in 1905 from 30 to 102 per cent and in 1913 from 33 to 112 per cent. Between 1895 and 1913 the differential in average earnings between engineering and six other branches of industry was reduced; in the same period differentials within ten different branches of industry increased.

5 On the decrease in earnings differentials between skilled and unskilled workers see G. Bry, *Wages in Germany*, Princeton, 1960, pp. 81ff. The proportion of skilled in the total workforce in Industrie and Handwerk was 65 per cent in 1895 but only 59 per cent in 1907; among male workers the proportion of skilled fell from 68 per cent to 61 per cent, among females from 53 per cent to 45 per cent; calculated from *StdDtR*, 211, 1913, pp. 251. For a definition of the concepts 'skilled' and 'unskilled' workers, see *StdDtR*, 202, 1909, p. 41ff.

6 Cf. K. Schönhoven, *Expansion und Konzentration. Studien zur Entwicklung der Freien Gewerkschaften im Wilhelminischen Deutschland 1880-1914*, Stuttgart, 1980.

7 The average non-agricultural employee nominally earned (1890) 650M, (1900) 784M and (1913) 1,083M per annum. In constant terms (based on 1895) he received (1890) 636M, (1900) 737M and (1913) 834M. Employees with a yearly income of more than 3000M per annum are not included. From calculations by Desai (pp. 112, 125; has figures also for years not included here). Desai corrects the earlier calculations of Kuczynski and Bry, according to whom real earnings stagnated post-1907, at the latest, and in part declined. Bry (esp. pp. 329, 353, 356)

relies heavily on J. Kuczynski, *Germany 1800 to the Present Day*, London, 1945. These figures are only slightly revised in *idem, Die Geschichte der Lage der Arbeiter unter dem Kapitalismus*, 4, Berlin, 1967, pp. 326–60; and similarly, without taking into account the results since published by Desai which do not correspond with his own, in *idem, Klassen und Klassenkämpfe im imperialistischen Deutschland und in der BRD*, Frankfurt, 1972, pp. 262–3. The calculations of Desai are more reliable than those of Kuczynski and Bry, because he makes use (pp. 4ff.) of the systematic returns from insurance offices (instead of relying, as they do, on single heterogeneous wage and earnings returns); because he draws in more branches of industry than Kuczynski and Bry (pp. 108ff.); and, above all, because through the additional inclusion of clothing, heating and lighting costs (pp. 1–2, 117) he has constructed a wider cost of living index than have those who limit themselves to the cost of food and rent. See also R. Gommel, *Realeinkommen in Deutschland. Ein internationaler Vergleich (1810–1914)*, Nuremberg, 1979.

8 See the survey of household costs of average income families in the German Reich, processed in Kaiserl. Statist. Amt, Abt. f. Arbeiterstatistik, *Reichsarbeitsblatt*, special issue 2, Berlin, 1909, pp. 48, 56–7.

9 See Kuczynski, *Geschichte*, 4, pp. 385–9, 398–9; Umbreit and C. Lorenz, *Der Krieg und die Arbeitsverhältnisse*, Stuttgart, 1928, pp. 5–10, 37–40; W. Zimmermann, 'Die Veränderungen der Einkommens- u. Lebensverhältnisse der deutschen Arbeiter durch den Krieg', in R. Meerwarth, *et al., Die Einwirkung des Krieges auf Bevölkerungsbewegung, Einkommen und Lebenshaltung in Deutschland*, Stuttgart, 1932, pp. 330f.; G.A. Ritter, *Staat, Arbeiterschaft und Arbeiterbewegung in Deutschland*, Berlin, 1980; *idem, Sozialversicherung in Deutschland und England. Entstehung und Grundzüge im Vergleich*, Munich, 1983. (To be published in English as *Social Security in Germany and England. Origins and Structure*, Leamington Spa, 1985.)

10 In the 1880s this relationship was apparently the reverse. See A. Jeek, *Wachstum und Verteilung des Volkseinkommens*, Tübingen, 1970, pp. 129, 215ff., 221. But it has less meaning for a class analysis if (as in Hoffmann, pp. 86–7; H. Nussbaum, 'Zur Imperialismustheorie Lenins', in *JbfWG*, IV 1970, p. 56; Groh, 'Je eher, desto besser!', p. 519) one compares 'work income' with 'capital income' and sees that the proportion of 'work income' to total income declined strongly before 1914. This tells us little for a class analysis, however, because self-employed incomes, which apparently grew very little, are included in the total 'work incomes'. For this criticism, see Jeek, pp. 123–4.

11 Regarding the decline in the proportion of lower incomes, the following are in agreement: K. Helfferich, *Deutschlands Volkswohlstand 1888-1913*, 4th ed., Berlin, 1914, pp. 130ff.; R. Wagenführ, *Die Industriewirtschaft*, Berlin, 1933 pp. 10–11, who disagrees with Helfferich and stresses the more rapid increase of the highest incomes. In any case one may see in the decrease in the proportion of those with lower incomes a potentially progressive growth in mass spending power and the domestic consumer market, which was not curtailed by rising prices; Groh's arguments must be regarded with some scepticism, when he talks of a growing 'weakness of purchasing power among broad sections' in the years before 1914, basing this mainly on the supposed stagnation of real wages and presenting it as an important determining factor of the 'systems' inherent problem' in Wilhelmine society. See Groh, pp. 518–21.

12 In 1907–9, the wife of a skilled worker earned on average 3.5 per cent, that of an unskilled worker 7.7 per cent of the total family income. See 'Erhebung von Wirtschaftsrechnungen minderbemittelter Familien im Deutschen Reiche' in *Reichsarbeitsblatt*, special issue 2, Berlin, 1909, p. 45. For the insufferable circumstances arising from wives at work in families with many children, see the

graphic description in N.T.W. Bromme, *Lebensgeschichte eines modernen Fabrikarbeiters*, 1905, new edition, Frankfurt, 1971. See also K. Saul *et al.* (eds.), *Arbeiterfamilien im Kaiserreich*. *Materialien zur Sozialgeschichte in Deutschland 1871-1914*, Düsseldorf, 1982; H. Rosenbaum, *Formen der Familie*. *Untersuchungen zum Zusammenhang von Familienverhältnissen, Sozialstruktur und sozialem Wandel in der Deutschen Gesellschaft des 19. Jahrhunderts*, Frankfurt, 1982, pp. 381-475; H. Reif, 'Soziale Lage und Erfahrungen des alternden Fabrikarbeiters in der Schwerindustrie des westlichen Ruhrgebiets während der Hochindustrialisierung', in *Archiv für Sozialgeschichte*, 22, 1982, pp. 1-34.

13 See J. Kuczynski, *Studien zur Geschichte des Kapitalismus*, Berlin, 1957, pp. 155ff.

14 By comparison with a similarly advanced capitalist society in contemporary America, the fundamental social class structure of Germany is very pronounced. For this, see J. Kocka, *White-collar Workers in America 1890-1940. A Social-Political History in International Perspective*, London, 1980. The memoirs of contemporary workers and factory supervisors contain much material on this question. See Bromme; K. Fischer, *Denkwürdigkeiten u. Erinnerungen eines Arbeiters*, Leipzig, 1903-4; P. Göhre, *Drei Monate Fabrikarbeiter u. Handwerksbursche*, Leipzig, 1891; M. Wettstein-Adelt, *3½ Monate Fabrik-Arbeiterin*, Berlin, 1893; see also the survey by A. Levenstein, *Die Arbeiterfrage*, Munich, 1912. On the very slight chances for upward social mobility of workers, see H. Kaelble, *Soziale Mobilität und Chancengleichheit im 19. und 20. Jahrhundert. Deutschland im internationalen Vergleich*, Göttingen, 1983, to be published as *Social Mobility and Equality in the 19th and 20th Centuries*, Leamington Spa, 1985.

15 See the relevant articles in D. Fricke (ed.), *Die bürgerlichen Parteien in Deutschland. Handbuch der Geschichte der bürgerlichen Parteien und anderer bürgerlicher Interessenorganisationen vom Vormärz bis zum Fahre 1945*, 2 vols., Berlin, 1968-70.

16 Cf. H.-U. Wehler, *The German Empire*; H.-J. Puhle, *Agrarische Interessenpolitik u. preussischer Konservatismsus im wilhelminischen Reich (1893-1914)*, Hanover, 1966; D. Stegmann, *Die Erben Bismarcks*; K. Wernecke, *Der Wille zur Weltgeltung*, Düsseldorf, 1970; H.-U. Wehler, *Krisenherde des Kaiserreichs 1871-1918*, Göttingen, 1970; V.R. Berghahn, *Der Tirpitz-Plan*, Düsseldorf, 1971. For the politics of the Mittelstand see H.A. Winkler, *Mittelstand, Demokratie u. Nationalsozialismus*, Cologne, 1972, chap. 4; J. Kocka, *Unternehmensverwaltung und Angestelltenschaft*, Stuttgart, 1969, pp. 536ff. For the labour movement see G.A. Ritter, *Die Arbeiterbewegung im Wilhelminischen Deutschland*, 2nd ed., Berlin, 1963; E. Matthias, 'Kautsky u. der Kautskyanismus', *Marxismusstudien*, 2, 1957, pp. 151-97; G.Roth, *The Social Democrats in Imperial Germany*, Ottowa, 1963; P. Lösche, *Arbeiterbewegung u. Wilhelminismus*, *GWU*, 20, 1969, 519-33; H.-J. Steinberg, *Sozialismus u. deutsche Sozialdemokratie vor dem 1. Weltkrieg*, Hanover, 1967; D. Groh, 'Negative Integration und revolutionärer Attentismus', *Internationale Wissenschftl. Korrespondenz z. Geschichte d. Dt. Arbeiterbewegung*, 15, 1972, pp. 1-17; *idem*, 'Negative Integration u. revolutionärer Attentismus', *Die deutsche Sozialdemokratie am Vorabend des Ersten Weltkriegs (1909-1914)*, Berlin, 1973. Also see F. Boll, 'Die deutsche Sozialdemokratie zwischen Resignation und Revolution. Zur Friedensstrategie 1890-1919' in W.Huber, J.Schwertfeger, *Frieden, Gewalt und Sozialismus. Studien zur Geschichte der sozialistischen Arbeiterbewegung*, Stuttgart, 1976; G.A. Ritter, *Staat, Arbeiterschaft und Arbeiterbewegung in Deutschland. Vom Vormärz bis zum Ende der Weimarer Republik*, Berlin, Bonn, 1980. Essential: M.R. Lepsius, 'Parteiensystem u. Sozialstruktur' in *Geschichte u. Wirtschaftsgeschichte*. Festschrift for F. Lütge, Stuttgart, 1966, pp. 371-93.

17 In 1913 the Free Trade Unions had 2.5 million members, the Christion unions had 340,000 and the Liberal associations had just over 110,000. In 1900 the figures had

been 680,000, 79,000 and 92,000. From E. Lederer and J. Marschak, 'Die Klassen auf dem Arbeitsmarkt u. ihre Organisationen', *GdS*, 9/11, Tübingen, 1927, pp. 140–3. Thus five out of six organised workers belonged to Social Democratic organisations before the War.

18 In 1884 the SPD received 9.7 per cent of the votes in the Reichstag elections, in 1903 31.7 per cent and in 1912 34.8 per cent; from G.A. Ritter (ed.), *Historisches Lesebuch 2 (1871 to 1914)*, Frankfurt, 1967, pp. 366–7. On the preponderance of the proletarian voter: R. Blank, 'Die soziale Zusammensetzung der sozialdemokratischen Wählerschaft Deutschlands, *Archiv*, 20, 1905, pp. 507ff. See also the following overviews with extended bibliographies: H.J. Varain, *Freie Gewerkschaften, Sozialdemokratie u. Staat*, Düsseldorf, 1956; H. Grebing, *Geschichte der deutschen Arbeiterbewegung*, 6th ed., Munich, 1975; H. Wachenheim, *Die deutsche Arbeiterbewegung 1844 bis 1914*, Cologne, 1967; A. Klönne, *Die deutsche Arbeiterbewegung. Geschichte, Ziele, Wirkungen*, Düsseldorf, 1980.

19 On the history of the employers' associations: F. Tänzler, *Die deutschen Arbeitgeberverbände 1904–1929. Ein Beitrag zur Geschichte der deutschen Arbeitgeberbewegung*, n.p., 1929, 12–118 (written from the employers' point of view); equally rather uncritical is R. Leckebusch, *Entstehung und Wandlungen der Zielsetzungen, der Struktur und der Wirkungen von Arbeitgeberverbänden*, Berlin, 1966, pp. 15–60; G. Erdmann, *Die deutschen Arbeitgeberverbände im sozialgeschichtlichen Wandel der Zeit*, Neuwied, 1966. For figures on strikes, lockouts and the use of the police, see E. Lederer and J. Marschak, 'Die Klassen auf dem Arbeitsmarkt u. ihre Organisationen', pp. 177–8, 185.

20 Cf. H.A. Winkler (ed.), *Organisierter Kapitalismus. Voraussetzungen und Anfänge*, Göttingen, 1974.

21 A first attempt to quantify the trends in some collective protests in the nineteenth century is R. Tilly, 'Popular Disorders in Nineteenth-century Germany. A Preliminary Survey', *Journal of Social History*, 4, 1970/71, pp. 14–40; C. Tilly et al., *The Rebellious Century 1830–1930*, Cambridge, Mass., 1975, pp. 191–238.

22 In 1904, 575 wage agreements were concluded, in 1907, 5,324 and in 1914, 10,866 agreements which covered 133,702 firms with 1,282 million workers; see Umbreit and Lorenz, p. 33.

23 Strike figures are given in Lederer and Marschak, p. 177 (official figures) and H. Kaelble and H. Volkmann, 'Konjunktur und Streik während des Übergangs zum Organisierten Kapitalismus in Deutschland', *Zeitschrift für Wirtschafts- u. Sozialwissenschaften*, 92, 1972, p. 542 (union information); *ibid.*, pp. 529–41 on the structural changes of the strike movement under the influence of increasing organisation (esp. p. 534 for the absolute and relative increase in strikeless movements). Strike figures are given in K. Tenfelde and H. Volkmann (eds.), *Streik. Zur Geschichte des Arbeitskampfes in Deutschland während der Industrialisierung*, Munich, 1981, pp. 296–301.

24 The case of Siemens is followed up in Kocka, *Unternehmensverwaltung*, pp. 335ff; see also K. Saul, *Staat, Industrie und Arbeiterbewegung im Kaiserreich. Zur Innen- und Aussenpolitik des Wilhelminischen Deutschland 1903–1914*, Düsseldorf, 1974. Specifically on the 'yellow' movement, the latter with bibliographical information: H.P. Schafter, 'Die "Gelben Gewerkschaften" am Beispiel des Unterstützungsvereins der Siemens-Werke, Berlin', *VSWG*, 59, 1972, pp. 41–76; K. Mattheier, *Die Gelben. Nationale Arbeiter zwischen Wirtschaftsfrieden und Streik*, Düsseldorf, 1973.

25 Summarised in Umbreit and Lorenz, pp. 10–18.

26 See K.E. Born, *Staat und Sozialpolitik seit Bismarcks Sturz*, Wiesbaden, 1957, p. 242. Public consciousness of inaction became particularly clear at the beginning of 1914. See F. Fischer, *Krieg der Illusionen. Die deutsche Politik von 1911 bis 1914*,

Düsseldorf, 1969, p. 412.

27 Reaching a highpoint with the 'Kartell der schaffenden Stände', 1913. For this see especially Stegmann, *Die Erben Bismarcks*, Chaps. 5–9; but Stegmann is inclined to over-estimate the stability of the 'Kartell' and its real influence. See also H. Kaelble, *Industrielle Interessenpolitik in der Wilhelminischen Gesellschaft*, Berlin, 1967, chap. 3; Puhle, II, esp. pp. 143–64.

28 For the BdI and the Hansa-Bund see H. Nussbaum, *Unternehmer gegen Monopole*, Berlin, 1966; S. Mielke, *Der Hansa-Bund, 1912–1914*, Göttingen, 1976; H.P. Ullmann, *Der Bund der Industriellen*, Göttingen, 1976.

29 Cf. Wehler, *The German Empire*; V.R. Berghahn, *Modern Germany: Society, Economy and Politics in the Twentieth Century*, Cambridge, 1982; a differing view stressing the possibilities of an emerging camp in the middle of the political spectrum: G. Schmidt, 'Innenpolitische Blockbildungen am Vorabend des Ersten Weltkrieges', *Aus Politik u. Zeitgeschichte*, 13 May 1972, pp. 3–32.

30 Figures on the basis of Zimmermann, *Veränderungen*, pp. 350–1, who compiled them from the annual reports of factory inspectors in the various German states. There are slight discrepancies between Zimmermann's figures for separate branches of industry when added together, and the total sum arrived at by myself when checking his figures.

31 This tendency can be seen if one takes into account the figures for 1916 as given in Zimmermann, *Veränderungen*, p. 372; more precise comparisons seem difficult because of changes in the mode of calculation. The results correspond with information from other sources, which indicate that efforts to provide adequately for workers in essential industries increased after the battles in the summer of 1916, the 'Hindenburg programme' and the Auxiliary Service Law.

32 There were ca. 8 million people in the army and navy in 1918. In 1910 there were 16,665 million men aged between 15 and 60 in Germany. From L. Grebler and W. Winkler, *The Cost of the World War to Germany and to Austria-Hungary*, New Haven, 1940, p. 76; F.H. Will, *Das Handwerk als Kriegslieferant*, Hanover, 1923, p. 40.

33 See Wagenführ, p. 21.

34 In the middle of 1916, 1.19 million conscripts were granted deferment in order to work in trades essential to the war effort, 1.89 million in the middle of 1917 and 2.42 million in the middle of 1918; of these the majority most probably worked in industry and mining. See E.v. Wrisberg, *Erinnerungen an die Kriegsjahre im Kgl. Preussischen Kriegsministerium*, Vol. 2, *Heer und Heimat*, Leipzig, 1921, pp. 90–1, 80–126 (on questions of labour provision generally).

35 During the War ca. 260,000 Polish workers were 'recruited'; according to official sources there were ca. 500,000 workers from previously Russian areas in Germany in 1918, 150,000 Belgian workers were 'recruited' during the War and between October 1917 and February 1918 a further 61,500 were forcibly deported from Belgium to Germany. Figures according to F. Zunkel, 'Die ausländischen Arbeiter in der deutschen Kriegswirtschaftspolitik des Ersten Weltkriegs', in G.A. Ritter (ed.), *Entstehung u. Wandel der modernen Gesellschaft*. Festschrift für Rosenberg, Berlin, 1970, pp. 280–311, esp. 291–310. See also Grebler and Winkler, pp. 30–1, and Wrisberg, p. 120. In 1916 ca. 260,000 prisoners of war were employed in industry and trade, and 79,000 German convicts (of whom most worked on the land).

36 Figures for women in factories in Schwarz, *Weltkrieg*, p. 163; M.-E. Lüders, 'Die Entwicklung der gewerblichen Frauenarbeit im Kriege', *Schmollers Jb.*, 44, 1920, H.1, pp. 241–67; H.2, pp. 253–77, esp. 276–7. The proportion of women in employment outside industry was even higher. According to medical insurance statistics, the proportion of women workers amongst the insured was about one-

third in 1914, but was over 50 per cent by 1918. See Wagenführ, p. 22. Further to
the question of women workers during the war, see: C. Lorenz, 'Die gewerbliche
Frauenarbeit während des Krieges' in Umbreit and Lorenz, pp. 307–91; M.-E.
Lüders, *Das unbekannte Heer*, Berlin, 1935; U. von Gersdorff, *Frauen im
Kriegsdienst 1914–1945*, Stuttgart, 1969, pp. 9–37 (excerpts from sources); S.
Bajohr, *Die Hälfte der Fabrik. Geschichte der Frauenarbeit in Deutschland 1914 bis
1945*, Marburg, 1979; A. Seidel *Frauenarbeit in Ersten Weltkrieg als Problem der
staatlichen Sozialpolitik. Dargestellt am Beispiel Bayerns*, Frankfurt, 1979.

37 According to the categories and calculations of Bry, pp. 193–4, based on figures
given in Zimmermann, p. 350. We have adopted Bry's three categories, although
they deviate slightly from those of other authors (such as R. Wagenführ), in order to
be able to use his wage calculations.

38 See Umbreit and Lorenz, p. 329. Up to July 1917 there were, in the area under the
authority of the Prussian AKs, a total of 101,178 deferred conscripts or servicemen
on leave who were recalled to military service. Their place in the labour force was
filled by 31,244 Auxiliary Service conscripts, 2,878 youths, 2,914 people over 60
and 64,143 women.

39 On the basis of the figures referred to in n.31.

40 After M. Frenzel, *Geschichte der Zentral-Werksverwaltung [Siemens-Schuckert-
werke] Berlin und ihrer Vorläufer 1899–1949*; also Ms 1953 SAA 68/Li 83), p. 69.
The SSW employed 27,700 people in July 1914 but this figure had fallen by 30 per
cent by October 1914. Through the changeover to armaments production and
various sorts of new construction the labour force then rose to 33,000 by July 1915,
or 130 per cent of the prewar level. The *male* labour force, however, remained at 70
per cent of prewar level. From *ibid*, pp. 61–2.

41 See *Jahresberichte der Preussischen Regierungs- und Gewerberäte und Bergbehörden
für 1914–1918*, Berlin, 1919 pp. 955–6

42 See Dr R. Zesch (ed.), 'Was ist geschehen zur Ermöglichung der Arbeit von
Ungelernten und Frauen?', Berlin im März 1933 (using official records) . . .',
National Archives Microcopy, T77, roll 343, no. 80665–80727: an overview of
relevant initiatives, suggestions and measures (including reorganisation of firms,
special training workshops and training practices for women and the unskilled in
large undertakings). I have to thank G.D. Feldman for access to this source. See
also Zimmermann, *Veränderungen*, p.359.

43 Bry, p.200; *ibid*, p.433, for similar results obtained by K. Kreiner from 479
Bavarian enterprises; Zimmermann, p. 382 (on shift-work earnings at Krupp), p.
398 (construction workers' rates in Berlin, Hamburg and Stettin), pp. 414–5
(summary); *Zahlen zur Geldentwentung in Deutschland 1914–1923*, Berlin, 1925,
p.40 (railwaymen, printers and compositors, miners); see also Bry, pp. 199 433–9.
Umbreit and Lorenz, pp. 120–1, underestimate the rise of nominal wages, working
on the basis of craft association statistics, which do not appear to have taken wage
supplements into account but which probably did include white-collar employees.
One must here take into account the fact that wage rates usually rose less steeply
than actual earnings because of the important part played by supplements and
overtime; and that the earnings of hourly-paid workers increased more slowly than
those paid by the week or the year.

44 Calculated by Bry, p. 207.

45 Inequality coefficient, *ibid*., p. 207; *ibid*., pp. 111 and 114 on the pre- and postwar
period.

46 See the tabulation of earnings by metal workers in Frankfurt and Berlin in 1918 in
O. Sperlich, *Arbeitslohn u. Unternehmergewinn in der Kriegswirtschaft*, Hamburg,
1938, pp. 15–16; the average weekly earnings (piece-work) in Berlin were 151M for
setters, 114M for toolmakers 106M for sheet metal workers 99M for turners, 95M

for mechanics, 94M for locksmiths, 94M for filers and millers, 87M for agricultural workers, 70M for assistants and 44M for women workers. The Frankfurt wages were lower: 'We only mention in passing – that there were exceptional wages earned by some individual metal workers – particularly skilled workers aimed to get 15,000M and more per annum', *ibid.*, p. 16. Bry, p. 202, and Zimmermann, *Veränderungen*, pp. 411-12, also take account of such exceptional cases; *ibid.*, p.379 for regional differences.

47 See Bry, pp. 200, 202-3, 206, 437, 438. The War industries were more likely to deviate from this predominant tendency than the peace industries: see *ibid.*, pp. 198, 199, 436. Qualified also in Kuczynski, *Geschichte*, 4, 369-71, whose contrary conclusions regarding the earnings differentials between men and women, p. 369, do not convince, even on his own figures, p. 368. See also Zesch, 'Was ist geschehen . . .', p. 60 (see n. 42 above), where Dr Zesch, by referring to the case as 'nearly grotesque', makes its untypical character quite plain. In July 1915 a typesetter in a publishing firm protested against the training of women. The case had a temporary success at the arbitration committee of the 'Tarifsamt der Buchdrucker' (the body responsible for setting wage rates for printers); the publisher was prohibited from 'diluting' (replacing expensive labour with cheaper) until January 1917.

48 See Bry, pp. 203-5. The metal industry also tended to have exceptions here.

49 See esp. F. Hesse, *Die deutsche Wirtschaftslage von 1914 bis 1923. Krieg, Geldblähe und Wechsellagen*, Jena, 1938; also G.D. Feldman *et al.* (eds.), *Die deutsche Inflation*, Berlin, 1982; C.-L Holtfrerich, *Die deutsche Inflation 1914-1923. Ursachen und Folgen in internationaler Perspektive*, Berlin, New York, 1980.

50 Columns (1) and (3) from *Zahlen zur Geldentwertung in Deutschland 1914-1923*, Berlin, 1925, p. 5: (2) and (4) from Bry, pp. 440-3, where (2) is based on Calwer's contemporary calculations on the basic rations issued to sailors in 200 towns and (4) on information from the Reich Statistical Office (*Zahlen zur Geldentwertung*, p. 40) on nominal and real wages in identical sectors of employment. On the discussion and calculation of the various indices, see Bry, pp. 208-9. Bry prepared this from information made available in the 1920s by the Reich Statistical Office and I believe them to be the most reliable.

51 See P. Quante, 'Lohnpolitik u. Lohnentwicklung im Kriege', *Zeitschrift d. Preussischen Landesamtes*, 59, 1919, pp. 323-84, esp. p. 368, where the increase in the outgoings of four-member workers' families between 1914 (average) and October 1918 is estimated at 175 per cent (Berlin), 149 per cent (Danzig), 159 per cent (Saxony) and 144 per cent (Rhine Province). This corresponds to an average increase to 256 where 1914 = 100. On the whole Quante's figures are accepted by Zimmermann, *Veränderungen*, pp. 462ff.; *ibid.*, pp. 429ff. for a critique of Calwer's figures, which are certainly much too low.

52 For example P. Graf Kielmansegg, *Deutschland u. der Erste Weltkrieg*, Frankfurt, 1968, pp. 68-9.

53 Unless one means their *relative* economic improvement as against other social groups, such as white-collar workers, who became even more impoverished. See Chap. 3 below.

54 See Bry, pp. 306-7.

55 See R. Knauss, *Die deutsche, englische u. französische Kriegsfinanzierung*, Berlin, 1923, pp. 23ff., 94ff., 174ff., P.-C. Witt, 'Finanzpolitik und sozialer Wandel in Krieg und Inflation 1918-1924' in Mommsen *et al.*, *Industrielles System und politische Entwicklung in der Weimarer Republik*, 1, 2nd ed., Düsseldorf, 1977, pp. 395-426.

56 From Bry, p. 211. Bry uses the index of the Reich Statistical Office (see Table above, p. 22, col. 4) and interpolates the monthly values using the monthly Calwer Index. Nominal earnings based on information above, pp. 20ff.

57 See G. Briefs, 'Kriegswirtschaftslehre u. Kriegswirtschaftspolitik', *HSt* 5, 4th ed., 1923, p. 989.
58 See A. Skalweit, *Die deutsche Kriegsernährungswirtschaft*, Stuttgart, 1927, p. 15.
59 According to expert contemporary estimates towards the end of the War the black market took up between a seventh and an eighth of the production of cereals, flour and potatoes, between a third and a quarter of milk, butter and cheese, and between a third and a half of eggs, meat and fruit. See W. Zimmermann, *Die gesunkene Kaufkraft des Lohnes und ihre Wiederherstellung*, Jena, 1919, p.5.
60 On the black market and hoarding, see Schwarz, pp. 156ff.; Ay, pp. 159ff. The increasing difficulties of converting money into goods may have contributed to the fact that savings reserves in savings banks increased markedly in the last two war years. See the figures in Zimmermann, *Veränderungen*, p. 469.
61 See MB, October 1916, pp. 4-5; Sperlich, *Arbeitslohn*, pp. 23-4; F.-A. Schilling-Voss, *Die Sonderernährung der Rüstungsarbeiter im Rahmen der Kriegswirtschaft 1914-18*, Hamburg, 1936. As time went on, industrial enterprises supported the black market more and more in order to be able to attract scarce labour with their distributions of food. At the beginning of 1918, from 4,000 to 12,000 workers were regularly supplied with food at Bayer-Leverkusen; see MB, 3 April 1918, p. 15. When government measures against large-scale black-marketeering (including the illegal provisioning in large enterprises) were announced in January 1918 and put into effect through a parliamentary order (largely unsuccessfully) the representatives of industry and the AKs warned the government against taking such a step because it would lead to a restriction on food hand-outs for armaments workers and thus to social unrest. See MB, 3 February 1918, p. 14; 3 March 1918, pp. 13ff.; 3 April 1918, pp. 15ff.
62 See n. 12 above.
63 See the overview on the relevant support systems, further developed during the War, in Umbreit and Lorenz, pp. 67-82; on the problem of family earnings, see Zimmermann, *Veränderungen*, pp. 412-13, 444, 468-73.
64 See *ibid.*, pp. 441, 457, 458, 435-44 with information on wartime household accounts.
65 See F. Brumm (ed.), *Deutschlands Gesundheitsverhältnisse unter dem Einfluss des Weltkrieges*, 1, Stuttgart, 1928, pp. 271-88.
66 In Zimmermann, *Die gesunkene Kaufkraft*, p.6.
67 In Nuremberg there was a shortfall of ca. 15,000 dwellings in 1918; see Schwarz, p. 162, n. 177.
68 See Bry, p. 432. In July 1914 the figures were 2.9 per cent; in August, 22.4 per cent; in September 15.7 per cent; in October 10.9 per cent; in November, 8.2 per cent; in December 7.2 per cent; in January 1915, 6.5 per cent; in February 5.1 per cent and, by March 1916, 3.3 per cent. They refer to unemployed or short-time-working members of Social Democratic trade unions in relation to the total membership of these unions. From 1915 (at the latest) they may be somewhat too high.
69 See Kuczynski, *Geschichte*, pp. 4, 389ff., 400ff.; Schwarz, p. 163. The actual work time in the 309 Nuremberg armaments factories was 60 hours per week for men, 56-7 for women. Short-time working continued throughout the war in some peace industries, such as some parts of the textile industry. See Umbreit and Lorenz, p. 65.
70 See L. Preller, *Sozialpolitik in der Weimarer Republik*, Stuttgart, 1949, pp. 9, 36.
71 K. Retzlaw, *Spartakus*, Frankfurt, 171, p. 72.
72 See generally U. Neff, *War and Human Progress*, Cambridge, Mass., 1950, p. 374.
73 *Wagenführ*, pp. 22, 23.
74 See Hesse, *Wirtschaftslage*, pp. 489-90.
75 See the information in Wagenführ, pp. 21-2; Sperlich, *Arbeitslohn*, p. 13; on the lower productivity of women: Umbreit and Lorenz, p. 340. On 11 April 1918 the managers of the S & H electric lamp factory reported to the S & H inspectors on production and

productivity during the War. According to this, the following number of electric
lamps were produced:

	Annually (in '000s)	Average per day	Average per worker per hour
1913/14	20,444	69,700	3.16
1914/15	13,316	45,300	3.74
1915/16	17,507	58,000	3.62
1916/17	19,310	63,800	3.34
1917/18 (until March)	14,981	76,700	3.19

In 1914/15 an important rationalisation of production was put through, putting an
end to the manufacture of unusual lamps. The plant was nearly always in full
production, but suffered occasionally from shortages of raw materials, coal and
labour and of industrial unrest. The rise in costs from the middle of 1914 to January
1917 were: 204 per cent for material; 73 per cent for wages; 122 per cent for overheads.
The plant did not sell on the open market but to another section of the firm for an
agreed price whose increase remained below rising costs. From the Minutes of the S
& H board meeting, 11 April 1918.

76 See Grabler/Winkler, pp. 33-4; Wagenführ, P. 23; Kuczynski, *Geschichte*, 4, pp.
397ff.
77 See Wagenführ, pp. 19, 23.
78 On the supply of raw materials see O. Goebel, *Deutsche Rohstoffwirtschaft im
Weltkrieg*, Stuttgart, 1930. The firm of KRA, founded by Walther Rathenau and
directed by him until May 1915, started with the supply of a few import-dependent
non-ferrous metals. As part of the Ka. they controlled ca. 300 non-agricultural raw
materials from 1917; in January 1917 (*ibid*. pp. 29, 173) there were 485 orders for raw
materials; on labour policy in particular: G.D. Feldman, *Army, Industry and Labor in
Germany 1914-1918*, Princeton, N.J., 1966; on the general problem: A. Schröter,
Krieg, Staat, Monopol 1914-18, Berlin, 1965; on food and agricultural policy: F.
Aereboe, *Der Einfluss des Krieges auf die landwirtschaftliche Produktion in Deutschland*,
Stuttgart, 1927; A. Skalweit, for an overview; the relevant chapters in Grebler and
Winkler; Kielmansegg; *DIEW*.
79 See A. Müller, *Die Kriegsrohstoffbewirtschaftung im Dienste des deutschen
Monopolkapitals*, Berlin, 1955, pp. 19, 26, 44, 68; A. Schröter, pp. 123ff.; *DIEW*, 2,
pp. 118ff.; *idem*, 3, pp. 466ff.; K. Helfferich, *Der Weltkrieg*, 2, Karlsruhe, 1924, pp.
115ff.; O. Goebel, pp. 120ff. A further example reported by W. Treue, 'Die Ilseder
Hütte u.der Staat in den Jahren 1916-1919', *Tradition*, 3, pp. 129-40, esp. 133-4.
State involvement leading to the founding of 'economically mixed' enterprises (esp.
in electricity supply, since before 1914) nevertheless signified some restriction on
private control.
80 Probably slightly exaggerated, but the quotation from *DAZ*, 16, 1917, 1. Beibl. (of 7
October) is typical: 'There is hardly an industrial plant in Germany that has not
planned significant enlargements in the course of the War'.
81 Figures in Goebell, p. 52.
82 On the strengthening of the authorities' influence in cooperative work with the
industrial self-administrative organisations see Goebel, pp. 21-2 (on the
changeover of directors in the KRA from Rathenau to Colonel Koeth), also pp.
112ff.; W.F. Bruck, 'Die Kriegsunternehmung. Versuch einer Systematik', *Archiv*,
48, 1920/1, pp. 572-3; E. Heymann, *Die Rechtsformen der militärischen
Kriegswirtschaft*, Marburg, 1921, pp. 31, 140ff.

83 There is much material and many different interpretations on this theme in the work of Goebel, Schröter, Haymann, Bruck (*Kriegsunternehmung*), Grebler and Winkler (esp. pp. 51-4), A. Müller, *DIEW*. See also W.F. Bruck, *Geschichte des Kriegsausschusses der Deutschen Baumwoll-Industrie*, Berlin, 1920; O. Sperlich, *Deutsche Kriegstextilwirtschaft*, Hamburg, 1936; K. Wiedenfeld, *Die Organisation der deutschen Kriegsrohstoffbewirtschaftung im Weltkrieg*, Hamburg, 1936; idem, *Zwischen Wirtschaft u. Staat*, Berlin, 1960. See also below, pp. 000-0.

84 See Grebler and Winkler, p. 39; Bruck, *Kriegsunternehmung*, pp. 566, 570.

85 See Grebler and Winkler, pp. 54-5; W. Hecht, *Organisationsformen der deutschen Rohstoffindustrie. Die Kohle*, Munich, 1924, pp. 3, 256; Schröter, pp. 134ff.; Goebel, p. 115ff.; R. Liefmann, *Kartelle u. Trusts*, 2nd ed., Berlin, 1918, p. 113, on the merger of the old spirits syndicate with the Reichsbranntweinstelle in 1916; other examples from the foodstuffs sector in: H. König, *Entstehung u. Wirkungsweise von Fachverbänden der Nahrungs- und Genussmittelindustrie*, Berlin, 1966, pp. 38-40, 49, 80, 119, 141-2, 196ff., 255ff.; H.V. Beckerath, *Kräfte, Ziele u. Gestaltungen in der deutschen Industriewirtschaft*, Jena, 1922 p. 10. On prewar development see E. Maschke, *Grundzüge der deutschen Kartellgeschichte bis 1914*, Dortmund, 1964; J. Kocka, *Unternehmer in der deutschen Industrialisierung*, Göttingen, 1975, Chap. V.

86 As they were in C. Bresciani-Turroni, *The Economics of Inflation*, 1931, 2nd ed., London, 1953, p. 262.

87 See Feldman, *Army*, pp. 158, 228ff., 248, 417ff., 496ff., 504-5.

88 On some methods of disguise see R. Fuchs, 'Die Kriegsgewinne der verschiedenen Wirtschaftszweige in den einzelnen Staaten anhand statistischer Daten dargestellt', unpublished Ph.D. thesis, Zurich, 1918, pp. 45-61.

89 Information from Reich Statistical Office, put together by Grebler and Winkler, p. 106.

90 See the Table *ibid.*, p. 105, that was checked, corrected and extended on the original. Source: *Frankfurter Zeitung*, 12 October 1916 to 3 February 1917, at irregular intervals, a series of articles on 'Industry in War time'. On the selection see *ibid.*, 12 October 1916, p. 4: the aim was 'to select a given number of particularly typical enterprises. . . . We will usually examine about 20 enterprises from every branch of industry, which are of general interest because of their size or for other reasons'. The categories are base capital; depreciation and write-offs before profits; profits without forward balance; dividends, bonus etc; depreciation of earnings including rises.

91 See Table in Fuchs, pp. 47ff., 85ff. Other examples of wartime profits, see A. Günther, 'Die Folgen des Krieges für Einkommen und Lebenshaltung der mittleren Volksschichten Deutschlands' in R. Meerwarth *et al.*, *Einwirkungen*, pp. 140-1; W. Richter, *Gewerkschaften, Monopolkapital und Staat im Ersten Weltkrieg und in der Novemberrevolution (1914-119)*, Berlin, 1959, pp. 96-7; Schröter, pp.132-3; Feldman, *Army*, pp. 63, 469ff.; H. Jaeger, *Unternehmer in der deutschen Politik (1890-1918)*, Bonn, 1967, pp. 229-32. The number of millionaires in Prussia was, in 1914, 91; 1915, 83; 1916, 134 (Günther, pp. 469-70).

92 From Sperlich, *Arbeitslohn*, pp. 32-3.

93 See Grebler and Winkler, p. 66.

94 See Grebler and Winkler, p. 38; Umbreit and Lorenz, p. 112.

95 This and similar examples are in the unpublished report by the Army Ordnance Office of 1933: Zesch, pp. 41ff.

96 The Siemens director Dihlmann wrote in the annual report of the SSW-Zentral-Werksverwaltung for 1916/17: 'At this point mention must be made of the new movement started by the ordnance office for the standardisation of norms of machine fabrication, triggered by the fact that the grenades delivered by the various

firms differed from each other because they were built according to different gauges. Attempts at standardisation spread quickly and were taken over by the VDI [Verein Deutscher Ingenieure] after it became clear that the so-called "Fabo" (Kgl. Fabrikenbüro in Spandau) could not cope with the task alone since the necessary specifications rapidly involved other industries, so that today the "Normenausschuss für die deutsche Industrie" (NADI), affiliated to the VDI, is attempting to solve the whole problem in a uniform manner . . .'. Quoted in Frenzel, *Geschichte der Zentral-Werksverwaltung*, SAA 68/Li 83, p. 69

97 See W. Groener, *Lebenserinnerungen*, Göttingen, 1957, p. 354; Briefs, pp. 992, 994, 1013; A.v. Mendelssohn-Bartholdy, *The War and German Society*, New Haven, 1937, pp. 391-2.

98 See Grebler and Winkler, pp. 38, 42-7; M. Schwarte (ed.), *Der grosse Krieg 1914 bis 1918*, 8, Berlin, 1921, pp. 85, 385-6, 393-4; Goebel, pp. 65-9.

99 Müller's presentation however overlooks that this *function* of the War Associations need not necessarily have corresponded with the *intention* of its founders and of the State officials, and in most cases probably did not, being rather a side effect of organisational changes whose chief purpose was the most rational production and distribution for the War.

100 In Goebel, p.98.

101 See G.D. Feldman, *German Business Between War and Revolution*, Festschrift H. Rosenberg, p. 319; on trade mark changes: K. Roesler, *Die Finanzpolitik des Deutschen Reiches im Ersten Weltkrieg*, Berlin, 1967, pp. 108, 11, 116-17. On the influential example of planned horizontal concentration in the chemical industry, which was greatly strengthened by the War, see W. Treue, 'Carl Duisbergs Denkschrift von 1915 zur Gründung der "Kleinen I.G." ', *Tradition*, 8, 1963, pp. 193-228. On the question of vertical and horizontal concentration in the iron and steel industry: G.D. Feldman, *Iron and Steel Industry in the German Inflation 1916-1923*, Princeton, 1977; also *ibid.* and H. Homburg, *Industrie u. Inflation. Studien u. Dokumente zur Politik der deutschen Unternehmer 1916-1923*, Hamburg, 1977.

102 See above p. 27.

103 Calculated from Zimmermann, *Veränderungen*, p. 350-1. With an average 8 per cent decrease in the total industrial labour force – see above – a loss of 5 per cent in mining still meant a small *relative* gain.

104 See Hoffmann, pp. 68-9, 205, whose figures, in contrast to those used here for the War, do include those of firms with less than ten employees.

105 See the annual index figures for production and consumer goods industries in *Wagenführ*, pp. 58-9; the long-term loss of mass spending power that took place is made clear when one considers that average workers' wages in Germany only regained the 1913 level in 1928, whereas in the USA in the same year they were nearly a third above the 1913 level. On the great economic, social and political significance of heavy industry in the Weimar Republic see H. Mommsen *et al.* (eds.), *Industrielles System und politische Entwicklung in der Weimarer Republik*, Düsseldorf, 1974, especially the essays by Feldman, Maier, Mommsen, Nocken, Petzina/Abelshauser and Weisbrod.

106 See Umbreit and Lorenz, pp. 64-5; Kuczynski, *Geschichte*, 4, pp. 391-2.

107 See Grebler and Winkler, p. 57. In the cotton industry in 1918 only seventy firms were graded as 'high efficiency units' (Höchstleistungsbetriebe) by the government, from a prewar total of 1700 spinning and weaving factories. In the glass and shoe industries ca. 50 per cent of the factories were closed. In 1913 there had been 3,786 breweries, in 1917 there were 2,192 and in 1918, 1,833. At the end of 1916 only 100 out of 668 soap factories were still in existence. See the calculations of former Oberbürgermeister Peppel on the 'Durchführung von Zusammenlegungen während des Krieges 1914-1918', 1937; National Archives Microcopy, T77, roll

343, no. 80728–80981, for the best review of the closures of 1917 to 1918 without, however, accurate statistical information. I am indebted to G.D. Feldman, Berkeley, for access to this source.

The work of SAZ, which was weakened by internal conflicts, from December 1916 to November 1917, appears to have brought about fewer closures than did the shortages of materials, workers and of actual contracts. At the end of 1917 its tasks were taken over in a very reduced form by the RWA.

108 Wagenführ, p. 23.
109 Goebel, p. 95. G. worked in the Kriegsamt as scientific expert on closures. Peppel stresses the powerlessness of the authorities, pp. 42ff., 60. The Ka. office in Düsseldorf wrote to the central Ka., 'that they did not have the means to close down firms, [that] the continuation of work could only be prevented by stopping the supply of coal and the withdrawal of labour, whereby the continuation of some plants could [still] not be avoided because they supplied themselves with coal directly in lorries loaded from the mines'. The closure measures lacked a clear and adequate legal basis (*ibid.*, pp. 8, 29-30); they were countered by the federalist structure of the Reich, the mistrust of parliamentary groups in the Reichstag and the lack of unity in the administration.
110 *Ibid.*, p. 119; on compensation, see n. 116 below.
111 The proportion of proprietors and self-employed in industry and craft declined from 36.6 per cent in 1882 to 25.7 per cent in 1895, 18.2 per cent in 1907 and 15.1 per cent in 1925. See *StdDtR*, 466, p. 194.
112 Peppel shows this in individual cases.
113 Table from Sperlich, *Arbeitslohn*, p. 32; in 1914, 119 new joint-stock companies were founded; in 1915, 58; in 1916, 89; in 1917, 111 and in 1918, 168.
114 Wagenführ (p. 23) includes them with the intermediate group, Bry (p. 193) with the peace industries.
115 See the tables in Sperlich, p. 35, who only includes joint-stock companies with more than 100,000M share capital in his calculations.
116 According to official internal reckoning, reproduced by Peppel, pp. 146-7, the average compensation paid per enterprise and year amounted to:
  in cotton (spinning), 35,000M
  in cotton (weaving), 24,000M
  in the cloth industry, 40-50,000M
  in worsted spinning, 200,000M (ranging from 36-700,000M)
  in the roofing-felt industry, 2,000M
  in the jute industry, 90-100,000M
  in the rubber industry, 120,000M
In 1917 and 1918 together ca. half a billion marks was paid out in compensation. On the compromise cooperative price policy of the authorities in this connection: *ibid.*, pp. 134-5. Not all firms closing down were compensated, only those who had previously joined suppliers' (or similar) organisations (*ibid*, pp. 124-5). See *ibid.*, p. 121: The Ka.d.Dt.Ind. ordered in 1917 that managers of the shut-down firms should be retained for the necessary maintenance of the plant. The actual practice is unclear. The Fourth AK (Magdeburg) spoke out in July 1918 concerning the widespread annoyance of the population about the constantly rising prices of consumer goods and at the same time against the generous price policy towards partly-closed industries (MB, 3 August 1918, p. 10).
117 As the Seventeenth AK (Danzig) in MB, 3 October 1918, p. 26.
118 See Wagenführ, p. 23, according to whose estimates the production of luxury goods fell from 100 (1913) to 92 (1914) to 88 (1915) to 84 (1916) to 67 (1917) and to 63 (1918). Figures for the total average: 100, 83, 67, 64, 62, 57.
119 See MB, 3 September 1918, p. 35 (Württemberger KM): the Fourth AK (Danzig)

was very similar, MB, 3 August 1918, p. 10.

120 See Zimmermann, *Veränderungen*, pp. 420–5.

121 MB, 3 August 1918, p. 12.

122 Thus the Eighteenth AK (Frankfurt) in MB, 3 February 1918, p. 17, on conditions in the summer of 1917.

123 Schwarz comes to a similar conclusion for Nuremberg, p. 188 and pp. 187-90 for telling examples of the luxurious life led by the rich during the War.

124 On this generally see T.R. Gurr, *Why Men Rebel*, Princeton, N.J., 1970, pp. 73ff., 59: '... the fewer the other satisfactions we have to fall back on, the greater is our discontent'.

125 Thus the Ninth AK (Altona) in MB, 15 April 1916, p. 10.

126 Thus AK Allenstein in MB, 3 March 1917, pp. 9-10.

127 Secret monthly 'Summaries of the Regional Command reports on the mood of the civil population' were used by the Prussian KM until October 1916. They were hectographed to begin with, printed from September 1916 onwards. The Ka. later distributed an edited version ('Summaries of the monthly reports of the Regional Command' (MB)) from 15 April 1916 to 3 October 1918; in these, extracts from the previous month's reports of the separate AKs were quoted and very briefly summarised. For example, 224 were sent out in August 1917. At first these summaries were made according to the Regional Command, later according to subject. The problems of food supply and distribution were dominant – especially in the first year. The selection of material by the KM or Ka., as well as its treatment at the AK, was no doubt influenced by the attitudes and prejudices of the writers or their superiors. An attempt was made to take this into account as far as possible when using the reports, without always expressly pointing this out. But the continuous and secret character of the MB, their evident effort to present their superiors with a realistic picture of the mood of the population as well as the fact – in contrast with most police reports – that they did not concentrate only or even primarily on phenomena that the authorities would wish to see suppressed, speaks for the value of this source of evidence. On the Regional Command and their powerful military commanders-in-chief generally: W. Deist (ed.), *Militär u. Innenpolitik*, Düsseldorf, 1970, pp. xlff. (Introduction); an enumeration of the twenty-one AKs in E.R. Huber, *Deutsche Verfassungsgeschichte seit 1789*, 4, Stuttgart, 1969, pp. 524–5.

128 See MB, 17 January 1917, pp. 7–8; similarly MB, 15 April 1916, p. 1; 22 May 1916, pp. 6–7, 8, 9; 14 June 1916, p. 1; 3 February 1917, p. 9; 3 March 1917, p. 19; 3 September 1918, pp. 28–9, 35, *passim*.

129 For example, see MB, 17 January 1917, p. 8 (Seventh AK, Münster).

130 This is the central thesis of J.C. Davies, 'Toward a Theory of Revolution', *American Sociological Review*, 27, 1962, pp. 5–19.

131 See, for the general connection between mobility and class tension: Coser, *Functions*, pp. 35ff.; on the general encouragement of mobility in war: S. Andreski, *Military Organisation and Society*, 2nd ed., Berkeley, 1968, pp. 134–5. See also, for embitterment over the rise of War profiteers, the report of the Berlin President of Police of 29 October 1918, partially quoted in Kuczynski, *Geschichte*, 4, pp. 355ff.; Mendelssohn-Bartholdy, p. 28. W. Schmidt, 'Das deutsche Handwerk im Weltkriege', unpublished Ph.D. thesis, Erlangen, 1927, Essen, 1929, pp. 56–7, writes of the rapid ascent of small craftsmen who profited from armaments contracts.

132 On the origins, aspects and functions of this, see O. Baumgarten, 'Der sittliche Zustand des deutschen Volkes unter dem Einfluss des Krieges', in *ibid. et al., Geistige und sittliche Wirkungen des Krieges in Deutschland*, Stuttgart, 1927, pp. 18, 44, *passim*; H. Lübbe, *Politische Philosophie in Deutschland*, Stuttgart, 1963, pp.

191ff; K. Schwabe, *Wissenschaft und Kriegsmoral*, Göttingen, 1969, pp. 34–44. On its preparation through the Press: K. Koszyk, *Pressepolitik im Ersten Weltkrieg*, Düsseldorf, 1968, pp. 84ff. See also: W. Gutsche (ed.), *Herrschaftsmethoden des deutschen Imperialismus 1897–98 bis 1917*. *Dokumente zur innen- und aussenpolitischen Strategie und Taktik der herrschenden Klassen des Deutschen Reiches*, Berlin, 1977; G. Schramm, 'Militarisierung und Demokratisierung. Typen der Massenintegration im Ersten Weltkrieg', *Francia*, 3, 1975, pp. 476–97.

133 It implied not only an abstention from all forms of class conflict between employers and workers but also brought about a temporary reduction in antisemitism (*ibid.*, p. 115 and W.E. Mosse (ed.), *Deutsches Judentum im Krieg u. Revolution 1916–1923*, Tübingen, 1971, pp. 411, 417, 513-4) and the end of disputes between employees' associations (*Archiv*, 41, 1916, pp. 591–2); it was probably also connected with the decline in the crime rate. See M. Liepmann, *Krieg u. Kriminalität in Deutschland*, Stuttgart, 1930, pp. 134, 156.

134 Amongst the numerous descriptions of the experiences of August 1914, see K.A. v. Müller, *Mars u. Venus, Erinnerungen 1914-1919*, Stuttgart, 1954, pp.12ff.; E. David, *Das Kriegstagebuch des Reichstagsabgeordneten . . .*; S. Miller (ed.), Düsseldorf, 1966, pp. 12ff., 48–9; P. Scheidemann, *Memoiren eines Sozialdemokraten*, 1, Dresden, 1928, pp. 259–60, 300, 307-8, 353.

135 See the summary in Grebing, pp. 139–47, in which the decision of 4 August is recognised as the continuation of the limited national integration of the labour movement before 1914. For the retrospective judgement of SPD policy in August 1914 by a member of Spartakus, see Retzlaw, p. 32; also, G. Schramm, 1914: Sozialdemokraten am Scheideweg', in C. Stern, H.A. Winkler (eds.), *Wendepunkte deutscher Geschichte 1848-1945*, Frankfurt, 1979, pp. 63–86.

136 See Schwabe, *Wissenschaft*, p. 41.

137 This is how *DAZ*, 13, 9 August 1914, interpreted the Burgfrieden ('the barriers have fallen'). Similarly, *ibid.* 15, 6 February 1916.

138 See Koszyk, p. 146, on a statement by the OHL on 26 November 1916.

139 See, for instance, MB, 15 April 1916, p. 18: the Regional Command in Kassel reported that it was very difficult to form a judgement on public opinion and mood, because censorship had a strong influence on statements of opinion and meetings were forbidden because of preserving the Burgfrieden.

140 See also K. Graf v. Westarp, *Konservative Politik im letzten Jahrzehnt des Kaiserreiches 2*, Berlin, 1935, pp. 23ff., which interpreted all attempts at 'Neuorientierung' as an offence against Burgfrieden. On censorship, see H.D. Fischer (ed.), *Pressekonzentration und Zensurpraxis im Ersten Weltkrieg*, Berlin, 1973; Deist, *Militär*, Chap. II (Sources) and Introduction, pp. xxxiff., liff.; Scheidemann, *Memoiren 1*, pp. 321, 326, 352, on the embittering effect of the state of siege and censorship in the SPD.

141 See Baumgarten, pp. 10–11. On 3 September 1918 the High Command in Marken issued an order forbidding the spreading of rumours. See Deist, *Militär*, pp. 1259ff.

142 See Baumgarten, *Der sittliche Zustand*, pp. 10–11. See Helfferich, 2, p. 156: the middle-class parties attempted to prevent the introduction of new taxes which would also have applied to war profits by an appeal to the necessity of the Burgfrieden. For a similar use of the concept of the Burgfrieden by the right-wing Vaterlandspartei, see K. Wortmann, *Geschichte der Deutschen Vaterlandspartei 1917-1918*, Halle, 1926, pp. 41, 70; Herzfeld, *Weltkrieg*, pp. 148–9.

143 See Dahrendorf, *Class*, pp. 223–31.

144 C. Haussmann's remark that 'a democratic species grew up in the War' must be regarded in this sense (*Schlaglichter*, Frankfurt, 1924, p. 154).

145 MB, 3 July 1917, pp. 17–18.

146 Groener, p. 360. He continued: 'It is hopeless and useless to strive against this

wave, but one needs to steer the waves in the right direction.' Groener, also, on 22 July 1917, quoted in Deist, *Militär*, p. 991: a similar picture, by Oberstleutnant Bauer in April 1918, *ibid.*, p. 1215.

147 *Kriegstagebuch*, p. 22 (11 August 1918).

148 Friederich Meinecke, 'Die deutschen Erhebungen von 1813, 1848, 1870 u. 1914' in *idem., Die deutsche Erhebung von 1914*, Stuttgart, 1914, p. 29.

149 SPD and union leaders in their dual-faced role between government and the masses directed their argument in their talks with the bureaucracy and the military to the purpose of preserving and enlarging their own power. For example: Cohen (Reuss) to Wahnschaffe, on 2 October 1914 (Memo, quoted in part in Kuczynski, *Geschichte*, 4, pp. 246–7).

150 *Kriegstagebuch*, pp. 30, 33 (1 and 3 September 1914); on p. 104 (8 February 1915) David noted with satisfaction that he had seen the first Social Democratic [military] lieutenant in a meeting of comrades; he continued: 'What the World War has managed to accomplish!'

151 His article 'Zeit zur Tat' from *Vorwärts* of 19 March 1917, reproduced in P. Scheidemann, *Der Zusammenbruch*, Berlin, 1921, p. 41.

152 See Ledebours' demand for women's voting rights in connection with the evidence for the achievements and sacrifices of working-class women in the War in *Prot. ü. d. Verhandlungen des Gründungs – Parteitags der USPD vom 6. bis 8. April 1917 in Gotha*. E. Eichhorn (ed.), Berlin, 1921, p. 80. This argument was ultimately too revisionist to be central to the radical rhetoric of the USPD.

153 See M. Weber, 'Wahlrecht u. Demokratie in Deutschland (1917)' in *idem, Gesammelte Politische Schriften*, Tübingen (2nd ed.) 1958 (3rd ed.) 1971, pp. 233–79, esp. p. 235; F. Meinecke, *Strassburg, Freiburg, Berlin 1901–1919. Erinnerungen*, Stuttgart, 1949, pp. 220, 223–4, 246–7.

154 See L. Stern (ed.), *Die Auswirkungen der Grossen Sozialistischen Oktoberrevolution in Deutschland*, Berlin, 1959, pp. 594-5; *ibid.*, pp. 571–2, for a similar attitude held by the State Secretary, Delbrück; K. Riezler, *Tagebücher, Aufsätze, Dokumente*, K.D. Erdmann (ed.), Göttingen, 1972, p. 64 (Erdmann's Introduction) on a similar attitude from the Chancellor's advisor Riezler; see also Westarp, p. 274, on the use of this type of argument by Ebert in April 1916 and Bethmann in July 1917.

155 See, for instance, the mistaken assessment of the situation by Oberstleutnant Bauer on 25 March 1918 in Deist, *Militär*, p. 1208; Bauer thought that the Social Democratic MPs were more radical and fanatical than 'our German working class who, as a mass, thought in nationalistic terms and who would not take part in a large-scale strike'.

156 See, for instance, the leading article in *DAZ*, 13, 25 October 1914. Other newspapers, for example *Vorwärts*, had given prominence to the 'alleged connection between war and voting rights or, more precisely, between the general obligation for military service and the general right to vote'. This will be rejected. 'Because times are hard, one is not concerned with rights but only with duties.'

157 See Westarp, pp. 232-3, with criticism of Bethmann's contrary conclusion.

158 See, for example, Hugenberg before the Ka.d.Dt.Ind in November 1917, Kapps' memo of May 1916, the remarks of the Alldeutschen Hopfen in January 1916 and those of the Prussian KM in March 1916 in Stegmann, *Erben*, pp. 455, 487, 490–1, 503. See also the observation by the SPD MP Heine on 1 May 1917: 'The Conservatives themselves know that annexation is impossible. They are only stirring things up for internal political reasons'. (From E. Matthias and E. Pikart (eds.), *Die Reichstagsfraktion der deutschen Sozialdemokratie 1898 bis 1918*, Düsseldorf, 1966, p. 255); see also Feldman, *Army*, pp. 135–6, 429ff.

159 See Retzlaw, pp. 56-7; K. Liebknecht, *Politische Aufzeichnungen aus seinem Nachlass*, Berlin, 1921, p. 10; see further R. Luxemburg, 'Zwei Osterbotschaften',

Spartakus, 5 May 1917, repr. in Inst. f. Marxismus- Leninismus b. Zk d. SED (ed.), *Spartakusbriefe*, Berlin, 1958, pp. 347ff.; 'Eine tragische Posse', *Spartakus*, 6 August 1917, *ibid.*, pp. 367–75; 'Zur Aufhebung des §153 der Gewerbeordnung', *Spartakus*, 9 June 1918, *ibid.*, p. 435.

160 On the appointment of Jules Guesde as Minister without Portfolio in Vivani's government, see Schulthess, *Europ. Geschichtskalender*, NF. 30, 1914, p. 687; on the visit of officials to Berlin trade union offices, initiated by Südekum: David, *Kriegstagebuch*, p. 67; T. Cassau, *Die Gewerkschaftsbewegung*, 2nd ed., Halberstadt, 1925, pp. 40–1, 44. At the outbreak of war the German trade unions did not receive 'the degree of respect, recognition and possibilities for cooperation that had been taken for granted by trade unions in England long before the War'.

161 See the extracts from the memo by Vice-Admiral Kraft, Director of Dockyards of the Reichsmarineamt, on the 'new orientation in labour policy', February 1917, in Deist, *Militär*, pp. 557–63; also the report of Umbreit, the former editor of *Vorwärts*, in Umbreit and Lorenz, pp. 145–92; Varain, pp. 73–9.

162 On this, also the limits of this process, see Feldman, *German Business*, pp. 322ff.; on the War Committee for the Metal Industry of Greater Berlin, which later served as a model: *idem.*, *Army*, pp. 76ff. Existing wage agreements frequently tended to work to the employees' disadvantage because of wartime price rises and they also prevented more frequent wage movements. See Preller, p. 15.

163 See above, pp. 71ff., 160–1..

164 See Huber, *Verfassungsgeschichte*, 4, p. 1141 (to §153); Preller, pp. 24, 50; Feldman, *Army*, pp. 473ff.

165 On this, see Conservative criticism in Westarp, pp. 222–7, which clearly shows how much the Conservatives experienced the government's action as a defeat for themselves and a victory for the trade unions; Inst. f. Marxismus-Leninismus b. ZK d.SED (ed), *Dokumente und Materialien zur Geschichte d.dt. Arbeiterbewegung*, 1, Berlin, 1958, pp. 258–9; Feldman, *Army*, pp. 121–2.

166 The best account of social policy during the War is in Preller, pp. 34–85.

167 On wartime taxation policy see Roesler; Sperlich, *Arbeitslohn*, pp. 38ff.

168 In more detail above, pp. 126ff.

169 See L. Bergsträsser, *Die preussische Wahlrechtsfrage im Kriege und die Entstehung der Osterbotschaft 1917*, Tübingen, 1924; R. Patemann, *Der Kampf um die preussische Wahlrechtsreform im Ersten Weltkrieg*, Düsseldorf, 1964.

170 See, for example, Ay, pp. 131ff. The Twentieth AK reported from Elbing in March 1917 that attempts had been made to prevent meetings in support of the 6th War Bonds, see MB, 3 April 1917, p. 6. The report continued: 'There are ever clearer signs that the influence of moderate workers' leaders is, as they themselves agree, on the wane . . .'.

171 See the police report of 15 September 1914 in Kuczynski, *Geschichte*, 4, p. 249, on the effects of the 'Kriegsstosses' on workers and Mittelstand.

172 See Mendelssohn-Bartholdy, p. 32; Schwarz, p. 156; on the importance of economic factors in collective discontent and protest in the twentieth century, see Gurr, pp. 66ff.

173 See, for instance, MB, 23 August 1916, p. 2; 3 September 1917, p. 3. By the autumn of 1918 this no longer applied; see MB, 3 October 1918, pp. 3–4.

174 This social configuration is quite clear in similar disturbances in Mainz and Wiesbaden in the spring of 1917; see MB, 3 May, 1917, p. 13; also Schwarz, p. 167, on the relative economic satisfaction of Nuremberg armaments workers; Kuczynski, *Geschichte*, 4 pp. 252ff.; Deist, *Militär*, pp. 248–9, 294ff., 387, 402–3, 405, 420, 425.

175 MB, 3 August 1917, p. 6; U. Daniel, 'Funktionalisierung von Frauen und Familien in der Kriegswirtschaft — Tendenzen und Gegentendenzen', Ms., Bielefeld, 1983.

176 See Preller, pp. 43–4; Kuczynski, *Geschichte* 4, pp. 378ff.; Deist, *Militär*, p. 695.
177 The best on this is Skalweit; also summary in Kielmansegg, pp. 177–82.
178 See Matthias and Pikart, *Reichstagsfraktion*, pp. 160–1, (14 March 1916).
179 See *ibid.*, pp. 197–8; MB, 14 June 1916, p. 14.
180 See Retzlaw, pp. 55–5, 60; MB, 3 March 1917, pp. 7, 9; *idem.*, 3 April 1917, pp. 7, 12, *pass.*: The dominance of economic motives in the growing discontent of the working class is stressed throughout, the 'people's morale has had to undergo the greatest test, in economic respects, with which it has been faced since the outbreak of the War' (thus the Regional Command in Strasburg, February 1917); *idem.*, 3 May 1917, pp. 9–17 and Deist, *Militär*, pp. 724–34 on the strike movement and its motives and causes; MB, 3 May 1917, for the text of a handbill – one of many – that was found inside an abbattoir in Buer. 'Comrades! I. Red United Comrades! With this letter I attest that you should not come to work tomorrow; let the damned fat-bellies give us more bread, so go on strike. II. Comrades! Do not work if we do not get 1½ lbs of bread. III. Also do no work if we do not get 15M per shift. – Start the strike on Saturday; we cannot work on turnips. All remain at home and do not work. Youths, do no work either.'
181. MB, 3 August 1917, p. 5.
182 MB, 3 February 1918, p. 13; in contrast the food situation was generally satisfactory, other AKs at this time expressing themselves less pointedly, although. in a similar vein. In September 1918 Friedrich Ebert commented 'that our people are more or less dressed in rags'. See E. Matthias and R. Morsey (eds.), *Der Interfraktionelle Ausschuss 1917/18*, Düsseldorf, 1959, II, p. 522.
183 Reported by the Regional Commands (specifically, from Frankfurt, in MB, 3 Feb 1917, p. 4) who, as Conservative observers, were otherwise inclined to reduce the many-layered discontents of the masses to the directly economic. See also Deist, *Militär*, pp. 1157ff.; Kuczynski, *Geschichte*, 4, pp. 284ff.
184 The MB of 3 June 1918 did not envisage any food problems, neither then nor in the immediate future; by July this had very clearly changed, see MB, 3 July 1918, e.g. pp. 3, 4: above all bread, potatoes and fruit were lacking. The MB of 3 September 1918 (esp. pp. 18–26, 31ff.) and 3 October 1918 (pp. 14ff.) do not report a worsening in this area, but stress the lack of clothing and housing and the beginning of a renewed shortage of coal.
185 High morale existed among the middle classes, not among the workers, wrote H. Delbrück in 1916 (see Schwabe, *Wissenschaft*, p. 129). Baumgarten estimates that the solidarity and readiness to go to war generated by the experiences of August 1914 lasted for eighteen months (*Wirkungen*, pp. 44–5). In Munich, according to Ay (p. 50) the first anti-war leaflet campaign of any size took place at Christmas 1915. The AK in Altona reported a generally good mood in March 1916, only in 'the poorer sections of the population' were 'faint-heartedness and war-weariness visible'.
186 See Retzlaw, pp. 36–7; Kuczynski, *Geschichte*, 4, pp. 260, 263–4.
187 MB, 3 October 1916, p. 3.
188 MB, 17 January 1917, pp. 4, 5.
189 MB, 3 June 1917, p. 22.
190 This observation recurs throughout the MB. See, for example, 3 October 1916 (p. 5), 3 November 1917 (p. 24), 3 September 1918 (p. 5); Retzlaw, p. 59.
191 See MB, 3 March 1917 (pp. 3ff), 3 November 1917 (p. 42), 3 April 1918 (p. 3): 'A sigh of relief went through the whole country when a powerful offensive was mounted in the West shortly before Easter . . .'. With the success of this offensive, however, the emotions it had generated no longer had a hold: see MB, 3 July 1918, pp. 3ff. It is well known that leading representatives of the SPD were not averse to moderate annexationist aims. See P. Lensch, *Der Arbeiter u. die deutschen Kolonien*,

Berlin, 1917; A. Ascher; '"Radical" Imperialists within German Social Democracy, 1912–1918', *Political Science Quarterly*, 76, 1961, pp. 555–75; Varain, pp. 98, 100–1; Grebing, pp. 147–8. Workers also were in no way immune to such tendencies, see MB, 3 June 1917, p. 26: the Münster AK reported a meeting of the Christian Metal Workers' Association in Düsseldorf on 13 May 1917, in which its voice was against a Scheidemann and for a Hindenburg peace; Stegmann, *Zwischen Repression*, pp. 381–4, on the limited success of the 'Freier Ausschuss für einen Deutschen Arbeiterfrieden' ('German Workers' Free Peace Committee with allegedly 65,000 members in 1917, 290,000 in January 1918), on the limited popular support for the DAAP, *ibid.*, pp. 392ff., 401.

192 In this he was also referring to other, previous difficulties over agitation.

193 Retzlaw, p. 65. This does not accord with L. Ay's opinion that influences on and changes in mood according to the progress of the War cannot be clearly established; see his 'Volksstimmung u. Volksmeinung als Voraussetzung der Münchener Revolution von 1918' in K. Bosl (ed.), *Bayern im Umbruch*, Munich, 1969, pp. 345–86, esp. 379.

194 According to the Ka. (MB, 3 July 1918, p. 3), which took stock with regard to the supposedly discouraging speech by Kühlmann on 23 June 1915.

195 See E. Kolb, *Die Arbeiterräte in der deutschen Innenpolitik 1918/1919*, Düsseldorf, 1962, pp. 15ff., with further evidence and a short description of the military and political events of September and October 1918. The report of the Stettin AK at the end of August (MB, 3 September 1918) states that morale had declined significantly in the previous six to eight weeks; in confirmation: *ibid.*, p. 3.

196 MB, 3 October 1918, p. 9.

197 In the joint session of the parliamentary SPD group in the Reichstag and the Party Committee on 23 September 1918 from: Matthias and Pikart, *Reichstagsfraktion*, 2, pp. 433–4.

198 Thus in MB, 3 September 1918 (pp. 4, 5), 3 October 1918 (pp. 3–4).

199 This is often underrated, as in Kolb (*Arbeiterräte*, pp. 15–24), and so the connection between hunger protests and peace movements on the one hand and the Revolution on the other is not sufficiently elaborated.

200 See MB, 14 June 1916, pp. 9, 16, 25, 26, 31ff.

201 See MB, 3 June 1918, p. 13 (AK Hanover): 'News about the distribution of dividends in large enterprises, particularly the armaments factories, [when] reported in the newspaper constantly arouses bad feeling'. Similarly, MB, 3 August 1918 (pp. 9. 12), 3 September 1918 (p. 3), 3 October 1918 (pp. 25–6) on the hatred of the trades people for the middlemen and their profits.

202 The MB repeatedly treated this subject as a major threat to the mood of the masses. See, for example, MB, 31 March 1917, p. 16 (AK Allenstein): 'The degree to which some people are enabled in present circumstances to better provide for themselves by illegal means, has led to greater agitation among the population in the economic field than the actual food shortages.' (See also Schwarz, pp. 158–9.

203 As AK Koblenz in MB, 3 October 1918, p. 28.

204. See n. 61 above.

205 See n. 59 above.

206 See MB, 3 October 1918, pp. 26–7 (AK Danzig), p. 18 (AK Karlsruhe).

207 MB, 3 April 1917, pp. 9–10.

208 MB, 3 August 1918, p. 10.

209 See Retzlaw, p. 51, on rumours in wartime, also: Ay, pp. 178ff.; S. Freud, *Zeitgemässes über Krieg u. Tod*, 1915, in *idem, Das Unbewusste. Schriften zur Psychoanalyse*, Frankfurt, 1960, pp. 187–213, 192; n. 141 above.

210 See Baumgarten, p. 46.

211 Thus MB, 3 August 1917, p. 11 (AK Karlsruhe on the mood of the rural population,

which was also directed against the large wages and salaries to be earned in the War industries).

212 Thus, the Stettin AK in October 1917 (MB, 3 November 1917, p. 20). See above for the spread of these ideas among the Social-Democratic sector of the working class towards the end of the War. On Spartakus: *Spartakusbriefe*, e.g., pp. 13ff (K. Liebknecht on the ideas of the right-wing Social Democrat E. David on 16 August 1916); *DIEW*, 2, pp. 413ff.

213 On the very limited degree of influence that Spartakus itself exerted on the Berlin working class, see the very valuable autobiography by Retzlaw, esp. pp. 45, 58, 64–5, 99; Kolb, *Arbeiterräte*, pp. 46–55, esp. p. 49.

214 In Ay, *Enstehung*, pp. 50, 54 and Baumgarten, p. 83; see also Schwarz p. 190.

215 Retzlaw, p. 51.

216 See n. 191 above; also Stegmann, *Erben*, p. 465, on the participation of 'yellow' workers' organisations in the annexationist 'Unabhängiger Ausschuss für einen Deutschen Frieden'; *ibid.*, pp. 509–10, esp. ns. 407, 410. On 1 September 1918 the Vaterlandspartei had 800,000 individual members (over 1 million if affiliated societies are included) which were organised into 2,536 local groups. On German war aims see: F. Fischer, *Griff nach der Weltmacht*, 3rd ed., Düsseldorf, 1964; W. J. Mommsen, 'Die Regierung Bethmann Hollweg und die Öffentliche Meinung 1914 bis 1917; *VfZ*, 17, 1969, pp. 117ff.

217 See Stegmann, *Erben*, p. 510; and Stresemann, 15 October 1917, on the financing of the Democratic pacifist line through left Liberal banking circles in D. Grosser, *Vom monarchischen Konstitutionalismus zur parlamentarischen Demokratie*, The Hague, 1970, p. 200, n. 332.

218 The associations are listed in Stegmann, pp. 506ff.; to these belonged, amongst others, the BdI, the CVDI, the Reichsdeutsche Mittelstands-Verband, the BdL, the Alldeutsche Verband, the 'Freie Ausschuss für einen Deutschen Arbeiter-frieden' and the 'Hauptausschuss nationaler Arbeiter- und Berufsverbände'.

219 The 'Ausschuss des deutschen (christlich-nationalen) Arbeiterkongresses', the 'Generalkommission der Gewerkschaften Deutschlands', the 'Interessen-gemeinschaft deutscher Reichs- und Staatsbeamtenverbände', the 'Soziale Arbeitsgemeinschaft der unteren Beamten im Reichs-, Staats- und Kommunal-dienst', the 'Verband der deutschen Gewerkvereine (H.-D.)', the 'Verband deutscher Handlungsgehilfen' and the 'Verein der deutschen Kaufleute'; see: *Um Freiheit und Vaterland. Erste Veröffentlichung des Volksbundes für Freiheit und Vaterland*, Gotha, 1918, p. 45; see also Varain, p. 102; Stegmann, *Erben*, pp. 510–11; *idem, Zwischen Repression*, p. 389.

220 See Stegmann, *Erben*, pp. 496ff; *Um Freiheit und Vaterland* (see n. 219 above), pp. 44–5; see also Meinecke, *Strassburg*, p. 235. It is well known that the dividing line between annexationist and non-annexationist was not absolutely identical with that between opponents and supporters of internal reform, that there also existed 'liberal imperialists' (G. Stresemann, for example) who linked their foreign policy annexation plans with demands for internal reforms; but they probably formed a minority among the annexationists.

221 See n. 158 above, with evidence on social-imperialist lines of thought; conversely, Matthias and Pikart, *Reichstagsfraktion*, p. 255, on the internal political purpose of SPD demands for a negotiated peace. That the connection could go the other way with internal political reforms being sought primarily as the means for foreign policy aims can be seen in Stresemann and Max Weber.

222 See Ay, p. 131–2.

223 Quoted in Kuczynski, *Geschichte*, 4, p. 258; see also *ibid.*, pp. 269ff.; Ay, pp. 26–7, 31–6, 64, 156ff., 185ff.

224 See information from the Spartakus group on 12 August 1916 on demonstrations

and strikes against the sentencing of Karl Liebknecht, in *Dokumente und Materialien*, pp. 432–41.
225 Schwarz (p. 168) identifies this politicisation as only from the beginning of 1918 in Nuremburg.
226 MB, 2 April 1917, p. 4; see also Scheidemann's talk with Wahnschaffe on 14 April 1917, in Scheidemann, *Memoiren*, 1, p. 400.
227 See the 'demands of Leipzig workers of 16 April 1917' and a report on the April strike by the Berlin police in *Dokumente und Materialien*, 1, pp. 612–13; n. 180 above; H. Scheel, 'Der Aprilstreik in Berlin' in *Revolutionäre Ereignisse u. Probleme in Deutschland während der Periode der Grossen Sozialistischen Oktoberrevolution 1917/18*, Berlin, 1957, pp. 1–88.
228 See the Free Trade Unions' analysis of strikes, which was censored at the time, in Varain, p. 105; also A. Rosenberg, *Enstehung der Weimarer Republik*, Frankfurt, 1961, pp. 183–9. Rosenberg points out (p. 182) that the aims of the strike movement at the beginning of 1918 largely corresponded with those of the strike in Leipzig in April 1917. See MB, 3 February 1918, p. 4, where the Koblenz AK wrote: 'Nowadays the mood is dominated not by economic but almost entirely by political factors'; *idem.*, p. 5, where the Magdeburg AK stressed the influence of 'Russian democratising propaganda and the voting rights discussion'; *idem*, pp. 6–7, where the Württemberg KM refers to the 'propaganda speeches' by Wilson and Lloyd George. See W. Boldt, 'Der Januarstreik in Bayern mit bes. Berücksichtigung Nürnbergs', *Jb. f. Fränkische Landesforschung*, 25, 1965, pp. 5–42; W. Bartel, 'Der Januarstreik in Berlin', in *Revolutionäre Ereignisse*, pp. 141–83.
229 MB, 3 June 1918, pp. 4, 5; 3 July 1918, pp. 4–5.
230 MB, 3 July 1918, p. 6; Roesler, pp. 112ff.
231 See MB, 3 October 1918, p. 7: the Dresden AK reported that 'three questions dominate the situation: the food situation, parliamentarisation and the question of peace'.
232 See MB, 3 August 1918, p. 13: The Police President of Berlin is reported as regarding the results up until then of the voting rights Bill as a contributory factor in the 'quite considerable discontent' among the working class in July; MB, 3 October 1918, p. 8: the Kassel AK reported that political questions at home – voting rights, the Chancellory crisis and the conditions for the SPD's entry into the government – are the causes of agitation among the population. See also Kolb, *Arbeiterräte*, pp. 21ff.
233 MB, 3 October 1918, p. 7.
234 *Ibid.*, p. 8.
235 Thus the Ka. office in Leipzig in Kuczynski, *Geschichte*, 4, p. 277.
236 It was just such a transposition which appears to have taken place on a large scale during the last months of the War. See the Koblenz AK report, n. 234 above; also Stresemann to Bassermann on 9 April 1917, with the demand 'that thoughts which are now entirely directed towards food must be diverted by a political act' (Matthias and Morsey, *Der Interfraktionelle Ausschuss*, 1, pp. xix–xx); such a suggestion can only be made if one is convinced of the possibility of making such partial substitutions of the causes of tension and discontent. This is also applicable to Groener who pleaded, after the April strike of 1917, for feeding the masses with votes rather than with non-existent meat and bread. See Feldman, *Army*, p. 319.
237 Such a connection is claimed (on little evidence) for Nuremberg. See Schwarz, pp. 167–72.
238 See the research by Tormin; Kolb; v. Oertzen; ns. 248, 249 below.
239 Certainly the fact the war workers were better able to afford strikes and protests than industrial workers in the peace industries, with their minimum wages, will

have had some influence. This phenomenon possibly also points to the fact that economic need as such was not the primary driving force behind the readiness to protest and the discontent that we are investigating here. One can perhaps assume that resignation and apathy were more likely responses in cases of extreme deprivation, rather than readiness for energetic protest. It seems to me unlikely that the protest of well-paid skilled workers can be interpreted as a form of status protest against the growing erosion of their economic and social advantages over other workers.

240 Feldman, Kolb and Rürup, p. 88, speak of the resentment of poorer workers against better-paid munitions workers; this may have existed. In the sources used here, this is only recorded as the resentment of agricultural against industrial workers. If the preferential treatment through special allowances for separate categories of heavy work was regarded as unfair by other workers – as occurred more frequently in 1916-17, according to the MB – then the resulting discontent was directed, as far as can be seen, against the centre of distribution or the authorising authority rather than against better-off colleagues (or at least, not openly)! It appears to me to be totally exaggerated to talk of a 'dissolution of the working class as a class' into two 'clearly distinct and diverging levels of armament and non-armament worker', as Schwarz (p. 174) does for Nuremberg, without sufficient evidence, in his otherwise very useful study.

241 Lock-outs were more or less non-existent. The numbers of those on strike declined also. The above figures from the Reichsstatistik (see Lederer and Marschak, p. 177). The trade union strike statistics give lower figures for the War but show roughly the same relative trend: 1915-60 strikes; 1916-139; 1917-189; 1918-163; 1919-3,604. From Corr.bl., 30, 1920, Statist. Beil., p. 120.

242 See, above all, S. Miller, *Burgfrieden und Klassenkampf. Die deutsche Sozialdemokratie im Ersten Weltkrieg*, Düsseldorf, 1974.

243 For the history of the USPD see (besides Schorske's well-known volume and E. Prager, *Geschichte der USPD*, Berlin, 1921; 4th ed., Bonn, 1980), H. Krause, *USPD*, Cologne, 1975; D.W. Morgan, *A History of the German Independent Party 1917-1922*, Ithaca/N.Y., 1976; R. Wheeler, *USPD u. Internationale*, Berlin 1975; Miller, *Burgfrieden*, pp. 156ff., *passim*. See also Kolb, *Arbeiterräte*, pp. 36-45, for a correct emphasis of the heterogeneity of this Party, which was not a direct continuation of the pre-War party line but which was primarily held together by its rejection of the SPD's war policy as well as by its wish for an immediate negotiated peace; U. Ratz, *Georg Ledebour 1850-1947*, Berlin, 1969, pp. 151-78; W. Benz and H. Graml (eds.), *Die revolutionäre Illusion. Zur Geschichte des linken Flügels der USPD. Erinnerungen von Curt Geyer*, Stuttgart, 1976; G.F. Knopp, 'Einigungsdebatte und Einigungsaktion in SPD und USPD 1917-1920 unter besonderer Berücksichtigung der "Zentralstelle für Einigung der Sozialdemokratie"', Ph.D. diss., Würzburg, 1975.

244 The figures are valid for 31 March. On 31 March 1918 membership was 249,000, rising to 1,012,000 a year later. From *Prot. über die Verhandlungen des Parteitags der SPD . . . Würzburg, 1917*, Berlin, 1917, p. 10; *Prot. über die Verhandlungen des Parteitags der SPD . . . Weimar . . . 1919*, Berlin, 1919, p. 54.

245 *USPD. Prot. über die Verhandlungen des ausserordentlichen Parteitages . . . 1919 in Berlin*, Berlin, n.d., p. 50.

246 'Prot. Parteitag SPD 1919', p. 16 (report by the Party Executive).

247 As in Nuremburg according to Schwarz, pp. 252ff.

248 Schwarz (pp. 170-2) believes — on the basis of very little empirical evidence — that the Nuremberg USPD mainly consisted of individuals from those industries that did not profit from the War and that the better-earning armaments workers who wished for reform tended to remain in the SPD (see also *ibid.*, pp. 174, 226-9).

Admittedly it must be remembered that a very clear radicalising process took place in the Nuremberg SPD. In the Munich USPD, Ay (pp. 192-3, 195) has confirmed a high proportion of tradesmen and intellectuals and reports that the artisans amongst the USPD membership came chiefly from the peace industries. Against this, it is well known that the 'revolutionary shop stewards' and their groups working within the Berlin USPD were drawn from well-paid skilled armament workers. See P. v. Oertzen, *Betriebsräte in der Novemberrevolution*, Düsseldorf, 1963, pp. 69ff. There was a particularly strong radical minority who favoured the USPD in the Metalworkers' Association. See n. 254. Ebert, in October 1918, thought that: 'Behind the self employed there were always only the indispensable people from the munitions industry. Those are the people for peace at any price'. In E. Matthias and R. Morsey, *Die Regierung des Prinzen Max von Baden*, Düsseldorf, 1962, p. 267; this also needs confirmation, however.

249   On the shop stewards, see R. Müller, *Vom Kaiserreich zur Republik*, 2 vols., Berlin, 1924, 1925 (M. was leader of the 'revolutionary shop stewards' in Berlin); E. Barth, *Aus der Werkstatt der Revolution*, Berlin, 1919, Kolb, *Arbeiterräte*, pp. 38-45; 56-60, on the emergence of workers' councils in Germany during the strikes of April 1917 and January 1918. On the overall problem, see also v. Oertzen, esp. pp. 69ff. On Spartakus, see the partisan work by Badia, the short critical representation by G. Schmidt and (with a further bibliography), *DIEW*, 3, pp., 62ff, 135ff, 285ff, 493ff; also the relevant sections in: *Geschichte der deutschen Arbeiterbewegung*, Vols. 2, 3; Kolb, *Arbeiterräte*, pp. 47ff, estimates that the group had 1,000 members at most and criticises (pp. 410-14) the strong over-valuation and exaggerated significance of the Spartakus group in the greater part of GDR literature, a criticism that is still largely appropriate today.

250   On the conflict-reducing policy of the trade unions see also W. Richter, *Gewerkschaften Monopolkapital u. Staat im Ersten Weltkrieg*, Berlin, 1959; and, further, Feldman, Kolb and Rürup, pp. 84-91, on the overall problems.

251   See Kolb, *Arbeiterräte*, pp. 49-51, on details; also the very impressive description of police persecution by Retzlaw, who himself lived 'illegally' and sometimes in hiding (pp. 52-3, 85-109). See also the description of the Regional Command in Marken (MB, 23 August 1916, pp. 2-3). After this, Berlin metal workers to some extent ignored the influence of their party and union leaders and supported Spartakus; they refused overtime despite special financial allowances. Detention and military conscription were the methods the authorities used to deal with the leaders. 'The movement was deprived of some of its best people in this way; those who remained became timid because one was never sure, from the callous way the military authorities set about things, that one would not be locked up.'

252   Similar reports are frequent in the MB, but the effect of intimidation remains unclear. On the role of fear in the working class, see also Retzlaw, pp. 46, 47. Loss of wages through strikes was also harder to bear, because of the shortages, than it had been before the War. *Ibid.*, p. 57: 'Released from military service, the union executive feared for their existence at every conflict.' See also Feldman, *Army*, pp. 449-50, 455, on the successful suppression of the strike at the beginning of 1918.

253   See also H.-J. Bieber, *Gewerkschaften in Krieg und Revolution*, 2 vols., Hamburg, 1982; S. Greiffenhagen, 'Die württembergischen Sozialdemokraten im Ersten Weltkrieg und in der Weimarer Republik (1914-1933)', in J. Schadt and W. Schmierer (eds.), *Die SPD in Baden-Württemberg und ihre Geschichte*, Stuttgart, 1979, pp. 160-91; J. A. Moses, 'Carl Legien und das deutsche Vaterland im Weltkrieg 1914-1918', *GWU*, 26, 1975, pp. 595-611; H. Potthoff, *Gewerkschaften und Politik zwischen Revolution und Inflation*, Düsseldorf, 1979; M. Scheck, *Zwischen Weltkrieg und Revolution. Zur Geschichte der Arbeiterbewegung in Württemberg 1914-1920*, Cologne/Vienna, 1981; R. Sigel, 'Die Lensch-Cunow-

Haenisch-Gruppe. Ihr Einfluss auf die Ideologie der deutschen Sozialdemokratie im Ersten Weltdrieg', *IWK*, 11, 1975, pp. 421–36; V. Ullrich, *Die Hamburger Arbeiterbewegung am Vorabend des Ersten Weltkriegs bis zur Revolution 1918/19*, 2 vols., Hamburg, 1976; *idem*, 'Weltkrieg und Novemberrevolution. Die Hamburger Arbeiterbewegung 1914–1918', in J. Berlin (ed.), *Das andere Hamburg*, Cologne, 1981, pp. 181–208; *idem*, 'Massenbewegungen in der Hamburger Arbeiterschaft im Ersten Weltkrieg', in A. Herzig, D. Langewiesche and A. Sywottek (eds), *Arbeiter in Hamburg*, Hamburg, 1982, as well as the *Habilitationsschrift* by G. Mai.

254 See F. Opel, *Der Deutsche Metallarbeiterverband während des ersten Weltkriegs u. der Revolution*, Hanover, 1957, pp. 35–75; pp. 65–9 (on the meeting of the Association in 1917 where the main executive resolution was accepted only by 64 votes to 53). On other Associations: Umbreit and Lorenz, pp. 178–82, who write from the point of view of the General Commission, i.e. the central organisation of all Social Democratic ('free') trade unions, formed in 1890 and headed by Carl Legien.

255 On the drawing together and the measures taken in common by the Social Democratic, Christian and Liberal trade unionists in their efforts to improve the distribution of food to the population, the treatment and implementation of the HDG, the fight against the 'yellows' and, from 1917, on voting rights and general political questions (in the Volksbund für Freiheit und Vaterland, for example), see Umbreit and Lorenz, pp. 164ff.; Varain, pp. 91–2, 105–6, 107–8.

256 As in *Corr. bl.*, 18, 1918, p. 2 (for 5 January).

257 The *Corr. bl.* clearly reflects the increasing politicisation of trade union demands. A comparison of the annual review at the beginning of 1915, 1916 and 1917 with that of 5 January 1918 provides a quick insight into this process and the broadening of union demands. See also *Corr. bl.*, 27, 1917, pp. 153–5 ('on the present situation'), 21 March, where this change is more clearly expressed for the first time. On the question of monopoly and resulting from a series of articles and discussion: *ibid.*, 17, 1917, pp. 147–9 (petition to the Reich Chancellor); H. Cunow *et al.*, *Monopolfrage u. Arbeiterklasse*, Berlin, 1917, pp. 83ff., 87ff.; also as the similar Point 12 in 'Sozialpolitisches Arbeiterprogramm' by the trade unions (*Corr. bl.*, 18, 1918, pp. 4–8 and again in Umbreit and Lorenz, pp. 217–26, summarised by Varain, pp. 109–10). This programme is the most accessible source on the aims of the trade unions in 1918, which were only modified in negotiations with entrepreneurs and with the resultant ZAG.

258 See above, pp. 46f.

259 This is how the chairman of the General Commission, Carl Legien, paraphrased the immediate objectives of the trade unions at the Reich Conference of the SPD in 1916 (in Varain, p. 76).

260 See Umbreit and Lorenz, pp. 52–169.

261 *Corr. bl.*, 29, 1919, Statist., Beil., p. 87.

262 On the transformation of trade-union ideology in the crucial first year of the war see [E. Lederer], 'Die Gewerkschaftsbewegung im Jahre 1914 . . .', in *Archiv*, 39, 1915, pp. 610–41, esp. 636ff. ('It is as if the conception of the State as a class State had been completely obliterated from trade-union ideology').

263 On this, see Varain, pp. 71–117 (summary); Feldman, *Army* (comprehensive); Umbreit and Lorenz (from the viewpoint of the General Commission); *Geschichte der deutschen Arbeiterbewegung*, 2, 3 (a Marxist-Leninist interpretation).

264 The thesis of the 'betrayal' of the working class and its interests by trade-union and party leaders, used in particular by Marxist-Leninist historians, is unproductive and impedes rational discussion and analysis. It is to be found, e.g., in W. Rasse, *Zur Geschichte der deutschen Gewerkschaftsbewegung 1914–1917 und 1917–1919*, Berlin, n.d.

265 See Robert Michels, *Zur Soziologie des Parteiwesens in der modernen Demokratie*.

Untersuchungen über die oligarchischen Tendenzen des Gruppenlebens, 1st ed. 1911, 2nd ed., Stuttgart, 1957; see also H.A. Winkler on Robert Michels, in H.-U. Wehler (ed.), *Deutsche Historiker*, 4, Göttingen, 1972, pp. 65–80.
266   In Umbreit and Lorenz, pp. 66–7.
267   In *Corr.bl.*, 20, 1920, Statist. Beil., pp. 78, 103.
268   *Ibid.*, 20, 1920, Statist. Beil., pp. 78, 97. Varain's figures (n. 2, p. 97) are not correct.
269   See on this the furious remarks of the Spartakist Retzlaw (p. 58).
270   See also Cassau, pp. 163ff.; Preller, p. 32.
271   See above, pp. 126ff.
272   See particularly the surveys by Nussbaum (*Unternehmer*), Kaelble (*Industrielle Interessenpolitik*) and H. Jaeger.
273   One may think of the deep-seated differences between the CVDI and the BdI, between the 'Kartell der schaffenden Stände' and the Hansa-Bund.
274   See Leckebusch, pp. 48–60, on the corresponding and increasing organisational rapport among employers; Nussbaum, *Unternehmer*, p. 160, *passim*; Stegmann, *Zwischen Repression*, pp. 359–60, *passim*.
275   *DAZ*, 13, 2 August 1914; on Burgfrieden rhetoric, *ibid.*, 9 August 1914: '. . . the barriers have fallen which separated the political parties from one another, there is neither a right nor a left, we want to be a united band of brothers, to be parted neither by need nor danger. Entrepreneurs and workers take each other by the hand . . .'.
276   See, similarly, on the attitude of the Bavarian upper classes, Ay, p. 85.
277   Emil Kirdorf at the general meeting of the Gelsenkirchen Bergwerks-AG in the spring of 1915, in *Corr.bl.*, 25, 1915, p. 190 (quoted therein from the *Post*); also *DAZ*, 15, 6 February 1916, on the expectation that the class war would, in the long term, become milder leading to a permanent strengthening of the feeling of national solidarity; the assessment of the German working class by Oberstleutnant Bauer, n. 155 above; Riezler, p. 183 (entry of 7 July 1914): the Conservative party leader Heydebrand expects a 'strengthening of partriarchal order and sentiment' from the War.
278   Kirdorf, in the spring of 1915, in *Corr.bl.*, 25, 1915; see also Stegmann, *Zwischen Repression*, pp. 377–8.
279   This line of argument is especially clear in Westarp, pp. 265–6, 279, 365.
280   See Feldman, *Army*, p. 136, on similar expectations by Hugenberg, late 1914; n. 158 abbre; Schwabe, *Wissenschaft*, pp. 156–7; Ay, pp. 60, 85–6, on Kapp. Conversely, the shipping magnate, Ballin; see L. Cecil, *Albert Ballin*, Hamburg, 1969, pp. 275–6.
281   See above; there is important new data in, Stegmann, *Zwischen Repression*, pp. 375–405, esp. 385ff. On *ibid.*, pp. 385–6, it may be commented that one should not regard the Vaterlandspartei solely as a 'new edition' of the manufacturers' cartel; it had wider aims as well as a much broader base. The Hansa-Bund and the BdI no longer stood aloof. The confrontations between Liberal and Conservative mass movements, so characteristic of 1913, became blurred and were even suspended, while the chances of attracting *white-collar* workers receded. The continuity here should not be overstated.
282   See Umbreit and Lorenz, pp. 51ff., 169. A review of the *Corr.bl.*, doubtless a reliable source in this respect, does not reveal any additional branches in which similar War committees and study groups arose voluntarily. As a concrete example see, for example, the study group for the building trade, *Corr.bl.*, 25, 1915, pp. 375–9.
283   See Feldman, *Army*, pp. 79, 382 (Borsig, Silverberg and Sorge); pp. 218, 241–2, 322 (Stresemann); p. 325 (Rieppel). See also K. Gossweiler, *Grossbanken, Industriemonopole und Staat*, Berlin, 1971, pp. 57–64. Basing himself on Lenin,

Kuczynski and Gutsche, Gossweiler differentiates between two 'factions' among entrepreneurs during the War, at least when dealing with the workers' question and the unions; essentially, however, he presents evidence for W. Rathenau's flexible ideas on reform without making sufficiently clear that these were representative of one 'faction' of industrialists.

284 As was the case at the founding of the 'Kriegsausschuss für die Metallbetriebe Gross-Berlins' in February 1915, but which found few imitators until the HDG. On this, *Corr.bl.*, 25, 1915, pp. 114–15; 26, 1916, p. 416 ('Paritätische Schlichtungskommissionen'); Feldman, *Army*, pp. 75–9. On the HDG, see above, pp. 135ff.

285 See, for instance, *DAZ*, 15, 6 February 1916 (leading article); P. Osthold, *Die Geschichte des Zechenverbandes 1908-1933*, Berlin, 1934, pp. 149, 213, 227 (on similar arguments by Hugenberg among others).

286 See Kirdorf's criticism of government policy on foreign, domestic and (especially) labour issues during the spring of 1915 in *Corr.bl.*, 25, 1915, p. 190; see also above, pp. 138ff.

287 That this manner of thinking (a loyal, dependable working class and a radical officialdom) formed the basis for the later myth of the 'stab in the back', can only be referred to in passing here.

288 In a circular of 26 April 1915, quoted in *Corr.bl.*, 25, 1915, p. 292.

289 See the refusals in *DAZ*, 16, 7 January 1917 ('Arbeitsgemeinschaft') 15, 25 June 1916 ('Organisation und Gleichberechtigung') and 16 July 1916 (against the representation of labour in the employment offices); more on this theme by the general secretaries of the 'Vereinigung' (Tänzler) on 13 October 1917 (in *Corr.bl.*, 28, 1918, pp. 30ff.), who are strongly against cooperation on an equal basis, and the 'new orientation'.

290 From *DAZ*, 41, 1916, cited in *Corr.bl.*, 26, 1916, p. 454.

291 Reproduced in Leckebusch, pp. 214–23, esp. p. 216 (on the abolition of the HDG), p. 218 (on the demand that enterprises should be managed only by the entrepreneur), pp. 219–19 (on the freedom of the work contract) and p. 223 (against government conciliation offices). On the other hand (p. 223) workers' committees when presented specific aims of the employees were now accepted.

292 See n. 24 above for further titles on this theme generally.

293 Work has been done on the effect of this in the mining industry. See W. Berg, ' "Herr im Hause" oder Emanzipation der Arbeitnehmer', diss., Freiburg, 1972, pp. 64–5; see also P. Osthold, *Die Geschichte des Zechenverbandes 1908-1933*, Berlin, 1934, pp. 163ff. The HDG weakened the jurisdiction of the entrepreneur in this field; on this, *Corr.bl.*, 27, 1917, pp. 101–2, 165–6.

294 See Deist, *Militär*, pp. 635ff., esp. p. 638, n. 7; in this report, some officers expressed certain reservations against the militarisation of firms (esp. p. 637; similarly in Groener; *ibid.*, p. 731). In fact, this militarisation in industry, in which the worker was subject to wartime controls, frequently took place even where there were no major strikes, especially in the Upper Silesian coal, iron and steel industry. See, for example MB, 3 June 1917, p. 24.

295 See, for example, Kocka, *Unternehmensverwaltung*, pp. 347–63. Generally, see L.H.A. Geck, *Die sozialen Arbeitsverhältnisse im Wandel der Zeit*, Berlin, 1931.

296 The south German textile industrialist Semlinger was opposed to too many forcible closures and the subsequent redistribution of work in 1917. Amongst other reasons, because social arrangements in many factories 'had led to a very friendly relationship between employer and employee, which prevented or allowed party political dissensions to be more easily overcome; it is to be feared that a displaced horde of workers of all political persuasions, who would regard their new situation with discontent and mistrust, could disturb and destroy the existing friendly and

mutually satisfying relationship in a very short time'; quoted in Peppel, pp. 96–7. See also Mendelssohn Bartholdy, p. 202; H.J. Teuteberg, *Geschichte der industriellen Mitbestimmung in Deutschland*, Tübingen, 1961, pp. 490ff.

297 See Umbreit and Lorenz, pp. 113ff.; on the significance of the entrepreneurs' disruption of the centralisation of employment offices see also Stegmann, *Zwischen Repression*, p. 359.

298 These (admittedly dubious) figures in Lederer and Marschak, pp. 186–7. That some entrepreneurs did not desist completely from encouraging the 'yellows' at the beginning of the War, contrary to trade-union expectations during the Burgfrieden, is shown by the employment policy of S & H which continued to seek a strengthening of its 'Unterstützungsvereins', as described and criticised in *Corr.bl.*, 11 April 1914, pp. 24, 615–16. 24, 615f.); see also Schäfer, *Die 'Gelben Gewerkschaften' pp. 68–9*.

299 See Stegmann, *Erben*, pp. 478–9; *idem, Zwischen Repression*, pp. 377–8. On the support of the Vereinigung Deutscher Arbeitgeberverbände for the 'yellow' Hauptausschuss nationaler Arbeiter- und Berufsverbände, see *DAZ*, 16, 1917, initially on 4 January, then repeatedly. See also the letter from the Vereinigung, 10 November 1916 (repr. *Corr.bl.*, 26, 1916, p. 535), which makes clear the non-confrontationist economic policy of the organisation, refers to a large meeting of 'yellow' trade unionists in Berlin on 1 October 1915 and requests readers' contributions such as had been received in the last year of peace but not apparently subsequently.

300 From 133,000 to 145,000 (in Lederer and Marschak, p. 187).

301 See Feldman, *Army*, pp. 322, 379–80; Deist, *Militär*, pp. 1207–8, 1212; Stegmann, *Zwischen Repression, pass.*

302 In Lederer and Marschak, p. 187. Membership of the 'yellows', out of 1,000, was: 1916, 145; 1917, 142; 1918, 42; 1919, 150 and 1923, 283.

303 In MB, 3 April 1917, p. 12. The concept 'blood oranges' – yellow outside, red inside – was used by contemporaries to describe those only externally 'yellow'.

304 In the last MBs references to the sharp tension between trade unions and the entrepreneurs became more and more distinct. Thus the Leipzig AK reported (MB, 3 April 1918, p. 19), that the increasingly active unions phrased their demands as ultimatums and thereby brought about 'well-justified bitterness and energetic opposition from the employers'. The Fourteenth AK in Karlsruhe wrote: 'The behaviour and demands of the trade unions is becoming more and more domineering, so that there is great discontent among the employers' (MB, 3 August 1918, p. 13). The slightly later report of the Second AK (Stettin) stated exaggeratedly but significantly: 'The trade unions have been brought to almost absolute power through the Auxiliary Service Law . . . their tyranny will bring the employers to the point where they will rather close their firms'. The possibility of great social conflict after the War was a very real one (MB, 3 September 1918, p. 33).

305 See Cecil, pp. 279ff., 286. How little prospect the social-imperialist line had, despite its increasing antisemitism and pre-fascism in the spring and autumn of 1918, is clearly shown in Stegmann, *Zwischen Repression*, pp. 391, 401.

306 On this, see above, pp. 138ff.

307 The continuity thesis, which was mostly put forward by employers, is not acceptable: *Fünfundzwanzig Jahre Arbeitnordwest 1904–1929*, Berlin, 1929, pp. 64–5. Admittedly there had been previous isolated and quickly terminated high-level discussions between entrepreneurs and union representatives in the heavy industry in the Ruhr – for example between Stinnes and Vogler on one side and Bauer, Leipart and Schulte on the other, during the summer of 1916. See W. Berg, pp. 126–7, taken from von Osthold, p. 262 and *Fünfundzwanzig Jahre*

Arbeitnordwest, p. 75; on further inconclusive talks in the summer of 1917: Feldman, *German Business*, pp. 323–4. See also H. v. Raumer, 'Unternehmer u. Gewerkschaften in der Weimarer Zeit', *Deutsche Rundschau*, 80, 1954, pp. 425ff.

308 See Lederer, *Die sozialen Organisationen*, p. 77, where the equalising of entrepreneurs' interests owing to wartime conditions is highlighted.

309 On the details see: Feldman, *Army*, pp. 167, 227–8, 273ff., 278, 282, 394, 396, 422; *idem, German Business*, pp. 318–19; Schröter, pp. 94ff., 99, 103–4, 114, 118; DIEW, 3, pp. 336ff., 570. Mistrust and bitterness by South German industrialists against the Prussian class comrades were often reported in the MB. See for example the report of the Württemberg KM, 31 August 1917, p. 17: 'Württemberg industry and craft will not allow itself to be economically harmed in favour of North German competitors. There is already an irrepressible bitterness in these circles about the well-known view that industry should be confined entirely to the coal areas and that [those in] south Germany should be shut down'. These fears were by no means groundless. Whereas, as shown above, the labour force in industrial firms with ten or more workers declined by about 8 per cent, in corresponding Prussian firms the decline was less than 2 per cent! In the annual reports of the Königl. Preussische Regierungs- und Gewerberäte, 1913, p. 775; and *ibid.*, 1914–18, p. 1589, the number of industrial enterprises with ten or more workers was 3,633,618 (1913) and 3,570,550 (1918). The figures appear comparable with each other and with those given above, from the same source. If these figures are correct, they show that the War led to a relative increase in the density of industrial activity in Prussia at the expense of other German states. See also Grebler and Winkler, p. 48, who demonstrate the increasing significance of the mid-German industrial area through the use of migration figures.

310 On similar tendencies before 1914, see Kocka, *Unternehmensverwaltung*, p. 382. The literature is full of evidence for this wartime trend for economic organisation, whose negative effect on the 'small ones' of the industrial world has been referred to above. See König, pp. 49, 80–1, 141–2, 196ff., 255–6. The detailed examination of the 'Willensbildungsprozess' in such organisations (which was ultimately more decisive than economic opportunity), that would be needed to analyse the shifting degrees of mutal adjustment between groups, between the private and government sectors, has not yet been carried out.

311 This is an aspect of the process which M. Weber describes as the 'victorious advance of the bureaucracy in the World War' ('Parlament und Regierung im neugeordneten Deutschland', in *idem, Politische Schriften*, p. 318); on the problem of the industrial bureaucracy in Wilhelmine Germany, see Kocka, *Unternehmensverwaltung*, pp. 547ff. Within the entrepreneurial structure of the Siemens' enterprises clear tendencies towards the further centralisation of control during the War are identifiable. See the setting up during the War of the joint committees formed by S & H and SSW (in SAA, 50/Lg 625) to which, according to the Minutes of the executive board meeting of 6 August 1914, hitherto independent workshops and sections were to be subordinated. The single fact that the authorities, War societies and committees called for more and more specifications (in order to calculate prices, for example) meant that the firm's accounting had to become strongly centralised (see Minute Vst. SSW, 22 March 1918, 2 and repetitions). This could be carried out only partially during the War owing to the shortage of office staff. S & H and SSW also set up a series of new offices in order to cope with the greatly-increased correspondence with the authorities. See, for instance, Frenzel, p. 65 (SAA, 68/Li 83), on the setting-up of a 'wartime raw materials office' by SSW in October 1916; this was to provide evidence of the need for the raw materials which were being applied for; it would represent the firm *vis-*

á-vis the War Societies and would intercept the 'rapid fire of economic rules and regulations'.

312 See *MkdI*, 1, 14 August 1914, p. 2; 6, 5 September 1914, pp. 53–9; the founding proclamation of the Ka.d.Dt.Ind is also published in *Corr.bl.*, 24, 1914, p. 511; see also W. Gutsche, 'Die Entstehung des Kriegsausschusses der deutschen Industrie u. seine Rolle zu Beginn des ersten Weltkrieges, *ZfG*, 18, 1970, pp. 877–98.

313 See *MkdI*, 45, 15 May 1915 ('Zur Frage einer kriegswirtschaftlichen Zentralorganisation').

314 See Gutsche (*Entstehung*, pp. 879, 883ff., 996), who convincingly demonstrates the superior power of the large enterprises over the majority of smaller ones and (pp. 886ff.) brings out the continuous conflict between CVDI and BdI on subordinate questions. See also the references in Schröter, *Krieg*, p. 140; *DIEW*, 1, pp. 405ff.

315 See *DAZ*, 15, 1916, suppl. of 21 December; *MKdI*, 201, 4 May 1918, p. 2969.

316 See Kaelble, *Industrielle Interessenpolitik*, pp. 170–4.

317 See *Corr.bl.*, 26, 1916, p. 471. The General Commission took the decision of industrial Associations as the occasion to call for a tighter organisation of all workers' trade unions. See also J. Herle, 'Deutscher Industrierat. Seine Entstehung und Organisation', *MKdI*, 203, 18 May 1918, pp. 2989–92. Herle was Business Manager of the 'Industrierat' and of the Ka.d.Dt.Ind.

318 See *ibid.*, p. 2991, on its first full session in February 1918.

319 *MKdI*, 241, 18 February 1919, pp. 3390–5; 250, 12 April 1919, pp. 3490–1 (on the first meetings of the Reich association in February and April 1919). See, generally, F. Hauenstein, 'Die ersten Zentralverbände', in F. Berg (ed.), *Der Weg zum industriellen Spitzenverband*, Darmstadt, 1956, pp. 71ff.

Chapter 3. The Polarisation of the Mittelstand

1 In *Std.Dt.R.*, 35, 1914, pp. 14f. Included here are 579,469 C2s, that is, skilled workers in trade or clerks, sales people and sales assistants, contrary to the official classification of 1907 but corresponding with the otherwise general usage of the time and with the legal regulation of 1911. Not included in this figure are civil servants (see below), members of the army, those in 'personal service' (mostly servants) and a very small number of managerial employees (directors, managing officers, estate administrators, etc.). On problems with these statistics, see Hartfiel, pp. 27–51, whose figures are not, however, adopted here. The number of wage labourers is to be taken as excluding salesmen and clerks, as well as those in 'personal service' in so far as they lived at their masters, and without dependants. The figure of 6.2 million industrial workers estimated above (see above, p. 12) referred only to industrial enterprises with more than ten employees, and is therefore smaller.

2 See K.M. Bolte, 'Angestelltenfrage im Licht der Zahlen' in H. Bayer (ed.), *Der Angestellte zwischen Arbeiterschaft u. Management*, Berlin, 1961, p. 67.

3 Only 87,631 of 562,716 organised commercial and bank employees, but 91,934 out of 137,332 organised technicians and as many as 28,720 out of 28,767 organised office workers belonged at the end of 1913 to so-called non-parity associations (which exluded the self-employed). Some associations, such as the nationalistic anti-semitic DHV (1913: 123,092 members) and the more liberal Verband Deutscher Handlungsgehilfen (1913: 90,507 members) did allow the self-employed to join, but pursued a clear and active interest-orientated policy that was to some extent more aggressive than that of some non-parity associations. Figures from *Reichsarbeitsblatt*, special issue 11, Berlin, 1915, II, pp. 22ff.

4 For a detailed history of white-collar workers to 1914, with bibliography, J. Kocka,

Die Angestellten in der deutschen Geschichte 1850–1980, Göttingen, 1981; *idem, White-collar Workers in America 1890–1940. A Social-political History in International Perspective*, London, 1980.

5 See O. Hintze, 'Der Beamtenstand' in *idem, Soziologie u. Geschichte gesammelte Abhandlungen 2*), 2nd ed., Göttingen, 1964, p. 68, who estimates the figure at 1.2 million in 1911; and the estimate of 1.5 million (1912) and nearly 2 million (1917) in F. Winters, *Die Deutsche Beamtenfrage*, Berlin, 1918, p. 14; see also F. Falkenberg, *Die Deutsche Beamtenbewegung nach der Revolution*, 2nd ed., Berlin, 1920, p. 17, who estimates that the figure had already reached 2 million by 1914. The occupational statistics do not allow for an exact separation between civil servants and professionals, who together numbered 3.4 million in 1907. These estimates include court and administration officials (390,000, according to Hintze), churchmen, officers and teachers as well as civil servants on the railways, the post office, etc., and probably local authority officials as well.

6 Hintze, p. 68, who offers an altogether excellent introduction to the historical, legal and sociological aspects of German civil service status before the War; pp. 121ff. on the problem of the traditional civil service status as applied to the new civil servants in rapidly expanding service sectors (e.g. railway and post office), which had little to do with the exercise of superior authority. See G. Kalmer, 'Beamtenschaft u. Revolution' in Bosl (ed.), pp. 203ff., who shows that in Bavaria full civil service status, originally fought for a group of administrative and legal civil servants who exercised public authority, was sought after, but not immediately achieved by other categories of civil servants. For a general overview, see H. Hattenbauer, *Geschichte des Beamtentums*, Cologne, 1980.

7 *Ibid.*, p. 208f.

8 See Winters, pp. 7–19, 31–49, 81ff.; Falkenberg, pp. 7–17, also 13ff. on the programme of the Bund der Festbesoldeten which also organised white-collar workers. In Bavaria in 1910 ca. 70 per cent of all civil servants were organised (Kalmer, p. 208).

9 As a good introduction in English cf. S. Volkov, *The Rise of Popular Anti-Modernism in Germany: The Urban Master Artisans, 1873–1896*, Princeton, N.J., 1978. See also J. Kocka, 'Craft traditions and the German labour movement in the 19th century' in G. Crossick *et al.* (eds.), *The Power of History: Essays for Eric Hobsbawm*, Cambridge, 1984 (forthcoming).

10 See *Std.Dtr.*, 466, 1937, pp. 188, 192 and above, p. 183, n. 2.

11 See W. Wernet, *Handwerkspolitik*, Göttingen, 1952, p. 77; J. Wein, *Die Verbandsbildung im Einzelhandel*, Berlin, 1968, p. 91.

12 See H.A. Winkler, 'Der rückversicherte Mittelstand', in Rüegg and Neuloh (eds.), pp. 163–79; *idem, Mittelstand*, pp. 40–64; Wernicke; E. Steinberg, *Die Handwerker-Bewegung in Deutschland, ihre Ursachen und Ziele*, Stuttgart, 1897; a survey of the 'mittelstandisch' legislation, in Huber, *Verfassungsgeschichte*, 4, pp.1010–14.

13 Wein, *Die Verbandsbildung*, with detailed descriptions of the many associations.

14 Gloomy assessments and predictions on the development of small-scale crafts and trades in the age of industrialisation also predominated in contemporary social science and in both left- and right-wing journalism. Actual development varied very greatly from branch to branch. See W. Fischer, 'Die Rolle des Kleingewerbes im wirtschaftlichen Wachstumsprozess in Deutschland 1850–1914' in F. Lütge (ed.), *Wirtschaftliche u. soziale Probleme der gewerblichen Entwicklung im 15. – 16. und 19. Jahrhundert*, Stuttgart, 1968, pp. 131–42; A. Noll, 'Wirtschafliche u. soziale Entwicklung des Handwerks in der zweiten Phase der Industrialisierung' in Rüegg and Neuloh (eds.), pp. 193–212.

15 See Winkler, *Der rückversicherte Mittelstand*, pp. 167ff.

16 G. Schmoller in 1897 was one of the first to propose this combination. In his view, a member of the Mittelstand had to earn between 1800 and 8000M annually and possess 'some' monetary means. 'The concept "Mittelstand" covers a whole range of different aspects and characteristics: it is connected with ideas on the distribution of incomes and fortunes and with concepts of honour, of social rank, of technical and human education, attitude to life, and occupational divisions; everyone who uses this word, applies it as a sort of average of this range of ideas but with their own upper and lower limits within the range.' ('Was verstehen wir unter dem Mittelstand? Hat er im 19. Jahrhundert zu- oder abgenommen?' in *Verhandlungen des 8. Evang.-soz. Kongresses*, Göttingen, 1897.) *Ibid.*, pp. 134f., 157f. and, on the 'neuen Mittelstand', p. 153f., 160. On the history of the concept, see Winkler, *Mittelstand*, pp. 21–5.

17 See H.J. Puhle, *Interessenpolitik*, pp. 98ff.; Stegmann, *Erben*, pp. 143ff., 176ff., 360ff. *passim*.; Winkler, *Der rückversicherte Mittelstand*, pp. 169ff.

18 On the need of the white-collar workers to distance themselves from manual workers, see Kocka, *Unternehmensverwaltung*, pp. 513–44; on the stand by artisans and small retail shopkeepers against 'capital' see also: H. Böttger, *Vom alten u. neuen Mittelstand*, Berlin, 1901, esp. p. 44; Wernicke, pp. 963ff.; Th. Brauer, 'Mittelstandspolitik' in *GdS* 9, II, pp. 376f. Further on the Mittelstand movement, see L. Müffelmann, *Die moderne Mittelstandsbewegung*, Leipzig, 1913; J. Wernicke, 'Mittelstandsbewegung', in *HSt.*, 6, 4th ed., 1925, pp. 594–602; E. Grünberg, *Der Mittelstand in der kapitalistischen Gesellschaft*, Leipzig, 1932; Th. Geiger, *Die soziale Schichtung des deutschen Volkes*, Stuttgart, 2nd ed., 1967, esp. pp. 84ff., 98ff.

19 From a survey of the Verein für Handlungs-Kommis in 1858. The Chamber of Commerce in Frankfurt/M. had recommended to its members on 2 August of that year to only pay white-collar workers earning up to 3000M, 33 per cent of their salary, and those who earned more, 25 per cent. See E. Steinitzer, 'Der Krieg u. die Angestellten' in *Jb. d. Angestelltenbewegung 1914/15*, pp. 182f. Other examples in *Corr. bl.*, 24, 1914, pp. 639f. and 25, 1915, pp. 90f.; *Archiv*, 41, 1916, pp. 584ff., esp. 589, 602f.

20 *Ibid.*, 44, 1917/18, p. 321. similar figures for the following years are unfortunately lacking. See A. Günther, *Die gesunkene Kaufkraft des Lohnes und ihre Wiederherstellung* II, Jena, 1919, p. 44.

21 See above, pp. 19ff. This is probably also true in the unlikely case that the stated annual earnings did not include wartime price-rise supplements; in any case, these were very low. Stegmann, *Repression*, p. 378, is incorrect in this respect. The Siemens' white-collar workers did not receive the otherwise regular annual earnings increment in 1915. See SAA Vst. S&H/SSW 24.1.1916, pt 1. The yearly increments were only reinstituted in February 1916.

22 In SAA 11 Lr 544 and Vst. SSW, 29 July 1918. After further raising the allowances, these consisted from 1 July 1918 of 120M per month for married male white-collar workers, 80M for single men, 80M for all females, and 50M for all those under nineteen years of age. On the wages at Siemens in 1912, see Kocka, *Unternehmensverwaltung*, p. 573. The child allowances for the first and second child were 30M, for the third and subsequent children, 35M. Price-rise supplements had existed at Siemens since 1912 (15 or 20M per month) and were thus not a response to wartime inflation. See SAA Vst. SSW, 26 October 1917, pt 2. Siemens and AEG were regularly in dispute over the payment of supplements. An exceptional raising of the basic wage (by 5 per cent) was only once planned during the War at Siemens, at least as far as can be seen from the Minutes of the board of directors' meetings. See SAA Vst. SSW, 14 August 1917. the annual regulation of wages, based primarily on seniority, took place every February, with the exception of 1915.

23 This argument by Borsig (1918) in Feldman, *Army*, p. 468. After the passing of the

Auxiliary Service Act (HDG), the arbitration committee forced AEG, in the autumn of 1917, to give their white-collar workers an assurance that the abolition or reduction in supplements would only become effective after a three-month time limit. Since Siemens and AEG had an agreement on equability, each firm gave their white-collar workers the same assurance. See SAA Vst SSW, 26 October 1917, pt 2.

24 See DHW 25, 1918, p. 40. According to this survey, the average annual income of clerks was: on 1 August 1914, 2393M; on 31 December 1914, 2266M; on 31 December 1915, 2632M; on 31 December 1917, 2829M. See also Schwarz; according to this source the earnings of technical and commercial white-collar workers in Nuremberg rose by only 20 per cent from the beginning of the War to November 1917.

25 Minutes of a meeting with representatives of the Society of Master-craftsmen on 7 July 1917, in SAA 11 Lr 544. The master-craftsmen spoke with 'discontent' and 'bitterness'. The Society had already asked for a wage rise, on 27 June 1916. 'We therefore allow ourselves to request the management to sympathetically review our wage situation and to improve it in keeping with the times', (*ibid.*).

26 See S. Aufhäuser, *Weltkrieg u. Angestelltenbewegung*, Berlin, 1918, p. 40; Kocka, *Unternehmensverwaltung*, pp. 490ff. On the relative movement of the earnings of white-collar and manual workers in one large enterprise up to 1914.

27 See *DIBZ*, 13, 1917, p. 197.

28 See DHW, 25, 1918, p. 39: 'Whereas the military and civil authorities, as well as the employers, made countless concessions, the professional associations of white-collar workers had to struggle constantly for the economic and social rights of the latter. The workers' wage demands were almost completely fulfilled, and there are countless examples of workers in armaments factories who, without exception, obtained higher incomes than white-collar workers in the same firm. We have consistently protested against this low valuation of mental work in countless public meetings and petitions'.

29 From tables compiled by the socio-political section at Siemens, in SAA 4/Lf 837. 'Manual' and 'white-collar' workers do not include youths: 'Normalbeteiligte' are certain higher white-collar workers, distinguished by their method of payment: the figures for 1914 are lacking in the tabulation.

30 See M. Victor, 'Verbürgerlichung des Proletariats u. Proletarisierung des Mittelstands', *Die Arbeit*, 8, 1931, p. 23; G. Bry, *Wages*, p. 362; F.W. Fischer, 'Die Angestellten, ihre Bewegung u. ihre Ideologien', PhD dissertation, Heidelberg, 1931, p. 39; R.K. Burns, 'The Comparative Economic Position of Manual and White-Collar Employees', *Journal of Business* , 27, Chicago, 1954, pp. 257–67; Bureau International du Travail, *Fluctuations des salaires dans differents pay de 1914 à 1922*, Geneva, 1923, pp. 74f.

31 Figures on money devaluation in Germany, 1914–1923, prepared in the Statist. Reichsamt, (*Wirtschaft und Statistik*, Sh. 1, 5, Berlin, 1925, p. 43).

32 MB, 8 September 1916, p. 3.

33 MB, 17 November 1916, p. 8.

34 Cf., for example, MB, 3 February 1917, p. 9; 3 May 1917, pp. 20f.; 3 June 1918, p. 33; 3 September 1918, p. 34; see also Ay, *Entstehung einer Revolution*, pp. 94ff.

35 Winters, pp. 51, 52; see also Kalmer, p. 212.

36 In SAA 29/Le 932, 1.

37 This from the Danzig AK, in MB, 3 April 1917, p. 7. Qualified technicians were most lacking, the Strasburg AK reported: *ibid*. See also MB, 3 January 1918, p. 36; 'There is quite particular indignation over the law [the HDG] among educated people because of the unreasonable demand that subordinate work is to be done.'

38 Figures in *Archiv*, 41, 1916, pp. 574f.

39 See the statement by the chairman of the Hamburger Verein für Handlungs-

Commis von 1858 in C. Köhler, *Die Privatbeamtempolitik nach dem Kriege*, Bonn, 1916, p. 9.

40 See DHW, 24, 1917, pp. 35f. '. . . the average income of clerks has hardly been raised, with the exception of that for the younger employees. But it is precisely the present payments to younger workers which shows that a real improvement in the whole system of wages can only be brought about through the pressure of circumstances. Younger workers are not only more sought after, but are also the most mobile, since they are mostly unmarried. They can exploit the war situation without having to fear that this will harm their future. Typists and stenographers are those who most easily rise higher. They have the advantage, as with craft workers, to be evaluated less for their personality and more for their mechanical skills, so that their performance is more easily measureable than is that of the ordinary commercially-trained employee. All these reasons result in the fact that some principals authorise wage rates for younger workers which they would earlier not have dreamt to be possible.' Put differently, the overstrained manual workers in short supply in wartime industries achieved advantages which had previously been reserved as privileges of the white-collar workers. Thus the S & H/SSW board of directors decided on 20 June 1918 that the right to a vacation should no longer be restricted to the firm's long-serving workers (SAA Vst, pt 3).

41 See Köhler, pp. 33f.; Falkenberg, pp. 46f. – there were barely 10,000 women employed in the Prussian railway administration in 1914, but by 1918 there were 100,000. See MB, 3 April 1917, p. 7, where the Magdeburg AK reported that 'there is a general over-supply of women for written and accounts work and for chamber and kitchen work in military employment'.

42 On this, see MB, 3 June 1918, p. 25; 3 July 1918, pp. 12, 14, 18; 3 August 1918, pp.5ff.

43 It had already made a stand before 1914, both for the better securing of rights of association and coalition and against the arrogance of some entrepreneurs. On the mixture of anti-conservative radicalism and expansive, anti-Socialist, racially-tinged chauvinism, which in some aspects anticipated later National Socialist ideologies during the last two decades of the Kaiserreich, see I. Hamel, *Völkischer Verband u. nationale Gewerkschaft. Die Politik des Deutschnationalen Handlungs-gehilfen-Verbandes 1893–1933*, Frankfurt, 1966.

44 On employers' regulations regarding the Butib, the DTV and the DHV, as well as the permanent refusal by most entrepreneurs to recognise white-collar associations as negotiating partners, see *Archiv*, 44, 1917/18, pp. 329ff. Further, *DIBZ* 11, 1915, pp. 91ff.; 13, 1917, pp. 85ff.; 14, 1918, pp. 10ff., 22, 101ff.; *DHW*, 25, 1918, pp. 35, 40. The employers had repeatedly stressed the differences between manual and white-collar workers even before 1914 (as had the middle-class type white-collar organisations), as well as the contradictory relationship between their 'civil servant' character and their union-like behaviour. They remained firm in this view, criticising every collective action by white-collar workers. See *DAZ* 13, 1914, against the Butib (19 July); 15, 1916, against the DTV and the Werkmeister-Verband (5 March) 16, 1917: the DTV demands 'breathe the air of class-conflict' (14 October); 17, 1918, 'the white-collar workers on the war-path' (1 September), and against the DHV (14 September).

45 See the examples of intervention by the authorities in police officers' associations in Winters, pp. 22f., 84f.; also Kalmer, p. 214.

46 Thus the chairman of the Verband Deutscher Handlungsgehilfen in *DIBZ*, 14, 1918, p. 7. Similarly, the chairman of the 58er Verein, see Kohler, pp. 19ff., although at the same time (*ibid.* p. 11) he has to admit to a 'certain intensification of opinion' among his colleagues.

47 See the DHV chairman, Bechly, 'Die Missachtung geistiger Arbeit' in *DHW*, 24,

1917, pp. 33ff. The wages question, he wrote, 'is and remains a question of power . . . even if one by no means has to think immediately of violent conflicts such as strikes or other forms of wage battle' it is nevertheless not possible to resolve it 'without a certain amount of pressure'. In July 1917 Bechly spoke of the impoverishment of white-collar workers as a 'systems failure' (*ibid.*, p. 89).

48 Minimum earnings became a major demand of the Arbeitsgemeinschaft Kaufmännischer Verbände, founded in 1916, to which all the larger clerks' associations (except the socialist Zentralverband) belonged. See the minimum rate demands, reproduced in *DHW*, 24, 1917, p. 91. 49. See *DHW*, 24, 1917, pp. 89f.; 26, 1919, pp. 53f.: 'Ein erfolgreicher Riesenstreik'. The article carried the motto 'All the wheels will stop, if your strong arm wants it'.

50 Concessions by the management after intervention by the War Office averted this. See *DHW*, 25, 1918, p. 19.

51 See Ay, pp. 101f., 198; Schwarz, p. 184.

52 One of the very few, and unsuccessful, white-collar strikes before the War was undertaken by Butib in 1911. White-collar workers often acted as strike breakers and took over the work of those on strike. See Ph. Lotmar, 'Die Streikarbeit', in *Jb.d. Angestelltenbewegung 1914/15*, p. 83 (an example from 1912). On white-collar strikes in 1919, see *Archiv*, 47, 1920/21, pp. 602f.

53 *DHW*, 25, 1918, p. 48.

54 The management appears to have often resurrected and reactivated social clubs. In the white-collar magazines of 1917 and 1918 there is lively criticism of the 'yellows'. See also the document by the business manager of the ('yellow') association of Krupp Beamten: A. Heinrichsbauer, *Die Privatangestellten der Grossbetriebe u. ihre Organisation*, Essen, 1918; Aufhäuser, pp. 105ff.; *Archiv*, 44, 1917/18, pp. 340f.

55 Quoted from a strictly confidential circular from Moritz Müller, the Hamburg publisher and entrepreneur of *Die Hanse*, containing an (incomplete) list of firms which supported *Die Hanse* with contributions of up to 4500M annually (including, among others, Borsig, Krupp, S&H, SSW, AEG, Bank für Handel und Industrie, Werft Blohm & Voss, Vulkan-Werke, Singer Nähmaschinenfabrik and Iduna-Versicherungs-AG). The circular was published in the *Bergarbeiter-Zeitung*, 36, 7 September 1918. I am indebted to W. Berg for this reference. On the history of one non-confrontationist association during the War, see H. Spethmann, *Der Verband technischer Grubenbeamten 1886–1936. Eine Festschrift*, Gelsenkirchen, 1936, esp. pp. 120ff.

56 See above, n. 54. The *Bergarbeiter-Zeitung*, 7 September 1918, published a sharp criticism of *Die Hanse* by the semi-official *Norddeutsche Allgemeine Zeitung*, 389, 1 August 1918. See also Stegmann, *Repression*, p. 391, on sceptical assessments of the success of the 'yellows', with further evidence. See also below, n. 61.

57 See Umbreit and Lorenz, p. 180 and above, p. 63.

58 See Ay, pp. 102, 192f., for Munich; Schwarz, p. 185 for Nuremberg.

59 See Retzlaw, p. 44.

60 He anticipated less trouble from the better-paid armaments workers. MB, 3 September 1918, p. 32.

61 In addition, the Vereinigung Deutscher Privatbeamten- und Angestellten-Verbände was founded on 3 November 1917; this consisted mainly of associations which had been orientated towards mutual aid and insurance (as well as sociable) functions, rather than towards trade union or social policy matters (for example, the Magdeburger Deutsche Privatbeamten Verein). The Vereinigung was rejected as 'yellow' by other organisations, but defended itself against the charge.

62 See *DIBZ*, 13, 1917, pp. 7f., 35, 145; *DHW*, 25, 1918, pp. 6, 19.

63 The Arbeitsgemeinschaft zur Herbeiführung eines einheitlichen Angestellten-rechts, founded in 1913, incorporated associations with different occupational

bases, chiefly technicians. During the War it became more and more union-orientated, broadened its purposes and changed into the Arbeitsgemeinschaft freier Angestelltenverbände (AfA) in the autumn of 1917. In contrast, the moderate Arbeitsgemeinschaft technischer Verbände and the Mittelstand-like Arbeitsgemeinschaft Kaufmännischer Verbände kept their occupational homogeneity during the War. See the Table, p. 96. It was only after the Revolution that a clear threefold division of white-collar organisations crystallised according to ideological differences (parallel with the workers' unions), so that occupation ceased to be a classificatory criterion. On the agreement between the three federations in July 1917, see *Reichsarbeitsblatt*, S., 16, 1918, p. 12, A review of the organisational history is given in Hartfiel, pp. 140ff.

64 See the plea by the DHV for 'Kaufmannskammern' (Chambers of Commerce) in *DHW*, 25, 1918, pp. 2, 19. At the same time, however, it refused to be included in the Handelskammern (trade associations of the self-employed).

65 The numbers of those expressing these views in Butib grew in the second half of the War. See *DIBZ*, 13, 1917, p. 39. After the editor of the *Correspondenzblatt der Generalkommission*, P. Umbreit, had demanded a firm partnership between white-collar and manual workers – one must not stop 'half way through the journey' (*Die deutschen Gewerkschaften im Weltkriege*, Berlin, 1917, p. 87) – Butib reacted positively: *DIBZ*, 13, 1917, pp. 199ff. Butib then turned towards the Social Democratic trade unions, although a rather left-wing minority split off in 1915. See *Corr. bl.*, 25, 1915, pp. 227, 451.

66 See *DIBZ*, 13, 1917, pp. 52–5.

67 Admittedly not all white-collar associations by a long way joined the Volksbund. See above, p. 55, and Stegmann, *Repression*, pp. 389f.

68 See *DHW*, 25, 1918, p. 19 and above, n. 64 on the evasive attitude of the DHV on this question. This association did not become reality.

69 This means, of course, that white-collar associations were less estranged from their members than were the trade unions, so that their statements may be more reliably used as a source for the changing views of white-collar workers.

70 Put together from *Reicharbeitsblatt*, s.i. 11, 1919, II, pp. 22ff.; 16, 1918, II, pp. 8ff.; 19, 1919, II, pp. 8ff., 40ff.; 22, 1920, II, p. 29ff. The numbers were processed in the Statist. Reichsamt (Abt. f. Arbeiterstatistik) and are based on information given by the associations. Some small associations who, in more than one instance, gave no information, have not been included in the following Table, but are mentioned in ns. 71 and 73. Their non-inclusion is unlikely to have altered the general picture to any extent.

71 In addition, the following belonged to the AKV: Allg. Dt. Buchhandlungsgehilfen-Verband, Leipzig; Buchhaltungsgehilfen-Verein, Leipzig; Deutscher Bankbeamten-Verien, Berlin. See n. 70 above.

72 The Deutsche Chorsänger-Verband, Mannheim (1884) incorporated the Ballett-Union, Mannheim (1912) into its association in 1916. The figures given for 1913 and 1915 cover the membership of both associations.

73 In addition, the AFA included the Allgemeiner Verband d. Dt. Bankbeamten, Berlin; Allgemeine Vereinigung Dt. Buchhandlungsgehilfen, Berlin; Dt. Steigerverband, Essen; Dt. Vorzeichner-Verband, Dortmund; Verband der Kunstgewerbezeichner, Berlin; Verband technischer Schiffsoffiziere, Hamburg; Verein Dt. Kapitäne und Schiffsoffiziere der Handelsmarine. See n. 71 above.

74 The figure is not available. In order to maintain comparability, the corresponding figure for 1913 was used, which indicates the general trend.

75 At the end of 1918 the Deutsche Techniker-Verband was incorporated into the Bund der technisch-industriellen Beamten.

76 For 1918, the Deutscher Polier-Bund gave its total membership figures, including

the self-employed, as 6,200. In accordance with the declared proportion of self-employed to white-collar employees in the previous year, half the number are assumed to be white-collar employees.

77 See the report by the AfA chairman: S. Aufhäuser, 'Die Freie Angestellten- und Arbeiterbewegung. Speech at the first national conference of technical white-collar workers and officials on 14.6.1920', Berlin, 1920, esp. pp. 11ff.

78 This applies particularly to the DHV. On its further development, see Hamel; on its liberal outlook, Gewerkschaftsbund der Angestellten (ed.), *Epochen der Angestelltenbewegung 1774–1930*, Berlin, 1930, pp. 167ff.

79 The increase and intensity of attacks on the 'united mass of capital' and on the 'master in my own house' attitude may be followed particularly clearly in the *DHW*, 1916–18, even if the DHV kept to the goal of future industrial harmony, to be achieved through social policy and the re-education of the entrepreneurs without changing relationships of production. See for instance *DHW*, 24, 1917, p. 81.

80 See above, Chap. 2, ns. 237, 238, on the cooperation of white-collar workers in the Munich and Nuremberg USPD; *Archiv*, 47, 1920/21, pp. 585–619 on the behaviour of white-collar associations at the time of the Revolution. It seems to me that E. Lederer sees the shift to the left of white-collar workers rather too much as an opportunistic adaptation to the Revolution and too little as a consequence of the War and the changes it had brought about, which had been long in the making. See also v. Oertzen, pp. 227ff.

81 Thus the Württemberg KM in MB, 3 July 1917, p. 21 (where there are also similar reports from other places); see also MB, 3 June 1917, p. 17, for the same argument from the Frankfurt AK, and MB, 3 September 1918, p. 34.

82 MB, 3 July 1918, p. 22.

83 See also Deist, *Militär*, pp. 700ff., 856 (for April and August 1917).

84 One needs to read of the laborious ascent of a middle-grade post office official or a rural postman, in the period before 1914, in Winters, pp. 39ff., 42ff., in order to understand what was now being threatened or destroyed in social and psychological terms at the small- and middle-grade official level. See also Schwarz, pp. 179ff.

85 Riezler, p. 247 (on 17 February 1915).

86 The MB constantly drew attention to this, as on 3 August 1917, p. 16 and 3 November 1917, pp. 21ff.

87 Communicated by V. AK (Posen) in MB, 3.10.1918, p. 27.

88 MB, 3 June 1918, p. 25. The Ka. commented (*ibid.*), 'The mood of the Mittelstand continues to be calm, but depressed'.

89 According to the Civil Service official, Winters, p. 89.

90 See W. Elben, *Das Problem der Kontinuität in der deutschen Revolution*, Düsseldorf, 1965, although admittedly only in relation to the top ranks of the civil service.

91 Stegmann, *Zwischen Repression*, pp. 385–414 shows that such elements were not altogether lacking.

92 Schwarz, p. 194.

93 See Winters, pp. 89–90, on the railway civil servants: 'Here nearly every group has its organisation, from the company secretary to the lowest level official, although there are also organisations which contain several classes of official. Even those belonging to one and the same class have formed several organisations existing side by side . . .' and divided according to section of the county, type of service, manner of entry into the service and other criteria.

94 See A. Falkenberg, 'Die Interessengemeinschaft deutscher Reichs- u. Staatsbeamtenverbände', *Beamten-Jahrbuch*, 4, 1917, pp. 93–6. The Interessengemeinschaft made contact with the Verband deutscher Beamtenvereine, which had existed since 1892 (with ca. 288,000 members at the beginning of 1917), and cooperated with it from September 1917 in the Reichsarbeitsausschuss of both organisations. The

Verband deutscher Beamtenvereine was primarily concerned with pensions and other welfare arrangements for civil servants, but was not a Standesvertretung, undertaking social and general policy matters for its members. On this basis a division of work was agreed between it and the politically-activating Interessengemeinschaft. For further details about both organisations, see K. Ritter v. Scherf, 'Die Entwicklung der Beamtenbewegung u. ihre Interessenvertretung', Ph.D. thesis, Greifswald, 1919, pp. 87ff., 99–104; Winters, pp. 96–101.

95 See Falkenberg, *Beamtenbewegung*, p. 69, for a listing of the relevant civil service associations.

96 See *idem*, 'Interessengemeinschaft', p. 95; *idem, Beamtenbewegung*, pp. 20f., twenty of the affiliated associations of the Interessengemeinschaft which did not accept individual members but only occupational associations.

97 Stated in 1917 by F. Winters, the moderate editor of the *Deutschen Postzeitung* (*Die deutsche Beamtenfrage*, p. 24), who at the same time drew attention to progress towards parliamentarisation in the Reich. On the political activity of the Interessengemeinschaft see v. Scherf, pp. 101–4.

98 Clearly, and in detail: Winters, pp. 22–30; H. Potthoff, 'Zur Frage: Beamtenverein u. Politik', *Beamten-Jahrbuch*, 4, 1917, pp. 174–6. This *Vierteljahrsschrift f.d. gesamte Beamtenbewegung*, which began appearing after 1914, was closely allied to the Interessengemeinschaft. It was brought out by H. Potthoff, the former Liberal MP and A. Falkenberg, later a SPD member of the Reichstag. Falkenberg was at the same time the editor of *Gemeinschaft*, the organ of the Interessengemeinschaft. This annual journal published articles by, amongst others, Liberal and Social Democratic politicians, such as 'Der Beamte im Volksstaat' by F. Naumann (1917), pp. 169–73 and 'Vom Segen der Selbsthilfe' by H. Peus (*ibid.*, 70–4). See also, on similar tendencies in Bavaria, Kalmer, pp. 211–20. On the Volksbund für Freiheit und Vaterland see above, Chap. 2, n. 212.

99 See n. 98 above and, on Bavaria, Kalmer, pp. 215, 217, 220.

100 This expression is used by M. Doeberl, see Kalmer, pp. 250ff.

101 See Falkenberg, *Beamtenbewegung*, pp. 23ff., 50ff.; Kalmer, pp. 220–49.

102 In *StdDtr*, 466, 1937, pp. 188ff. On the division into 'war' and 'peace' industries: above, p. 18. The figures refer to technical units and not only to independent entrepreneurs, whose number was somewhat lower, but the information is adequate for comparative purposes.

103 In F. H. Will, *Das Handwerk als Kriegslieferant*, Hanover, 1923, p. 40. R. Fichte, *Die grosse Zeit im Deutschen Handwerk*, Berlin, 1922, pp. 15ff., is also based on Handwerkskammer reports. Figures on closures in individual districts have been aggregated.

104 See *HWZ*, 17, 1917, p. 48.

105 MB, 3 February 1917, p. 9. The Posen AK added (*ibid.*): 'Some small craft businesses, particularly carpenters, plumbers, locksmiths and tailors have little work or earnings.'

106 Quoted by R. Peppel (a retired Oberbürgermeister) in 'Die Durchführung von Zusammenlegungen (Stillegungen) in der Industrie während des Krieges 1914–1918', I, National Archives Microcopy, T77, Roll 343, 80728–80981, 6.

107 See *NHWZ*, 22, 1917, pp. 37f., 58f., 137f.; 23, 1918, p. 2; *HWZ*, 16, 1916, pp. 291f.; 17, 1917, p. 63. The eighteenth Handwerks- und Gewerbekammertag, the annual convention of the local and regional craft boards, brought out guidelines for closures in the woodworking industries (*ibid.*, pp. 163f.). Peppel (see n. 106 above) stressed the very limited success of the closures, which he regarded as due mainly to the inefficiency of the administration.

108 Evidently, even the authorities directly involved did not have exact figures at their disposal. On the great power, still increasing at the end of 1917, of the Ka.d.Dt.Ind.

on closures decisions see Peppel (n. 106 above), pp. 21, 31. See also MB, 3 August 1917, p. 17, where the Württemberg War Ministry warned against acting too rigorously against small-scale businesses within the state: 'They on the whole suffer more from the War than do other groups since many of these businesses have either closed down entirely or have had to be greatly reduced . . . Turning the screw too tight over closures of Württemberg firms would doubtless lead to very unpleasant consequences', especially if this strengthened the impression that this was occurring in favour of the Prussian industrial areas. On this see above, p. 73, and below, n. 308.

109 See on this *Corr.bl.*, 27, 1917, pp. 177ff.; W. Schmidt, 'Das deutsche Handwerk im Weltkriege', PhD dissertation, Erlangen, 1927, Essen, 1929, pp. 18ff.; *Mitteilungen der Handwerkskammer zu Münster*, 1917, p. 182 (with figures for 1914–17).

110 See Fichte, pp. 11f., 27ff., 33.

111 See MB, 15 April 1916, p. 7, where the Sixth AK in Breslau reported complaints by large and small traders on their exclusion from access to food supplies since this was increasingly being dealt with on a centralised and communalised basis; similarly, MB, 26 September 1916, pp. 11, 13. The Secretary of State of the new Reich Economic Office stated in the Reichstag on 13/14 March (Sten.Ber. Reichstag, 311, pp. 435ff.), 'The business Mittelstand has suffered most of all; added to this is the fact that this section is not accorded the sympathy which is offered to the artisanal section.' See, similarly, F. Schär, *Umgestaltung u. Neuorientierung des Handels infolge des Krieges*, Berlin, 1916, pp. 14f.; Schmidt, p. 32; Grebler and Winkler, pp. 54, 94.

112 On the economic success and progress of at least some craft association branches before 1914 (contrary to the general impression) see W. Fischer, *Rolle*; Noll, pp. 193–217. The fact that artisans were amongst those to suffer most under the War is presented in a generally indiscriminating way in later discussions. See Feldman, *Army*, pp. 464f.; *DIEW*, 3, p. 332; Ay, pp. 98ff.; Schwarz, p. 178f.; Winkler, *Mittelstand*, pp. 27f., 61.

113 Quoted in W. Schmidt, p. 35, who mentions such complaints by craft associations, at the same time warning against generalisations based on this.

114 Wernet, p. 77.

115 See *Std.DtR*, 466, 937, pp. 188ff. for details. On the slower decline in the proportion of self-employed out of the total engaged in business from 1907 to 1925 (in comparison with 1895 to 1907) see *ibid.*, p. 194. The proportion of self-employed even increased in some branches of the economy, namely, trade and transport; industry, stone, mining; iron and steel; electrical engineering; rubber and asbestos; building; water, gas and electricity; publishing and catering.

116 See A. Günther, 'Die Folgen des Krieges für Einkommen u. Lebenshaltung der mittleren Volksschichten Deutschlands' in R. Meerwarth *et al.*, *Die Einwirkungen des Krieges auf Bevölkerungsbewegung, Einkommen u. Lebenshaltung in Deutschland*, Stuttgart, 1932, p. 236.

117 MB, 3 August 1917, p. 16f.

118 MB, 3 November 1917, p. 22.

119 See Col. M. Bauer, *Der grosse Krieg in Feld und Heimat*, Tübingen, 1921, p. 153.

120 Both the Prussian Ministry for Public Works (28 August 1914) and the War Ministry (5 November 1914) issued corresponding recommendations and decisions. See Fichte, pp. 24, 28. Regarding the protest of the Ka.d.Dt.Ind. against the negotiation of orders through the craft associations, see *MkdI*, 12, 26 September 1915, p. 114. The industry and trade organisation also protested against the preference shown to craft (Fichte, pp. 46ff.). See also the gratified announcement of success by Obermeister Rahardt, the chairman of the Berlin craft association in *HWZ*, 17, 1917, p. 182.

220   *Notes*

121 The demand which followed from this, to change this policy in order to concentrate resources on to more productive enterprises – above, pp. 34f. – remained relatively ineffective. In November the SAZ was dissolved and closure decisions were handed over to the RWA which acted with increasing restraint up to the end of the War. See Peppel (n. 106 above), pp. 18ff.; quoted by Groener, *ibid.*, p. 6.

122 Thus the Ka. in MB, 3 November 1917, p. 21.

123 The 5 per cent turnover tax which was imposed in 1918, against the opposition of large-scale industry (and the SPD!), contained certain concessions which favoured the Mittelstand by adding a fictitious turnover from one finishing stage to another, which had the effect of hurting large rather than small enterprises. See Sten.Ber. Reichstag, 325, 1918, pp. 2649f.; Roesler, *Finanzpolitik*, p. 117.

124 See, on this, the Conservative MP Hammer on 14 December 1917 in *Wörtliche Berichte über die Verhandlungen des Preussischen Abgeordnetenhauses*, 7, p. 7176.

125 See Rahardt in *HWZ*, 17, 1917, pp. 181f. who wrote that despite decreasing membership numbers – 'as in our industrial cartel' – the craft organisations had become stronger from year to year. 'Der grosse Lehrmeister Krieg' had prepared the way for the founding of credit and distribution cooperatives. On the details of these craft organisations and their success see Fichte, pp. 81–93; W. Schmidt, pp. 37–58. The changes are underestimated, however, in Winkler, *Mittelstand*, e.g. p. 73.

126 See Wernet, pp. 73, 77; Fichte, pp. 76f.

127 See Brauer, pp. 378f.; Wein, pp. 121f.; *HWZ*, 14, 1914, p. 131. On the relatively moderate pre-war attitude of the Handwerks–und Gewerbekammertag, the annual convention of the local and regional craft boards, see the speech by its general secretary Meusch, *NHWZ*, 19, 1914, pp. 143–5.

128 On this see F. Schürholz, *Entwicklungstendenzen im deutschen Wirtschaftsleben zu berufsständischer Organisation u. ihre soziale Bedeutung*, Mönchen-Gladbach, 1922, pp. 49-56; Winkler, *Mittelstand*, pp. 84f. *Ibid.*, pp. 88-89, on the postwar revival of (largely unsuccessful) demands for a legally-guaranteed and compulsory organisation which would follow on from the prewar social-protectionist tradition but without providing for the possibility of state intervention; this was, of course, in contrast to the wartime organisations and despite the strengthening of the self-administering craft associations. On parallel emphases in the small-scale traders' specialist associations ('Erst das Fach, dann der Stand') which emerged both during and after the War (noting, however, the renewal of Mittelstand ideology towards the end of the Weimar Republic) see Wein, pp. 137, 139, 140f.

129 See above, n. 112. In January 1916, after carefully considering both the positive and negative effects of the War on small craftsmen, the *HZW* (16, 1916, pp. 27f.) concluded that the latter predominated. By the end of 1917 it expressed itself more definitely still (*HZW*, 17, 1917, p. 182). For the positive aspects (such as improvement in quality and in organisation) see Fichte, p. 93, and W.Schmidt, pp. 56ff. Imprecise contemporary discussions of the 'War-induced plight' of the Mittelstand contributed (indeed, still contribute) to a lack of differentiation between the overall decline in the position of white-collar workers and civil servants (the 'new' Mittelstand) and the less homogeneous group of small-scale self-employed workers (the 'old' Mittelstand); indeed the position of some of the latter groups was much improved by the War.

130 MB, 3 June 1917, p. 17 (XVIII AK, Frankfurt/Main).

131 *Ibid.* (XIV AK, Karlsruhe). See also *ibid.* the argument of XIX AK in Leipzig and MB, 3 November 1917, p. 21, on a corresponding attitude by the Ka.

132 MB, 8 February 1918, p. 6. Most speak indiscriminately of 'the Mittelstand' in this connection (in the MB and elsewhere), which greatly limits the force of their statements.

133 *NHWZ*, 23, 25 May 1918, quoted in Winkler, *Mittelstand*, p. 65.
134 See P. Molt, *Der Reichstag vor der improvisierten Revolution*, Cologne, 1963, pp. 210ff.
135 See Ay, pp. 192ff.; Schwarz, pp. 185, 229.
136 In G.A. Ritter, 'Kontinuität u. Umformung des deutschen Parteiensystems 1918-1920' in H. Rosenberg. The following Table from the Appendix shows that, among the SPD and USPD party members in the Reichstags of 1912 and 1920 and in the National Assembly of 1919, there were:

| | 1912 | 1919 | | 1920 | |
	SPD	SPD	USPD	SPD	USPD
Owners of independent craft businesses	9	7	1	3	4
Higher civil servants in State or Reich service	–	–	–	1	–
Medium or lower civil servants in State or Reich service	–	3	–	2	–
Municipal civil servants	2	2	–	–	–
White-collar workers in the private sector (without managers)	–	3	–	5	5
Teachers	–	1	–	3	–

In 1912, 9 out of 21, in 1919, 8 out of 17 and in 1921, 7 out of 19 MPs in the SPD/USPD were artisans or small-scale businessmen. It was very different among white-collar workers; in 1912 there were no MPs from this occupational group in the Reichstag. In the National Assembly of 1919, 5 out of 6, and in the Reichstag of 1920, all 10 MPs whose occupation was given as 'white-collar worker' were in the SPD/USPD.

137 This is grossly exaggerated, being argued on far too narrow an evidential base, at least for the members of the 'old' Mittelstand; see Schwarz, p. 186. More appropriately, but an inaccurate assessment, in Winkler, *Mittelstand*, pp.70f.
138 See Ay, p. 101. The MB speak frequently of 'widespread' longing for peace, including much of the Mittelstand, as on June 1917, p. 22, and 3 September 1918, p. 6 (the XVIII AK in Frankfurt/Main).
139 See Stegmann, *Erben*, p. 506 and above, pp. 55f.
140 See Winkler, *Mittelstand*, p. 63.
141 See the evidence in ns. 103–10 above. On the discrimination against artisans in deferments see *Archiv*, 40, 1915, p. 121; *NHWZ*, 22, 1917, pp. 37f. The Handwerks- und Gewerbekammertag warned against all attempts to 'close down craft businesses in order to place their workers and equipment at the disposal of industry'; *HWZ*, 17, 1917, p. 48, on the competition between industry and craft for raw materials.
142 *NHWZ*, 20, 1917, p. 78.
143 See *ibid.*, 22, 1917, pp. 58f. (against joint decision making by employees), 66 (against equality of rights of employees), 118 (against social policies too much favouring the worker), 133 (the problem of apprentices), 139 (against the raised demands of the Christian trade unions); *ibid*, 23, 1918, pp. 33f. (against trade union demands for more rights for apprentices), 77 ('Mittelstand and Social Democracy'), 109 (against the revision of § 153 of the craft regulations), 117f. (against the proposed Arbeitskammergesetz). In contrast the moderately liberal *HWZ* expressed itself with much more restraint, only cautiously condemning the

Berlin armaments strike (18 and 25 May, 1917).
144 See above, pp. 69f.
145 See *Corr. bl.*, 27, 1917, pp. 174-74, 191.
146 See the evidence in Winkler, *Mittelstand*, pp. 65-72.
147 See *NHWZ*, 22, 1917, pp. 58f.; *HWZ*, 1917, p.78.
148 Thus an interpolation, on 13 March 1918, by Irl, the Centre MP, who often spoke up in the Reichstag for the interests of the smaller craftsmen. See Sten. Ber. Reichstag, 311, p. 4345.
149 *Ibid.*, P. 4372, for this comment by the Conservative MP, Kapp.
150 See *NHWZ*, 22, 1917, p. 95, 117f., 122f., 142., 181ff.; *ibid.*, 23, 1918, pp. lf., 13, 15, 18, 36, 77, 111.
151 These however, were still apparent in the *NHWZ* in 1918. See, for example, *NHWZ*, 23, 1918, pp. 97f., 129f. The change of emphasis discussed here was neither abrupt nor complete, but gradual and tendential.
152 Especially clearly stated by Peters, the legal representative of the Düsseldorf Craft Association, see *NHWZ*, 23, 1918, pp. 160f., 165f., 170f. Similarly the memorandum of the 1918 Handwerks- und Gewerbekammertag, published *ibid.*, on 21 and 28 September, 5 and 12 October ('Measures for the reconstruction of craft'). Similarly, *HWZ*, 15/22 July: 'The use of military and bureaucratic maxims in economic life is a contradiction of the nature of the economic struggle'. See also Mitteilungen of the Münster Craft Association, esp. 5, 1917, Nos. 7, 12 (Minutes of the plenary meeting of 14 March 1917): 'Cooperative self-organisation of craft instead of state monopolies and compulsory syndicalisation is the aim.'
153 See above, pp. 138ff.
154 Both the *NHWZ* and *DAZ* spoke out against state intervention and coercion with articles that, in part 'quoted' one another word for word. See, for example, *NHWZ*, 22, 1917, (17 November) and *DAZ*, 16, 1917, (23 December), against plans by August Müller. The rejection of the government's proposed Arbeitskammergesetz also used almost identical arguments. See *DAZ*, 17, 1918, (13 January and, with reference to relevant personal statements, 11 August).
155 On the beginning of this process before the War, see E. Lederer, *Die wirtschaftlichen Organisationen*, Leipzig, 1913, p. 105; on its speed-up during the War: *idem, Die sozialen Organisationen*, 2nd ed., Leipzig, 1922, pp. 91-114.
156 *DAZ*, 17, 1918, supplement of 28 July.
157 See Winkler, *Mittelstand*, p. 67; *ibid*, pp. 70f., on a similarly argued offer of cooperation from a Craft Association representative to large-scale industry, December 1918.
158 See W. Kulemann, *Genossenschaftsbewegung, 1, Berlin, 1922, p. 84; R. Wilbrandt, Kapitalismus u. Konsumenten. Konsumvereinspolitik, GdS*, 9, II, pp. 411-56, esp. 430ff.; Wein, pp. 61, 91ff., 104ff. The 'consumer association danger' was in the forefront of the activities of various associations of the self-employed Mittelstand immediately prior to the War. See *Jb. d. Angestelltenbewegung*, 1914/5, p. 67.
159 See *ibid.*, pp. 186f.; W. Albrecht, *Landtag u. Regierung in Bayern am Vorabend der Revolution von 1918*, Berlin, 1968, pp. 99, 111. In 1913 the DHV had rejected the consumer associations on purely ideological grounds (*DHW*, 20, 1913, pp. 217-19). Necessity altered this preconception. See also Ay, p. 100. On the attitude of the employers' associations see *DAZ*, 16, 1917, AM 8.4: 'Through cooperatives to the socialist state'.
160 On this see above, pp. 126ff. above.
161 See above, n. 155 and Wein, pp. 134ff. on small-scale trade.
162 See the brief overview on the 1920s in J. Kocka, 'The First World War and the 'Mittelstand': German artisans and white-collar workers', in *J Cont Hist*, 8, 1973, 1, pp. 101-23, esp 121-3. *Idem, Die Angestellten in der deutschen Geschichte 1850-1980,*

Göttingen, 1981, pp. 142–70; H. Speier, *Die Angestellten vor dem Nationalsozialismus*, Göttingen, 1977.
163 In 1930 Gedag had 592,000 members, AfA 480,000 and the Liberal Union of White-collar Workers (GdA) 385,000. In Fischer, *Die Angestellten*, pp. 44f.
164 Cf. Kocka, *Die Angestellten in der deutschen Geschichte*, pp. 148–58; *idem*, *White-collar workers in America*. Richard Hamilton's attempt to question these results is not successful (*Who voted for Hitler?*, Princeton, 1984). The latest stage of the debate may be found in M. Prinz, 'Vom "neuen Mittelstand" zum "Volksgenossen". Ausprägung und Entwicklung der Kragenlinie in der deutschen Sozialstruktur 1880-1945', PhD dissertation, Bielefeld, 1983. Prinz's work is the best and most comprehensive analysis of white-collar workers in the Weimar Republic and the Third Reich that has so far been written (to appear 1985).
165 'Das soziale Antlitz des Deutschen Reiches' in *idem*, *Aufsätze zur Soziologie*, Tübingen, 1953, p. 221.
166 See Winkler, *Mittelstand*, chaps. III–VIII.

Chapter 4. Class-society and State

1 MB, 3 May 1917, p. 23.
2 See O.v. Kiesenwetter, *Fünfundzwanzig Jahre wirtschaftspolitischen Kampfes. Geschichtliche Darstellung des Bundes der Landwirte*, Berlin, 1918, p. 194; similarly, the Catholic Bavarian farmers' leader, Heim in G. Heim and S. Schlittenbauer, *Ein Hilferuf der deutschen Landwirtschaft*, Regensburg, n.d. [1916], pp. 68ff.; F. Münch, 'Die agitatorische Tätigkeit des Bauernführers Heim' in K. Bosl (ed.), *Bayern im Umbruch*, Munich, 1969, pp. 301–44, esp. 314. See also F. Aereboe, *Der Einfluss des Krieges auf die landwirtschaftliche Produktion in Deutschland*, Stuttgart, 1927, pp. 32-5. The HDG stipulated that those required for duty under the Auxiliary Service Law who had worked in the agricultural sector before 1 August 1916 should not transfer to another sector (not even one covered by the HDG).
3 See Aereboe, pp. 126, 128.
4 See Prince Max v. Baden, *Erinnerungen u. Dokumente*, G. Mann and A. Burckhardt (eds.), 2nd ed., Stuttgart, 1968, p. 548, n. 1, on the 'Bolshevism' of agricultural workers in Lower Pomerania, who for weeks 'had already been discussing the division of the masters' estates on the Russian model' (communication to Max v. Baden at the beginning of November); further, E.v. Oldenberg-Januschau, *Erinnerungen*, Leipzig, 1936, pp. 208-9, on the 'spirit of revolt' in his estate district in November 1918.
5 See Aereboe, pp. 124-9; W. Mattes, *Die bayerischen Bauernräte*, Stuttgart, 1921, pp. 33-6; Kiesenwetter, pp. 233-4, 238-9. At the beginning of 1918 K., who was an official of the BdL, turned sharply against the Vereinsgesetz-Novelle being extended to cover rural areas. He did not recognise that the workers' conflict was already causing his Association major problems, the more so since he hoped, together with Frh. v. Wagenheim for a 'German peace', for annexation and its socially 'reconciling' effect. See also, and more recently: H.Muth, 'Die Entstehung der Bauern- u. Landarbeiterräte im Nov. 1918 u. die Politik des Bundes der Landwirte', *VfZ*, 21, 1973, pp. 1-38.
6 See the report for the Saarbrücken AK in MB, 3 May 1917, p. 22, on the local farmers' deep-seated resentment of large landowners in the East, who (allegedly) delivered less and were allowed to sell what they did not deliver at higher prices. In January 1917 the Fifth AK (Posen) had reported a 'perceptibly heightened feeling lately among the small farmers against the landowners' (MB, 3 February 1917, p. 11). See also Mattes, p. 56, on complaints by Bavarian farmers about the

preferential treatment of the larger land owners, especially owners of entailed estates.

7 See, for example, on the National-Liberal orientated 'Deutscher Bauernbund', which turned towards the FVP during the War, *Die bürgerlichen Parteien in Deutschland*, 1, pp. 415-21, esp. 418. Also Mattes, pp. 56-9, 63, on the Catholic Bavarian Farmers' Association and its demands, which were directed against unrestricted large-scale land ownership, and whose left wing, under the leadership of Gandorfer, advocated a negotiated peace in July 1918.

8 See T. v. Bethmann Hollweg, *Betrachtungen zum Weltkriege*, 2, Berlin, 1921, pp. 171-2.

9 The main points of attack and causes for complaint are in Helm and Schlittenbauer, pp. 5-19, 46-56, 61ff.; extracts from letters from the small- and medium-sized farmers who made up the greater part of their organisation in *idem*, pp. 91-120, 127-35, esp. 118-20; examples of the frequently recurring descriptions of the mood in the countryside in the MB, 15 July 1918, pp. 2-3, 26; 8 September 1916, pp. 5-6; 3 August 1917, pp. 10ff.; 3 November 1917, pp. 27ff.; 3 June 1918, pp. 26-7; 3 August 1918, pp. 15ff.; for the views of the other side, see the memoirs of Oldenburg-Januschau, the radical Junker, pp. 145-72; the semi-official criticism of the War economy by the BdL, in Kiesenwetter, pp. 173-232; the criticism of the conservative Westarp, pp. 365-431. W. was close to the BdI.. This is not the place to investigate either the details of government intervention or the justification for the complaints and criticisms by the agricultural sector. For this see, above all, A. Skalweit, *Die deutsche Ernährungswirtschaft*, Stuttgart, 1927, and Aereboe, pp. 29-107, whose judgement, however, appears to be biased towards the agricultural interest; this also colours the factual but very enlightening analysis by v. Westarp.

10 Confirmed by Lederer, *Soziale Organisationen*, 2nd ed., 1922, pp. 144ff.

11 See Kiesenwetter, p. 223ff.; 'Die Bürgerlichen Parteien in Deutschland', Vol. I, pp. 122-49, esp. 145-6; Stegmann, *Erben*, pp. 456ff., 465ff., 504ff.; pp. 55f., above.

12 With Westarp, it is possible to speak of a change in Conservative policy on this question, with the reasons for which need reconsideration. See Westarp, pp. 386ff., 390-1, 397, 406, 410-19. The move against the 'compulsory economy' and 'state socialism' also dominates Kiesenwetter's account, see esp. pp. 188-9, 210-11, 217-21, 230; see further the speeches by Rötger (CVDI), Wangenheim and Roesicke (BdL) at the 1917 'Kriegstagung des BdL' in *Bund der Landwirte, Kgr. Bayern*, 19, Munich, 1917, on 25 February and 4 March; *ibid.*, 20, Munich, 1918, on 28 July ('Who is to blame for our economic policy?'), 29 September and 27 October; further, see Oldenburg-Januschau, pp. 145-72, 193-204, esp. 196 (his speech at the BdL meeting at Zirkus Busch in February 1918).

13 See Kiesenwetter, p. 220 (quoted by Roesicke from the Reichstag, 11 May 1917), pp. 210-11.

14 See the report of the meeting on this theme of the Dt. Handelstag, the Ka.d.Dt.ind, the Dt. Landwirtschaftsrat and the Dt. Handwerks- und Gewerbekammertag, on 28 September 1914, in *DAZ*, 13, 4 October 1914. *Ibid.*, 15, 12 March 1916, on the very conciliatory expression of contrast about the labour force. See also *MKdI*, 216, 17 August 1918, pp. 3165-6, for a reprint of 'Landwirtschaft und Industrie. Eine zeitgemässe Betrachtung über ihre innigen Wechselbeziehungen'.

15 See above, Chap. 2, n. 217, and pp. 55f.; Kiesenwetter, pp. 249-58, esp. 256-7, on a petition of December 1917 against the granting of general voting rights in Prussia. This petition was signed by the Associations in the 1913 Kartell, with the exception of the Ka.d.Dt.Ind., the BdI and the Hansa-Bund, who nevertheless made common cause with other Kartell Associations over the question of war aims and of resistance to government intervention.

16 Lederer (*Soziale Organisationen*, pp. 114ff.) took the maintenance of large-scale

agrarian power for granted. R. Lewinsohn (Morus), *Die Umschichtung der europäschen Vermögen*, Berlin, 1926, pp. 159ff., points to agricultural profits and their justification in the rising wartime inflation. See Aereboe, pp. 84ff.; Grebler and Winkler, pp. 85ff., on the loss of capital and the long-term damage done to agriculture during the war. H. Rosenberg, 'Zur sozialen Funktion der Agrarpolitik im Zweiten Reich', in *idem, Probleme der deutschen Sozialgeschichte*, Frankfurt, 1969, p. 77, sees the War as initiating the decline of the Junkers. More differentiating is A. Günther, 'Die Folgen des Krieges für Einkommen u. Lebenshaltung der mittleren Volksschichten Deutschlands' in Meerwarth *et al.*, pp. 259ff.

17 MB, 8 September 1916, p. 5.

18 MB, 3 December 1916, pp. 5, 6.

19 See, for example, MB, 17 January 1917, p. 8; 3 March 1917, pp. 15ff.; 3 June 1917, pp. 18–19; 3 November 1917, p. 17; 3 September 1918, p. 29.

20 Seen clearly in the quotation, p. 121 above, by a Pomeranian farmer's wife; see also Ay, *Entstehung*, pp. 109–22, 151.

21 See, on the Bavarian hatred of Prussia, which was strengthened by the presence of rich tourists from the North, Ay, pp. 108–9, 119–20, 134–48; MB, 3 September 1918; above, Chap. II, n. 298.

22 See MB, 3 December 1916, pp. 12–13; 17 January 1917, pp. 6–7; 3 February 1917, p. 5; 3 March 1917, pp. 5–6; 3 April 1917, p. 5; 3 May 1917, pp. 7ff.; 3 September 1918, pp. 14ff.; 3 October 1918, pp. 11ff.

23 Generally on the connection between (decreasing but real) group differences between Jews and non-Jews on the one hand and the potential for aggression and protest arising from quite different sources on the other, see E. G. Reichmann, *Hostages of Civilisation*, Boston 1951.

24 MB, 3 February 1917, pp. 7–8; for further examples, MB, 8 September 1916, p. 3; 7 November 1916, p. 4; 3 December 1916, p. 10.

25 See W. Jochmann, 'Die Ausbreitung des Antisemitismus' in W. E. Mosse (ed.), *Deutsches Judentum in Krieg und Revolution 1916–1923*, Tübingen, 1971, pp. 424–7. Jochmann is able (pp. 409–42) to display extensive material on antisemitism during the War.

26 See *ibid.*, p. 438, *pass.*

27 See *ibid.*, pp. 436–42; Stegmann, *Repression*, pp. 396ff. On the tradition of antisemitic manipulation by radical-Conservative politicians, see Puhle, *Interessenpolitik*, pp. 125–40.

28 On the DAAP and its failure, see Stegmann, *Repression*, pp. 394ff.

29 See O. Baumgarten *et al., Geistige u. Sittliche Wandlungen des Krieges in Deutschland*, Stuttgart, 1927, pp. 15, 70ff.; on the narrowing of earnings differentials between young and old, see p. 21 above. Further: W. Flitner, 'Der Krieg u. die Jugend', in Baumgarten, p. 291 (on the partial reduction in traditional teacher-pupil differences).

30 *Ibid.*, pp. 296–302, esp. p. 346; M. Buber-Neumann, *Von Potsdam nach Moskau*, Stuttgart, 1957, pp. 29ff., on the politicisation of the 'Wandervögel'.

31 See E. Foerster, 'Die Stellung der evangelischen Kirche', in Baumgarten, pp. 89–148, 122ff.

32 See A. Rademacher, 'Die Stellung der katholischen Kirche', in Baumgarten, pp. 149–216, 179, 204ff. In so far as both churches had identified themselves to a large extent with the old system and made themselves partially responsible for propaganda functions for the State during the War – this was less the case for the Catholic than for the Protestant church – they were identified with those who lost the War. The influence of the clergy among the upper classes probably diminished because of the War; see A. Günther, *Folgen*, pp. 116ff. On the churches as means of

propaganda: E. Lederer, 'Zur Soziologie des Weltkriegs', *Archiv*, 39, 1915, p. 374; Ay, pp. 89–94; W. Pressel, *Die Kriegspredigt 1914 bis 1918 in der evangelischen Kirche Deutschlands*, Göttingen, 1967; H. Missalla, '*Gott mit uns.*' *Die deutsche Katholische Kriegspredigt 1914–1918*, Munich, 1968.

33 See Mendelssohn-Bartholdy, pp. 6ff., 27.

34 This refers more to the mostly inactive fleet than to the army. See D. Horn, *The German Naval Mutinies of World War I*, New Brunswick, N.J., 1969; on the army: *Archiv*, 41, 1916, pp. 914–15; Baumgarten, p. 54; Ay, pp. 102–9.

35 This is repeatedly stressed in the MB, as on 8 September 1916, p. 8; 3 January 1917, p. 24; 3 September 1918, p. 5; see also the comments by Grober on Ludendorff in E. Matthias and R. Morsey (eds.), *Die Regierung des Prinzen M. v. Baden*, Düsseldorf, 1962, p. 228.

36 See above, pp. 75, 110.

37 How decisive the initiatives of the State's bureaucracy were for the development of the Prussian-German class structure before 1848 is shown by R. Koselleck, *Preussen zwischen Reform u. Revolution*, Stuttgart, 1967; how greatly the formation of white-collar workers into a social stratum in the last decades before the first World War depended on state legislation and its power for social definition is shown in Kocka, *Unternehmensverwaltung*, pp. 513–44.

38 See M. Weber, *Wirtschaft u. Gesellschaft*, Cologne, 1964, pp. 39–40; M. Draht, 'Der Staat der Industriegesellschaft', *Der Staat*, 5, 1966, pp. 273 94; O. Stammer and P. Weingart, *Politische Soziologie*, Munich, 1972, pp. 37–9.

39 See. H.-J. Puhle, 'Parlament, Parteien u. Interessenverbände 1890–1914', in M. Stürmer (ed.), *Das Kaiserliche Deutschland*, p. 343.

40 This inadequacy, owing to a lack of historical depth marked J. Habermas, *Strukturwandel der Öffentlichkeit*, Neuwied, 2nd ed. (1965), 5th ed. (1971); equally, the important essay by C. Offe, 'Politische Herrschaft und Klassenstrukturen. Zur Analyse spätkapitalistischer Gesellschaftsstrukturen', in G. Kress and K. Senghaas (eds.), *Politikwissenschaft*, Frankfurt, 1972, pp. 135–64, esp. p. 140. On the historical situation before 1914: H.-U. Wehler, *The German Empire*.

41 See Huber, *Verfassungsgeschichte*, 4.

42 See W. Zapf, *Wandlungen der deutschen Elite*, Munich, 1965, pp. 38ff.; Kaelble, *Sozialer Aufstieg*.

43 These assertions could only be backed up by a thorough analysis of the Wilhelmine system, which cannot be carried out here. See also the first section in Chap. 2 above, with further bibliography.

44 See Chap. 1, n. 2, above.

45 See K. Helfferich, *Der Weltkrieg*, 2, Berlin, 1919, pp. 239–40; Skalweit, pp. 165–6; on the changes in the Reichstag at the beginning of the War, see E. Pikart, 'Der deutsche Reichstag u. der Ausbruch des Ersten Weltkriegs', *Der Staat*, 5, 1955, pp. 51ff. In order to prevent political discussions in the Reichstag the government, from November 1914, gave promises of a 'Neuorientierung'. Although these promises were not at first made public, they show that the Reichstag was not totally excluded during 1914 and 1915. See E. Matthias and R. Morsey (eds.), *Der Interfraktionelle Ausschuss 1917/18*, 1, Düsseldorf, 1959, p. xiii. Government representatives conferred with leaders of the parliamentary parties with Südekum and with other members of the SPD leadership before taking important decisions, more than they had done before the War.

46 See J. V. Bredt, *Der Deutsche Reichstag im Weltkrieg*, Berlin, 1926, pp. 45ff.; Grosser, pp. 102, 122ff., deals with the motives of the parties on this step – partly annexationist (National Liberals), partly internal reformist (SPD).

47 See, amongst others, R. B. Armeson, *Total Warfare and Compulsory Labor*, The Hague, 1964, pp. 78–94, 105, 108–9. On the 15th Committee: *RGBI* 1916, pp.

1333ff., 9; the (characteristic) criticism by Westarp, pp. 461-2.

48 See U. Bermbach, *Vorformen parlamentarischer Kabinettsbildung in Deutschland*, Cologne, 1967; Grosser, pp. 109-110.

49 To this belonged the rapid introduction of general and equal voting rights in Prussia; a moderate foreign policy on the basis of the German reply to the Pope's 'Friedensnote' (but not on the basis of the continuing peace resolutions by the government majority); the lifting of political censorship and the 'Section 153' trade regulations and a pro-trade union Works Council Law. See Matthias and Morsey, *Der interfraktionelle Ausschuss*, 1, pp. 143, 248-9, 573; *ibid.*, 2, pp. 426-9, for Scheidemann and Ebert in July 1918 on the non-fulfilment of this programme (except for the revision of Section 153).

50 See, on the partial fulfilment of this long-standing SPD demand, *ibid.*, 2, p. 220, n. 48; Westarp, pp. 501ff.

51 See, above all, Bredt, pp. 198-217, 348-67; Matthias and Morsey, *Der Interfraktionelle Ausschuss*, 1, xi-xxxix; *idem*, 2, pp. 126-52 (esp. 146), where the authors bring out the weakness and heterogeneity of the Reichstag majority between July 1917 and July 1918 and thereby correct the usual all too strong emphasis on the actual extent of parliamentarisation during the War.

52 We have made frequent references above to the almost consistently negative attitude of the entrepreneurs' organisations towards any tendencies to a 'Neuorientierung'. On the attitude of the Conservative party, where the interests of the agrarian and heavy industrial sectors were best represented, see Westarp, pp. 467ff., 483ff., 500ff., 610-15, 655ff.; on the anti-parliamentary attitude of the industrially committed right wing of the National Liberals and the Centre, see Grosser, pp. 117, 119ff., 168ff., 175-6; H. Thieme, *Nationaler Liberalismus in der Krise*, Boppard, 1963, esp. pp. 30-7. The group around Stresemann and the industrial, mercantile and banking interests which were influential in the FVP nevertheless show that a minority in the entrepreneurial camp did not share the dominant hostility to the 'Neuorientierung'.

53 See esp., Grosser, pp. 103-26, 152-80; Ritter, *Kontinuität*.

54 See esp., Bermbach, *Vorformen*; *idem*, 'Aspekte der Parlamentarismus-Diskussion im Kaiserlichen Reichstag', *PVS*, 8, 1967, pp. 51-70.

55 See L. Bergsträsser, *Die preussische Wahlrechtsfrage im Kriege u. die Entstehung der Osterbotschaft 1917*, Tübingen, 1929; R. Patemann, *Der Kampf um die preussische Wahlrechtsreform*, Düsseldorf, 1964.

56 See, amongst others, Puhle, *Parlament*, pp. 342-3, 362-3.

57 See Matthias and Morsey, *Der Interfraktionelle Ausschuss*, 1, pp. xiii-xiv.

58 See, above all, Deist, *Militär*, pp. lii-lxv, esp. lxiv, where earlier exaggerated ideas about the 'Ludendorff dictatorship' are corrected; *ibid.*, pp. 803-19 with sources on the 'vaterländischen Unterricht' ('patriotic lessons') of April 1917 to Oct. 1918; *ibid.*, pp. 919ff., 937ff., 947-8, 950-1, 957ff., on his probably relatively minimal effectiveness. See also Grosser, pp. 134-49, esp. 148, on Scheidemann's remark in April 1918 that '. . . the constitutional situation in which we live is after all only military absolutism, tempered by fear of a parliamentary scandal'.

59 See H. Jaeger, *Unternehmer in der deutschen Politik (1890-1918)*, Bonn, 1967, on the proportion of entrepreneurs who were leading political figures.

60 See. J. Kochka, 'Industrielles Management. Konzeptionen u. Modelle in Deutschland vor 1914', *VSWG*, 56, 1969, p. 362.

61 See O. Most, *Zur Wirtschafts- u. Sozialstatistik höherer Beamter in Preussen*, Leipzig, 1916; *idem*, 'Zur Wirtschafts- und Sozialstatistik des höheren Beamtentums in Preussen', *Schmollers Jb.*, 39, 1915, pp. 214ff.

62 As well as the studies mentioned in n. 61 above, see F. Maas, 'Über die Herkunftsbedingungen geistiger Führer', *Archiv*, 41, 1916, pp. 144ff., where the

proportion of 'intellectual leaders originating in the practical sphere' (statesmen, economists, the military, businessmen), and whose fathers belonged to the 'lower orders', is given as 7.9 per cent. Those coming from civil service (25.8 per cent), landowning (19.8 per cent) and military (19.6 per cent) families preponderated over those coming from families in trade and industry (11.7 per cent). Unfortunately this group is not subdivided further, but the elitist selection procedures of the time for civil service and military careers allow one to assume that entrepreneurs and businessmen were more likely to come from the 'lower orders' than were statesmen and military personnel. Handbooks were used as sources in the survey, with 'fame' or being known to the public as the selection criteria. The proportion of MPs from the 'lower orders' was naturally greater under the conditions of a general suffrage and a large workers' party. See W. Kremer, 'Der soziale Aufbau der Parteien u. des deutschen Reichstags 1871-1918', diss., Cologne, Emsdetten, 1934; K. Demeter, 'Die soziale Schichtung der deutschen Parlamente seit 1848', *VSWG*, 39, 1952, pp. 1ff. But, given the powerlessness of Parliament and the limited participation by the SPD in the decision-making process, this was of little significance.

63 See above, pp. 155ff.

64 See R. Merton, *Erinnernswertes aus meinem Leben das über das Persönliche hinausgeht*, Frankfurt, 1955 (M. was the son of the founder of the Frankfurt 'Metallgessellschaft' and worked for this enterprise until 1914). On the Junior Director of AEG, see, amongst others, W. O. Henderson, 'Rathenau. A Pioneer of the Planned Economy', *EHR*, 4, 1951, pp. 98, 108. W. von Moellendorff was an engineer at AEG, Sorge was a director at Krupp, K. Helfferich, formerly Director of the Deutschen Bank, became Secretary of State in the Reich Treasury at the beginning of 1915, and State Secretary at the Ministry of the Interior in June 1916. See K. Helfferich, *Der Weltkrieg*, 2, Berlin, 1919, pp. 115ff., on the changes made in the direction of his office at the Treasury in comparison with his predecessor. Many other examples may be found in, *Wegweiser durch die Deutsche Kriegswirtschaft. Geschäftsführung des Kriegsausschusses der deutschen Industrie*, Steinmann-Bucher (eds.), Berlin, n.d.; A. Müller, *Die Kriegsrohstoffbewirtschaftung 1914-1918 im Dienste des deutschen Monopolkapitals*, Berlin, 1955, pp. 17-18, 33-4, 80, *pass.*; A. Schröter, *Krieg, Staat, Monopol 1914-1918*, Berlin, 1965; Jaeger, pp. 216ff.

65 See Riezler, pp. 401-2 (25 January 1917). See, on this contrast between the 'traditional' and new 'radical militarism', G. D. Feldman, 'Les fondements politiques et sociaux de la mobilisation économique en Allemagne (1914-1918)', *Annales ESC*, 24, 1969, pp. 120-1, 126-7. See also Deist, *Militär*, pp. xvii, on the failure to integrate technical education sufficiently into officer training.

66 See Groener, p. 335; Skalweit, pp. 184-5; Feldman, *Army*, pp. 235-6.

67 See *ibid.*, pp. 353-4, on Schlickes' difficulties at the metal workers' annual conference in 1917.

68 See *RGBI*, 1916, pp. 1333ff.; also in Umbreit and Lorenz, pp. 239-45.

69 See the very informative study (even though marked by the ideological conditions under which it was carried out) by H. Dierkopf, 'Vorgeschichte, Entstehung u. Auswirkungen des Vaterländischen Hilfsdienstgesetzes v. 5. Dez. 1916', PhD diss., Halle, 1937; Armeson; Feldman, *Army*, pp. 197-249; Deist, *Militär*, pp. 459-647 (for the sources).

70 See Feldman, *Army*, pp. 186ff., on the early history; Deist, *Militär*, pp. 503 (n. 7, on the OHL's first brief version of 28 October 1916 that did, however, acknowledge the moderating influence of Groener), 513 (on Ludendorff's original idea); *ibid.*, p. 503 (n. 8, on Groener's version of the events of 28 October); *ibid.*, pp. 506 (n. 1), 514 (on Groener's statement to the state representatives in the Bundesrat, 9 November 1916 - its explicit function and the Reichstag's aspirations in this role); E. Ludendorff (ed.), *Urkunden der Obersten Heeresleitung über ihre Tätigkeit 1916-18*,

Berlin, 1921, pp. 81–2.
71 On 9 November 1916, according to Deist, *Militär*, p. 513; pp. 502–6 (esp. 505) on Groener's conversation with Prussian ministers on 29 October. For Helfferich, whose proposal placed greater reliance on voluntarism (*ibid.*, p. 504, n. 17) concern about the interests of those entrepreneurs outside wartime and heavy industry is likely to have played a role.
72 *Ibid.*, pp. 515–6, n. 4, for Helfferich's attitude.
73 *Ibid.*, pp. 516–36, for the Minutes of the meeting of the Prussian Ministry of State, 1 December 1916: 'One could almost say that Social Democrats, Poles, Alsatians and the workers' secretariats had made this law. The changes thereby introduced into the law deviate so basically from the compromises discussed by the Ministry of State that another consultation seems indispensable'. Thus Helfferich, *ibid.*, p. 527; for Bethmann's attitude, *ibid.*, p. 536.
74 On the parliamentary process up to the final version, see n. 69 above on the bibliography in Deist, *Militär*. See *ibid.*, pp. 506ff., on the proposal of 30 October which emerged from the discussion between the OHL and the Prussian Ministry of State; *ibid.*, pp. 515–19; on the Prussian Ministry of State's plan after private prior negotiations with party, employer and union representatives. This is roughly how the presentation went in the Bundesrat; see also the similar account in Umbreit and Lorenz, pp. 148–51. This version, with all its compromises (equal representation on arbitration committees, no workers' committees within companies, no Reichstag participation, no equivalent to the important subsequent last sentence of §9), sought to anticipate party criticism – see, esp., Deist, *Militär*, p. 518, n. 10. It may be compared with the much more far-reaching final version, *RGBl*, 1916, pp. 1333ff.
75 See HDG, §§ 11ff.; O. Neuloh, *Die deutsche Betriebsverfassung bis zur Mitbestimmung*, Tübingen, 1956, pp. 81ff., 105–6.
76 On submission of an 'important reason', also if the move to another Hilfsdienst firm would bring about 'an appropriate improvement in living conditions', the Hilfsdienst worker was entitled to a pass allowing him to be re-engaged by another Hilfsdienst firm (see HDG, §9). §10, para. 1, made provision for 'economic organisations' to draw up lists of proposals according to which the arbitration committees of the Ka. would be set up.
77 See Matthias and Pikart, *Die Reichstagsfraktion der deutschen Sozialdemokratie 1898 bis 1918*, 2, Düsseldorf, 1966, pp. 231–40; E. David, *Das Kriegstagebuch des Reichstagsabgeordneten . . . 1914 bis 1918*, Düsseldorf, 1966, pp. 206–12.
78 See Armeson, pp. 8–2, 85.
79 See the speech by Hugo Haase on 2 December 1916, in E. Prager, *Geschichte der USPD*, Berlin, 1921, p. 121; Armeson, pp. 92–3 (A. interprets the law rather too much as a sacrifice for the working class and as the product of the military-industrial complex).
80 On the backward-looking standpoint of the General commission, see Umbreit and Lorenz, pp. 145–57. For the employers' standpoint, see *Fünfundzwanzig Jahre Arbeitnordwest 1914–1929*, Berlin, 1929, pp. 79ff.; Osthold, pp. 235ff., 254, 256. Groener, the head of the Ka. had already commented (14 December 1916) that: 'In [his] opinion it was the entrepreneurs who were more frightened of the law than the workers' (Deist, *Militär*, p. 541). See also *ibid.*, p. 573; H. v. Stein, *Erlebnisse u. Betrachtungen aus der Zeit des Weltkrieges*, Leipzig, 1919, pp. 109–10, a negative assessment of the HDG by the Prussian Minister of War); Westarp, pp. 453–63; Feldman, *Army*, pp. 308ff., 325, 410. See also n. 86 below and pp. 91f. above.
81 Thus Jaeger, p. 260, although he also mentions some deviant examples. Entrepreneurial discontent with political authorities is exemplified in R. Leckebusch, *Entstehung u. Wandlungen der Zielsetzungen, der Struktur und der*

Wirkungen von Arbeitgeberverbänden, Berlin, 1966, pp. 52-3, 141-50. Leckebusch refers chiefly in her evidence to the relationship of the employers' association to the political parties, not to the decisively important administration. We cannot enter here into the many divergences and conflicts that existed among the entrepreneurial class before 1914, in which attempts were often made to mobilise the power of the state against opponents or competitors.

82 See *MKdI*, 45, 15 May 1915. The somewhat divergent demands of some industrialists for a central agency to deal with problems arising from the transitional economy (see *DIEW*, 2, pp. 134-5) stressed throughout the necessity for a far-reaching industrial self-administration through the participation of the associations or of individuals from trade and industry even, if necessary, in a centralised form. The demands for an 'economic General Staff' (*ibid.*, p. 481), insofar as they existed in industry, were rarely aimed at an enlargement of the state authorities' power. See *DAZ*, 15, 16 January 1916, warning of 'state schematicism and bureaucratism', esp. in the field of social policy; *ibid.*, 19 March, for 'economy in the administration', against bureaucracy and the broadening of its functions in the economic sphere.

83 See Feldman, *Army*, pp. 55-6, 60-1, 65ff., 87ff.

84 *Vossische Zeitung*, No. 3, 1 October 1916, in *DAZ*, 15, 15 October 1916. *Ibid.*, 1 October, 'On the dismantling of state socialism'. 'The businessman has been turned into a functionary . . . We have descended far too deeply into the civil service world of state socialism . . .'

85 See Armeson, pp. 34ff.

86 See the communication of the Ka.d.Dt.Ind. to the Reich Chancellor, 30 November 1916, in which the 'setting aside of the obligatory standing workers' committees' and the 'reversion of the so-called arbitration committees to a simple military complaints authority in consultation each time with an employer and a genuine [*sic*!] employee' was unsuccessfully demanded. Published in *DAZ*, 15, 3 December 1916. On later criticism of the HDG: *ibid.*, 16. 2 September 1917. On the rejection of the HDG by a powerful industrialist, see A. Rotth, *Wilhelm von Siemens*, Berlin, 1922, p. 183.

87 Thus *ibid.*, 16, 4 March 1917; a further attack on the bureaucracy on 11 March.

88 See *ibid.*, 15 March.

89 'Ein Mahnwort Krupps', ('A warning by Krupp'), speech on 5 February 1917, at the German Museums Committee, Munich in *DAZ*, 16, 25 February 1917.

90 *Ibid.*, 15 July (Minutes).

91 *Ibid.*, 21 October.

92 *Ibid.*, 23 September, 'Against Communism'; similarly 4 November (Minutes): 'On bureaucratism'; 11 November, 'Where are we heading?'. See also Cecil, pp. 272-3.

93 See above, pp. 109-11, 118-19, on similar attitudes on the part of small-scale tradesmen and agricultural entrepreneurs. See also L. Preller, *Sozialpolitik in der Weimarer Republik*, Stuttgart, 1949, pp. 18-19, 20, 23.

94 On this, F. Zunkel, *Industrie u. Staatssozialismus. Der Kampf um die Wirtschaftsordnung in Deutschland 1914-1918*, Düsseldorf, 1974. Zunkel's findings confirm the thesis of the predominant opposition between industry and the authorities and treats this in a broad, differentiated and stimulating way, but one which is not of further interest here.

95 See *MKdI*, 20 July, 28 September, 19 and 26 October 1918, on the transitional economy; *DAZ*, 17, 3 July 1918 (Minutes): Hugenberg, speaking at the General Meeting of the 'Vereins der bergbaulichen Interessen' against monopolisation under state supervision; *ibid.*, 11 August: criticism of a mass state, of Parliament and of the parties; *ibid.*, 29 September (Minutes): 'Dismantling the War economy'. Further examples of differences between the authorities and industry in Feldman,

Army, pp. 322, 347, 379ff., 420, 437-8, 477.

96 On this see Feldman, 'German Business' in *Entstehung u. Wandel*, pp. 312-41. F. rightly brings out ZAG's two-faced stand (against the masses and the State) in entrepreneurial consciousness.

97 As in a social-political programme, set up in October 1908, of the 'Verein Deutscher Arbeitgeberverbände', affiliated to the BdI, for which see Leckebusch, p. 150, n. 94 above.

98 Contemporaries throughout conceived of 1914 as a change in this respect. See *DIBZ*, 11, 1915, pp. 196-7. Up to the War the employers had had the State as an ally against the workers' movement; the War changed that. See also Umbreit and Lorenz, p. 30.

99 On this concept (deriving from Lenin) and its application to research in the early twentieth century, see J. Kuczynski, *Zur Frühgeschichte des deutschen Monopolkapitals und des staatsmonopolistischen Kapitalismus*, Berlin, 1962, pp. 173ff.; above all, H. Nussbaum, 'Zur Imperialismusttheorie W.I Lenins u. zur Entwicklung des deutschen Imperialismus bis 1914', *JbfWG*, 1970, IV, pp. 25-65. D. Baudis and H. Nussbaum, *Wirtschaft und Staat in Deutschland vom Ende des 19. Jahrhunderts bis 1918/19*, Berlin, 1978.

100 The redistribution of the population's income in the interest of the ruling class is not the 'starting point' for him 'but rather the natural accompaniment' of the War economy.

101 The competition between monopolistic groups, such as that between the coal, iron and steel industries and the 'younger monopolies' of electricity, chemicals etc. as well as that between the War and 'peace' industries, was intensified during the War. See Schröter, pp. 92-3; *DIEW*, 1. 397; *ibid.*, 2, pp. 126, 130ff. 481ff.; *ibid.*, 3, p. 570. An example of such decisions is the Hindenburg programme, which mainly promoted the interests of heavy industry while restricting other sectors. The conflicts between large and small firms, and between monopolies and those sectors not yet monopolised can be understood in these terms.

102 See the beginning of Chap. 1, above.

103 On the political and ideological conditions of the history of the GDR, see Kocka, *Theorieprobleme*, pp. 322-3. See Schröter, *Krieg*, pp. 10ff.; Kuczynski, *Geschichte*, 4, p. 268; above all, *DIEW*, 2, pp. 471ff.: these studies show no appreciation of the fact that the decided improvements, which meliorated the compulsion exercised by the law and which led to an enlargement of power for the organised working class at the entrepreneurs' expense, were put through (mainly by the trade unions and the SPD majority against the opposition of the entrepreneurs) by changing the Parliamentary Bill. They assess the law, in a one-sided manner, as increasing the oppression and exploitation of the worker, and as 'depriving the working class of its rights' (*DIEW*, p. 474).

105 See *DIEW*, p. 140. In confirmation, we may quote K. Liebknecht's remark that in the war the 'immediate dependence of the State on large-scale private capital would be strengthened' (*DIEW*, p.273).

106 This analysis by Lenin is quoted approvingly. See *DIEW*, 2, p. 488; Schröter, p. 110: 'The Hilfsdienstgesetz was the most important means whereby, as Lenin described it, Germany was turned into a penitentiary for the workers'. Similarly, the otherwise more strongly differentiated contribution by Nussbaum, *Imperialismustheorie*, p. 57.

107 Such as Fricke's article on the BdL in *Die bürgerlichen Parteien in Deutschland*, pp. 145-6, where, astonishingly, quite central attacks against state interventionism shown in the relevant sources (Kiesenwetter, Oldenburg-Januschau, Westarp, etc.) are simply disregarded.

108 This is more or less how Kuczynski (*Geschichte*, 4, pp. 202ff.), without any evidence, interprets a pointed anti-state comment by Stresemann – as a remark which was

directed less against the State than against those entrepreneurs and competitors whose interest were served by state intervention.

109 See, for example, Schröter, p. 103, on the negative reaction of 'peace' industry entrepreneurs to attempts by the State to initiate mergers which would have greatly favoured War industries.

110 Without sufficient evidence, differentiating between a 'liberalising-imperialist' monopoly-capital group (especially the electrical industry, machine construction, chemicals, components, shipping, commercial capital) and a 'conservative-imperialist' group (chiefly the iron, coal, steel and heavy industry of Rhine-Westphalia) (*DIEW*, 1, pp. 363ff.) may have a certain heuristic value in the analysis of entrepreneurial attitudes to trade union and 'Neuorientierung' questions, and also to questions on war aims.

111 Lederer perceptively observed this during the first year of the War (*idem, Soziologie des Weltkriegs*, pp. 359ff., see also R. Hilferding, 'Das historische Problem', *ZfP*, N.F., 1, 1954, pp. 293ff. Certain expressions of this view can also be found in the Marxist-Leninist orientated literature. See Kuczynski, *Geschichte*, 4, p. 204: 'since the means also begin to develop an "own life" . . .'; *DIEW*, 2, pp. 135-6, 481; Nussbaum, *Imperialismustheorie*, pp. 51, 64. These examples do not, however, prevent incorrect interpretations, as shown in the last section; they are not integrated into the authors' overall theories, although this should be possible precisely in following K. Marx: 'Der achtzehnte Brumaire des Louis Bonaparte', *MEW*, 8, pp. 185, 196ff.

112 In August 1917 there were already 1,044 price checking offices in Germany, Grebler and Winkler, p. 60. The number of government regulations dealing with economic and economically relevant matters had arisen to over 1,000 by the end of 1917 (*MkdI*, 173, p. 2690).

113 See *Handbuch f.d. Deutsche Reich*, 39, 1914, pp. 189ff.; *ibid.*, 44, 1918, pp. 128ff., 160ff., 444ff.: in 1914, 192 civil servants were working in the Reichsamt des Innern; in 1918, 92 worked there, while 217 and 104 respectively worked in the Reichswirtschaftsamt and the Kriegsernährunsamt (whose range of work to a limited degree had still been acknowledged by the Innenamt in 1914). See Schröter, pp. 154-57, for a list of wartime economic authorities.

114 See E. Forsthoff, *Rechtsfragen der leistenden Verwaltung* (1938), Stuttgart, 1959; *idem, Lehrbuch des Verwaltungsrechts*, 1, 8th ed., Munich, 1961, pp. 31ff., 35ff., 41ff., on the general problem.

115 See p. 209, n. 311, above. In all these respects, the War simply speeded up tendencies that were already recognisable before 1914.

116 State authorisation required for the re-establishment of joint-stock companies can serve as an example (notification of November 1917, *RGBI*, p. 987; see *DAZ*'s indignation over this, 11 January 1917, 'Where are we going to?'). Most of the entrepreneurial protests mentioned above against too much state intervention are connected with interventions of this sort.

117 See, on Delbrück: *DIEW*, 1, p. 411; W.v. Moellendorff, *Deutsche Gemeinwirtschaft*, Berlin, 1916. For the socio-economic plans of Riezler, the Chancellor's adviser, see Riezler, pp. 213, 261, 358-9 (7 October 1914, 26 March 1915, 14 June 1916) and, above all, pp. 524–40, esp. 535ff. ('Domestic and Foreign policy in 1916'). On the attitude of the trade unions, see above, p. 64.

118 See Andreski, pp. 99ff.

119 See above, pp. 44–5. On Stresemann, see also T. Eschenburg, *Die improvisierte Demokratie*, Munich, 1963, pp. 155ff.; W.J. Mommsen, *Max Weber u. die deutsche Politik 1890 to 1920*, Tübingen, 1959, pp. 96ff., 115ff.; Schwabe, pp. 138ff. See also the attitude of the DHV, in which aggressive nationalism and annexationism was combined with demands for domestic social and legal reforms: 'Man is the most valuable possession of the State . . . a strong . . . Reich Wehrmacht [is] not possible

without a healthy and strong people and without its protection through social reform'. On the other hand: 'A powerful social reform is only possible in a strong Reich' (*DHW*, 21, 1914, p. 141).

120 See Chap. 2, ns. 158, 280 above. On the long tradition and basic significance of such social-imperialist integration policy see, above all, H–U. Wehler, *Bismarck u. der Imperialismus*, 3rd ed., Cologne, 1972, esp. pp. 115ff.

121 See Scheidemann, *Memoiren*, 1, p.309.

122 See, among many examples, the expectations given in David, *Kriegstagebuch*, pp. 23ff., 223, 226, 227, 247, 249, 286ff.; Riezler, p.183 (7 July 1914, on Bethmann's viewpoint), 359, 402.

123 For fundamental treatment, see also Nussbaum, *Imperialimustheorie*, pp. 64–5.

124 On the Burgfrieden phase, see Feldman, *Army*, p. 30. On 'corporatism', cf. P. C. Schmitter, 'Modes of Interest Intermediation and Models of Social Change in Western Europe' in *Comparative Political Studies*, 10, 1977, pp. 7–38.

125 See above, pp. 64–6.

126 For examples of industrial, craft and agrarian criticism of bureaucracy, see above, pp. 109–11, 118–19, 138. See also Armeson, p. 30, on C. Duisberg's corresponding criticism in 1916; in general, see also Mendelssohn Bartholdy, pp. 30ff. Criticism of the military was more restrained and only became more noticeable in the last phase of the War; but see *Fünfundzwanzig Jahre Arbeitnordwest*, pp. 73–4, and Rieppel's criticism (MAN) of the uneconomic attitude and practice of the military in Groener, pp. 349–50.

127 How quickly and (apparently) easily the entrepreneurial class parted from the Wilhelmine system in October and November 1918 is shown by the dispassionate and adaptable articles in their newspapers. See *DAZ*, 17, 13 October 1918: 'The employer under the new change of course'; *ibid.*, 24 November 1918: 'New Paths'.

128 Thus also Baumgarten, p. 50. On the discussion of tax policy and its social distribution effects, see Roesler, pp. 71–4, 103–30, esp. 128ff.;*DIEW*, 2, pp. 120ff. A thorough study of the 'Willensbildungprozesse' in the field of tax legislation is still lacking.

129 See Feldman, pp. 158, 496ff.; Roesler, pp. 66, 100ff.

130 See J. Plenge, *1789 and 1914*, Berlin, 1916, esp. pp. 16ff., as an example of the frequent glorification of German organisational talent (on p. 20, a comparison with Great Britain). In their review Grebler and Winkler (p. 24) share this misconception: 'Nowhere was "totalitarian mobilisation" so thorough as in Germany, the country of organisers and systematizers . . .'. See also Marwick, p. 168.

131 See O. Goebel, *Deutsche Rohstoffwirtschaft im Weltkrieg*, Stuttgart, 1930, p. 93: the War Office had less power than the British Ministry of Munitions, established in 1915; K. Koszyk, *Pressepolitik im Ersten Weltkrieg*, Düsseldorf, 1968, p. 233, on the successful censorship and disciplining of the press in England; R. Levinsohn, *The Profits of War Through the Ages*, New York, 1937, p. 149, on the closer control of war profits in Great Britain; on this also, *idem, Die Umschichtung*, pp. 307ff. See also Feldman, *Army*, pp. 169, 173, 206, 218ff., 228, 483.

132 See Goebel, p. 93, 153; Armeson, p. 106; Mendelssohn Bartholdy, pp. 116ff.; Groener, pp. 333, 336, 342; Skalweit, pp. 164, 180; Koszyk, p. 183; Feldman, *Army*, pp. 503ff.; Bermbach, *Vorformen*, pp. 16ff.; Deist, *Militär*, xl–li.

133 See Bethmann Hollweg's corresponding remark on 31 October 1919, quoted in G.A. Ritter, 'Regierung und Parlament in Grossbritannien seit dem 17. Jahrhundert', *PVS*, 5, 1964. p. 24, n. 16; see also W.J. Mommsen, 'Die Regierung Bethmann Hollweg u. die öffentliche Meinung 1914-1917',*VfZ*, 17, 1969, p. 118; Armeson, p.93, on the weakness of the government without a parliamentary majority in the argument about the HDG; Albrecht, who shows that the Bavarian

government (with its extremely modest Reichskammer reform) was brought down by the privileged Conservatives, pp. 269ff. More generally, he stresses the weakness of the monarchist-constitutional government, see the summary on pp. 429ff.

134 On the limits of Ludendorff's domestic political power, see also Feldman, *Army*, 407ff., 456, 496ff.; Deist, *Militär*, xiv, xx. For the unconvincing thesis on Ludendorff's military dictatorship, which certainly needed to be defined, see H.-U. Wehler, '"Absoluter" und "totaler" Krieg', *PVS*, 10, 1969, pp. 246–7. Armeson's position (pp. 110, 136) that, with certain qualifications, Germany had fought a total war is even less appropriate.

135 On the following see, above all, Feldman, *Les fondements*, esp. pp. 122ff. His line of thought is very close to ours.

136 For the Merton memorandum of 12 July 1917, which was in favour of profit controls and was supported by Groener, the subsequent intriques by some heavy industrialists, the fall of Groener as chief of the War Office and the disappearance of the memorandum, see Armeson, pp. 126ff.; Feldman, *Army*, pp. 390ff. The memorandum is given in Merton, pp. 29–35. The information that Groener did indeed support the contents of the memo, but as a soldier (*sic!*) did not want to bring it before the Reichstag throws a glaring light on the connection between the social distribution of power and the constitutional problems of the Reich. See D. Groener-Geyer, *General Groener*, Frankfurt, 1955, p. 62. See Armeson, p. 71, and Feldman, *Army*, pp. 417ff., on the readiness of the trade unions to accept far-reaching military control which, since it would have at the same time restricted the power of the entrepreneurs, was therefore blocked. See Ludendorff, *Urkunden*, p. 140; Feldman, *Army*, pp. 496ff. on the later attempts at control by the OHL which also failed because of entrepreneurial opposition.

137 The issue of industrial bonds and preference shares and the later re-establishment of limited companies were all subject to official authorisation, although the issue of ordinary shares and, naturally, prices and profits as the main source of investment capital at that time, were not. See n. 116 above; Roester, p. 138.

138 Thus the deputy Prussian War Minister, 18 December 1915, quoted in *DIEW*, 2, p. 122.

139 See the provocative open letter of August 1916 by the radical Junker Oldenburg-Januschau in *Erinnerungen*, pp. 152–7, esp. p. 155: 'Every person who is offered a good price likes to deliver, even if they don't do this out of patriotism'. See also Westarp, pp. 387ff.

140 Thus, quite openly, Oldenburg-Januschau in August 1917 (p. 170); also the observation in Retzlaw, p. 92.

141 See, for example, Feldman, *Army*, pp. 480ff. on the strike threat at the Daimler works, whereupon the army moved in; *idem*, p. 486, on the flat refusal by some entrepreneurs to keep to the conditions of the HDG.

142 Even those military ranks and persons (such as Groener) who tried to cooperate with the working class in the interests of internal consolidation (especially in economic and social respects) were politically mostly Conservative and set against too far-reaching reforms. See *ibid.*, pp. 124ff., 340ff.

143 On the concept of 'respective conditions' of state action, see O. Kirchheimer, 'Restriktive Bedingungen u. revolutionäre Durchbrüche', in *idem*, *Politische Herrschaft*, Frankfurt, 1967, pp. 30ff.; J. Bergmann *et. al.*, 'Herrschaft, Klassenverhältnis und Schichtung' in T.W.Adorno, (ed.), *Spätkapitalismus oder Industriegesellschaft?*, Stuttgart, 1969, pp. 67–99, esp. 69–73. There the 'restrictive conditions' of state action are seen 'in the necessity to maintain private control over the means of production' and in the 'private power of control over industrial large enterprises and the investment decisions coordinate with that power' (p. 72). In

contrast, the historically variable content of these 'restrictive conditions' needs to be stressed here.

144 See especially the work by H.-U. Wehler, M. Stürmer, F. Fischer, D. Stegmann and V. Berghahn.

145 See E. Kehr, 'Klassenkämpfe u. Rüstungspolitik im kaiserlichen Deutschland', in *idem, Der Primat der Innenpolitik*, 2nd ed., Berlin, 1970, pp. 87–110; this theme is taken up again and continued by Groh, *PVS*, 13. pp. 501-21.

146 Feldman, *Fondements*, is excellent on this.

147 See, for example, *Corr. bl.*, 16, 1916, p.2; *DIBZ*, 13, 1917, pp. 52–5; in a common petition, white- and blue-collar workers' association protested against the then-current practice on food policy and demanded the strengthening of the War Food Office.

148 Thus already in MB, 15 April 1916, p. 20 (AK Kassel); *ibid.*, 14 June 1916, pp. 5, 7 (AAK Stettin).

149 Thus the Eighteenth AK (Frankfurt) in MB, 3 August 1917, p. 13, on the rural population.

150 Thus the Seventh AK (Breslau) and the Twentieth AK (Allenstein) in MB, 17 November 1916, pp. 5, 6.

151 Thus the Eighteenth AK (Frankfurt) and the Nineteenth AK (Leipzig) in MB, 3 November 1917, p. 18.

152 *Ibid.*, p. 21.

153 MB, September 1918, p. 6.

154 The report diagnosed a 'collapse of trust in the wisdom of state guidance'. *Ibid.*, pp. 9–10.

155 Report by Seventh AK (Münster) in MB, 23 August 1916, p. 13.

156 See MB, 3 June 1918, pp. 25, 33; 3 July 1918, pp. 12, 14, 15, 18; 3 August 1918, pp. 5ff., 24.

157 See the Eighteenth AK (Frankfurt) in MB, 3 August 1917, pp. 18–19: '. . . the people will continue to become unnecessarily irritated if gendarmes - as unfortunately often happens - over-zealously confiscate trifling amounts of foodstuffs which they find in the luggage of travellers'. Similarly, the Stettin AK in MB, 3 October 1918, on the black market, in which it was always only the small dealer who got caught.

158 MB, 3 August 1917, p. 17.

159 MB, 3 October 1918, pp. 25-6.

160 Thus the Danzig AK, *ibid.*, pp. 26-7.

161 *Ibid.*, p. 34.

162 See Umbreit and Lorenz, pp. 105, 108; Baumgarten, pp. 26-7; M. Liepmann, *Krieg u. Kriminalität in Deutschland*, Stuttgart, 1930, pp. 10, 22, 25ff., 142-3; Mendelssohn Bartholdy, pp. 30ff. 108, 195, 201. Cassau (pp. 308-9, 310) remarks that the German war-conditioned criticism of bureaucracy corresponded with a growing criticism of Parliament in England.

163 See Marwick, P. 202.

164 See Umbreit and Lorenz, p. 98; Feldman, *Army*, pp. 99ff., 105-6, 109. 265-6, 417-18. This admiration for the military fitted into the general mood which , especially during the first years of the war was ready to accept soldiers and the military as the norm in all areas of life. See Liepmann, pp. 109, 115–16; Baumgarten, pp. 76ff.; Koszyk, p. 120.

165 The MB first reported the declining trust in the OHL in August 1918; see MB, 3 September 1918 ('High command in the Marken'). Previously they had repeatedly contrasted the high faith in the military leadership with the declining confidence in the civil administration and political leadership. See also Mendelssohn Bartholdy, pp. 196ff.

166 See the report of the Berlin President of Police, 29 October 1918, quoted in part in Kuczynski, *Geschichte*, 4, pp. 355ff.; Ay, pp. 159ff.; Baumgarten, pp. 26-7, 63-4; Liepmann, p. 62.
167 See MB, 3 June 1918, p. 33.
168 Thus the Seventeeth AK (Danzig) in MB, 3 August 1918, p. 12; similarly, the Koblenz AK in MB, 3 October 1918, p. 28.
169 *Ibid.*, 3 October 1918, p. 30. 'In some cases the victim of the robbery is later anonymously sent a carefully calculated repayment'.
170 *Ibid.*, p. 30.
171 *Ibid.*, p. 8.
172 See also C. Johnson, *Revolutionstheorie*, Cologne, 1971, pp. 46, 117ff., 141 (on the analysis of a pre-revolutionary situation generally, the basic features of which existed in Germany from the summer of 1918).
173 See A. Rosenberg, *Entstehung*, pp. 223ff.; R. Rürup, *Probleme der Revolution in Deutschland 1918/19*, Wiesbaden, 1968, pp. 12ff. See also C.L. Bertrand (ed.), *Revolutionary Situations in Europe, 1917-1922: Germany, Italy, Austria, Hungary*, Montreal, 1977; F.L. Carsten, *Revolution in Mitteleuropa 1918-1919*, Cologne 1973; D. Dähnhardt, *Revolution in Kiel. Der Übergang vom Kaiserreich zur Weimarer Republik 1918/19*, Neumünster, 1978; G.D. Feldman, 'Socio-Economic Structure in the Industrial Sector and Revolutionary Potentialities, 1917-1922', in C.L. Bertrand (ed.), pp. 169ff.; E. Kolb, K. Schönhoven (eds.), *Regionale und lokale Räteorganisationen in Württemberg 1918/19*, Düsseldorf, 1976; H. Krause, *Revolution und Konterrevolution 1918/19 am Beispiel Hanau*, Kronberg/Ts., 1974; I. Materna, *Der Vollzugsrat der Berliner Arbeiter- und Soldatenräte 1918/19*, Berlin, 1978; W.J. Mommsen, 'Die deutsche Revolution 1918-1920. Politische Revolution und soziale Protestbewegung', *GG*, 4, 1978, pp. 362-91; R. Rürup (ed.), *Arbeiter- und Soldatenräte im rheinisch-westfälischen Industriegebiet. Studien zur Geschichte der Revolution 1918/19*, Wuppertal, 1975; W. Ruge, *Novemberrevolution. Die Volkserhebung gegen den deutschen Imperialismus und Militarismus 1918/19*, Berlin, 1978; *idem, Revolutionstage November 1918*, Berlin, 1978. But now this old thesis has been revived, without good reason, in H. Schulze, *Weimar. Deutschland 1917-1933*, Berlin, 1982, pp. 141-70.
174 See *Corr.bl.*, 28, 1918, pp. 463-6, on the (basically correct) reference to the continuity in their own policy towards entrepreneurs before the War, during the War and in the ZAG. On the founding of ZAG see, above all, Feldman, *German Business*.

Chapter 5. Methodological Epilogue

1 Cf. E.J. Hobsbawm, 'From Social History to the History of Society', in *Daedalus (Historical Studies Today)*, Winter 1971, Cambridge, Mass., pp. 20-45. Hobsbawm's concept of the 'history of society' is comparable to the German concept of 'Gesellschaftsgeschichte'. Cf. J. Kocka, 'Theory and Social History: Recent Developments in West Germany' in *Social Research*, 47, 1980, pp. 426-57, esp. 449-55.
2 Greatly simplified, this would be the process recommended by an analytical theory of science. See statements by R. König and H. Albert in R. König (ed), *Handbuch der Empirischen Sozialforschung*, 1, Stuttgart, 1967, pp. 8-9, 58.
3 Above all, in the analysis of structure and function of the political process, a growing gap between model and reality became apparent, which was explainable by taking further thought on the matter (the specific role of the state in a class society under wartime conditions) see Chap. 4, sect. 4 above. We have also explained and

interpreted changes which conformed to the model by considerations not provided for in the model (for example, in Chap. 2, sect. 4, the five factors which facilitated the transformation of valid class opposition into class tensions). Concepts and considerations not covered by the model were also introduced at several points in order to relate the outcome of the inquiry to a diversity of research problems of current interest, which were in no way incorporated in the model (see, for example, p. 154, above, on the problem of social-imperialism and its reverse side).

4 See, for example, at the beginning of Chap. 4 above.

5 See, on this, the criticism of the concept of state monopoly capitalism in Chap. 4, sect. 3, above. See also Wehler, *Bismarck*, pp. 15–16, on the necessity for 'a sheaf of theories' for historical research. It is significant (and only consistent) that this particular methodological insight should be criticised by dogmatists. See H. Schleier, 'Zum Verhältnis von Historismus, Strukturgeschichte und sozialwissenschaftlichen Methoden in der gegenwärtigen Geschichtsschreibung der BRD', in E. Engelberg (ed.), *Probleme der marxistischen Geschichtswissenschaft. Beiträge zu ihrer Theorie und Methode* (licenced ed.), Cologne, 1972, p. 324; H.–D. Kittsteiner, 'Theorie und Geschichte' in *Kritik der bürgerlichen Geschichtswissenschaft*, II (=*Das Argument*, 75), Berlin, 1972, pp. 29–30. See also n. 6. below.

6 Reference must at least be made to the fact that these statements imply a particular conception of the relationship between knowledge and the reality to be known, according to which only a partial knowledge is possible and reality is structured in a multi-faceted manner, allowing scientific knowledge only a limited interpretative space. See J. Kocka, *Sozialgeschichte*, Göttingen, 1977, pp. 9-47.

7 See Wehler's Introduction in *idem* (ed.), *Geschichte u. Soziologie*, p. 22. This applies particularly to wartime 1914–18, where the situation of extreme shortages and needs lent a particularly prominent weight to economic factors and considerations.

8 See Chap. 1, n. 27, above.

9 There was an intensive debate on this book when it was first published. For a comment on these comments see my postscript to the 2nd German edition (1978), pp. 233–9. Among the reviews in English see C. Maier in *Journal of Social History*, 9, 1976, pp. 583–8; W.J. Mommsen in *Journal of Modern History*, 47, 1975, pp. 530–8; J.A. Moses in *Australian Journal of Politics and History*, 22, 1976, pp. 317–20; G.D. Feldman in *Journal of Interdisciplinary History*, 7, 1976/77, pp. 164-9; K.H. Jarausch in *Societas*, 5, 1976, n. 4.

10 Cf. M. Weber, *Gesammelte Aufsätze zur Wissenschaftslehre*, 3rd ed., Tübingen, 1968, p. 191, on the notion of 'ideal type'. See also W.J. Mommsen, '"Verstehen" und "Idealtypus". Zur Methodologie einer historischen Sozialwissenschaft', in *idem, Max Weber. Gesellschaft, Politik und Geschichte*, Frankfurt, 1974, pp. 208-32. A Weberian use of a Marxian class concept can also be found in J. Kocka, *Lohnarbeit und Klassenbildung. Arbeiter und Arbeiterbewegung in Deutschland 1800-1875*, Berlin, 1983.

11 Some of them are discussed in Kocka, *Theory*, (quoted in n. 1 above).

12 Comparative attempts in G. Schramm, 'Minderheiten gegen den Krieg. Motive und Kampfformen 1914 bis 1918 am Beispiel Grossbritanniens und seines Empire', in *Geschichte und Gesellschaft*, 6, 1980, pp. 164ff.; D. Baudis, 'Deutschland und Grossbritannien in der Zeit des ersten Weltkrieges. Versuch einer vergleichenden Betrachtung einiger Aspekte der wirtschaftlichen und sozialen Entwicklung', in *Jahrbuch für Wirtschaftsgeschichte*, 1981/111, pp. 49-78; *ibid.*, 1981/IV, pp. 205-16.

13 Cf. H.-A. Winkler (ed.), *Organisierter Kapitalismus. Voraussetzungen und Anfänge*, Göttingen, 1974. See also J. Kocka, 'Organisierter Kapitalismus im Kaiserreich?' in *Historische Zeitschrift*, 230, 1980, pp 614-31.

Afterword

1 The following are the criticisms I am aware of which contain more than just a description of the contents: B. Adolff, in *Stuttgarter Zeitung*, 136, 16 June 1974; K.-L. Ay, in *Zeitschrift für bayerische Landesgeschichte*, Vol. 37, 1974, pp. 956–62; K.J. Bade, in *Das Historisch-Politische Buch*, Vol. 22, 1974, pp. 178–9; W. Baumgart, in *VSWG*, Vol. 63, 1976, pp. 525–7; F. Blaich, in *Jahrbücher für Nationalökonomie und Statistik*, Vol. 189, 1975, pp. 455–6; K. Büchi, in *Schweizerische Zeitschrift für Geschichte*, Vol. 24, 1974, pp. 165–7; W. Conze, in *Neue Politische Literatur*, Vol. 19, 1974, pp. 506–8; G.D.Feldman, in *Journal of Interdisciplinary History*, Vol. 7, 1976/77, pp. 164–9; J. Flemming, in *Frankfurter Rundschau*, 201, 1 September 1975; E. Hannisch, in *Zeitgeschichte*, (Jg. 1), 1974, pp. 129–30; H. Haumann, in *Das Argument*, 99, 1976, pp. 875–7; D. Herz-Eichenrode, in *PVS*, Vol. 17, 1976, pp. 578–9; A. Hillgruber, in *HZ*, Vol. 220, 1975, pp. 757–8; K.H. Jarausch, in *Societas*, Vol. 5, 4, 1976; B. Kaulisch, in *Deutsche Literaturzeitung* (Jg. 97), 1976, pp. 59–62: C. Landauer, in *American Historical Review*, Vol. 80, 1975, pp. 670–1; C. Maier, in *Journal of Social History*, Vol. 9, 1976, p. 583–8; W.J. Mommsen, in *Journal of Modern History*, Vol. 47, 1975, pp. 530–8; J.A. Moses, in *Australian Journal of Politics and History*, Vol. 22, 1976, pp. 317–20; E. Ohno, in *Keizai-Ronsō*, Vol. 116, Kyoto, 1975, pp. 140–7; G. Schramm, in *GG* (Jg. 2), 1976, pp. 244–60; D. Stegmann, in *Archiv für Sozialgeschichte*, Vol. 15, 1975 pp. 511–12; G. Stollberg, in *Internationale Wissenschaftliche Korrespondenz zur Geschichte der deutschen Arbeiterbewegung*, Vol. 10, 1974, pp. 519–21; W.-H. Struck, in *Nassauische Annalen* (Jg. 86), 1975, pp. 373–4; M. Stürmer, in *Frankfurter Allgemeine Zeitung*, No. 199, 29 August 1974; M. Stürmer, in *German Studies*, Vol. 8, 1975, pp. 188–91; W. Stump, in *Vierteljahresschrift f. Sozialrecht*, Vol. 3, 1975, H. 1/2; S. Volkov, in *Jahrbuch des Instituts für Deutsche Geschichte*, Vol. 4, 1975, pp. 527–30; H.A. Winkler, in *Militärgeschichtliche Mitteilungen*, Vol. 18, 1975, pp. 158–60; P.-C. Witt, in *GG* (Jg. 2), 1976, pp. 118–24; C. Wurm, in *Historisches Jahrbuch*, Vol. 95, 1975, pp. 228–30.

2 On the concept, see J. Kocka, *Sozialgeschichte. Concept – development – problems*, Göttingen, 1977, pp. 97ff.

3 This seems to me to be the chief disadvantage of an otherwise and in many respects impressive attempt at synthesis by W. Conze. See *idem*, 'Sozialgeschichte' in H. Aubin and W.Zorn (eds.), *Handbuch der deutschen Wirtschafts-und Sozialgeschichte*, Vol. 2, Stuttgart, 1976, pp. 426–84, 602–84. It falls apart into his separate sections; this may be due to the author's abstention from the use of all-embracing theories.

4 A criticism intended for the 1978 *Jahrbuch für Wirtschaftsgeschichte* was not available to me at time of this comment.

5 See Kocka, *Sozialgeschichte*, pp. 9–47.

6 See *ibid*., pp. 86ff.

7 'It is true that the value of historical generalization begins where discrepancies must be explained between fact and description. But thereafter the hostorian must seek to narrow the gap either by amending or overturning his theories; Kocka seems less vexed by the explanatory lacunae than the liberal or neo-kantian social scientist would be.' C. Maier, p. 587.

8 See, on further aspects of the application of theory in historical science, J. Kocka (ed.), *Theorien in der Praxis des Historikers*, Göttingen, 1977 (=*GG*, special issue 3).

9 See *idem, Angestellte zwischen Faschismus und Demokratie. Zur politischen Sozialgeschichte der Angestellten; USA 1890–1940 im internationalen Vergleich*, Göttingen, 1977, pp. 56–7, 356, n. 102; in supplement to above, p. 95.

10 See T.W. Mason, *Arbeiterklasse und Volksgemeinschaft. Dokumente und Materialien zur deutschen Arbeiterpolitik 1936–1939*, Opladen, 1975, pp. 1–173 (Introduction

by M.). Mason analyses the similarities less than he describes how much leading National Socialists were aware of the similarity of the problem situation (esp. pp. 1–16).

11 See similarly W.–H. Struck; also Winkler, p. 160, on the 'integral nationalism' which unfolded during the War and which I really did not pay enough attention to.

12 In answer to C. Wurm's criticism, it must be conceded that this study was concerned with the internal political and social-historical conditions of the Revolution and not with a total analysis. For this reason the role of the military revolt as a trigger was not pursued further. On the other hand the claim by W. Baumgart, that the clarification of the social and structural historical conditions of the Revolution unintentionally rehabilitates the 'stab in the back' legend, does not seem reasonable to me. Demonstrating the inner reasons and conditions for the Revolution does not mean denying the military reasons and conditions for the collapse. The analysis of the reasons for the Revolution has nothing to do with the inflammatory accusations of large sections of the Weimar right-wing groups against the 'November criminals'.

13 See also my criticism on the use of state monopoly capitalism premises by GDR historians in H.A. Winkler (ed.), *Organisierter Kapitalismus. Voraussetzungen und Anfänge*, Göttingen, 1974, pp. 24–9.

14 One could also recommend supplementing the conflict-theoretical initial model from this point of view, as discussed in the previous section.

Bibliography

1. Unpublished sources

Peppel, Oberbürgermeister, i. R., 'Die Durchführung von Zusammenlegungen(Stillegungen) in der Industrie während des Krieges 1914–1918. Darstellung u. Beurteilung'. 1. T.: Überblick über den Verlauf der Zusammenlegungen (abgeschlossen im Okt. 1937). National Archives microcopy, T77, Roll 343. Records of Headquarters, German Armed Forces, High Command (Oberkommando der Wehrmacht/OKW), 80728–80981 (in the collection of Departmental Records Branch, The Adjutant-General's Office, RG 1026)

Siemens-Archiv-Akten [SAA]. W.-v.-Siemens-Institut, Munich. Diverse Einzelstücke aus: 4/Lf 837; 11/Lg 625; 29/Le 932, 1; 50/Lg 625; Protokolle der Vorstandssitzungen S&H/SSW 1914–18; M. Frenzel, Geschichte der Zentral-Werksverwaltung (ZW) Berlin u. ihre Vorläufer 1893–1949. Ed. ms. 1953 (= 68/Li 83)

Zesch, Dr. R., (ed.), 'Was ist geschehen zur Ermöglichung der Arbeit von Ungelernten u. Frauen? Unter Benutzung amtlicher Akten u. Mitteilungen des VDI. Berlin im März 1933. Aus Bücherei d. Heereswaffenamtes Tit. Secr. Nr. 15. National Archives microcopy T77, Roll 343. Records of Headquarters, German Armed Forces, High Command (Oberkommando der Wehrmacht/OKW), 80665–80727 (in collection: Departmental Records Branch. The Adjutant-General's Office, RG 1026)

Zusammenstellungen aus den Berichten der stellvertretenden Generalkommandos über die Stimmung in der Zivilbevölkerung, – from Sept. 1916 under the title: Zusammenstellungen der Monats-Berichte der stellvertretenden Generalkommandos [MB]. 15. 4. 1916–3. 8. 1917 in Generallandesarchiv, Karlsruhe. Abt. 456. Bd. 70; 3. 8. 1917–3. 10. 1918 in Bayer. Hauptstaatsarchiv, Munich. Abt. IV (Kriegsarchiv). MKr. 12851–12853

2. Periodicals

Deutsche Arbeitgeber-Zeitung. Zentralblatt deutscher Arbeitgeber-Verbände, 13–17, Berlin, 1914–18 [*DAZ*]

Archiv für Sozialwissenschaft u. Sozialpolitik, 38–45, Tübingen, 1914–18
[*Archiv*]

Beamtenjahrbuch. Vierteljahrsschrift für die gesamte Beamtenbewegung, 1–4,
Stuttgart, 1914–17

Bund der Landwirte. Königreich Bayern, 16–20, Munich, 1914–18

Correspondenzblatt der Generalkommission der Gewerkschaften Deutschlands,
24–29, Berlin, 1914–19 [*Corr.bl.*]

Frankfurter Zeitung, 1917–18

Handbuch f. d. Deutsche Reich. Reichsamt d. Innern (ed.), 39–44, Berlin,
1914–18

*Deutsche Handels-Wacht. Zeitschrift der Berufsgenossenschaft Deutschnationaler
Handlungsgehilfen-Verband*, 20–26, Hamburg, 1913–19 [*DHW*]

*Handwerks-Zeitung. Amtliches Organ der Handwerkskammern zu Berlin u.
Frankfurt/Oder. Offizielles Publikationsorgan des Zentral-Ausschusses
vereinigter Innungsverbände Deutschlands. Redaktion: Handwerkskammer
zu Berlin*, 14–17, Berlin. 1914–17 [*HWZ*]

*Nordwestdeutsche Handwerks-Zeitung. Amtliches Organ der Handwerkskammern
zu Altona, Aurich, Flensburg, Hannover, Harburg, Hildesheim u.
Stadthagen. Organ des Nordwestdeutschen Handwerker-Bundes*, 19–23,
1914–18 [*NHWZ*]

*Deutsche Industriebeamten-Zeitung. Zeitschrift f. d. sozialen Interessen der
technischen Privatangestellten. Organ des Bundes der technisch-industriellen
Beamten*, 10–14, Berlin, 1914–18 [*DIBZ*]

Jahrbuch der Angestelltenbewegung, Berlin, 1914–15

Statistisches Jahrbuch für das Deutsche Reich. Kaiserl. Statistisches Amt (from
1919: Stat. Reichsamt) (ed.), 35–44, Berlin, 1914–24/25

Mitteilungen der Handwerkskammer zu Münster, 2–6, Münster, 1914–18

Mitteilungen des Kriegsausschusses der deutschen Industrie, 1–250, Berlin, 14
August 1914–12 April 1918 [*MKdI*]

Reichsarbeitsblatt. Special issues 2–22, Berlin, 1907–20 *Reichsgesetzblatt*,
Berlin, 1914–18 [*RGBI*]

Schulthess' Europäischer Geschichtskalender, N. F. 30–34, 1914–18, Munich,
1917 ff.

Stahl u. Eisen. Zeitschrift f. d. deutsche Eisenhüttenwesen, 34–38, Düsseldorf,
1914–18

Statistik des Deutschen Reichs, Berlin [*StdDtR*]

3. **Published sources and bibliography**

Adelmann, G. (ed.), *Quellensammlung zur Geschichte der sozialen Betriebsverfassung. Ruhrindustrie*, I, Bonn, 1960

Aereboe, F., *Der Einfluß des Krieges auf die landwirtschaftliche Produktion in Deutschland*, Stuttgart, 1927

Albert, H., *Traktat über kritische Vernunft*, 2nd ed., Tübingen, 1969

Albertin, L., *Liberalismus u. Demokratie am Anfang der Weimarer
Republik. Eine vergleichende Analyse der Deutschen Demokratischen Partei
u. der Deutschen Volkspartei*, Düsseldorf, 1972

Albrecht, W., *Landtag u. Regierung in Bayern am Vorabend der Revolution von 1918. Studien zur gesellschaftlichen u. staatlichen Entwicklung Deutschlands 1912 bis 1918*, Berlin, 1968

Andexel, R., *Imperialismus. Staatsfinanzen, Rüstung, Krieg. Probleme der Rüstungsfinanzierung des deutschen Imperialismus*, Berlin, 1968

Andreski, S., *Military Organisation and Society*, 2nd ed., Berkeley, 1968

Armeson, R. B., *Total Welfare and Compulsory Labor. A Study of the Military-Industrial Complex in Germany During World War I*, The Hague, 1964

Aron, R., 'Social Structure and Ruling Class', *British Journal of Sociology*, 1, 1950, quoted in L. A. Coser, *Political Sociology*, New York, 1966, pp.48–100

Ascher, A., '"Radical" Imperialism within German Social Democracy', *Political Science Quarterly*, 76, 1961, pp. 555–75

Aubin, H. and Zorn, W. (eds.), *Handbuch der deutschen Wirtschafts- und Sozialgeschichte*, Vol. 2, *Das 19. u. 20. Jahrhundert*, Stuttgart, 1976

Aufhäuser, S., *Weltkrieg und Angestelltenbewegung*, Berlin, 1918

—, *Die freie Angestellten- u. Arbeiterbewegung. Referat, dem Ersten ordentlichen Bundestag der technischen Angestellten u. Beamten, 14. 6. 1920*, Berlin, 1920

Ay, K.-L., *Die Entstehung einer Revolution. Die Volksstimmung in Bayern während des Ersten Weltkrieges*, Berlin, 1968

Badia, G., *Le Spartakisme. Les dernières années de R. Luxemburg et de K. Liebknecht, 1914–1919*, Paris, 1967

Bajohr, S., *Die Hälfte der Fabrik. Geschichte der Frauenarbeit in Deutschland 1914 bis 1945*, Marburg, 1979

Baltrusch, F., *Die Arbeitsgemeinschaft der industriellen u. gewerblichen Arbeitgeber und Arbeitnehmer Deutschlands*, Cologne, 1920

Bartel, W., *Die Linken in der deutschen Sozialdemokratie im Kampf gegen Militarismus u. Krieg*, Berlin, 1958

Barth, E., *Aus der Werkstatt der deutschen Revolution*, Berlin, [1919]

Basler, W., *Deutschlands Annexionspolitik in Polen u. im Baltikum 1914–1918*, Berlin, 1962

Baudis, D., 'Die Arbeiterausschüsse im Mansfelder Kupferschieferbergbau in der Zeit des Ersten Weltrieges', *JbfWG*, III, 1962, pp. 28–53

Bauer, M., *Der Große Krieg in Feld u. Heimat. Erinnerungen u. Betrachtungen*, 2nd ed., Tübingen, 1921

Baumgart, W., *Deutsche Ostpolitik 1918*, Munich, 1966

—, (ed.), *Von Brest-Litovsk zur deutschen Novemberrevolution. Aus den Tagebüchern, Briefen u. Aufzeichnungen von A. Paquet, W. Groener u. A. Hopman. März bis Nov. 1918*, Göttingen, 1971

Baumgarten, O., *et al.*, *Geistige u. Sittliche Wirkungen des Krieges in Deutschland*, Stuttgart, 1927

Bechtel, H., *Wirtschaftsgeschichte Deutschlands im 19. u. 20. Jahrhundert*, Munich, 1956

Beckerath, H. v., *Kräfte, Ziele u. Gestaltungen in der Industriewirtschaft*, Jena, 1922

—, *Der moderne Industrialismus*, Jena, 1930
Beiträge zur Kriegswirtschaft. Volkswirtschaftl. Abt. des Kriegsernährungsamtes (ed.), 1–68, Berlin, 1916–1920
Bendix, R. and Lipset, S. M. (ed.), *Class, Status and Power*, 2nd ed., New York, 1966
Benz, W. and Graml, H. (eds.), *Die revolutionäre Illusion. Zur Geschichte des linken Flügels der USPD. Erinnerungen von Curt Geyer*, Stuttgart, 1976
Berg, F. (ed.), *Der Weg zum industriellen Spitzenverband*, Darmstadt, 1956
Berg, W., '"Herr im Hause" oder Emanzipation der Arbeitnehmer. Die betrieblichen u. gesellschaftlich-politischen Beziehungen zwischen Unternehmern, Angestellten u. Arbeitern im Ruhrkohlenbergbau während des Ersten Weltkrieges', diss., Freiburg, 1972
Berghahn, V. R., *Der Tirpitz-Plan. Genesis u. Verfall einer innenpolitischen Krisenstrategie unter Wilhelm II*, Düsseldorf, 1971
—, *Modern Germany: Society, Economy and Politics in the Twentieth Century*, Cambridge, 1982
Bergmann, J. *et. al.* 'Herrschaft, Klassenverhältnis u. Schichtung', in T. W. Adorno (ed.), *Spätkapitalismus oder Industriegesellschaft?*, Stuttgart, 1969, pp. 67–87
Bergsträßer, L., *Die preußische Wahlrechtsfrage im Kriege u. die Entstehung der Osterbotschaft 1917*, Tübingen, 1929
Berlau, A. J., *The German Social Democratic Party 1904–1921*, New York 1949
Bermbach, U., *Vorformen parlamentarischer Kabinettsbildung in Deutschland. Der Interfraktionelle Ausschuß 1917/18 u. die Parlamentarisierung der Reichsregierung*, Cologne, 1967
—, 'Aspekte der Parlamentarismus-Diskussion im kaiserlichen Reichstag – Die Erörterung im Interfraktionellen Ausschuß 1917–1918', *PVS*, 8, 1967 pp. 51–70
Bernstein, E., 'Klasse u. Klassenkampf', *Sozialistische Monatshefte*, 9, 1905, pp. 857–64
Berthold, L. and Neef, H., *Militarismus und Opportunismus gegen die Novemberrevolution*, Berlin, 1978
Bertrand, C.L. (ed.), *Revolutionary Situations in Europe, 1917–1922: Germany, Italy, Austria, Hungary*, Montreal 1977
v. Bethmann Hollweg, T., *Betrachtungen zum Weltkriege*, 2 vols., Berlin, 1919, 1921
Bieber, H.-J., *Gewerkschaften in Krieg und Revolution*, Hamburg, 2 vols. 1982
Blaich, F., *Staat und Verbände in Deutschland zwischen 1871 und 1945*, Wiesbaden, 1979
Blank, R., 'Die soziale Zusammensetzung der Sozialdemokratischen Wählerschaft Deutschlands,' *Archiv*, 20, 1905, pp. 507ff.
Böttger, H., *Vom alten u. neuen Mittelstand*, Berlin, 1901
Boldt, W., 'Der Januarstreik 1918 in Bayern mit besonderr Bertücksichtigung Nürnbergs', *Jb f. Fränkische Landesforschung*, 25, 1965, pp. 5–42
Boll, F., 'Die deutsche Sozialdemokratie zwischen Resignation und Revolution. Zur Friedensstrategie 1890–1919', in W.Huber and J.Schwertfeger (eds.),

Frieden, Gewalt und Sozialismus. Studien zur Geschichte der sozialistischen Arbeiterbewegung, Stuttgart, 1976

—, *Frieden ohne Revolution? Friedensstrategien der deutschen Sozialdemokratie vom Erfurter Programm 1891 bis zur Revolution 1918*, Bonn, 1980

—, *Massenbewegungen in Niedersachsen 1906–1920. Eine sozialgeschichtliche Untersuchung zu den unterschiedlichen Entwicklungstypen Braunschweig und Hannover*, Bonn, 1981

Born, K. E., *Staat u. Sozialpolitik seit Bismarcks Sturz. Ein Beitrag zur Geschichte der innenpolitischen Entwicklung des Deutschen Reiches 1890–1914*, Wiesbaden, 1957

Bosl, K., 'Gesellschaft u. Politik in Bayern vor dem Ende der Monarchie. Beiträge zu einer sozialen und politischen Strukturanalyse', *Zs. f. bayerische Landesgeschichte*, 28, 1965, pp. 1–31

—, (ed.), *Bayern im Umbruch. Die Revolution von 1918, ihre Voraussetzungen, ihr Verlauf u. ihre Folgen*, Munich, 1969

Bottomore, T. B., *Classes in Modern Society*, London, 1955

Bracher, K. D., *Die deutsche Diktatur. Entstehung, Struktur, Folgen des Nationalsozialismus*, Cologne, 1969 (transl. as *The German Dictatorship: The Origins, Structure and Consequences of National Socialism*, Harmondsworth, 1971)

Brauer, T., 'Mittelstandspolitik', *GdS*, 9, II, Tübingen, 1927, pp. 368–410

Braybon, G., *Women Workers in the First World War. The British Experience*, London, 1981

Brecht, A., *Aus nächster Nähe. Lebenserinnerungen 1884–1927*, Stuttgart, 1966

Bredt, J. V., *Der Deutsche Reichstag im Weltkrieg*, Berlin, 1926

Bresciani-Turroni, C., *The Economics of Inflation. A Study of Currency Depreciation in Post War-Germany 1931*, 2nd ed., London, 1953

Briefs, G., 'Kriegswirtschaftslehre u. Kriegswirtschaftspolitik', *HSt*, 5, 4th ed., 1923, pp. 984–1022

Brockhusen-Justin, H.-J. v., *Der Weltkrieg u. ein schlichtes Menschenleben*, Greifswald, 1928

Brodnitz, G., 'Die Wirtschaftsblockade im Weltkrieg', *Schmollers Jb.*, N.F. 43, 1919/3, pp. 87–122

Bromme, M. T. W., *Lebensgeschichte eines modernen Fabrikarbeiters*, 1905, (new ed., Frankfurt, 1971)

Bruck, W. F., *Geschichte des Kriegsausschusses der Deutschen Baumwoll-Industrie. Zugleich Abriß der Baumwollwirtschaft während des Krieges*, Berlin, 1920

—, 'Die Kriegsunternehmung. Versuch einer Systematik', *Archiv*, 48, 1920/21, pp. 547–95

—, *Social and Economic History of Germany from William II to Hitler 1888–1938*, New York, 1938 (2nd ed., 1962)

Bry, G., *Wages in Germany 1871–1945*, Princeton, 1960

Buber-Neumann, M., *Von Potsdam nach Moskau. Stationen eines Irrweges*, Stuttgart, 1957

Buchner, E., *Kriegsdokumente. Der Weltkrieg 1914 in der Darstellung der zeitgenösischen Presse,* 1–9, Munich, 1915–18

v. Bülow, B. Fürst, *Denkwürdigkeiten, 3: Weltkrieg u. Zusammenbruch,* F. v. Stockhammern (ed.), Berlin, 1931

Bumm, F. (ed.), *Deutschlands Gesundheitsverhältnisse unter dem Einfluß des Weltkrieges,* 2 vols., Stuttgart, 1928

Bur, L., *Die Umwälzung der deutschen Volkswirtschaft im Kriege,* Strasburg, 1919

Burchardt, L., *Friedenswirtschaft u. Kriegsvorsorge. Deutschlands wirtschaftliche Rüstungsbestrebungen vor 1914,* Boppard, 1968

—, 'Walther Rathenau u. die Anfänge der Deutschen Rohstoffversorgung im Ersten Weltkrieg', *Tradition,* 15, 1970, pp. 169–96

—, 'Eine neue Quelle zu den Anfängen der Kriegswirtschaft in Deutschland 1914', *Tradition,* 16, 1971, pp. 72–7

Bureau International du Travail, *Fluctuations des salaires dans différents pays de 1914 à 1922,* Genf, 1923

Burns, R. K., 'The Comparative Economic Position of Manual and White-Collar Employees', *Journal of Business,* 27, 1954, pp. 257–67

Busch, R., 'Imperialismus und Arbeiterliteratur im Ersten Weltkrieg', *AfS,* 14, 1974, pp. 293–350

Calkins, K. R., *Hugo Haase. Demokrat und Revolutionär,* Berlin, 1976

Carsten, F. L., *Revolution in Mitteleuropa 1918–1919,* Cologne, 1973

Cartarius, U. (ed.), *Deutschland im Ersten Weltkrieg,* Munich, 1982

Cassau, T., *Die Gewerkschaftsbewegung. Ihre Soziologie u. ihr Kampf,* Halberstadt, 1925

Cecil, L., *Albert Ballin. Wirtschaft u. Politik im deutschen Kaiserreich 1888–1918,* Hamburg, 1969 (transl. as *A. Ballin. Business and Politics in Imperial Germany 1888–1918,* 1967)

Claß, H. *Wider den Strom. Vom Werden u. Wachsen der Opposition im alten Reich,* Leipzig, 1932

Cole, G. D. H., *Studies in Class Structure,* London, 1955

Conze, W., *Polnische Nation u. deutsche Politik im Ersten Weltkrieg,* Cologne, 1958

Cordes, G. (ed.), *Krieg, Revolution, Republik. Eine Dokumentation,* Ulm, 1978

Coser, L. A., *The Functions of Social Conflict,* 1956 (2nd ed., Glencoe, 1964)

—, *Continuities in the Study of Social Conflict,* New York, 1967

Dähnhardt, D., *Revolution in Kiel. Der Übergang vom Kaiserreich zur Weimarer Republik 1918/19,* Neumünster, 1978

Dahrendorf, R., *Class and Class Conflict in Industrial Society,* Stanford, 1959 (revised and extended transl. of *Soziale Klassen u. Klassenkonflikte in der industriellen Gesellschaft,* 1957)

—, *Gesellschaft u. Freiheit. Zur soziologischen Analyse der Gegenwart,* Munich, 1961

—, *Gesellschaft u. Demokratie in Deutschland,* Munich, 1965

—, *Konflikt u. Freiheit. Auf dem Weg zur Dienstklassengesellschaft,* Munich, 1972

David, E., *Die Sozialdemokratie im Weltkrieg*, Berlin, 1915
—, *Das Kriegstagebuch des Reichstagsabgeordneten E. David, 1914–1918*, E. Matthias and S. Miller (eds.), Düsseldorf, 1966
Davies, J. C., 'Toward a Theory of Revolution', *American Sociological Review*, 27, 1962, pp. 5–19
— (ed.), *When men revolt and why. A reader in political violence and revolution*, New York, 1971
Deist, W., 'Die' Politik der Seekriegsleitung u. die Rebellion der Flotte Ende Oktober 1918', *VfZ*, 14, 1966, pp. 341ff.
—, 'Eine Kontroverse zwischen dem Reichskanzler u. dem Oberbefehlshaber in den Marken im Sommer 1915', *Militärgeschichtliche Mitteilungen*, 5, 1969, pp. 101–19
— (ed.), *Militär u. Innenpolitik im Weltkrieg 1914–1918*, 2 vols., Düsseldorf, 1970
—, 'Armee und Arbeiterschaft 1905–1918', *Francia*, 2, 1974, pp. 458–81
Delbrück, C, v., *Die wirtschaftliche Mobilmachung in Deutschland 1914*, J. v. Delbrück (ed.), Munich, 1924
Demeter, K., 'Die soziale Schichtung der deutschen Parlamente seit 1848', *VSWG*, 39, 1952, pp. 1ff.
Desai, A. V., *Real Wages in Germany 1871–1913*, Oxford, 1968
Deuerlein, E., *Der Bundesratsausschuß für die auswärtigen Angelegenheiten 1870 bis 1918*, Regensburg, 1955
Deutschland im Ersten Weltkrieg, 3 vols., Berlin, 1968–9; (vol. 1, 3rd ed., 1971; vols. 2, 3, 2nd eds., 1970)
Dieckmann, W., *Die Behördenorganisation in der deutschen Kriegswirtschaft 1914 bis 1918*, Hamburg, 1937
Dierkopf, H., 'Vorgeschichte, Entstehung u. Auswirkung des vaterländischen Hilfsdienstgesetzes vom 5. Dezember 1916. Ein Beitrag zur Wirtschafts- und Sozialgeschichte des Weltkriegs', Ph.D. thesis, Halle, 1937
Dix, A., *Wirtschaftskrieg u. Kriegswirtschaft*, Berlin, 1920
Dokumente u. Materialien zur Geschichte der deutschen Arbeiterbewegung, Inst. f. Marxismus-Leninismus beim ZK der SED, (ed.), Series II/1, Berlin, 1958; II/2, Berlin, 1957
Donner. O., *Die Kursbildung am Aktienmarkt*, Berlin, 1934
Drabkin, J. S., *Die Novemberrevolution in Deutschland 1918/19*, 2 vols., Berlin, 1968
Draht, M., 'Der Staat der Industriegesellschaft. Entwurf einer sozialwissenschaftlichen Staatstheorie', *Der Staat*, 5, 1966, pp. 273–84
Duisberg, C., *Abhandlungen, Vorträge u. Reden aus den Jahren 1882–1921*, Berlin, 1923

Ebert, F., *Schriften, Aufzeichnungen, Reden*, 2 vols., Dresden, 1926
Eckstein, H. (ed.), *Internal War: Problems and Approaches*, New York, 1965
Eckardt, G., *Industrie u. Politik in Bayern 1900–19. Der Bayerische Industriellen Verband als Modell des Einflusses von Wirtschaftsverbänden*, Berlin, 1976
Elben, W., *Das Problem der Kontinuität in der deutschen Revolution. Die Politik der Staatssekretäre u. der militärischen Führung vom Nov. 1918 bis*

Feb. 1919, Düsseldorf, 1965

Elm, L., *Zwischen Fortschritt u. Reaktion. Geschichte der Parteien der liberalen Bourgeoisie in Deutschland 1893–1918*, Berlin, 1968

Elster, K., *Von der Mark zur Reichsmark. Die Geschichte der deutschen Währung in den Jahren 1914 bis 1924*, Jena, 1928

Engel, J., 'Der Wandel in der Bedeutung des Krieges im 19. u. 20. Jahrhundert', *GWU*, 19, 1968, pp. 468–86

Epochen der Angestelltenbewegung 1774–1930, Gewerkschaftsbund der Angestellten (ed.), Berlin, 1930

Epstein, K., 'Der Interfraktionelle Ausschuß u. das Problem der Parlamentarisierung 1917–1918', *HZ*, 191, 1960, pp. 562–84

—, *Matthias Erzberger u. das Dilemma der deutschen Demokratie*, Berlin, 1962 (transl. as M. *Erzberger and the Dilemma of German Democracy*, 1959)

Erdmann, G., *Die deutschen Arbeitgeberverbände im sozialgeschichtlichen Wandel der Zeit*, Neuwied, 1966

Erdmann, K.-D., 'Zur Beurteilung Bethmann Hollwegs', *GWU*, 15, 1964, pp. 525–40

Ereignisse, Revolutionäre . . . u. Probleme in Deutschland während der Periode der Großen Sozialistischen Oktoberrevolution 1917/1918. Beiträge zum 40. Jahrestag der Großen Sozialistischen Oktoberrevolution, Berlin, 1957

Erhebung von Wirtschaftsrechnungen minderbemittelter Familien im Deutschen Reiche, Kaiserl. Statist. Amt. Abt. f. Arbeiterstatistik (ed.) (= *Reichsarbeitsblatt*, special issue 2), Berlin, 1909

Erzberger, M., *Erlebnisse im Weltkrieg*, Stuttgart, 1920

Eschenburg, T., *Die Improvisierte Demokratie*, Munich, 1963

Evans, R. J., *The Feminist Movement in Germany, 1894–1933*, London, 1976

Facius, F., *Wirtschaft u. Staat. Die Entwicklung der staatlichen Wirtschaftsverwaltung in Deutschland vom 17. Jahrhundert bis 1945*, Boppard, 1959

Falkenberg, A., *Die deutsche Beamtenbewegung nach der Revolution*, 2nd ed., Berlin, 1920

Feldman, G. D., *Army, Industry and Labor in Germany 1914–1918*, Princeton, 1966

—, 'Les fondements politiques et sociaux de la mobilisation économique en Allemagne (1914–1916)', *Annales E. S. C.*, 24, 1969, pp. 102–27

—, 'German Business Between War and Revolution: The Origins of the Stinnes-Legien Agreement', in G. A. Ritter (ed.), *Enstehung u. Wandel der modernen Gesellschaft. Fs. H. Rosenberg*, Berlin, 1970, pp. 312–41

—, 'Die Freien Gewerkschaften und die Zentralarbeitsgemeinschaft 1918–1924', in H. O. Vetter (ed.), *Vom Sozialistengesetz zur Mitbestimmung*, Cologne, 1975, pp. 229–52

—, *Iron and Steel in the German Inflation 1916–1923*, Princeton,1977

—, 'The Origins of the Stinnes-Legien Agreement: A Documentation', *IWK*, 19/20, 1972, pp. 45–102

—, 'Socio-Economic Structure in the Industrial Sector and Revolutionary Potentialities, 1917–1922', in C. L. Bertrand (ed.), *Revolutionary Situations in Europe, 1917–1922: Germany, Italy, Austria, Hungary*, Montreal, 1977, pp. 160ff.

—, 'Wirtschafts- und sozialpolitische Probleme der deutschen Demobilisierung) 1918/19', in H. Mommsen *et al.* (eds.), *Industrielles System und politische Entwicklung in der Weimarer Republik*, 2 vols., 2nd ed., Düsseldorf, 1977, pp. 618–36

—, (ed.), *Die deutsche Inflation*, Berlin, 1982

— and Homburg, H., *Industrie und Inflation. Studien und Dokumente zur Politik der deutschen Unternehmer 1916–1923*, Hamburg, 1977

Feldman, G. D., Kolb, E. and Rürup, R., 'Die Massenbewegungen der Arbeiterschaft in Deutschland am Ende des Ersten Welkrieges (1917–1920)', *PVS*, 13, 1972, pp. 84–105

— and Büsch, O. (eds.), *Historische Prozesse der deutschen Inflation 1914–1924*, Berlin, 1978

Fichte, R., *Die große Zeit im Deutschen Handwerk. Die Grundlagen der gegenwärtigen Wirtschaftsorganisationen des Deutschen Handwerks u. seine Beteiligung an den Heereslieferungen im Weltkriege*, Berlin, 1922

Fischer, F., *Griff nach der Weltmacht. Die Kriegszielpolitik des kaiserlichen Deutschland 1914/18*, Düsseldorf, 1961 (2nd ed., 1962; 3rd ed., 1964; special edition, 1967) (transl. as *Germany's War Aims in the First World War*, London 1967)

—, *Weltmacht oder Niedergang. Deutschland im Ersten Weltkrieg*, Frankfurt, 1965

—, *Krieg der Illusionen. Die deutsche Politik von 1911 bis 1914*, Düsseldorf, 1969 (transl. as *War of Illusions*, London, 1974)

—, (ed.), *Der Erste Weltkrieg und das deutsche Geschichtsbild. Beiträge zur Bewältigung eines historischen Tabus*, Düsseldorf, 1977

—, 'Der Stellenwert des Ersten Weltkriegs in der Kontinuitätsproblematik der deutschen Geschichte', *HZ*, 229, 1979, pp. 25–53

—, *Bündnis der Eliten. Zur Kontinuität der Machtstrukturen in Deutschland 1871–1945*, Düsseldorf, 1979

—, *Juli 1914: Wir sind nicht hineingeschlittert. Das Staatsgeheimnis um die Riezler-Tagebücher*, Reinbek, 1983

—, 'Die Angestellten, ihre Bewegung u. ihre Ideologien', Ph.D. thesis, Heidelberg, 1931

Fischer, H. D. (ed.), *Pressekonzentration und Zensurpraxis im Ersten Weltkrieg*, Berlin, 1973

Fischer, K., *Denkwürdigkeiten u. Erinnerungen eines Arbeiters*, P. Göhre (ed.), 2 vols., Leipzig, 1903, 1904

Fischer, W., 'Die Rolle des Kleingewerbes im wirtschaftlichen Wachstumsprozeß in Deutschland 1850-1914', in F. Lütge (ed.), *Wirtschaftliche u. soziale Probleme der gewerblichen Entwicklung im 15.-16. u. 19. Jahrhundert*, Stuttgart, 1968, pp. 131–42.

—, 'Staatsverwaltung u. Intersssenverbände im Deutschen Reich 1871–1914', in *Interdependenzen von Politik und Wirtschaft. Festgabe f. G. von Eynern*, Berlin, 1967, pp. 431–56

—, and P. Czada, 'Wandlungen in der deutschen Industriestruktur im 20. Jahrhundert. Ein statistisch-deskriptiver Ansatz', in G. A. Ritter (ed.), *Enstehung u. Wandel der modernen Gesellschaft. Fs. H. Rosenberg*, Berlin, 1970, pp. 116–65

Forsthoff, E., *Rechtsfragen der leistenden Verwaltung*, 1938 (Stuttgart, 1959)
—, *Lehrbuch des Verwaltungsrechts*, 1, 8th ed., Munich, 1961
Um Freiheit u. Vaterland. Erste Veröffentlichung des Volksbundes für Freiheit u. Vaterland, Gotha, 1918
Freud, S., 'Zeitgemäßes über Krieg u. Tod (1915), in *idem, Das Unbewußte. Schriften zur Psychoanalyse*, Am. Mitscherlich (ed.), Frankfurt, 1960, pp. 187–213
Freyberg, J. v., *et al.*, *Geschichte der deutschen Sozialdemokratie 1863-1975*, Cologne, 1975
Fricke, D., *Die deutsche Arbeiterbewegung 1869–1914*, Berlin, 1976
Friedensburg, F., *Kohle u. Eisen im Weltkrieg u. in den Friedensschlüssen*, Munich, 1934
—, *Das Erdöl im Weltkrieg*, Stuttgart, 1939
Friedländer, S., 'Die politischen Veränderungen der Kriegszeit und ihre Auswirkungen auf die Judenfrage', in W. E. Mosse (ed.), *Deutsches Judentum in Krieg u. Revolution 1916–1923*, Tübingen, 1971, pp. 27–65
Fuchs, R., 'Die Kriegsgewinne der verschiedenen Wirtschaftszweige in den einzelnen Staaten anhand statistischer Daten dargestellt', Ph.D. thesis, Zurich, 1918
Fülberth, G. and J. Harrer, *Die deutsche Sozialdemokratie 1890-1933. Arbeiterbewegung und SPD*, Neuwied, 1974
Fünfundzwanzig Jahre Arbeitnordwest 1904-1929. Arbeitgeberverband f. d. Bezirk d. nordwestl. Gruppe d. Vereins Deutscher Eisen- u. Stahlindustrieller (ed.), Berlin, 1929
Fürstenberg, C., *Die Lebensgeschichte eines deutschen Bankiers*, H. Fürstenberg (ed.), Berlin, 1931

Gantzel, K. J., Kress, G. and Rittberger, V., *Konflikt — Eskalation — Krise. Sozialwissenschaftliche Studien zum Ausbruch des Ersten Weltkrieges*, Düsseldorf, 1972
Gebhard, G., *Ruhrbergbau. Geschichte, Aufbau u. Verflechtung seiner Gesellschaften u. Organisationen*, Essen, 1957
Geck. L. H. A., *Die sozialen Arbeitsverhältnisse im Wandel der Zeit. Eine geschichtliche Einführung in die Betriebssoziologie*, Berlin, 1931
Geiger, T., *Die soziale Schichtung des deutschen Volkes. Soziographischer Versuch auf statistischer Grundlage*, Stuttgart, 1932 (2nd ed., 1967)
—, 'Zur Theorie des Klassenbegriffs u. der proletarischen Klasse', 1930, repr. in *idem, Gesammelte Arbeiten zur Soziologie*, Neuwied, 1962, pp. 206-92
Geiss, I., *Der polnische Grenzstreifen 1914 bis 1918. Ein Beitrag zur deutschen Kriegszielpolitik im Ersten Weltkrieg*, Lübeck, 1960
—, (ed.), *Julikrise u. Kriegsausbruch 1914. Eine Dokumentensammlung*, 2 vols., Hanover, 1963, 1964
—, *Juli 1914. Die europäische Krise u. der Ausbruch des Ersten Weltkrieges*, Munich, 1965
—, 'Die Fischer-Kontroverse', in *idem, Studien über Geschichte u. Geschichtswissenschaft*, Frankfurt 1972, pp. 108-98
—, *Das Deutsche Reich und die Vorgeschichte des Ersten Weltkriegs*, Munich, 1978

—, *Das Deutsche Reich und der Erste Weltkrieg*, Munich, 1978
— and Wendt, B.-J. (eds.), *Deutschland in der Weltpolitik des 19. u. 20. Jahrhunderts. Fs. F. Fischer*, Düsseldorf, 1973
Gerlach, H. v., *Die große Zeit der Lüge*, Charlottenburg, 1926
Gersdorff, U.v., *Frauen im Kriegsdienst 1914–1945*, Stuttgart, 1969
—, 'Frauenarbeit u. Frauenemanzipation im Ersten Weltkrieg, *Francia*, 2, 1975, pp. 502–23
Geschichte der deutschen Arbeiterbewegung, Inst. f. Marxismus-Leninismus beim ZK der SED (ed.), 1–3, Berlin, 1966
Goebel, O., *Deutsche Rohstoffwirtschaft im Weltkrieg. Einschließlich des Hindenburg-Programms*, Stuttgart, 1930
Göhre, P., *Drei Monate Fabrikarbeiter u. Handwerksbursche*, Leipzig, 1891
Göppert, H., 'Die Sozialisierungsbestrebungen in Deutschland nach der Revolution', *Schmollers Jb*, 45, pt. 2, 1921, pp. 9–44
Görlitz, W. (ed.), *Regierte der Kaiser? Kriegstagebücher, Aufzeichnungen u. Briefe des Chefs des Marinekabinetts G. A. v. Müller 1914–1918*, Göttingen, 1959
Goodspeed, D. J., *Ludendorff. Soldat, Diktator, Revolutionär*, Gütersloh, 1968 (transl. as *Ludendorff*, Toronto, 1966)
Gossweiler, K., *Großbanken, Industriemonopole, Staat. Ökonomie u. Politik des staatsmonopolistischen Kapitalismus in Deutschland 1914–1932*, Berlin, 1971
Grebing, H., *Geschichte der deutschen Arbeiterbewegung*, 6th ed., Munich, 1975
Grebler, L. u. and Winkler, W., *The Cost of the World War to Germany and Austria-Hungary*, New Haven, 1940
Greenwald, M. W., *Women, War and Work. The Impact of World War I on Women Workers in the United States*, Westport, 1980
Greiffenhagen, S., 'Die württembergischen Sozialdemokraten im Ersten Weltkrieg und in der Weimarer Republik (1914-1933)', in J. Schadt and W. Schmierer (eds.), *Die SPD in Baden-Württemberg und ihre Geschichte*, Stuttgart, 1979, pp. 160–91
Groener, W., *Lebenserinnerungen. Jugend, Generalstab, Weltkrieg. F. F. v. Gaertringen* (ed.), Göttingen, 1957
Groener-Geyer, D., *General Groener — Soldat u. Staatsmann*, Frankfurt, 1955
Groh, D., 'The "Unpatriotic Socialists" and the State', *JContHist*, I, IV, pp. 151–77
—, 'Negative Integration u. revolutionärer Attentismus. Die Sozialdemokratie im Kaiserreich', *Internationale Wissenschaftliche Korrespondenz zur Geschichte der deutschen Arbeiterbewegung*, 15, April 1972, pp. 1–8
—, ' "Je eher, desto besser!" Innenpolitische Faktoren für die Präventivkriegsbereitschaft des Deutschen Reiches 1913/14', *PVS*, 13, 1972, pp. 501–21
—, *Negative Integration und revolutionärer Attentismus. Die deutsche Sozialdemo-kratie am Vorabend des Ersten Weltkrieges*, Berlin, 1973
Grosser, Dieter, *Vom monarchischen Konstitutionalismus zur parlamentarischen Demokratie. Die Verfassungspolitik der deutschen Parteien im*

letzten Jahrzehnt des Kaiserreiches, The Hague, 1970

Grünberg, E., *Der Mittelstand in der kapitalistischen Gesellschaft*, Leipzig, 1932

Gündell, G., *Die Organisation der deutschen Ernährungswirtschaft im Welt-kriege*, Leipzig, 1939

Günther, A., *Die gesunkene Kaufkraft des Lohnes u. ihre Wiederherstellung, II: Kriegslöhne u. -preise und ihr Einfluß auf Kaufkraft u. Lebenskosten*, Jena, 1919

—, *Lebenshaltung des Mittelstandes. Statistische u. theoretische Untersuchungen zur Konsumtionslehre*, Munich, 1920

—, 'Die Folgen des Krieges für Einkommen u. Lebenshaltung der mittleren Volksschichten in Deutschland', in R. Meerwarth, A. Günther and W. Zimmermann, *Die Einwirkungen des Krieges auf Bevölkerungsbewegung, Einkommen u. Lebenshaltung in Deutschland*, Stuttgart, 1932, pp. 99–279

Gurr. T. R., *Why Men Rebel*, Princeton, 1970

Gutsche, W., 'Bethmann Hollweg u. die Politik der "Neuorientierung". Zur innenpolitischen Strategie und Taktik der deutschen Reichsregierung während des Ersten Weltkrieges', *ZfG*, 13, 1965, pp. 209–34

—, 'Die Beziehungen zwischen der Regierung Bethman Hollweg und dem Monopolkapital in den ersten Monaten des Ersten Weltkrieges', Ph.D. thesis, Berlin, 1967

—, 'Die Entstehung des Kriegsausschusses der deutschen Industrie u. seine Rolle zu Beginn des Ersten Weltkrieges', *ZfG*, 18, 1970, pp. 877–98

—, (ed.), *Herrschaftsmethoden des deutschen Imperialismus 1897/98 bis 1917. Dokumente zur innen- und außenpolitischen Strategie und Taktik der herrschenden Klassen des Deutschen Reiches*, Berlin, 1977

Habermas, J., *Strukturwandel der Öffentlichkeit. Untersuchungen zu einer Kategorie der bürgerlichen Gesellschaft*, 2nd ed., Neuwied, 1965 (5th ed., 1971)

—, *Erkenntnis u. Interesse*, Frankfurt, 1968

—, *Legitimationsprobleme im Spätkapitalismus*, Frankfurt, 1973

Hahlweg, W., *Der Diktatfrieden von Brest-Litowsk 1918 u. die bolschewistische Weltrevolution*, Münster, 1960

Hamel, I., *Völkischer Verband und nationale Gewerkschaft. Die Politik des Deutschnationalen Handlungsgehilfen-Verbandes 1893–1933*, Frankfurt, 1967

Hammer, K., *Deutsche Kriegstheologie 1870–1918*, Munich, 1971

Handbuch der Empirischen Sozialforschung, R. König (ed.), 2 vols., Stuttgart, 1967

Hardach, G., *Der Erste Weltkrieg 1914–1918*, Munich, 1973

Harms, B. (ed.), *Kriegswirtschaftliche Untersuchungen aus dem Institut für Seeverkehr u. Weltwirtschaft an der Universität Kiel*, 17 parts, Jena, 1915–18

— (ed.), *Strukturwandlungen der Deutschen Volkswirtschaft*, 2 vols., Berlin, 1928

Hartfiel, G., *Angestellte u. Angestelltengewerkschaften in Deutschland. Entwick-lung und Situation von beruflicher Tätigkeit, sozialer Stellung u. Verbandswesen der Angestellten in der gewerblichen Wirtschaft*, Berlin, 1961

Haußmann, C., *Schlaglichter. Reichstagsbriefe u. Aufzeichnungen*, U. Zeller (ed.), Frankfurt, 1924

Hecht, W., *Organisationsformen der deutschen Rohstoffindustrie: Die Kohle*, Munich, 1924

Heim, G. and Schlittenbauer, S., *Ein Hilferuf der deutschen Landwirtschaft. Überreicht von der Zentralstelle der Bayerischen Christlichen Bauernvereine in Regensburg*, Regensburg [1916]

Heinrichsbauer, A., *Die Privatangestellten der Großbetriebe u. ihre Organisation*, Essen, 1918

Helfferich, K., *Deutschlands Volkswohlstand 1888-1913*, 4th ed., Berlin, 1914

—, *Reden u. Aufsätze aus dem Kriege*, Berlin, 1917

—, *Der Weltkrieg*, 3 vols., Berlin, 1919

Henderson, W. O., 'Walter Rathenau. A Pioneer of the Planned Economy', *FHR*, 4, 1951/52, pp. 98-108

Hennig, E., *Monopolgruppentheorie in der DDR, Leviathan. Zeitschrift für Sozialwissenschaft*, 1, 1973, pp. 135-51

Hennig, E., *et al* (eds.), *Karl Marx/Friedrich Engels. Materialien zur Rekonstruktion der marxistischen Staatstheorie*, Frankfurt, 1974

Henning, F.-W., *Die Industrialisierung in Deutschland 1800-1914*, Paderborn, 1973

—, *Das Industrialisierte Deutschland 1914-1972*, Paderborn, 1974

Herzfeld, H., *Die deutsche Sozialdemokratie u. die Auflösung der nationalen Einheitsfront im Weltkriege*, Leipzig, 1928

—, *Der Erste Weltkrieg*, Munich, 1968

Hesse, F., *Die deutsche Wirtschaftslage von 1914 bis 1923. Krieg, Geldblähe u. Wechsellagen*, Jena, 1938

Hesse, K., *Der kriegswirtschaftliche Gedanke*, Hamburg, 1935

Heuss, T., *Friedrich Naumann*, 2nd ed., Stuttgart, 1949

—, *Erinnerungen. 1905-1933*, 2 vols., Tübingen, 1963, 1967

Heymann, E., *Die Rechtsformen der militärischen Kriegswirtschaft als Grundlage des neuen deutschen Industrierechts*, Marburg, 1921

Hildebrand, K., *Bethmann Hollweg. Der Kanzler ohne Eigenschaften? Eine kritische Bibliographie*, Düsseldorf, 1970

Hilferding, R., 'Probleme der Zeit', *Die Gesellschaft*, 1, 1924, 1-17

—, 'Das historische Problem', *ZfP*, N. F. 1, 1954, pp. 293-324

Hillgruber, A., *Deutschlands Rolle in der Vorgeschichte der beiden Weltkriege*, Göttingen, 1967

Hindenburg, P. v. *Aus meinem Leben*, Leipzig, 1920

Hintze, O., 'Der Beamtenstand', 1911, in *idem, Soziologie u. Geschichte*, G. Oestreich (ed.), *Collected Essays*, 2nd vol., 4th ed., Göttingen, 1964, pp. 66-125

Hirschfeld, M., *Sittengeschichte des Weltkrieges*, 2 vols., Leipzig, 1930

Höfle, A., *Privatangestellte u. Neuorientierung*, Berlin, 1918

Hoffmann, W. G., *Das Wachstum der deutschen Wirtschaft seit der Mitte des 19. Jahrhunderts*, Berlin, 1965

Holtfrerich, C.-L., *Die deutsche Inflation 1914-1923. Ursachen und Folgen in internationaler Perspektive*, Berlin and New York, 1980

Hoop, E., *Die Innenpolitik der Reichskanzler Michaelis u. Graf Hertling*, PhD thesis, Kiel, 1951

Horn, D. (ed.), *The German Naval Mutinies of World War I*, New Brunswick, 1969

Huber, E. R. (ed.), *Dokumente zur deutschen Verfassungsgeschicht*. Vol. 2: *1851–1918*, 2nd ed., Stuttgart, 1964

—, *Dokumente zur deutschen Verfassungsgeschichte*. Vol. 3: *Dokumente der Novemberrevolution und der Weimarer Republik 1918–1933*, Stuttgart, etc., 1966

—, *Deutsche Verfassungsgeschichte seit 1789*. Vol. 4: *Struktur u. Krisen des Kaiserreichs*, Stuttgart, 1969

—, *Deutsche Verfassungsgeschichte seit 1789*. Vol. 5: *Weltkrieg, Revolution und Reichserneuerung 1914–1919*, Stuttgart, 1978

Huldermann, B., *A. Ballin*, Oldenburg, 1922

Hurwitz, S. J., *State Intervention in Great Britain. A Study of Economic Control and Social Response 1914–1919*, 2nd ed., London, 1968

'Immediatbericht des preußischen Ministers des Innern, v. Loebell, vom 22. Nov. 1915', introduction and commentary by J. Schellenberg, *Jb f. Geschichte*, 1, 1967, pp. 229–60

Inst. f. Gesellschaftswissenschaften beim ZK der SED, *Der Imperialismus der BRD*, Berlin, 1972

Jaeger, H., *Unternehmer in der deutschen Politik (1890–1918)*, Bonn, 1967

Jahresberichte der Königlich Preußischen Regierungs- u. Gewerberäte und Bergbehörden für 1913 (official publ.), Berlin, 1914

Jahresberichte der Preußischen Regierungs- u. Gewerberäte und Bergbehörden für 1914–1918, Ministerium für Handel und Gewerbe (ed.) (official publ.), Berlin, 1919

Janoska-Bendl, J., *Methodologische Aspekte des Idealtypus. M. Weber u. die Soziologie der Geschichte*, Berlin, 1965

Jannsson, W., *Arbeiterinteressen u. Kriegsergebnis*, Berlin, 1915

Janßen, K.-H., *Macht u. Verblendung. Die Kriegszielpolitik der deutschen Bundesstaaten, 1914–1918*, Göttingen, 1962

—, *Der Kanzler u. der General. Die Führungskrise um Bethmann Hollweg u. Falkenhayn 1914–1916*, Göttingen, 1967

Jarausch, K. H., *The Enigmatic Chancellor. Bethmann Hollweg and the Hybrid of Imperial Germany*, New Haven, 1973

—, (ed.), *Quantifizierung in der Geschichtswissenschaft*, Düsseldorf, 1976

Jeck, A., *Wachstum u. Verteilung des Volkseinkommens. Untersuchungen u. Materialien zur Entwicklung der Einkommensverteilung in Deutschland 1870–1913*, Tübingen, 1970

Jochmann, W., 'Die Ausbreitung des Antisemitismus', in W. E. Mosse (ed.), *Deutsches Judentum in Krieg u. Revolution 1916–1923*, Tübingen, 1971. pp. 409–510

Johann, E. (ed.), *Innenansicht eines Krieges. Bilder – Briefe – Dokumente, 1914 bis 1918*, Frankfurt, 1968

Johnson, C., *Revolutionstheorie*, Cologne, 1971 (transl. as *Revolutionary Change*, 1966)

Jürgensen, K., ' "Deutsche Abende — Flensburg 1914." Ein Beitrag zum Verhältnis von Volk, Staat u. evangelischer Kirche nach Ausbruch des Ersten Weltkrieges', *GWU* 20, 1969, 1–16

Kachulle, D. (ed.), *Die Pöhlands im Krieg. Briefe einer Arbeiterfamilie aus dem Ersten Weltkrieg*, Cologne, 1982

Kaelble, H., *Industrielle Interessenpolitik in der wilhelminischen Gesellschaft. Centralverband deutscher Industrieller 1895–1914*, Berlin, 1967

—, 'Sozialer Aufstieg in Deutschland 1850–1914' *VSWG*, 60, 1973, pp. 41–71

—, and Volkmann, H., 'Konjunktur u. Streik während des Übergangs zum Organisierten Kapitalismus in Deutschland', *Zeitschrift für Wirtschafts- u. Sozialwissenschaften' (hitherto Schmollers Jb)*, 92, 1972, pp. 513–44

—, et al., *Probleme der Modernisierung in Deutschland. Sozialhistorische Studien zum 19. und 20. Jahrhundert*, Opladen, 1978

Kalmer, G., 'Beamtenschaft u. Revolution', in K. Bosl (eds.), *Bayern im Umbruch. Die Revolution von 1918, ihre Voraussetzungen, ihr Verlauf u. ihre Folgen*, Munich, 1969, pp. 201–61

Karbe, A., *Die Frauenlohnfrage und ihre Entwicklung in der Kriegs- und Nachkriegszeit*, Rostock, 1928

Kautsky, K., *Sozialdemokratische Bemerkungen zur Übergangswirtschaft* Leipzig, 1918

Keilpflug, E., 'Die Gehaltserhöhungen der bayerischen Beamten im Kriege und die Lebensmittelteuerung', *JNS*, 111, 1918, pp. 59–69

Kehr, E., *Der Primat der Innenpolitik. Gesammelte Aufsätze zur preußisch-deutschen Sozialgeschichte im 19. u. 20. Jahrhundert*, 2nd ed., Berlin, 1970

Keßler, H. Graf, *W. Rathenau, sein Leben u. sein Werk*, Wiesbaden, 1928 (rept. 1962)

Kielmansegg, P. Graf, *Deutschland u. der Erste Weltkrieg*, Frankfurt, 1968

Kiesenwetter, O. v., *Fünfundzwanzig Jahre wirtshaftspolitischen Kampfes. Geschichtliche Darstellung des Bundes der Landwirte. Zum 18. 2. 1918*, for the BdL, Berlin, 1918

Kirchheimer, O., *Politische Herrschaft. Fünf Beiträge zur Lehre vom Staat*, Frankfurt, 1967

Kitchen, M., *The Silent Dictatorship. The Politics of the German High Command under Hindenburg and Ludendorff, 1916–1918*, London, 1976

Klass, G. v., *A. Vögler*, Tübingen, 1957

—, *H. Stinnes*, Tübingen, 1958

Klein, F. (ed.), *Studien zum deutschen Imperialismus vor 1914*, Berlin, 1976

—, 'Krieg – Revolution – Frieden, 1914–1920', *ZfG*, 28, 1980, pp. 544–54

Kluge, U., *Soldatenräte und Revolution. Studien zur Militärpolitik in Deutschland 1918/19*, Göttingen, 1975

Knauss, R., *Die deutsche, englische u. französische Kriegsfinanzierung*, Berlin, 1923

Knopp, G. F., 'Einigungsdebatte und Einigungsaktion in SPD and USPD 1917–1920 — unter besonderer Berücksichtigung der "Zentralstelle für Einigung der Sozialdemokratie" '. Ph.D. thesis, Würzburg, 1975

Koch, H. W. (ed.), *The Origins of the First World War. Great Power Rivalry and German War Aims*, London, 1972

Kocka, J., *Angestellte zwischen Faschismus und Demokratie. Zur Politischen Sozialgeschichte der Angestellten: USA 1890–1940 im internationalen Vergleich*, Göttingen, 1977
—, 'The first world war and the "Mittelstand": German artisans and white-collar workers', *JConHist*, 8, 1973, pp. 101–24
—, 'Gegenstandsbezogene Theorien i. d. Geschichtswissenschaft: Schwierigkeiten u. Ergebnisse der Diskussion', in *idem* (ed)., *Theorien in der Praxis des Historikers*, *GG*, special issue 3, Göttingen, 1978, pp. 178–88
—, 'Industrielles Management. Konzeptionen u. Modelle in Deutschland vor 1914', *VSWG*, 56, 1969, pp. 32–72
—, 'Karl Marx u. Max Weber im Vergleich. Sozialwissenschaften zwischen Dogmatismus und Dezisionismus', in H.-U. Wehler (ed.), *Geschichte u. Ökonomie*, Cologne, 1973, pp. 54–84
—, *Sozialgeschichte. Begriff – Entwicklung – Probleme*, Göttingen, 1977
—, 'Art. "Sozial- und Wirtschaftsgeschichte"', *SDG*, 6, 1972, pp. 3–7
—, 'Theorieprobleme der Sozial- u. Wirtschaftsgeschichte. Begriffe, Tendenzen und Funktionen in West u. Ost', in H.-U. Wehler (ed.), *Geschichte u. Soziologie*, Cologne, 1972, pp. 305–30
—, *Unternehmensverwaltung u. Angestelltenschaft am Beispiel Siemens 1847–1914. Zum Verhältnis von Kapitalismus und Bürokratie in der deutschen Industrialisierung*, Stuttgart, 1969
—, 'Vorindustrielle Faktoren in der deutschen Industrialisierung. Industriebürokratie und "neuer Mittelstand"', in M. Stürmer (ed.) *Das Kaiserliche Deutschland*, Düsseldorf, 1970 (2nd ed., 1977), pp. 265–86
—, 'Weltkrieg u. Mittelstand. Handwerker u. Angestellte in Deutschland 1914–1918', *Francia*, 2, 1974, pp. 431–57
—, 'Zur Problematik der deutschen Angestellten 1914–1933', in H. Mommsen *et al.* (eds.), *Industrielles System und politische Entwicklung in der Weimarer Republik*, Düsseldorf, 1974 (2nd ed., 1977), pp. 792–810
Köhler, C., *Die Privatbeamtenpolitik nach dem Kriege*, Bonn, 1916
Köllner, L. and Kutz, M., *Wirtschaft und Gesellschaft in den beiden Weltkriegen. Berichte und Bibliographien (Berichte des Sozialwissenschaftlichen Instituts der Bundeswehr, H.22)*, Munich, 1981
König, H., *Entstehung u. Wirkungsweise von Fachverbänden der Nahrungs- u. Genußmittelindustrie*, Berlin, 1965
Koistinen, P. A. C., 'The "Industrial-Military Complex" in Historical Perspective: World War I', *BHR*, 41, 1967, pp. 378–403
Kolb, E., *Die Arbeiterräte in der deutschen Innenpolitik 1918/19*, 2nd (ext.) ed., Frankfurt, 1978
—, (ed.), *Vom Kaiserreich zur Republik*, Cologne, 1972
—, and Schönhoven, K. (eds.), *Regionale und lokale Räteorganisationen in Württemberg 1918/19*, Düsseldorf, 1976
Koschnitzke, R., 'Die Innenpolitik des Reichskanzlers v. Bethmann Hollweg im Weltkrieg', Ph.D. thesis, Kiel, 1951
Kosselleck R., *Preußen zwischen Reform u. Revolution. Allgemeines Landrecht, Verwaltung u. soziale Bewegung 1791–1848*, Stuttgart, 1967
Koszyk, K., *Zwischen Kaiserreich u. Diktatur. Die sozialdemokratische Presse 1914 bis 1933*, Heidelberg, 1958

—, *Deutsche Pressepolitik im Ersten Weltkrieg*, Düsseldorf, 1968
Krause, H., *Revolution und Konterrevolution 1918/19 am Beispiel Hanau*, Kronberg/Ts., 1974
—, *USPD. Zur Geschichte der Unabhängigen Sozialdemokratischen Partei Deutschlands*, Frankfurt, Cologne, 1975
Kremer, W., 'Der soziale Aufbau der Parteien u. des deutschen Reichstags, 1871 bis 1918', Ph.D. thesis, Cologne, Emsdetten, 1934
Kruck, A., *Geschichte des Alldeutschen Verbandes 1890-1939*, Wiesbaden, 1954
Kuczynski, J., *Studien zur Geschichte des deutschen Imperialismus, I: Monopole u. Unternehmerverbände*, 2nd ed., Berlin, 1952
—, *Studien zur Geschichte des Kapitalismus*, Berlin, 1957
—, *Zur Frühgeschichte des deutschen Monopolkapitals u. des staatsmonopolistischen Kapitalismus*, Berlin, 1962
—, *Die Geschichte der Lage der Arbeiter unter dem Kapitalismus, I, 4: Darstellung der Lage der Arbeiter in Deutschland, 1900-1917/18*, Berlin, 1967
—, *ibid., 5: Darstellung der Lage der Arbeiter in Deutschland, 1917/18-1932/3*, Berlin, 1966
—, *Klassen u. Klassenkämpfe im imperialistischen Deutschland u. in der BRD*, Frankfurt, 1972
Kuhn, T. S., *Die Struktur wissenschaftlicher Revolutionen* (1962), Frankfurt, 1967 (2nd ed., Chicago, 1970)
Kulemann, W., *Die Berufsvereine, I: Geschichtliche Entwicklung der Berufsorganisationen der Arbeitnehmer u. Arbeitgeber aller Länder 1–3: Deutschland*, 2nd ed., Jena, 1908
—, *Genossenschaftsbewegung*, I, 1: *Geschichtlicher Teil, Darstellung der Entwicklung in alten Kulturländern sowie der internationalen Beziehungen*; 2: *Systematischer Teil. Die Kulturbedeutung der Genossenschaftsbewegung*, Berlin, 1922

Lambers, H., *Die Revolutionszeit in Hagen. Die politische Entwicklung von 1917 bis 1924 in Hagen u. Haspe. Regionalanlyse der politischen Ereignisse, des Parteienverhaltens u. der Wahlen in der Revolutionsperiode*, Hagen, 1963
Lange, P., *Die Neuorientierung der Gewerkshaften*, Leipzig, 1917
Laqueur, W., 'Revolution', *IESS*, 13, 1968, pp. 501–7
Laslett, P., 'History and the Social Sciences', *IESS*, 6, 1968, pp. 434–40
Laursen, K. and Pedersen, J., *The German Inflation 1918-23*, Amsterdam, 1964
1914-1918. L'autre Front. Etudes coordonnées et rassamblées par Patrick Fridenson. Cahiers du 'Mouvement Social', 2, Paris, 1977
Leckebusch, R., *Enstehung u. Wandlungen der Zielsetzungen, der Struktur u. der Wirkungen von Arbeitgeberverbänden*, Berlin, 1966
Lederer, E., *Die Privatangestellten in der modernen Wirtschaftsentwicklung*, Tübingen, 1912
—, *Die wirtschaftlichen Organisationen*, Leipzig, 1913
—, 'Die Organisation der Wirtschaft durch den Staat im Kriege', *Archiv*, 40, 1915, pp.118–46
—, 'Zur Soziologie des Weltkriegs', *Archiv*, 1915, pp. 347–84
—, 'Die ökonimische Umschichtung im Kriege, I. u. II', *Archiv*, 45, 1918/

258   *Bibliography*

19, pp. 1.–39, 430–63
—, *Die sozialen Organisationen*, 2nd ed., Berlin, 1922
—, *Umschichtung der Einkommen u. des Bedarfs*, Berlin, 1928
— and Marschak, J., 'Die Klassen auf dem Arbeitsmarkt u. ihre Organisationen', *GdS*, 9/11, Tübingen, 1927, pp. 106–258
Leibrock, O., *Arbeitsgemeinschaft*, Leipzig, 1920
Leipart, T., *K. Legien*, Berlin, 1929
Leonhard, S., *Unterirdische Literatur im revolutionären Deutschland während des Weltkrieges*, Frankfurt, 1968 (repr. of the Berlin edition of 1920)
Lenin, W. I., *Werke*, 40 vols., from the 4th Russian ed., Berlin, 1955ff.
Lensch, P., *Die deutsche Sozialdemokratie u. der Weltkrieg*, Berlin, 1915
—, *Der Arbeiter u. die deutschen Kolonien*, Berlin, 1917
Lepsius, M. R., 'Parteiensystem u. Sozialstruktur. Zum Problem der Demokratisierung der deutschen Gesellschaft', in W. Abel *et al.*, (eds.), *Wirtschaft, Geschichte u. Wirtschaftsgeschichte. Fs. F. Lütge*, Stuttgart, 1966, pp. 371–93
Levenstein, A., *Die Arbeiterfrage mit besonderer Berücksichtigung der sozialpsychologischen Seite des modernen Großbetriebes u. der psycho-physischen Einwirkungen auf den Arbeiter*, Munich, 1912
Lewinsohn, R., *Die Umschichtung der europäischen Vermögen*, Berlin, n.d.
—, *The Profits of War through the Ages*, New York, 1937
Liebknecht, K., *Klassenkampf gegen den Krieg*, Berlin, 1919
—, *Politische Aufzeichnungen aus seinem Nachlaß. Geschrieben in den Jahren 1917 bis 1918*, F. Pfemfert (ed.), Berlin, 1921
—, *Gesammelte Reden u. Schriften*, 8–9, Inst. f. Marxismus-Leninismus beim ZK der SED (ed.), Berlin, 1966, 1971
Liefmann, R., *Die Kartelle in u. nach dem Kriege*, Berlin, 1918
—, *Kartelle u. Trusts u. die Weiterbildung der volkswirtschaftlichen Organisation* (3rd ed., 1918), 4th ed., Stuttgart, 1920
Liepmann, M., *Krieg u. Kriminalität in Deutschland*, Berlin, 1930
Lipset, S. M., *Political Man. The Social Basis of Politics*, New York [1960] 1963 (transl. as *Soziologie der Demokratie*, Neuwied, 1962)
—, *Revolution and Counterrevolution*, New York, 1968
Lloyd, E. M. H., *Experiments in State Control*, Oxford, 1924
Lösche, P., *Der Bolschewismus im Urteil der deutschen Sozialdemokratie*, Berlin, 1967
—, 'Bericht über die innenpolitische Entwicklung während des Krieges' [1915], *Jb. f. d. Geschichte Mittel- u. Ostdeutschlands*, 18, 1969, pp. 216–53
—, 'Arbeiterbewegung u. Wilhelminismus. Sozialdemokratie zwischen Anpassung u. Spaltung', *GWU*, 20, 1969, pp. 519–33
Lorenz, C., 'Die gewerbliche Frauenarbeit während des Krieges', in P. Umbreit and C. Lorenz, *Der Kriege u. die Arbeiterverhältnisse*, Stuttgart, 1928, pp. 307–91
—, *Die Statistik in der Kriegswirtschaft*, Hamburg, 1936
Lotz, W., *Die deutsche Staatsfinanzwirtschaft im Kriege*, Berlin, 1927
Lucas, E., *Die Sozialdemokraten in Bremen während des Ersten Weltkrieges*, Bremen, 1969
Ludendorff, E., *Meine Kriegserinnerungen, 1914–1918*, Berlin, 1919

—, (ed.), *Urkunden der Obersten Heeresleitung über ihre Tätigkeit 1916/18*, Berlin, 1921

Lübbe, H., *Politische Philosophie in Deutschland*, Basle, 1963

[Luebbering, H.,] *Handwerksfragen zur Kriegszeit*, Mönchen-Gladbach, 1915

Lüders, M.-E., 'Die Entwicklung der gewerblichen Frauenarbeit im Kriege', 2 pts., *Schmollers Jb.*, 44, 1920, pt. 1, pp. 241–67; pt. 2, *ibid.*, pp. 253–77

—, *Das unbekannte Heer. Frauen kämpfen für Deutschland 1914–1918*, Berlin, 1935

Lütge, F., 'Die deutsche Kriegsfinanzierung im Ersten und Zweiten Weltkrieg', in *Fs. R. Stucken*, Göttingen, 1953, pp. 553–7

—, *Deutsche Sozial- u. Wirtschaftsgeschichte*, 3rd ed., Berlin, 1966

Lüthgen, H., *Das Rheinisch- Westfälische Kohlensyndikat in der Vorkriegs-, Kriegs- u. Nachkriegszeit u. seine Hauptprobleme*, Leipzig, 1926

Luxemburg, R., *Ausgewählte Reden u. Schriften*, Marx-Engels-Lenin-Inst. beim ZK der SED (ed.), 2 vols, Berlin, 1951

—, *Politische Schriften*, Leipzig, 1968

Maas, F., 'Über die Herkunftsbedingungen geistiger Führer'. *Archiv*, 41, 1916, pp. 144–86

Mai, Gerlind, *Die innenpolitische Stellung und Bedeutung der Militär-befehlshaber in den Anfangsjahren des Ersten Weltkriegs 1914/15. Unter besonderer Berücksichtigung des X. Armeekorps (Hannover)*, Marburg, 1975

Mai, Gunther, *Kriegswirtschaft und Arbeiterbewegung in Württemberg 1914–1918*, Stuttgart, 1983

—, 'Burgfrieden und Sozialpolitik in Deutschland in der Anfangsphase des Ersten Weltkriegs (1914/15)', *Militärgeschichtliche Mitteilungen*, 2, 1976, pp. 21–50

—, 'Die Sozialstruktur der württembergischen Soldatenräte 1918/19', *IWK*, 14, 1978, pp. 3–28

Maier, C. S., 'Between Taylorism and Technocracy: European Ideologies and the Vision of Industrial Productivity in the 1920s', *JContHist*, 5, 1970, pp. 27–61

—, *Recasting Bourgeois Europe: Stabilization in France, Germany, and Italy in the Decade after World War I*, Princeton, 1975

Mammach, K., *Der Einfluß der russischen Februarrevolution u. der Großen Sozialistischen Oktoberrevolution auf die deutsche Arbeiterklasse, Febr. 1917–Okt. 1918*, Berlin, 1955

Marwick, A., *The Deluge. British Society and the First World War*, London, 1965

—, *War and Social Change in the Twentieth Century. A Comparative Study of Britain, France, Germany, Russia and the United States*, London, 1974

—, *Women at War: 1914–1918*, Glasgow, 1977

Maschke, E., *Grundzüge der deutschen Kartellgeschichte bis 1914*, Dortmund, 1964

Mason, T. W., 'The primacy of politics — Politics and economics in National Socialist Germany', in S. J. Woolf (ed.), *The Nature of Fascism* (London, 1968), Vintage Books, ed., 1969, pp. 165–95

—, *Arbeiterklasse und Volksgemeinschaft. Dokumente und Materialien zur deutschen Arbeiterpolitik 1936-1939*, Opladen, 1975

Materna, I., *Der Vollzugsrat der Berliner Arbeiter- und Soldatenräte 1918/19*, Berlin, 1978

Matthias, E., 'Kautsky u. der Kautskyanismus. Die Funktion der Ideologie in der deutschen Sozialdemokratie vor dem Ersten Weltkriege', *Marxismusstudien*, 2, Tübingen, 1957, pp. 151–97

— and Morsey, R. (eds.), *Der interfraktionelle Ausschuß 1917/18*, 2 vols., Düsseldorf, 1959

—, *Die Regierung des Prinzen M. v. Baden*, Düsseldorf, 1962

— and Pikart, E. (eds.), *Die Reichstagsfraktion der deutschen Sozialdemokratie, 1898-1918*, 2 vols., Düsseldorf, 1966

Mattes, W., *Die bayerischen Bauernräte. Eine soziologische u. historische Untersuchung über bäuerliche Politik*, Stuttgart, 1921

Marx, K. and Engels, F., *Werke*, Berlin, 1957ff [= *MEW*]

Mauke, M., *Die Klassentheorie von Marx u. Engels*, K. Heymann *et al.* (eds.), Frankfurt, 1970

Prince M. v. Baden, *Erinnerungen u. Dokumente*, G. Mann and A. Burckhardt (eds.), Stuttgart, 1968

Meerwarth, R., Günther, A., and Zimmerman, W., *Die Einwirkungen des Krieges auf Bevölkerungsbewegung, Einkommen u. Lebenshaltung in Deutschland*, Stuttgart, 1932

Mehnert, G., *Evangelische Kirche u. Politik 1917-1919*, Düsseldorf, 1959

Meinecke, F., 'Die deutschen Erhebungen von 1813, 1848, 1870 u. 1914', in idem., *Die deutsche Erhebung von 1914*, Stuttgart, 1914, pp. 9–38

—, 'Das deutsche Bürgertum im Kriege', in idem., *Politische Schriften u. Reden*, G. Kotowski (ed.), Darmstadt, 1958, pp. 247–51

—, *Straßburg, Freiburg, Berlin 1901-1919. Erinnerungen*, Stuttgart, 1949

Mendelssohn Bartholdy, A., *The War and German Society*, New Haven, 1937

Merton, R., *Erinnernswertes aus meinem Leben, das über das Persönliche hinausgeht*, Frankfurt, 1955

Messerschmidt, M., *Militär und Politik in der Bismarckzeit und im Wilhelminischen Deutschland*, Darmstadt, 1975

Michels, R., *Zur Soziologie des Parteiwesens in der modernen Demokratie. Untersuchungen über die oligarchischen Tendenzen des Gruppenlebens (1911)*, W. Conze (ed.), Stuttgart, 1957 (new ed., 1925)

Mielke, S., *Der Hansa-Bund für Gewerbe, Handel und Industrie 1912-1914*, Göttingen, 1976

Mihaly, J., . . . *Da gibt's ein Wiedersehen! Kriegstagebuch eines Mädchens 1914-1918*, Freiburg/Heidelberg, 1982

Miliband, R., 'Marx and the State', *The Socialist Register*, 1, 1965, pp. 278–96

—, *The State in Capitalist Society*, London, 1969

Miller, S. *Burgfrieden u. Klassenkampf. Die deutsche Sozialdemokratie im Ersten Weltkrieg*, Düsseldorf, 1974

—, *Das Problem der Freiheit im Sozialismus*, Frankfurt, 1964

—, *Die Bürde der Macht. Die deutsche Sozialdemokratie 1918-1920*, Düsseldorf, 1978

Missalla, H., *'Gott mit uns' – Die deutsche katholische Kriegspredigt 1914-1918*,

Munich, 1968

v. Moellendorf, W., *Deutsche Gemeinwirtschaft*, Berlin, 1916

Molt, P., *Der Reichstag vor der improvisierten Revolution*, Cologne, 1963

Mommsen, H. (ed.), *Sozialdemokratie zwischen Klassenbewegung und Volks-partei*, Frankfurt, 1974

—, *Arbeiterbewegung und Nationale Frage*, Göttingen, 1979

—, (ed.), *Arbeiterbewegung und industrieller Wandel*, Wuppertal 1980

— and Borsdorf, V. (eds.), *Glück auf Kameraden! Die Bergarbeiter und ihre Organisation in Deutschland*, Cologne, 1979

—, *et al.* (eds.), *Industrielles System u. politische Entwicklung in der Weimarer Republik*, Düsseldorf, 1974 (2nd ed., 1977)

Mommsen, W. J., *Max Weber u. die deutsche Politik 1890–1920*, Tübingen, 1959

—, 'Die deutsche Kriegszielpolitik 1914–1918. Bemerkungen zum Stand der Diskussion', in *Kriegsausbruch 1914*, Munich, 1967, pp. 60–100

—, 'Die deutsche Öffentliche Meinung u. der Zusammenbruch des Regierungssystems Bethmann Hollwegs im Juli 1917, *GWU*, 19, 1968 pp. 656–71

—, 'Die Regierung Bethman Hollweg u. die öffentliche Meinung 1914–1917', *VfZ*, 17, 1969, pp. 117–59

—, 'Die deutsche Revolution 1918–1920. Politische Revolution und soziale Protestbewegung', *GG*, 4, 1978, pp. 362–91

Morgan, D. W., *The Socialist Left and the German Revolution. A History of the German Independent Party 1917–1922*, Ithaca, N.Y., 1976

Morrow, J., 'Industrial Mobilization in World War I. The Prussian Army and the Aircraft Industry', *Journal of Economic History*, 37, pp. 36–52

Morsey, R., *Die deutsche Zentrumspartei 1917–1923*, Düsseldorf, 1966

Moses, J. A. 'Carl Legien und das deutsche Vaterland im Weltkrieg 1914–1918', *GWU*, 26, 1975, pp. 595–611

Mosse, W. E. (ed.), *Deutsches Judentum in Krieg u. Revolution 1916–1923*, Tübingen, 1971

Most, O., *Zur Wirtschafts- u. Sozialstatistik höherer Beamter in Preußen*, Leipzig, 1916

—, 'Zur Wirtschafts. u. Sozialstatistik des höheren Beamtentums in Preußen', *Schmollers Jb.*, 39, 1915, pp. 181–218

Müller, A., *Die Kriegsrohstoffbewirtschaftung 1914–1918 im Dienst des deutschen Monopolkapitals*, Berlin, 1955

v. Müller, K. A., *Mars u. Venus. Erinnerungen 1914–1919*, Stuttgart, 1954

Müller, R., *Vom Kaiserreich zur Republik: Ein Beitrag zur Geschichte der revolutionären Arbeiterbewegung während des Weltkrieges*, Vienna, 1924

Müller, W. and Neusüss, C., 'Die Sozialstaatsillusion u. der Widerspruch von Lohnarbeit u. Kapital', *Probleme des Klassenkampfs*, special issue 1, Berlin, June 1971, pp. 7–70 (orig. in *Sozialistische Politik 2,6/7*, 1970, pp. 4–67

Neck, R., *Arbeiterschaft und Staat im Ersten Weltkrieg 1914–1918*, 2 vols. Vienna, 1964, 1968

Nef, J. U., *War and Human Progress*, Cambridge/Mass., 1950

Nestriepke, S., *Die Gewerkschaftsbewegung*, 2 vols., Stuttgart, 1920, 1921
Nettl, P., R. *Luxemburg*, Cologne, 1967
Neuloh, O., *Die deutsche Betriebsverfassung u. ihre Sozialformen bis zur Mitbestimmung*, Tübingen, 1956
Nicolai, W., *Nachrichtendienst, Presse u. Volksstimmung im Weltkrieg*, Berlin, 1920
Nimtz, W., *Die Novemberrevolution 1918 in Deutschland*, Berlin, 1962
Nipperdey, T., *Die Organisation der deutschen Parteien vor 1918*, Düsseldorf, 1961
Noll, A., 'Wirtschaftliche u. soziale Entwicklung des Handwerks in der zweiten Phase der Industrialisierung', in W. Rüegg and O. Neuloh (eds.), *Zur Soziologischen Theorie u. Analyse des 19. Jahrhunderts*, Göttingen, 1971, pp. 193–212
Nussbaum, H., *Unternehmer gegen Monopole. Über Struktur u. Aktionen antimonopolistischer bürgerlicher Gruppen zu Beginn des 20. Jahrhunderts*, Berlin, 1966
—, 'Zur Imperialismustheorie W. I. Lenins u. zur Enterwicklung staatsmonopolistischer Züge des deutschen Imperialismus bis 1914', *JbfWG*, 1970/IV, pp. 25 65
—, and Baudis, D., *Wirtschaft und Staat in Deutschland vom Ende des 19. Jahrhunderts bis 1918/19* (Vol. 1 of H. Nussbaum and L. Zumpe (eds.), *Wirtschaft und Staat in Deutschland. Eine Wirtschaftsgeschichte des staatsmonopolistischen Kapitalismus in Deutschland vom Ende des 19. Jahrhunderts bis 1945*, 3 vols., Vaduz/Liechtenstein, 1978)

O'Boyle, L., 'The German Independent Socialists during the First World War', *AHR*, 56, 1950/51, pp. 824–31
v. Oertzen, P., *Betriebsräte in der Novemberrevolution*, Düsseldorf, 1963 (2nd ed., Berlin, 1976)
Offe, C., 'Politische Herrschaft u. Klassenstrukturen. Zur Analyse spätkapitalistischer Gesellschaftstrukturen', in G. Kress and D. Senghaas (eds.), *Politikwissenschaft*, Frankfurt, 1972, pp. 135–34
—, *Strukturprobleme des kapitalistischen Staates. Aufsätze zur Politischen Soziologie*, Frankfurt, 1972
v. Oldenburg-Januschau, E., *Erinnerungen*, Leipzig, 1936
Opel, F., *Der Deutsche Metallarbeiterverband während des Ersten Weltkrieges u. der Revolution*, Hanover, 1975
— and Schneider, D., *75 Jahre Industriegewerkschaft. 1891 bis 1966. Vom Deutschen Metallarbeiterverband zur Industriegewerkschaft Metall*, 3rd ed., Cologne, 1980
Osthold, P., *Die Geschichte des Zechenverbandes 1908–1933*, Berlin, 1934
Ott, H., 'Kriegswirtschaft und Wirtschaftskrieg 1914–1918, verdeutlicht an Beispielen aus dem badisch-elsässischen Raum', in *Geschichte, Wirtschaft, Gesellschaft. Fs. C. Bauer zum 75. Geb.*, Berlin, 1974

Parkinson, R., *Tormented Warrior. Ludendorff and the Supreme Command*, London, 1978
Patemann, R., *Der Kampf um die preußische Wahlrechtsreform im Ersten*

Weltkrieg, Düsseldorf, 1964
Die bürgerlichen Parteien in Deutschland. Handbuch der Geschichte der bürgerlichen Parteien u. anderer Interessenorganisationen vom Vormärz bis zum Jahre 1945, D. Fricke (ed.), 2 vols., Berlin, 1968, 1970
Payer, F., *Von Bethmann Hollweg bis Ebert*, Frankfurt, 1923
Petzina, D., *et al.*, *Sozialgeschichtliches Arbeitsbuch. 3: Materialien zur Statistik des Deutschen Reiches 1914–1945*, Munich, 1978
Pikart, E., 'Der deutsche Reichstag u. der Ausbruch des Ersten Weltkriegs', *Der Staat*, 5, 1966, pp. 47–70
Pinner, F., *Deutsche Wirtschaftsführer*, Charlottenburg, 1924
Plenge, J., *1789 u. 1914. Die symbolischen Jahre in der Geschichte des politischen Geistes*, Berlin, 1916
Pogge v. Strandmann, H. and Geiss, I., *Die Erforderlichkeit des Unmöglichen. Deutschland am Vorabend des Ersten Weltkrieges*, Frankfurt, 1965
Politik im Krieg 1914–1918. Studien zur Politik der deutschen herrschenden Klassen im Ersten Weltkrieg, F. Klein (ed.), Berlin, 1964
Popplow, U., 'Göttingen in der Novemberrevolution 1918/19', *Göttinger Jahrbuch*, 24, 1976, pp. 205–42
Potthoff, H., *Gewerkschaften und Politik zwischen Revolution und Inflation*, Düsseldorf, 1979
Prager, E., *Geschichte der USPD. Entstehung und Entwicklung der Unabhängigen Sozialdemokratischen Partei Deutschlands*, Berlin, 1921 (repr. as *Das Gebot der Stunde. Geschichte der USPD*, 4th ed., Berlin, 1980)
Prager, M., 'Gewerkschaftspolitik der Privatangestellten', *Süddeutsche Monatshefte*, 11/II, 1914, pp. 90–112
—, 'Die wirtschaftliche soziale Lage der Privatangestellten', *Süddeutsche Monatshefte*, 11/II, 1914, pp. 608–22
Preller, L., *Sozialpolitik in der Weimarer Republik*, Stuttgart, 1949 (repr., Kronberg Ts., 1978
v. Preradovich, N., *Die Führungsschichten in Österreich u. Preussen (1804–1918). Mit einem Ausblick bis zum Jahre 1945*, Wiesbaden 1955
Pressel, W., *Die Kriegspredigt 1914–1918 in der evangelischen Kirche Deutschlands*, Göttingen, 1967
Protokoll über die Verhandlungen des Parteitages der Sozialdemokratischen Partei Deutschlands, Würzburg 14.–20. Oktober 1917, Berlin, 1917
Protokoll über Verhandlungen des Parteitages der Sozialdemokratischen Partei Deutschlands, Weimar 10.–15. Juni 1919, Berlin, 1919
Pross, H., *Jugend, Eros, Politik. Die Geschichte der deutschen Jugendverbände*, Munich, 1964
Puhle, H.-J., *Agrarische Interessenpolitik u. preußischer Konservatismus im Wilhelminischen Reich (1893–1914). Ein Beitrag zur Analyse des Nationalismus in Deutschland am Beispiel des Bundes der Landwirte und der Deutsch-Konservativen Partei*, Hanover, 1966
—, 'Parlament, Parteien u. Interessenverbände 1890–1914', in M. Stürmer (ed.), *Das Kaiserliche Deutschland, Politik u. Gesellschaft 1870–1918*, Düsseldorf, 1970, pp. 340–77

264   *Bibliography*

Quante, P., 'Lohnpolitik u. Lohnentwicklung im Kriege', *Zeitschrift des Preußischen Statistischen Landesamtes*, 59, 1919, pp. 323–84

Quidde, L., *Der deutsche Pazifismus während des Ersten Weltkriegs 1914–1918. Aus dem Nachlaß Ludwig Quiddes*, K. Holl (ed.), Boppard, 1979

Raase, W., *Zur Geschichte der deutschen Gewerkschaftsbewegung 1914–1917 u. 1917 bis 1919*, Berlin, n.d.

Rakenius, G. W., *Wilhelm Groener als erster Generalquartiermeister. Die Politik der Obersten Heeresleitung 1918/19*, Boppard, 1977

Rathenau, W., *Gesammelte Schriften*, 5 vols., Berlin, 1925

—,*Briefe*, 2 vols., Dresden, 1926

—,*Politische Briefe*, Dresden, 1929

—,*Schriften aus der Kriegs- u. Nachkriegszeit*, Berlin, 1929

—,*Tagebuch 1907–1922*, H. Pogge v. Strandmann (ed.), Düsseldorf, 1967

—,'Die Organisation oder Rohstoffversorgung', lecture, 20 December 1915, in ms. outline

v. Raumer, H., 'Unternehmer u. Gewerkschaften in der Weimarer Zeit', *Deutsche Rundschau*, 80, 1954, pp. 425–34

Ratz, U., *Georg Ledebour 1850–1947. Weg and Wirken eines sozialistischen Politikers*, Berlin, 1969

—,*Sozialreform und Arbeiterschaft. Die 'Gesellschaft für soziale Reform' und die sozialdemokratische Arbeiterbewegung von der Jahrhundertwende bis zum Ausbruch des Ersten Weltkriegs*, Berlin, 1980

Rauh, M., *Die Parlamentarisierung des Deutschen Reiches*, Düsseldorf, 1978

Rauscher, E., *Die Umstellung von der Friedens- auf die Kriegsfertigung*, Hamburg, 1937

Reichert, J., *Die Arbeitsgemeinschaft der industriellen u. gewerblichen Arbeitgeber und Arbeitnehmer Deutschlands*, Berlin, 1919

—,*Entstehung, Bedeutung u. Ziel der 'Arbeitsgemeinschaft'*, Berlin, 1919

Reichmann, E. G., *Die Flucht in den Haß. Die Ursachen der deutschen Judenkatastrophe, Frankfurt*, n.d. (transl. as *Hostages of Civilisation*, 1951)

—,'Der Bewußtseinswandel der deutschen Juden', in W. E. Mosse (ed.), *Deutsches Judentum in Krieg u. Revolution 1916–1923*, Tübingen, 1971, pp. 511–612

Reichsarchiv, *Der Weltkrieg 1914–1918*, 14 vols., Berlin, 1925–44 (Vols. 13, 14, 2nd ed., Bonn, 1956)

Reiß, K.-P. (ed.), *Von Bassermann zu Stresemann. Die Sitzungen des nationalliberalen Zentralvorstandes 1912–1917*, Düsseldorf, 1967

Retzlaw, K., *Spartakus. Aufstieg u. Niedergang eines Parteiarbeiters*, Frankfurt 1971 (2nd ed., 1972)

Reulecke, J. (ed.), *Arbeiterbewegung an Rhein u. Ruhr*, Wuppertal, 1974

—,'Der Erste Weltkrieg u. die Arbeiterbewegung im rheinisch-westfälischen Industriegebiet', in idem (ed.), *Arbeiterbewegung an Rhein u. Ruhr*, Wuppertal, 1974, pp. 205–39

—,*Die wirtschaftliche Entwicklung der Stadt Barmen von 1910–1925* (= *Bergische Forschungen*, Vol. 10), Neustadt, 1973

—,'Wirtschaft und Bevölkerung ausgewählter Städte im Ersten Weltkrieg (Barmen, Düsseldorf, Essen, Krefeld)', in idem (ed.), *Die deutsche Stadt im*

Industriezeitalter. Beiträge zur modernen deutschen Stadtgeschichte, Wuppertal, 1978, pp. 114-26

—, 'Städtische Finanzen und Kriegswohlfahrtspflege im Ersten Weltkrieg unter besonderer Berücksichtigung der Stadt Barmen', *Zeitschrift für Stadtgeschichte*, 2, 1975, pp. 48-79

Richter, W., *Gewerkschaften, Monopolkapital u. Staat im Ersten Weltkrieg u. in der Novemberrevolution (1914-1918)*, Berlin, 1959

Riezler, K., *Tagebücher, Aufsätze, Dokumente*, K. D. Erdmann (ed.), Göttingen, 1972

Ritter, G., *Staatskunst u. Kriegshandwerk. Das Problem des Militarismus in Deutschland. 2: Die Hauptmächte Europas u. das Wilhelminische Reich (1890 bis 1914)*, Munich, 1960; *3: Die Tragödie der Staatskunst. Bethmann Hollweg als Kriegskanzler (1914-1917)*, Munich, 1964; *4: Die Herrschaft des deutschen Militarismus u. die Katastrophe von 1918*, Munich, 1968

Ritter, G. A., *Die Arbeiterbewegung im Wilhelminischen Reich. Die sozialdemokratische Partei u. die freien Gewerkschaften 1890-1900*, 2nd ed., Berlin, 1963

—, 'Regierung u. Parlament in Großbritannien seit dem 17. Jahrhundert', *PVS*, 5, 1964, pp. 20-30

—, (ed.), *Historisches Lesebuch*, 2 (1871-1914), Frankfurt, 1967

—, 'Kontinuität u. Umformung des deutschen Parteiensystems 1918-1920', in *idem* (ed.), *Entstehung u. Wandel der modernen Gesellschaft. Fs. H. Rosenberg*, Berlin, 1970, pp. 342-76

—, *Arbeiterbewegung, Parteien und Parlamentarismus. Aufsätze zur deutschen Sozial- und Verfassungsgeschichte des 19. und 20. Jahrhunderts*, Göttingen, 1976

—, *Staat, Arbeiterschaft und Arbeiterbewegung in Deutschland. Vom Vormärz bis zum Ende der Weimarer Republik*, Berlin, 1980

— and Miller, S. (eds.), *Die deutsche Revolution 1918-1919*, Frankfurt, 1968,

Roesler, K., *Die Finanzpolitik des Deutschen Reiches im Ersten Weltkrieg*, Berlin, 1967

Röseler, K., 'Unternehmer in der Weimarer Republik', *Tradition*, 13, 1968, pp. 217-40

Rosenberg, A. *Entstehung der Weimarer Republik*, Frankfurt, 1961

Rosenberg, H., *Probleme der deutschen Sozialgeschichte*, Frankfurt, 1969

Roth, G., *The Social Democrats in Imperial Germany. A Study in Working-Class Isolation and National Integration*, Totowa, 1963

Rotth, A., *W. v. Siemens*, Berlin, 1922

Rürup, R., *Probleme der Revolution in Deutschland 1918/19*, Wiesbaden, 1968

—, (ed.), *Arbeiter- und Soldatenräte im rheinisch-westfälischen Industriegebiet. Studien zur Geschichte der Revolution 1918/19*, Wuppertal, 1975

Ruge, W., 'Massenbewegungen und politische Kräfte in Europa 1917 bis 1920/21', *ZfG*, 20, 1972, pp. 302-24

—, *Novemberrevolution. Die Volkserhebung gegen den deutschen Imperialismus und Militarismus 1918/19*, Berlin, 1978

—, *Revolutionstage November 1918*, Berlin, 1978

Runciman, W. G., *Relative Deprivation and Social Justice. A Study of Attitudes to Social Inequality in Twentieth-Century England*, Berkeley, 1966

Ryder, A. J., *The German Revolution of 1918. A Study of German Socialism in War and Revolt*, Cambridge, 1967

Sachwörterbuch der Geschichte Deutschlands u. der deutschen Arbeiterbewegung, 2 vols., Berlin, 1970

Saul, K., *Staat, Industrie u. Arbeiterbewegung im Kaiserreich. Zur Innen- u. Außenpolitik des Wilhelminischen Deutschland 1903–1914* (= *Studien z. modernen Geschichte*, 16) Düsseldorf, 1974

Schäfer, H. P., 'Die "Gelben Gewerkschaften" am Beispiel des Unterstützungsvereins der Siemens-Werke', *VSWG*, 59, Berlin, 1972, pp. 41–76

—,*Industrie und Wirtschaftspolitik während des Ersten Weltkriegs in Baden*, Stuttgart, 1980

Schäfer, W., *NSDAP. Entwicklung und Struktur der Staatspartei des Dritten Reiches*, Hanover, 1956

Schär, F., *Umgestaltung und Neuorientierung des Handels infolge des Krieges*, Berlin, 1916

Scheck, M., *Zwischen Weltkrieg und Revolution. Zur Geschichte der Arbeiterbewegung in Württemberg 1914–1920*, Cologne/Vienna, 1981

Scheidemann, P., *Der Zusammenbruch*, Berlin, 1921

—,*Memoiren eines Sozialdemokraten*, 2 vols., Dresden, 1928

Scheler, M., '1789 u. 1914', *Archiv*, 42, 1916/17, pp. 586–605

Schellenberg, J., 'Probleme der Burgfriedenspolitik im Ersten Weltkrieg — Zur innenpolitischen Strategie u. Taktik der herrschenden Klassen Deutschlands von 1914 bis 1916', Ph.D. thesis, Berlin, 1967

v. Scherf, K. Ritter, 'Die Entwicklung der Beamtenbewegung u. ihre Interessenvertretung', Ph.D. thesis, Greifswald, 1919

Schieck, H., 'Der Kampf um die deutsche Wirtschaftspolitik nach dem Novembersturz 1918', Ph.D. thesis, Heidelberg, 1958

Schieder, T. (ed.), *Handbuch der europäischen Geschichte*, 6, Stuttgart, 1968

—,'Unterschiede zwischen historischer und sozialwissenschaftlicher Methode' (1970), in. H.-U. Wehler (ed.), *Geschichte u. Soziologie*, Cologne, 1972, pp. 283–304 Schieder, W. (ed.), *Erster Weltkrieg. Ursachen, Enstehung u. Kriegsziele*, Cologne/Berlin, 1969 (= *NWB*, 32)

Schiffers, R., *Der Hauptausschuß des Deutschen Reichstags 1915/18. Formen und Bereiche der Kooperation zwischen Parlament und Regierung.* Düsseldorf, 1979

—,*u. M. Koch (ed.), Der Hauptausschuß des Deutschen Reichstags 1915–1918* (= *Quellen zur Geschichte des Parlamentarismus und der politischen Parteien*, 9), 4 vols., Düsseldorf, 1981

Schilling-Voß, F.-A., *Die Sonderernährung der Rüstungsarbeiter im Rahmen der Kriegswirtschaft 1914/18.*, Hamburg, 1936

Schinkel, M., *Staatsmonopole während u. nach Beendigung des Krieges*, Hamburg, 1915

Schmidt, E.-H., *Heimatheer und Revolution 1918. Die militärischen Gewalten im Heimatgebiet zwischen Oktoberreform und Novemberrevolution* (= *Beiträge zur Militär- und Kriegsgeschichte*, 23, Militärgeschichtlichen Forschungsamt (ed.), Stuttgart, 1981

Schmidt, G., *Spartakus — R. Luxemburg u. K. Liebknecht*, Frankfurt, 1971

Schmidt, G., *Deutscher Historismus u. der Übergang zur parlamentarischen Demokratie. Untersuchungen zu den Politischen Gedanken von Meinecke, Troeltsch, Max Weber*, Lübeck, 1964

—, 'Innenpolitische Blockbildungen am Vorabend des Ersten Weltkrieges', *Aus Politik und Zeitgeschichte*, 13 May 1972, pp. 3–32

Schmidt, W., *Das deutsche Handwerk im Weltkriege*, Ph.D. thesis, Erlangen, 1927, Essen, 1929

Schmoller, G., 'Was verstehen wir unter dem Mittelstande? Hat er im 19. Jahrhundert zu- oder abgenommen?', *Verhandlungen des 8. Evang.-soz. Kongresses (10. u. 11. Juni 1897)*, Göttingen, 1897, pp. 132–85

Schneider, G., *Die Angestelltenbewegung im Lichte des Krieges und der Revolution*, Berlin, 1919

Schneider, M., *Die Christlichen Gewerkschaften 1894–1933*, Bonn, 1982

Schorske, C. E., *German Social Democracy 1905–1917. The Development of the Great Schism*, Cambridge, 1955

Schramm, G., 'Militarisierung und Demokratisierung. Typen der Massenintegration im Ersten Weltkrieg', *Francia*, 3, 1975, pp. 476–95

—, '1914: Sozialdemokraten am Scheideweg', in C. Stern and H. A. Winkler (eds.), *Wendepunkte deutscher Geschichte 1848–1945*, 1979, pp. 63–86

—, 'Minderheiten gegen den Krieg. Motive und Kampfformen 1914 bis 1918 am Beispiel Grossbritanniens und seines Empires', *GG*, 6, 1980, pp. 164–88

Schröder, E., *O. Wiedfeldt*, Essen, 1964

Schröter, A., *Krieg —Staat — Monopol. 1914 bis 1918. Die Zusammenhänge von imperialistischer Kriegswirtschaft, Militarisierung der Volkswirtschaft u. staatsmonopolistischem Kapitalismus in Deutschland während des Ersten Weltkrieges*, Berlin, 1965

Schüddekopf, O. E., *Der Erste Weltkrieg*, Gütersloh, 1977

Schürholz, F., *Entwicklungstendenzen im deutschen Wirtschaftsleben zu berufsständischer Organisation u. ihre soziale Bedeutung*, Mönchen-Gladbach, 1922

Schulz, G., *Zwischen Demokratie u. Diktatur. Verfassungspolitik u. Reichsreform in der Weimarer Republik, 1: Die Periode der Konsolidierung u. der Revision des Bismarckschen Reichsaufbaus 1919–1930*, Berlin, 1963

—, *Revolutionen und Friedensschlüsse*, Munich, 1967

Schulze, H., *Otto Braun oder Preußens demokratische Sendung*, Berlin, 1977

Schumacher, M. (ed.), *Erinnerungen u. Dokumente von J. V. Bredt 1914–1933*, Düsseldorf, 1970

—, *Mittelstandsfront und Republik. Die Wirtschaftspartei — Reichspartei des deutschen Mittelstandes 1919–1933*, Düsseldorf, 1972

Schwabe, K., 'Zur politischen Haltung der deutschen Professoren im Ersten Weltkrieg', *HZ*, 193, 1961, pp. 601–34

—, *Wissenschaft und Kriegsmoral. Die deutschen Hochschullehrer u. die politischen Grundfragen des Ersten Weltkrieges*, Göttingen, 1969

Schwarte, M. (ed.), *Der Weltkrieg in seiner Einwirkung auf das deutsche Volk*, Leipzig, 1918

—, (ed.), *Der große Krieg 1914–1918*, 8–10, Leipzig, 1921–3

Schwarz, K.-D., *Weltkrieg u. Revolution in Nürnberg*, Stuttgart, 1971

v. Seeckt, H., *Aus meinem Leben 1866–1917*, F. von Rabenau (ed.), Leipzig, 1938

Seidel, A., *Frauenarbeit im Ersten Weltkrieg als Problem der staatlichen Sozialpolitik, dargestellt an Beispiel Bayerns*, Frankfurt, 1979

Sheehan, J. J., 'Quantification in the Study of Modern German Social and Political History', in V. R. Lorwin and J. M. Price (eds.), *The Dimensions of the Past*, New Haven, 1972, pp. 301–31

Sichler, R. and Tiburtius, J., *Die Arbeiterfrage – eine Kernfrage des Weltkrieges*, Berlin [1925]

Siemens, G., *C. F. v. Siemens*, 2nd ed., Munich, 1962

Sigel, R., *Die Lensch–Cunow–Haenisch-Gruppe. Eine Studie zum rechten Flügel der SPD im Ersten Weltkrieg*, Berlin, 1976

Silverberg, P., *Reden u. Schriften*, F. Mariaux (ed.), Cologne, 1951

Skalweit, A., *Die deutsche Kriegsernährungswirtschaft*, Stuttgart, 1927

Skrzypczak, H., *Marx, Engels, Revolution*, Berlin, 1968

Snell, J. L., 'Socialist Unions and Socialist Patriotism in Germany 1914–1918', *AHR*, 59, 1953/54, pp. 66–76

Sombart, W., *Händler u. Helden*, Munich, 1915

Sonnemann, R., 'Über die Duisburg-Denkschrift aus dem Jahre 1915', *JbfWG*, 1966, III, pp. 119–45

Sorokin, P. A., *Fluctuations of Social Relationships. War and Revolution*, New York, 1937

Spartakusbriefe, Inst. f. Marxismus-Leninismus beim ZK der SED (ed.), Berlin, 1958

Sperlich, O., *Deutsche Kriegstextilwirtschaft*, Hamburg, 1936

—,*Arbeitslohn und Unternehmergewinn in der Kriegswirtschaft*, Hamburg, 1938

Spethmann, H., *Zwölf Jahre Ruhrbergbau. Aus seiner Geschichte von Kriegsanfang zum Franzosenabmarsch 1914–1925, 1: Aufstand und Ausstand bis zum zweiten Generalstreik April 1919*, Berlin, 1928

—,*Der Verband technischer Grubenbeamten 1886–1936*, Gelsenkirchen, 1936

Stammer, O. and P. Weingart, *Politische Soziologie*, Munich, 1972

Stegemann, B., *Die deutsche Marinepolitik 1916–1918*, Berlin, 1970

Steglich, W., *Die Friedenspolitik der Mittelmächte 1917/18*, 1, Wiesbaden, 1964

Stegmann, D., 'Zwischen Repression u. Manipulation: Konservative Machteliten u. Arbeiter- u. Angestelltenbewegung 1910-1918. Ein Beitrag zur Vorgeschichte der DAP/NSDAP', *ASG*, 12, 1972, pp. 351–432

—,*Die Erben Bismarcks. Parteien u. Verbände in der Spätphase des Wilhelminischen Deutschland 1897–1918*, Cologne, 1970

—, 'Hugenberg contra Stegmann. Die Politik der Industrieverbände am Ende des Kaiserreichs', *VfZ*, 24, 1976, pp. 329–78

v. Stein, H., *Erlebnisse u. Betrachtungen aus der Zeit des Weltkrieges*, Leipzig, 1919

Steinberg, E., *Die Handwerker-Bewegung in Deutschland, ihre Ursachen u. Ziele*, Stuttgart, 1897

Steinberg, H.-J., *Sozialismus u. deutsche Sozialdemokratie. Zur Ideologie der*

Partei vor dem 1. Weltkrieg, Hanover, 1967 (3rd ed., 1972)

Steiner, H., *Soziale Strukturveränderungen im modernen Kapitalismus. Zur Klassenanalyse der Angestellten in Westdeutschland*, Berlin, 1967

Steinitzer, E., 'Der Krieg u. die Angestellten', *Jb. d. Angestelltenbewegung*, 1914/15, pp. 177–95

Stern, F., *Bethmann Hollweg und der Krieg. Die Grenzen der Verantwortung*, Tübingen, 1968

Stern, L., *Der Einfluß der Großen Sozialistischen Oktoberrevolution auf Deutschland u. die deutsche Arbeiterbewegung*, Berlin, 1958

—,(ed.), *Archivalische Forschungen zur Geschichte der deutschen Arbeiterbewegung. 4/I–IV: Die Auswirkungen der Großen Sozialistischen Oktoberrevolution auf Deutschland*, Berlin, 1959

Stresemann, G., *Reden u. Schriften, 1897–1926*, 2 vols., Dresden, 1926

Stucken, R., *Deutsche Geld- u. Kreditpolitik 1914–1963*, 3rd ed., Tübingen, 1964

Stürmer, M., 'Staatsstreichgedanken im Bismarckreich', *HZ*, 209, 1969, pp. 566–615

—,(ed.), *Das kaiserliche Deutschland. Politik u. Gesellschaft 1870–1918*, Düsseldorf, 1970

—,*Das Ruhelose Reich. Deutschland 1866–1918*, Berlin, 1983

Studien zur Geschichte des deutschen Imperialismus von der Jahrhundertwende bis 1917, ed. by the Dept. '1900–17' of the Zentralinstitut für Geschichte of the Acad. of Sciences of the GDR, directed by W. Gutsche, Berlin, 1977 (= *Jb. für Geschichte*, 15)

Stump, W., *Geschichte u. Organisation der Zentrumspartei in Düsseldorf 1917–1933*

Syrup, F., *Hundert Jahre staatliche Sozialpolitik 1839–1939*, O. Neuloh (ed.), Stuttgart, 1957

Szabó, E., 'Krieg u. Wirtschaftsverfassung', *Archiv*, 39, 1915, pp. 643–88

Tänzler, F., *Die deutschen Arbeitgeberverbände 1904–1929*, Berlin, 1929

Tanter, R. and Midlarsky, M., 'A Theory of Revolution', *Journal of Conflict Resolution*, 11, 1967, pp. 264–80

Tennstedt, F., *Sozialgeschichte der Sozialpolitik in Deutschland. Vom 18. Jahrhundert bis zum Ersten Weltkrieg*, Göttingen, 1981

Teuteberg, H.-J., *Geschichte der industriellen Mitbestimmung. Ursprung u. Entwicklung ihrer Vorläufer im Denken u. in der Wirklichkeit des 19. Jahrhunderts*, Tübingen, 1961

Thieme, H., *Nationaler Liberalismus in der Krise. Die nationalliberale Fraktion des Preußischen Abgeordnetenhauses 1914–18*, Boppard, 1963

Thimme, R. and Legien, C. (eds.), *Die Arbeiterschaft im neuen Deutschland*, Leipzig, 1915

Thimme, F. (ed.), *Vom inneren Frieden des deutschen Volkes*, Leipzig, 1916

Thimme, H., *Der Weltkrieg ohne Waffen. Die Propaganda der Westmächte gegen Deutschland, ihre Wirkung u. ihre Abwehr*, Stuttgart, 1932

Tilly, C. et al., *The Rebellious Century 1830–1930*, Cambridge, Mass., 1975

Tilly, R., 'Popular Disorders in Nineteenth-Century Germany. A Preliminary Survey', *Journal of Social History*, 4, 1970/71, pp. 1–40

Timasheff, N. S., *War and Revolution*, J. F. Scheuer (ed.), New York, 1965
Tormin, W., *Zwischen Rätediktatur u. sozialer Demokratie*, Düsseldorf, 1954
Toynbee, A. J., *War and Civilization*, London, 1950
Treue, W., 'Die Ilseder Hütte u. der Staat in den Jahren 1916–1919', *Tradition*, 3, 1958, pp. 129–40
—, 'C. Duisbergs Denkschrift von 1915 zur Gründung der "Kleinen I. G." ', *Tradition*, 8, 1963, pp. 193–228
Trotnow, H., *Karl Liebknecht. Eine politische Biographie*, Cologne, 1980
Tumin, M. M., *Social Stratification. The Forms and Functions of Inequality*, Englewood Cliffs, 1967

Ullman, H.-P., *Der Bund der Industriellen. Organisation, Einfluß und Politik klein- und mittelbetrieblicher Industrieller im Deutschen Kaiserreich 1895–1914*, Göttingen, 1976
Ullrich, V., *Die Hamburger Arbeiterbewegung am Vorabend des Ersten Weltkriegs bis zur Revolution 1918/19*, 2 vols., Hamburg, 1976
—, 'Weltkrieg und Novemberrevolution. Die Hamburger Arbeiterbewegung 1914–1918', in J. Berlin (ed.), *Das andere Hamburg*, Cologne, 1981, pp. 181– 208
—, 'Massenbewegungen in der Hamburger Arbeiterschaft im Ersten Weltkrieg', in A. Herzig *et al.* (eds.), *Arbeiter in Hamburg*, Hamburg, 1982
—, *Kriegsalltag*, Hamburg, 1982
Umbreit, P., *Soziale Arbeiterpolitik u. Gewerkschaften*, Berlin, 1916
—, *Die deutschen Gewerkschaften im Weltkriege*, Berlin, 1917
Umbreit, P. and Lorenz, C., *Der Krieg u. die Arbeitsverhältnisse*, Stuttgart, 1928
Urlanis, B. Z., *Bilanz der Kriege. Die Menschenverluste Europas vom 17. Jahrhundert bis zur Gegenwart*, Berlin, 1965
[U.S.P.D.], *Protokoll über die Verhandlungen des Gründungs-Parteitags der U.S.P.D., 6–8 April 1917 in Gotha*, E. Eichhorn (ed.), Berlin, 1921
U.S.P.D., Protokoll über die Verhandlungen des a.o. Parteitages vom 2.–6. März 1919 in Berlin, Berlin n.d.

Vagts, A. 'M. M. Warburg u. Co. Ein Bankhaus in der deutschen Weltpolitik 1905 bis 1933', *VSWG*, 45, 1958, pp. 289–388
Varain, H.-J., *Freie Gewerkschaften, Sozialdemokratie u. Staat*, Düsseldorf, 1956
Vetter, H. O. (ed.), *Vom Sozialistengesetz zur Mitbestimmung. Zum 100. Geburtstag v. Hans Boeckler*, Cologne, 1975
Victor, M., 'Verbürgerlichung des Proletariats u. Proletarisierung des Mittelstandes', *Die Arbeit*, 8, 1931, pp. 17–31 Volkmann, E. O., *Der Marxisms u. das deutsche Heer im Weltkriege*, Berlin, 1925
Vondung, K. (ed.), *Kriegserlebnis. Der Erste Weltkrieg in der literarischen Gestaltung und symbolischen Deutung der Nationen*, Göttingen, 1980
Vorstand des Verbandes der Bergarbeiter Deutschlands (ed.), *Material zur Lage der Bergarbeiter während des Weltkrieges*, n.p., n.d. (*ca.* 1919)
Vring, T. von der, 'Der Verband der deutschen Buchdrucker im Ersten

Weltkrieg, in der Novemberrevolution und in der Inflationszeit (1914–1924), Die Geschichte einer Gewerkschaft während 10 Krisenjahren', Ph. D. thesis, Frankfurt, 1964

Wachenheim, H., *Die deutsche Arbeiterbewegung 1844 bis 1914*, 2nd ed., Cologne, 1972

Wagenführ, R., *Die Industriewirtschaft (=Vierteljahreshefte zur Konjunkturforschung*, special issue, 31), Berlin, 1933

Weber, A., *Der Kampf zwischen Kapital u. Arbeit*, 3rd and 4th eds., Tübingen, 1921

Weber, H., *Ludendorff u. die Monopole. Deutsche Kriegspolitik 1916–1918*, Berlin, 1966

Weber, M., *Wirtschaft u. Gesellschaft*, Cologne, 1964

—, *Gesammelte Aufsätze zur Wissenschaftslehre*, 3rd ed., Tübingen, 1968

—, *Gesammelte politische Schriften*, J. Winkelmann (ed.), 2nd ed., Tübingen, 1958 (3rd ed., 1971)

Wegs, R. J., *Die österreichische Kriegswirtschaft 1914–1918*, Vienna, 1979

Wegweiser durch die deutsche Kriegswirtschaft. Geschäftsführung des Kriegsausschusses der deutschen Industrie, Steinmann-Bucher (ed.), Berlin, n.d.

Wehler, H.-U., ' "Absoluter" und "totaler" Krieg', *PVS*, 10, 1969, pp. 220–48

—, *Krisenherde des Kaiserreichs 1871–1918. Studien zur deutschen Sozial- u. Verfassungsgeschichte*, Göttingen, 1970

—, *Bismarck und der Imperialismus*, Cologne, 1969 (4th ed., 1976)

—, *The German Empire, 1971–1914*, Leamington Spa, 1985

—, (ed.), *Geschichte u. Soziologie*, Cologne, 1972

Wein, J., *Die Verbandsbildung im Einzelhandel. Mittelstandsbewegung, Organisation der Großbetriebe, Fachverbände, Genossenschaften u. Spitzenverband*, Berlin, 1968

Wende, F., *Die belgische Frage in der deutschen Politik des Ersten Weltkriegs*, Hamburg, 1969

Das Werk des Untersuchungsausschusses der Deutschen Verfassungsgebenden Nationalversammlung u. des Deutschen Reichstages 1919–1930, IV. Reihe: Die Ursachen des deutschen Zusammenbruchs im Jahre 1918, 12 vols., Berlin, 1925ff.

Wernecke, K., *Der Wille zur Weltgeltung. Außenpolitik u. Öffentlichkeit im Kaiserreich am Vorabend des Ersten Weltkriegs*, Düsseldorf, 1970

Wernet, W., *Handwerkspolitik*, Göttingen, 1952

Wernicke, J., *Kapitalismus u. Mittelstandspolitik*, Jena, 1907 (2nd ed., 1922)

—, 'Mittelstandsbewegung', *HSt*, 6, 4th ed., 1925, pp. 594–602

v. Westarp, K. Graf, *Konservative Politik im letzten Jahrzehnt des Kaiserreiches, 2: 1914–1918*, Berlin, 1935

Wheeler, r., *USPD und Internationale. Sozialistischer Internationalismus in der Zeit der Revolution*, Berlin, 1975

—, 'Zur sozialen Struktur der Arbeiterbewegung am Anfang der Weimarer Republik. Einige methodologische Bemerkungen', in H. Mommsen *et al.* (eds.), *Industrielles System und politische Entwicklung in der Weimarer Republik*, 1, 2nd ed., Düsseldorf, 1977, pp. 179–89

Wieber, F. and Bechly, H., *Der Stand der Löhne u. Gehaltsfragen im Kriege*, Cologne, 1918

Wiedenfeld, K., *Die Organisation der Kriegsrohstoff-Bewirtschaftung im Weltkriege*, Hamburg, 1936

—,*Zwischen Wirtschaft u. Staat. Lebenserinnerungen*, Berlin, 1960

Wiehn, E., *Theorien der sozialen Schichtung*, Munich, 1968

v. Wiese, L., *Staatssozialismus*, Berlin, 1916

Wilbrandt, R., 'Kapitalismus u. Konsumenten. Konsumvereinspolitik', *GdS*, 9/11. Tübingen, 1927, pp. 411–56

Will, F. H., *Das Handwerk als Kriegslieferant*, Hanover, 1923

Williams, J., *The Home Fronts: Britain, France and Germany 1914–1918*, London, 1972

Williamson, J. G., *Karl Helfferich, 1872–1924. Economist, Financier, Politician*, Princeton, 1971

Winkler, H. A., 'Der rückversicherte Mittelstand. Die Interessenverbände von Handwerk u. Kleinhandel im deutschen Kaiserreich', in W. Rüegg and O. Neuloh (eds.), *Zur soziologischen Theorie u. Analyse des 19. Jarhunderts*, Göttingen, 1971, pp. 163–79

—,*Mittelstand, Demokratie u. Nationalsozialismus. Die politische Entwicklung von Handwerk u. Kleinhandel in der Weimarer Republik*, Cologne, 1972

—,*R. Michels*, in H.-U. Wehler (ed), *Deutsche Historiker*, 4, Göttingen, 1972, pp. 65–80

—,(ed.), *Organisierter Kapitalismus. Voraussetzungen und Anfänge*, Göttingen, 1974

—,*Die Sozialdemokratie und die Revolution von 1918/19. Ein Rückblick nach sechzig Jahren*, Berlin, 1979

Winters, F., *Die deutsche Beamtenfrage*, Berlin, 1918

Wirth, M., *Kapitalismustheorie in der DDR. Entstehung u. Entwicklung der Theorie des staatsmonopolistischen Kapitalismus*, Frankfurt, 1972

Witt, P.-C., *Die Finanzpolitik des Deutschen Reiches, 1903–1913*, Lübeck/Hamburg, 1970

—,'Finanzpolitik und sozialer Wandel. Wachstum und Funktionswandel der Staatsausgaben in Deutschland 1871–1933', in *Sozialgeschichte heute. Fs. H. Rosenberg z.70.Geb.*, Göttingen, 1974

—,'Finanzpolitik und sozialer Wandel in Krieg und Inflation 1918–1924', in H. Mommsen *et al.* (eds), *Industrielles System und Politische Entwicklung in der Weimarer Republik*, 1, 2nd ed., Düsseldorf, 1977, pp. 395–426

Wohlgemuth, H., *Deutschland und die deutsche Arbeiterbewegung von der Jahrhundertwende bis 1917*, 2nd ed., Berlin, 1964

—,*Die Entstehung der Kommunistischen Partei Deutschlands 1914 bis 1918*, Berlin, 1968 (2nd ed., 1978)

Wortmann, K., *Geschichte der Deutschen Vaterlands-Partei 1917–1918*, Halle, 1926

v. Wrisberg, E., *Erinnerungen an die Kriegsjahre im Königlich Preußischen Kriegsministerium. 1: Der Weg zur Revolution; 2: Heer u. Heimat; 3: Wehr u. Waffen, 1914–1918*, Leipzig, 1921, 1922

Zahlen zur Geldentwertung in Deutschland 1914–1923 (= *Wirtschaft u. Statistik*, 5, special issue 1), Statist. Reichsamt. (ed.), Berlin, 1925

Zapf, W., *Wandlungen der deutschen Elite. Ein Zirkulationsmodell deutscher Führungsgruppen 1919–1961*, Munich, 1965

Zechlin, E., *Die Deutsche Politik u. die Juden im Ersten Weltkrieg*, Göttingen, 1969

Zimmermann, W., *Der Krieg u. die deutsche Arbeiterschaft*, Jena, 1915

—,*Die gesunkene Kaufkraft des Lohnes u. ihre Wiederherstellung*, Jena, 1919

—, 'Die Veränderungen der Einkommens- u. Lebensverhältnisse der deutschen Arbeiter durch den Krieg', in R. Meerwarth, A. Günther and W. Zimmermann, *Die Einwirkung des Krieges auf Bevölkerungsberwegung, Einkommen u. Lebenshaltung in Deutschland*, Stuttgart, 1932, pp. 281–474

Zunkel, F., 'Die ausländischen Arbeiter in der deutschen Kriegswirtschaftspolitik des ersten Weltkrieges', G. A. Ritter (ed.), *Entstehung u. Wandel der modernen Gesellschaft. Fs. H. Rosenberg*, Berlin, 1970, pp. 280–311

—, 'Die Gewichtung der Industriegruppen bei der Etablierung des Reichsverbandes der Deutschen Industrie', in H. Mommsen *et al.* (eds.), *Industrielles System u. politische Entwicklung in der Weimarer Republik*, Düsseldorf, 1974, pp. 637–46

—,*Industrie und Staatssozialismus. Der Kampf um die Wirtschaftsordnung in Deutschland 1914–1918*, Düsseldorf, 1974

Index

Names

Baden, Max von, 130
Bassermann, J., 202
Bauer, M., 134, 197, 208
Baumgart, W., 239
Baumgarten, H., 199
Bismarck, O. von, 120
Bry, G., 183, 188

Class, H., 146
Conze, W., 171, 173
Coser, L., 182

Dahrendorf, R., 182
David, E., 44, 45
Delbrück, H., 144, 199
Desai, A. V., 183, 184
Dihlmann, — (director of Siemens), 192

Ebert, F., 61, 62, 199
Falkenberg, A., 218
Feldman, D., 6
Fischer, F., 5
Fricke, W., 231
Friedberg, R., 120

Groener, W., 44, 103, 105, 134, 136, 145, 202, 229, 234
Groh, D., 184
Gutsche, W., 207

Haase, H., 62
Hanisch, E., 172
Haumann, H., 172, 175, 176
Haussmann, C., 196
Heine, W., 197
Helfferich, K., 133, 136, 184
Hertling, G. von, 130
Hertz-Eichenrode, D., 172

Hillgruber, A., 171
Hindenberg, P. von, 36, 129, 131, 134, 200
Hollweg Bethmann, T. von, 45, 129, 136, 137
Horkheimer, M., 167
Hugenberg, A., 146

Jarausch, K., 172

Kaiser (Emperor), 43, 46, 57, 58, 129
Kaulisch, B., 172
Kehr, E., 154
Krupp, A., 12, 139
Kuczynski, J., 183, 184, 189, 207, 231

Lederer, E., 217
Legien, C., 64, 205
Leipart, T., 208
Lenin, V. I., 206, 231
Liebknecht, K., 50, 56, 176, 202, 231
Ludendorff, E., 36, 129, 131, 134, 150

Maier, C., 172, 173
Marx, K., 9, 172, 181, 182
Meinecke, F., 43, 45
Merton, R., 133, 234
Michaelis, G. von, 130
Moellendorff, W. von, 133, 144
Mommsen, W. J., 172
Müller, A., 134, 193
Muller, M., 215

Naumann, F., 43, 145
Noske, G., 52

Oppenheimer, F., 124

Payer, F. von, 130

275

Subject